PRAISE FOR

Clinical Supervision in Alcohol and Drug Abuse Counseling

"Powell's blended model of supervision is a presentation on the art of the practice of effective supervision in counseling. Dr. Powell provides the practical guidance and wisdom that all supervisors need to create a powerful and stimulating learning experience."

—Carina Borges, addiction counselor, director,
Chemical Dependency Office, Consultation and Treatment,
Lisbon, Portugal

"Dr. Powell has produced a compendium of sound, pragmatic techniques for effective clinical supervision based on decades of personal experience and best practices research. Here at St. Joseph's all clinical supervisors are trained in his approach. His professional reputation in the field of clinical supervision is unsurpassed and well deserved."

—Karl Kabza, president and CEO,
St. Joseph's Rehabilitation Center, Inc., Saranac Lake, New York;
former director, United States Marine Corps Substance Abuse Program

"Dr. Powell's dedication and commitment to the field of clinical supervision in alcohol and other drugs is unequaled. His leadership and guidance found in *Clinical Supervision in Alcohol and Drug Abuse Counseling* continues to set the standard for the field."

—Bernard Murphy, Pacific Institute for Research and Evaluation;
former clinical preceptor, U.S. Navy and Marine Corps

"The latest version of David Powell's classic book, *Clinical Supervision in Alcohol and Drug Abuse Counseling,* includes much more in-depth coverage of the most current knowledge and issues in clinical supervision practice. Drawing from his highly successful and diverse international clinical supervision training and consultation practice, David Powell seeks to help readers integrate and apply practical and invaluable lessons to their own supervisory experiences."

—Tony Ting, president, Association of
Professional Substance Abuse Counselors, Singapore

"Powell's book and his model of clinical supervision are the gold standard for supervision in the addictions field. Our field is better and our clients safer because of David's book and work. Do not just read this book—study it, use it as a guide in your work."
—Craig Nakken, author, *The Addictive Personality*

"As a former director of a treatment program in Australia, I would suggest to the reader that no one can effectively facilitate the complex issues facing treatment teams without this book at their beck and call."
—George Thompson, Clinical Living Solutions,
Somerville, Victoria, Australia

"One of the lesser known but great successes of clinical supervision over the past twenty-five years has been Dr. David J. Powell's innovative adaptation of this methodology to the U.S. Navy's alcohol treatment program. Under the title Clinical Preceptorship, it provided licensed and credentialed mentors to the Navy-trained counselors. Dr. Powell started this program in 1976 at the U.S. Naval Alcohol Rehabilitation Center in Norfolk, Virginia. Over the years, he has overseen its expansion to about fifty bases worldwide, from Iceland to Cuba and from Diego Garcia in the Indian Ocean to Sicily in the Mediterranean Sea. The program also operates on the U.S. Navy aircraft carriers. As a former commanding officer of the Naval Alcohol Rehabilitation Center, Norfolk, I have experienced the Clinical Preceptorship Program's great value to the counselors. Further, having the ability to confer with an impartial, knowledgeable person from outside of the organization is of inestimable value to the commanding officer—a person who may or may not have training in the substance abuse field. Dr. Powell's clinical supervision expertise and his vision created a program that helped save the military career and possibly the lives of thousands of Navy and Marine Corps personnel, including my own."
—Capt. Thomas J. Glancy Jr., United States Navy, retired

"David Powell has trained tens of thousands of substance abuse professionals worldwide in the fine art of clinical supervision. In addition to his vast expertise, his wisdom, warmth, and genuineness have all contributed to making *Clinical Supervision in Alcohol and Drug Abuse Counseling* the premier text in the field."
—Patricia A. Burke, faculty,
Rutgers Summer School of Alcohol and Drug Studies

"David Powell, internationally recognized leader in clinical supervision, has helped to significantly shape the way in which addiction policy makers and counseling professionals understand and perform critical supervisory functions. The blended model, described in *Clinical Supervision in Alcohol and Drug Abuse Counseling*, is user friendly and theoretically sound. More than nine hundred clinical supervisors throughout New York State attended his training and have incorporated the book's principles and techniques. This result is being seen in increasing qualitative patient care. Clinical supervisors are well advised to use this book as a foundation for their practice."

—Pamela Mattel, president,
Changing Dynamics Consulting and Training

"Clinical supervision is a significant part of quality alcoholism and drug abuse treatment. This comprehensive book, based on David Powell's blended model of clinical supervision, is of paramount importance to the alcoholism and drug abuse field today."

—Gail Gleason Milgram, director of education and training,
Center of Alcohol Studies, Rutgers University

"Powell's text on clinical supervision continues to be a mainstay in the development of supervisory skills for the counseling profession. This landmark guide has become the principal manual for trainers and clinicians who promote the practice of clinical supervision in addiction treatment."

—Thomas G. Durham, director,
Clinical Preceptorship Program for U.S. Navy and Marine Corps,
Danya International, Inc.

"Dr. Powell's text continues to be the foundational operational reference for our clinical supervisors. Even more useful has been the training conducted by David for our Provincial staff that further develops these essential concepts, strategies, and their applications."

—Dan Davies, senior clinical team leader,
Addiction Services, Saskatoon Health Region,
Saskatoon, Canada

Clinical Supervision in Alcohol and Drug Abuse Counseling

Principles, Models, Methods

David J. Powell

with Archie Brodsky

Revised Edition

JOSSEY-BASS
A Wiley Imprint
www.josseybass.com

Published by Jossey-Bass
A Wiley Imprint
989 Market Street, San Francisco, CA 94103-1741   www.josseybass.com

Jossey-Bass books and products are available through most bookstores. To contact Jossey-Bass
directly call our Customer Care Department within the U.S. at 800-956-7739, outside the U.S.
at 317-572-3986, or fax 317-572-4002.

Jossey-Bass also publishes its books in a variety of electronic formats. Some content that appears
in print may not be available in electronic books.

Library of Congress Cataloging-in-Publication Data

Powell, David J.
  Clinical supervision in alcohol and drug abuse counseling :
principles, models, methods / David J. Powell ; with Archie Brodsky.—
Rev. ed.
      p. ; cm.
Includes bibliographical references and index.
  ISBN 978-0-7879-7377-3 (alk. paper)
  1. Alcoholism counselors—Supervision of. 2. Drug abuse
counselors—Supervision of. 3. Alcoholics—Rehabilitation—Evaluation.
4. Narcotic addicts—Rehabilitation—Evaluation.
  [DNLM: 1. Alcoholism—rehabilitation. 2. Clinical Competence.
3. Counseling—methods. 4. Models, Theoretical. 5. Substance-Related
Disorders—rehabilitation. WM 55 P882c 2004] I. Brodsky, Archie.
II. Title.
  HV5276.P68 2004
  362.29'186—dc22   2003026855

10 9 8 7 6

Contents

Appendixes

Figures and Tables

Figures

Tables

Acknowledgments

This book has taken many years to become a reality, for it is based on thirty years of training clinical supervisors around the world in the alcoholism and drug abuse field. I have conducted one- to three-day workshops for supervisors in most states and many countries, and Archie and I are indebted to the supervisors who have participated in these workshops. We thank ETP and the National Association of Alcoholism and Drug Abuse Counselors for support in providing these workshops to thousands of supervisors. For the wisdom, humor, and insights shared by these trainees, we are grateful.

We are also indebted to our professional colleagues around the world who have listened to our ideas, challenged our thinking, told us when we were wrong, and stayed with the issue of clinical supervision as our thinking evolved. Special thanks are due to the U.S. Navy and Marine Corps for their involvement in the Clinical Preceptorship Program from 1976 to 2004. I am indebted to Archie Brodsky for his commitment to the behavioral health field and to ensuring that this book remain a quality text in the field.

Special thanks are due from me to Barbara Powell for her love, support, and encouragement throughout the writing of this book and for the hours, days, and weeks of lost time as this book was being born. Archie and I also thank those who showed limitless patience, generous support, and tireless assistance in the production of this book.

Dedication to the 2004 Edition

To the thousands of participants in my clinical supervision classes, who have taught me so much about the subject

Dedication to the 1993 Edition

To Heather and Kirstin Powell, my daughters, for their love and support despite losing many hours of time with their dad during the writing of this book

Introduction to
the 2004 Edition

I wrote *Clinical Supervision in Alcohol and Drug Abuse Counseling* in the early 1990s. Since then the alcohol and drug abuse and mental health fields, which we now refer to collectively as the *behavioral health field,* have undergone many changes. These include the expansion of managed care, the inclusion of co-occurring disorders in treatment, the changes in U.S. Department of Health and Human Services (HHS) regulations concerning confidentiality resulting from the enactment of the Health Insurance Portability and Accountability Act (HIPAA), the institutionalization of the substance abuse field, an increase in the number of states licensing and certifying counselors, the proliferation of credentialing requirements, court rulings affecting managers and supervisors, financial crises for many treatment programs, increased knowledge of what brings about change in people, and a greater emphasis on spirituality in counseling. We find ourselves not only in a new decade, century, and millennium but also in new times and uncharted waters.

The impact of the terrorist attacks of September 11, 2001, continues to unfold as the behavioral health field encounters new regulations affecting confidentiality and disclosure of information and new levels of anxiety for managers, staff, and clients. For most, the events of 9/11 brought a time of insecurity and nervousness. Many people sought anchors to give them a sense of security and made the effort to find what was in their control and to let go of what was not. On September 11, in a dramatic way, we all realized how little control we have over life (Powell 2003). Many turned to counseling and spiritual or religious pursuits to find answers to the perplexing, complex questions that resulted from that day. The revisions this book makes to the blended model of clinical supervision invite you to find a sense of your own inner self, significance, and voice.

Finally, in the years since the 1993 edition of this book was published, many people have spoken to me in my supervision classes about their ever-changing roles and the pressures of management today. I am grateful to my students who have informed and enlightened me about the changing role of supervisors, thus creating the basis for this new edition.

WHAT IS CHANGED IN THE BEHAVIORAL HEALTH FIELD?

Supervisors' responsibilities and tasks have changed in at least seven areas over the past decade.

The Role of Managers and Supervisors

First and foremost, the role of managers and supervisors has radically changed. Formerly, supervisors had more time to attend to the education and clinical sophistication of personnel. As a result of litigation, federal and state regulations, and managed care oversight, supervisors now find themselves absorbed in conformity and compliance issues, financial management ("keeping the beds filled and the census up"), legal backside covering, and the task of completing an endless array of mandated forms. Few supervisors have sufficient time to attend to the clinical knowledge and skills of counselors. Hence, it is more imperative than ever that managers allocate time for quality clinical supervision and training of personnel.

The Economics of Counseling

The economic and financial landscape has been irrevocably altered by managed care: payers and purchasers of services have a greater voice in care, patients have diminished autonomy in choosing providers and services, and funding crises are more frequent. After the exodus of clinicians in the mid-1990s from the mental health and substance abuse fields as a result of new regulations and oversight, the survivors were shell-shocked by the volume of work to be done by fewer providers and the lack of reimbursement for services rendered. Payers placed tight financial constraints on managers, including precertification for services, utilization review, provider profiling, and endless scrutiny. This too has radically altered what managers and supervisors have time to do. It should be pointed out that the effects of managed care and financial constraints are not unique to the behavioral health field but are also being felt in medicine, business, and government worldwide.

The Merging of Fields

State by state, the mental health and the alcohol and drug abuse fields are merging. Health care systems are treating patients with dual diagnoses—that is, both mental health and substance abuse disorders. New knowledge and new skills are required to meet this challenge. When systems merge, two people—a licensed mental health professional and a certified alcohol and drug abuse counselor— often vie for one job. In a field now driven by credentials, alcohol and drug abuse professionals often find themselves pushed out by the more highly credentialed mental health workers. Hence, it is essential that substance abuse managers and supervisors improve the knowledge, skills, and credentials of staff.

The Regulations

In the post-9/11 world, providers find themselves assaulted by an ever-changing range of requirements. The United States was attacked that day, and in the aftermath, Americans' civil liberties have been radically affected. In health care, the right to confidentiality has been drastically circumscribed. For example, in 2002 HHS instituted new regulations that permit law enforcement officials to review clinical records *without the knowledge or consent of clients.* So much for Title 42 of the Code of Federal Regulations, which formerly protected clients' rights to confidentiality and privacy. Although these and other regulations will surely be tested in the courts, they indicate that ongoing attention must be paid to a changing landscape of fundamental medical ethics and legal codes concerning patients' rights.

The Impact of Case Law

Case law is affecting criteria for counselor and supervisor competency; mandates for accountability; the necessity for supervisory contracting; supervisee selection, assignment, and liaison; clinical oversight (consent, relationships, confidentiality); and evaluation and documentation by supervisors.

The Credentialing Standards

Most states and several countries have established standards for credentialing supervisors in the alcohol and drug abuse field. The standards of the International Certification & Reciprocity Consortium (IC&RC) have been adopted by many states. To add teeth to these standards, state and federal funding sources have mandated that to be certified, counselors must be supervised by certified clinical supervisors. Some states now license alcohol and drug abuse counselors. Licensure of supervisors is not far away. Such credentialing results in a greater need for training and remaining current in the field to maintain one's certification.

The Spiritual Side of Healing

The original blended model emphasized cognitive, behavioral, and emotional qualities of counselors. In the past twenty years, clinicians have given more attention to the spiritual dimension of personal change as well. Building on the work of such founders of psychology as Gordon Allport, Carl Jung, and Abraham Maslow, authors such as M. Scott Peck, Gerald May, and Thomas Moore have encouraged medicine and psychology to acknowledge the importance of the soul and spirit in healing and health.

WHAT IS CHANGED IN CLINICAL SUPERVISION?

Beyond the changes in clinical supervision resulting from changes in the field of behavioral health, these additional changes must be considered.

Training and Education

First, supervisors are better educated and trained now than they were when I wrote the first edition of this book. Often driven by increased requirements for credentialing, training opportunities have increased since the early 1990s. Fifteen years ago I practically had to go into the streets to find people to attend my supervision workshops. Now they are oversold!

Understanding of Personal Change

Second, knowledge of what brings about change in a counseling and supervisory relationship has grown. Thanks to the landmark work of Hubble, Duncan, and Miller (1999), we have a clearer picture of the contribution made by the four major factors that account for change in a therapeutic relationship. Thirty percent of the change that occurs is related to the quality of the therapeutic relationships between the counselor and the client and between the counselor and the supervisor. Forty percent of the change derives from extratherapeutic factors. One such factor is the setting to which the client returns or the setting in which the supervisor works. Another is the client's or supervisee's stage of readiness for change (Prochaska, Norcross, and DiClemente 1994). The placebo effect—that is, the instillation of a sense of hope and expectancy—accounts for 15 percent of the change. Finally, only 15 percent of the change is derived from the technique used by the change agent (counselor or supervisor).

Although learning techniques of counseling and supervision is important, the quality of the relationship, what the client and counselor bring to that relationship, and the instillation of hope are far more critical to a positive outcome. Thus, the revised blended model draws on the work of Hubble, Duncan, and Miller (1999) and Prochaska, Norcross, and DiClemente (1994) as well as books such as Irvin Yalom's *The Gift of Therapy* (2002).

New and Revised Models

Third, the fundamental models of counseling and supervision developed decades ago—the psychodynamic, skills, and family therapy models—still provide the basis for much of what is written in the supervision literature. In addition, a number of new texts and models of supervision have been written since the mid-1990s, such as the interactional model of Shulman (1993), the systems model of Holloway (1995), the four-stage process model of Taibbi (1995), and the double-helix model of van Ooijen (2000). Just as some of these texts build on foundations previously set, this book builds on the solid foundational models in Chapters Six through Nine of the 1993 edition, revising and extending the blended model.

WHAT IS UPDATED AND REVISED IN THIS EDITION?

First, the entire 1993 edition is contained in this edition, with the exception that a few of the original appendixes have been omitted and a more current form for evaluating the supervisor in training has been supplied, along with a new appendix that discusses the use of the sociogram. New sections have been added to the ends of the chapters for which updates are necessary.

This edition provides the following revisions and updates:

The new blended model. Building on the foundation of the 1993 blended model, the new blended model integrates current knowledge about the way change occurs during therapy with the spiritual and contemplative aspects of supervision. The new blended model might also be termed a *contemplative model of supervision.* The new blended model is discussed at the end of the first edition text in Chapter Ten, "A Blended Model of Clinical Supervision for the Alcoholism and Drug Abuse Field."

Current legal and ethical concerns for supervisors. There have been many changes in the legal and ethical issues facing managers and supervisors, especially those concerning confidentiality, competence, contracting, clinical oversight, and evaluation and documentation. These changes are addressed following the first edition text of Chapter Fifteen, "Ethical and Legal Concerns." For a thorough review of the ethical and legal issues faced by supervisors, the reader is referred to Janet Elizabeth Falvey's book, *Managing Clinical Supervision: Ethical Practice and Legal Risk Management* (2002).

New directions for the future. Obviously much has changed in the behavioral health field since 1993, including the financial, political, social, and program trends of which counselors and supervisors need to be aware. Because the vision for the next decade laid out in the original Chapter Seventeen, "Directions for the Future," has largely come to pass, this concluding chapter has been renamed "New Directions for the Future" and entirely rewritten to suggest the trends that will matter through the decade to come.

Updated appendixes. Some older versions of forms have been omitted and one new form supplied, reflecting the changes in counselor credentialing requirements, legal and ethical concerns, and other areas covered in this edition.

Updated references. This edition retains the classic texts in the field cited in the 1993 edition and also cites newer texts. It offers an extensive current bibliography on clinical supervision, including all sources cited in the text.

Credentialing examination, certification, training, and academic organizations will find that this edition retains the main thrust of the 1993 edition. The earlier edition has been a primary text for the alcohol and drug abuse counseling field, used by supervisors in training and as a basis for credentialing examinations. This revision reflects both the development and refinement of the blended model, changes in legal and ethical issues and in management requirements, and trends in the fields of medicine and psychotherapy. Because the bulk of the text has not required revision, however, the reader is asked to update mentally the time frames referred to in text from the 1993 edition.

HOW TO USE THIS EDITION

This book is for clinical supervisors and managers and those who wish to become supervisors. It is meant to be accessible and helpful to all who seek to better understand the role of the supervisor in a clinical setting.

This is a professional text that requires readers to engage in continuous searching and disciplined practices to find their own model of supervision. In my training sessions I ask participants to define their models of counseling and supervision. Some, in frustration, simply state that they are "eclectic," which typically means, "I don't know what I do because I am always doing something different." Thus, defining their model of counseling and supervision is often a struggle for those who have never been asked to do so before. Simply reading through this book may be interesting, but little will change for readers unless they seriously consider and apply themselves to the steps of defining their model of supervision.

You can begin this task by completing the self-assessments found in the appendixes. Change will occur for you when you answer the questions, try the innovative techniques, and practice the skills offered herein. But change is not simply a mental or even behavioral process. It requires a shift in attitude, in the foundation of your practice of supervision. Ultimately, the new blended model encourages you to explore your spirit and basic questions about your clinical supervisory practice and connection to something greater than yourself.

It is recommended that you keep a journal when reading this book. Journaling enables you to apply ideas from this book to your personal journey in supervision and counseling. Put the journal on your desk and reflect and write in it about what you have read, always seeking to define your ever-changing, evolving model of counseling and supervision.

Everyone is unique. This book can provide a basic road map, but you need to adapt and apply it to your unique self. Instead of thinking about counseling and supervision in the abstract, explore your relationships with your supervisees. Instead of absorbing abstractions about clinical work, learn about the work you do and the type of supervisor you wish to become. Growth as a supervisor is an active process. Over time you will observe changes in your supervision, illuminated by the new blended model. A pattern will emerge. Seeing change will be enormously reinforcing in your growth process as a supervisor and counselor.

Like the supervisors it is intended for, the content of this book is a work in progress. This edition reflects the changes and updates that have occurred in the behavioral health field and in the state of knowledge about the change process. Future changes will also add to the refinement of the new blended model of clinical supervision.

Introduction to the 1993 Edition

In the dozen years since the publication of *Clinical Supervision: Skills for Substance Abuse Counselors* (Powell 1980a, 1980b), the content and process of clinical supervision have evolved, and the body of relevant knowledge has grown considerably. Organizations are changing, with the command-control structure in some instances giving way to more flexible, team-oriented management. Research findings are making their way into clinical training and supervision curricula at a slow but steady pace. An awareness of a variety of medical, psychiatric, ethical, and legal issues is increasingly recognized to be essential for supervisors. Drug and alcohol abuse must now compete for the counselor's attention with codependency, adult children of alcoholics, and a panoply of other "syndromes." Ethnic, cross-cultural, economic, and especially gender issues—power, hierarchy, discrimination, and sex role–stereotyped thinking—have been opened up for discussion. Developmental approaches to counselor training and supervision have been formulated, adding to the mix from which a comprehensive model of supervision for the substance abuse field must be synthesized.

At this crossroads in its history, the field of clinical supervision faces critical questions parallel to those that confront the counseling field as a whole. How can the expense of training and supervision be justified? Can theoretical models of supervision be made sufficiently comprehensive and flexible so that they can be adapted to the full range of clinical settings? How precisely can the standards and credentialing requirements for supervisors in the substance abuse field be formulated?

This book serves to update *Clinical Supervision: Skills for Substance Abuse Counselors* for a changing professional environment but has a more ambitious purpose as well: to articulate a model of clinical supervision designed specifically for substance abuse counseling. Until now, the available literature on clinical supervision has had limited applicability to actual practice in the substance abuse field. Having been written (for the most part) in and for academic or outpatient psychiatric settings, it has been insufficiently attuned to the pressures of everyday practice: budgets, censuses, reimbursement, and liabilities. And relying as it does on concepts imported from other mental heath disciplines, such as family therapy and psychoanalysis, this literature has not been tailored to the special circumstances and needs of substance abuse counseling.

Family therapists, psychologists, psychodynamic therapists, behavioral therapists, and so forth often treat substance abusers and conduct clinical supervision according to their own established bodies of theory and practice. Substance abuse treatment agencies, however, draw unsystematically from the models found in these disciplines; substance abuse counseling and supervision may have a mental health flavor, a family therapy flavor, a psychoanalytic flavor, or something else, depending on the individual and the agency. Such models are applicable to clinical work with drug and alcohol abusers, but they need to be synthesized and applied with precision and rigor.

This book makes the case for substance abuse counseling as a unique discipline with its own model of supervision. A practitioner of another mental health discipline who works with substance abusers or supervises counselors in a substance abuse treatment facility needs to do more than just superimpose a family therapy, psychodynamic, or cognitive-behavioral model on the issues surrounding substance abuse. Although the substance abuse model of supervision incorporates components taken from these disciplines, mental health practitioners must be aware of the broader integration of the substance abuse model, as well as the particular components they know from their own practice.

For clinical supervisors from other mental health fields, as well as supervisor trainees, trainers, and administrators, this book provides what is needed to apply these disciplines meaningfully to substance abuse. For those in the substance abuse field, it outlines a paradigm of supervision developed specifically for this field, together with guidelines for implementation.

In the next few years, new standards for counseling practice will be written, to include additional knowledge and skills beyond those expected of alcoholism and drug abuse counselors in the past. Staff members must become proficient in articulating treatment plans as well as in dealing with medical and psychiatric issues coexisting with and affecting substance abuse (such as AIDS, dual diagnosis, borderline behaviors, codependency, and family dynamics). Credentialing criteria will be expanded to reflect these increased demands. This book gives clinical supervisors guidance in acquiring the background, content knowledge, and instructive techniques necessary to meet the upgraded requirements for certification of their staff.

Furthermore, credentialing of clinical supervisors in the substance abuse field is a reality as states adopt the standards for certification promulgated by the International Certification & Reciprocity Consortium (IC&RC), formerly the National Certification Reciprocity Consortium (NCRC). The role delineation study conducted by the Columbia Assessment Services (Appendix B) and published by the National Certification Reciprocity Consortium (1992) establishes the tasks and competencies of alcohol and drug abuse clinical supervisors. State counselor certification groups increasingly are using these standards in their credentialing process. As a result, training of supervisors in these competencies is becoming the norm for the substance abuse field.

THE NEED FOR PROFESSIONALISM IN SUPERVISORY TRAINING AND PRACTICE

Until recently, supervisory training has been a neglected area in the mental health fields generally and in the substance abuse field specifically. According to Shemburg and Leventhal (1978), more than half of the clinicians affiliated with academic institutions spend 10 to 20 percent of their time in supervisory functions, and another 7 percent spend close to one-third of their time supervising. In nonacademic mental health centers, including alcoholism and drug treatment centers, this figure might rise above 50 percent for many clinicians, who would thus be spending half their time doing a job for which they have little or no training. As yet, few courses in supervision are offered in social work, professional psychology, or family therapy training programs. Borders and Leddick (1987) report that only one-third of the training programs for counselors in the United States provide training in supervision, a finding confirmed by Hess (1986) and Richardson and Bradley (1984). Even where such courses are offered, few trainees move into supervisory functions immediately after graduate school. As a rule, by the time they do take on supervisory roles, they have long since forgotten any limited training in supervision they may have had.

The lack of attention and priority given to supervision is reflected in the paucity of literature on the subject. In the professional journals of alcoholism and drug abuse counseling, articles on clinical supervision are scarce. In one prominent textbook, Lawson, Ellis, and Rivers's *Essentials of Chemical Dependency Counseling* (1984), less than one page is devoted to supervision. For the past decade, my initial efforts to pull together the principles of supervision in book form (Powell 1980a, 1980b) have had no competition. This relative paucity of literature and training programs in clinical supervision for substance abuse counselors has been symptomatic of the lack of recognized standards and credentialing authority in this area.

Currently the substance abuse field is following in the wake of other mental health professions in a belated recognition of the need for well-trained supervisors. During the late 1970s and 1980s, books on supervision appeared in the fields of psychoanalysis (Caligor, Bromberg, and Meltzer 1984; Lane 1990), social work (Kadushin 1976; Munson 1979, 1983), marriage and family therapy (Kaslow 1986a; Liddle, Breunlin, and Schwartz 1988; Whiffen and Byng-Hall 1982), and generic counseling (Association for Counselor Education and Supervision 1989; Bradley 1989; Hart 1982; Hess 1980; Mead 1990; Stoltenberg and Delworth 1987). This same decade saw the founding of the journal *Clinical Supervisor.* The American Association for Marriage and Family Therapy (AAMFT) formed its Commission on Supervision, which resulted in that organization's mandating supervisory training. In June 1987, the journal *Professional Psychology: Research and Practice* contained an extensive section on advances in psychotherapy supervision. Supervision came to be featured more prominently on the programs of major professional meetings.

What Alonso (1985) referred to as the "quiet profession" was becoming more vocal.

But why was it quiet for so long? Why did even psychologists, as Hess (1986, p. 51) put it, "tend to take psychotherapy supervision for granted"? Unlike private-sector business organizations, the helping professions have assumed that supervisory training somehow occurs serendipitously in the course of the general training of psychotherapists. Business management years ago recognized that running a machine and supervising machine operators are different tasks requiring different skills and knowledge. As a result, courses on supervision are offered regularly by business schools as well as by the American Management Association. In contrast, the human services professions have operated on the naive assumption that a good counselor automatically makes a good supervisor. That is equivalent to assuming that because one is a recovering alcoholic one will automatically be a good counselor. On the contrary, supervision, like counseling, is a profession with its own theories, practices, and standards. It requires individuals who are well informed, equipped with a core body of knowledge and skills, and properly credentialed (Alonso 1985). That is, it requires an attitude of professionalism.

CONSEQUENCES OF INADEQUATE SUPERVISORY TRAINING

In the early days of substance abuse counseling, so-called paraprofessional counselors typically felt defensive and fearful of oversight as a result of their lack of academic credentials. Often they did not know what supervision was, or if they did know, they did not seek it out. A study I conducted in 1975 revealed that 57 percent of alcoholism and drug abuse counselors were not receiving clinical supervision (Powell 1976). Moreover, when supervision was available, there was no assurance that it would be helpful. Counselors became supervisors by virtue of their therapeutic expertise, longevity of service, or mere survival in an agency. All too often, in line with the well-known Peter Principle, they were rising to the level of their incompetence.

The consequences of nonexistent or inadequate preparation of supervisors were readily observable in alcoholism and drug abuse treatment facilities in the 1970s and beyond. There have been a number of deleterious effects on counselors and supervisors alike (not to mention clients and agencies).

Errors in Supervision

Untrained supervisors who are forced to operate with only their clinical experience and instincts as guides are prone to certain characteristic errors. These include:

- Confusing clinical supervision with case management, thereby attending inappropriately to the client's rather than the counselor's needs.
- Falling back on what they do know—their counseling skills— so that they become counselors to the counselors, a form of role confusion that may give rise to boundary issues.
- Taking a laissez-faire attitude, even to the point of excessive familiarity or other serious boundary violations.
- Becoming judgmental, authoritarian, and demanding, to the edge of sadism.

Multigenerational Transmission

Aldrich and Hess (1983, p. 8) observed that the complex task of supervision is "too often performed with no more preparation than the neophyte supervisor trying to recall his own supervisory experiences." Unfortunately, counselors who are poorly supervised are thereby exposed to a poor model of supervision. When their turn comes to supervise, they adopt the behaviors that were modeled for them. Often supervisors fail to improve with experience because they "perpetuate the mistakes of their own supervisors" (Worthington 1987, p. 206). In this way, supervisory errors reverberate through the careers of generations of clinicians.

Supervisor Burnout

Inexperienced, poorly trained supervisors are likely to feel incompetent, inadequate to deal with their supervisees' problems, and overwhelmed by the sheer dimensions of their task. "If asked," notes Alonso (1985, p. 56), "new supervisors often will admit that they feel fraudulent and are terrified of being discovered as such." The result in too many cases is rapid burnout. "Many promising supervisors are so disheartened by finding themselves pressed into service with little or no supervisor training that they flee the role and are lost forever to the profession" (Alonso 1985, p. 5). Typically they move up or out. If they do not leave the field altogether, they look for the first opportunity to become an agency director, thus acting out the Peter Principle at a higher level.

Counselor Burnout

As supervisors muddle through their haphazard on-the-job training, supervisees are deprived of an essential asset in their personal and professional growth. As Alonso (1985, p. 59) puts it, "The unconscious silence about the supervisor's part of the process and its effect on him mitigates against the student finding reassuring guidelines around which to organize the expectations arising from this new venture." As a result, supervisees may become frustrated with their own practice; they may come to feel worthless, confused, and angry.

The factors that contribute to counselor burnout are readily apparent. A person fresh from school or from personal recovery experiences, with varying degrees of formal training and little or no experience in the complex tasks of counseling, is asked to guide people through major life crises—rape, family violence, sexual abuse, bereavement, and emotional collapse. No amount of schooling can prepare anyone for the gut-wrenching emotional reaction to the first case of child sexual abuse or suicide encountered. And for this the counselor is paid little more than a McDonald's employee. The average annual salary for an alcohol and drug abuse counselor in 2003 was $28,000 (Center for Substance Abuse Treatment 2003). Added to these frustrations are those engendered by long hours, heavy caseloads, bureaucratic conflicts, and an inability to influence organizational policy. Such obstacles prove daunting for many counselors in the absence of emotional support from a trained clinical supervisor.

As counselors move through Edelwich and Brodsky's (1980) cyclic stages of disillusionment leading to professional burnout—enthusiasm, stagnation, and frustration—supervisors need to learn to intervene so as to keep counselors from falling permanently into the final stage: apathy. Clinical supervision can provide a safety net that enables counselors to bounce back up from disappointments and frustrations. Most counselors need a mentoring and support system, which translates into a coach, cheerleader, handholder, and wise adviser. Since counselors, as a rule, have not been able to count on this support, it is not surprising that the average length of employment in treatment facilities has been only two years.

Misguided Hiring and Personnel Policies

Agencies generally have done a poor job of defining the profile of the counselors they are seeking to hire. Too many agencies are tacitly biased in favor of the young, energetic counselor with great potential for advancement. That preference makes sense if an agency can offer rapid upward mobility. In fact, the opportunities for advancement in most treatment facilities are very limited. Seeing this, the "mustang" counselor quickly becomes frustrated and bolts to a facility that promises a pay increase and greater opportunities for growth. Facilities would do better to hire fewer "mustangs" and more "mules"—counselors who do not aspire to be clinical directors but are content to do counseling. Here, too, the role of the clinical supervisor is crucial in conveying a realistic assessment of the agency's personnel needs and in keeping both the "mustangs" and "mules" appropriately motivated.

Staff Turnover

For all of the above reasons, staff turnover in substance abuse treatment facilities in the 1970s and 1980s was disastrously high—typically 30 to 50 percent annually. The average tenure in a counseling job in 2003 was merely two years (Center for Substance Abuse Treatment 2003). When counselors view an agency as merely a training ground for some other agency that will offer them a $2,000 raise in pay, the organizational climate that results is detrimental to team building, staff morale, and quality of care. No organization with such a high turnover rate can maintain a satisfactory level of efficiency, productivity, and continuity of care. This problem is exacerbated by an average turnover of supervisors and managers *every year* (Center for Substance Abuse Treatment 2003).

In the changing work environment of the 1990s, with the impact of managed care and the economic recession, a different pattern is emerging. Job hopping is less of a concern than it was for treatment centers because counselors feel compelled to hold on to their jobs. Agencies hold "golden handcuffs" on staff who may not be able to move elsewhere in a recessionary marketplace yet feel trapped by an employment situation where they receive little or no support or clinical supervision. An elite minority of "mustangs" can still maneuver for a better job (or, in some cases, step down to a less demanding one), but the far more numerous "mules" are bogged down in the mud.

Edelwich and Brodsky (1980) describe an exercise in which helping professionals are asked how they would feel if they found themselves working at the same job in the same agency ten years later. Typical responses are "No way!" and "The pits!" On reflection, however, many people concede that they may well be working at the same job in ten years. In the absence of skilled supervision, this contradiction in people's view of their work situation is a recipe for stagnation and apathy.

These conditions attest to a failure to treat clinical supervision of drug and alcohol abuse counselors as a truly professional endeavor involving a specified knowledge base, core competencies, and training and certification requirements. What other professionals would be allowed to practice their trade without training? Principle Two of the American Psychological Association (1981) ethics code stipulates that people be given training in the field in which they practice. Just as it is unethical to employ counselors who are not trained in counseling, so it is unethical to ask people to supervise without training them in supervision.

FACTORS PLACING A PREMIUM ON QUALITY SUPERVISION

A number of developments have made the substance abuse field, along with the other mental health professions, more cognizant of the need for high-quality clinical supervision. These professions are now being held accountable for their performance in unaccustomed ways and are discovering the central importance of clinical supervision in quality control. Treatment facilities now are subject to several kinds of external scrutiny:

Financial accountability. Agencies are accountable, first, to their funding sources. With health care costs rising to crisis levels, the undisciplined billing practices of many providers in the fields of psychotherapy and rehabilitation can no longer be tolerated. Managed care has made it necessary to articulate, monitor, and justify clinical decisions.

Ethical accountability. In reaction to the excesses and hypocrisies of recent decades, prominent figures in American life—business leaders, politicians, scientists, evangelists, sports stars—are feeling the spotlight of ethical scrutiny. Therapists and counselors are no exception. Highly publicized revelations of sexual involvements with clients have made ethics in the human services a legitimate public concern.

Legal accountability. In today's litigious climate, clinical or ethical lapses (real or perceived) entail legal liability. Legal actions are commonly brought against mental health professionals and treatment agencies on such grounds as misdiagnosis, failure to take reasonable precautions to protect against suicide or violence, and sexual or financial exploitation.

Accountability to accrediting and credentialing bodies. To meet the need for more disciplined, cost-effective operations, the accreditation of agencies and the credentialing of personnel (long taken for granted in the established mental health professions) have been adopted by the substance abuse treatment field. Facilities are now accredited by the Joint Commission on Accreditation of Healthcare Organizations (JCAHO) and the Commission on Accreditation of Rehabilitation Facilities (CARF). Counselor credentialing, as called for by the Birch and Davis (1986) report, has become the norm. Clinical supervision is a prerequisite for accreditation, certification, or licensing. Moreover, in line with the standards set forth by the

International Certification & Reciprocity Consortium, clinical supervisors themselves will now require credentialing.

These developments have contributed significantly to the evolution of the alcoholism and drug abuse treatment field. The mystique of the pioneer counselors has given way to a developing technology of counseling, which calls for a corresponding technology of training and supervision. Clinical models and approaches are better defined and more systematically implemented. Today's counselors have had undergraduate- and graduate-level training. More and more of them have been exposed to supervision, sometimes in other disciplines in which they were originally trained, and they demand supervision as a matter of course. For their part, supervisors now are more likely to have benefited from quality supervision themselves, so that they can model this experience for their supervisees.

This confluence of factors has given momentum to the professionalizing of clinical supervision. Good supervision internalizes the oversight imposed by outside authorities. Providing good supervision, already a clinical and ethical responsibility, is now a requirement for survival in a competitive market. Not surprisingly, then, individuals and agencies are demanding more and better supervisory training. Workshops on clinical supervision are being requested by state counselor organizations, proprietary treatment systems, counselor training groups, and college and university programs. Attendance at my own workshops has more than tripled over the past half decade.

BENEFITS OF SUPERVISION: THE EXPERIENCE OF THE CLINICAL PRECEPTORSHIP PROGRAM

The information in this book is derived in great part from sixteen years of experience with the Clinical Preceptorship Program (CPP), a comprehensive, integrated, skills-oriented supervisor training program developed and maintained by ETP Inc., through rigorous testing and ongoing adaptation. This unique, centrally coordinated program operates worldwide in both civilian and military counseling facilities. As of 1992, sixty-five highly trained preceptors were serving over a hundred sites, including at least eighty-five U.S. Navy alcoholism and drug abuse rehabilitation and counseling centers, twenty-one U.S. Marine Corps alcoholism and drug abuse counseling centers, and over two hundred civilian agencies. At each site, the CPP provides a minimum of eighty hours per year of individualized clinical supervision, including one-on-one as well as small-group sessions. The curriculum covers two general areas: counselor role and skill development. It includes the following components:

Basic helping skills: affective engagement, listening skills, communication techniques, appropriate confrontation.

Routine procedures: intake, history taking, assessment, treatment planning, record keeping.

Group counseling skills: group formation, climate setting, leadership styles, group dynamics, group process.

Professional ethics: confidentiality, respect, informed consent, maintaining boundaries.

The CPP has been the real-life laboratory in which the model of supervision outlined in this book has been developed. Its evaluation component has accumulated a decade and a half of data on the outcomes of clinical supervision and on counselor training needs. These data provide what is probably the best barometer of the current state of clinical supervisory training for substance abuse counselors.

Earlier studies (Aiken, Smits, and Lollar 1972; Henry, Sims, and Spray 1971; Kermish and Kushin 1969) showed that better clinical supervision led to greater job satisfaction and, in turn, to better staff retention rates. More recently, Frankel and Piercy (1990) demonstrated an isomorphic relationship between the effectiveness of the supervisor-counselor dyad and that of the counselor-client dyad. That is, when high-quality clinical supervision was provided, clients and their families became and remained more cooperative. Thus, good supervision can have a positive effect on client outcomes by improving the quality of counseling, a finding surely of interest to those who fund facilities and monitor the quality of care.

All of these studies have shown that the quality of the relationship between counselor and supervisor is the key ingredient in the counselor's training experience. A good supervisory relationship is one of the most satisfying aspects of the counselor's work—more important than pay, working conditions, or other forms of organizational support. The data collected by the CPP confirm these findings. Both military and civilian counselors view their supervisor as a primary resource for education, training, coaching, morale building, and consultation. The supervisor-preceptor gives the counselor a much-needed role model and support, an empathic listener and guide who encourages the counselor to achieve professional and personal growth.

Although the content of supervision is certainly important, nothing matters more to counselors than the process of open, professional sharing with a trusted, objective clinical expert. Some key features of this desirable relationship are the following:

- The openness of both supervisor and supervisee to feedback.
- The supervisor's helping the counselor feel relaxed and open to criticism.
- The supervisor's ability to listen and attend appropriately to the counselor, the counselor's therapeutic style, and the respective therapeutic orientations of the supervisor and supervisee.
- The consistency between the supervisor's and supervisee's therapeutic orientations.
- The emotional support provided by the supervisor.
- The sharing of clinical responsibilities by the supervisor and supervisee.

In line with these characterizations of the supervisory relationship, experienced counselors who were asked to describe what they had gained from a supervisor they especially valued gave the following responses:

"Accessibility—I could get to him when I needed him."

"She made me feel empowered."

"He showed that he was concerned about me as distinct from the client, and that gave me a feeling of validation."

"Her high expectations gave me standards to live up to."

"A sense of safety—a feeling of permission, trust, acceptance."

"She let me know it was OK to make mistakes."

"He encouraged me to make my own decisions. I felt that I'd be supported even if what I did turned out to be wrong."

"She wasn't wishy-washy. She gave me clear guidelines and wasn't afraid to tell me in a nice way, 'You screwed up.'"

"She gave regular feedback. You could tell where you were from week to week instead of waiting to get your head handed to you on the year-end evaluation."

The CPP has also studied the perceptions of supervisors and supervisees about the supervisees' skills, competencies, and further training needs. By and large, the two groups agree in their assessments of the supervisees' understanding of their limits, their skills in intake and record keeping, and their knowledge of alcoholism and drug abuse issues. Contrary to the supervisees' more confident self-perceptions, however, their supervisors see them as needing improvement in individual and (especially) group-counseling skills, as well as in some helping skills.

These findings replicate those of an earlier needs assessment (Powell 1976) to the effect that clinical supervision remains a greatly needed and underutilized form of training for alcoholism and drug abuse counselors. Moreover, they reaffirm the value of experiential learning for counselors, as well as the need for clinical supervisors to provide regular, consistent, and accurate feedback to counselors concerning their clinical knowledge and skills.

More specifically, the data point to three main recommendations concerning clinical supervision in the alcohol and drug abuse field:

1. Managers of treatment facilities need to be trained in the value of clinical supervision. The Center for Substance Abuse Treatment acknowledged this need by identifying clinical supervision as their top training priority for 2004 (Center for Substance Abuse Treatment 2003). The field as a whole needs to focus on the importance of clinical supervisory training. To appreciate its value, program managers need to be shown what high-quality clinical supervision is and what is required to provide it.

2. Clinical supervisors need more thorough training in how to supervise. Supervisors need not only better preparation for their new role and unfamiliar tasks but also ongoing supervision of their supervision.

3. More sophisticated mechanisms are needed for supervising counselors. These include some of the newer training technologies, such as videotaping, bug-in-the-ear (described in Chapter Twelve), satellite conferencing, structured internship programming, and interactive video training.

This book has been conceived as a step toward meeting these needs.

THE CONTENT AND ORGANIZATION
OF THIS BOOK

The three parts of this book comprise a rounded picture of the new model of supervision the book articulates for the alcoholism and drug abuse field. Part One lays the foundation by exploring what clinical supervision is and the role it plays in the provision of clinical services. After a review of historical definitions of supervision, a working definition is proposed for what I call the *blended model*. The remaining chapters in Part One present leadership principles for supervisors in today's changing organizational climate and then apply them to the demands of the supervisory role. Part One concludes with learning objectives for supervisors.

Part Two takes up the challenge of developing a model of clinical supervision for the alcoholism and drug abuse field. I first develop a framework for such a model, consisting of a set of layers or components that any model will have. The substance abuse field, being of recent origin, benefits from the experience of the older mental health professions. Therefore, I examine existing models of supervision (psychodynamic, skills, and family therapy) for their contributions to this new field of supervision. From those models, from a developmental approach to supervision, and from the principles and practice of the alcoholism and drug abuse field, the blended model is synthesized.

Part Three shows how the blended model is implemented in practice. Unlike some other forms of therapy, alcoholism and drug abuse counseling is conducted—and its practitioners are trained—mainly in public and private treatment agencies rather than academic institutions. With this crucial context in mind, the methods of day-to-day supervision are outlined: the initial contract and supervision plan, direct and indirect observation of the counselor at work, case presentation, feedback, intervention, and evaluation. Well-established procedures (for example, peer supervision, group supervision, role playing) as well as innovative techniques (for example, solution-focused supervision, in vivo supervision) are covered. Guidelines and specific instruments for counselor assessment are included. These chapters look at supervision from the perspectives of both content (what the supervisor and supervisee talk about) and context (time and budgetary constraints, organizational climate, and the need for sensitivity to issues such as gender and ethnicity). The growing impact of ethical and legal concerns on clinical practice is examined, along with the role of the supervisor in liability prevention. Finally, future directions are anticipated for this rapidly changing field.

The appendixes contain supervisor task analyses, as well as questionnaires, checklists, and sample forms for supervisor and counselor assessment. These instruments make it possible to assess supervisor training and performance from the perspectives of the supervisor, supervisor trainee, and supervisee.

In the interest of nonsexist language, the pronouns *he* and *she* will be used interchangeably in hypothetical examples.

Part One

Principles

Chapter One

A Historical Review of Supervision

A first step toward the recognition of clinical supervision as a profession in its own right—and, in turn, toward the consistent provision of high-quality supervision in treatment facilities—is to establish a clear, succinct, comprehensive, broadly applicable definition of supervision. There seem to be as many definitions as there are fields in which clinical supervision is practiced—perhaps even as many as there are people writing about supervision. On the basis of the following brief survey of some definitions employed by the mental health professions as well as by society as a whole, I will formulate a definition for the substance abuse field in the following chapter.

TRADITIONAL DEFINITIONS

The term *supervisor* has its roots in Latin; it means "looks over." It was originally applied to the master of a group of artisans. One hundred years ago, it was not uncommon for the master in a New England shop to have almost complete power over the work force. The master would bid on jobs, hire his own crew, work them as hard as he pleased, and make a living out of the difference between his bid price and the labor costs.

The other source of our notion of a supervisor was the person in charge of a group of towrope pullers or ditchdiggers. That person was literally the *foreman*, since he was up forward of the gang. His authority consisted mainly of chanting "One, two, three, up," which set the pace of the rest of the workers. In Germany a supervisor is still called a *Vorabeiter* ("fore worker"); in England the analogous term *charge hand* is used.

Today the supervisor's job combines some of the talents of the master (or skilled administrative artisan) with those of the foreman (or leader). As the term is generally understood, supervisors are front-line managers who normally report to middle managers. Supervisors plan, motivate, direct, and control the work of nonmanagerial employees at the operational level of the organization. Their responsibility is to see that staff carry out the plans and policies set by executives and middle managers.

LEGAL DEFINITIONS

Legal definitions of supervision are worth looking at as indicators of the social recognition, legitimacy, and authority of the occupation. According to the Taft-Hartley Act of 1947, a supervisor is

> any individual having authority, in the interest of the employer,
> to hire, transfer, suspend, lay off, recall, promote, discharge,
> assign, reward, or discipline other employees, or responsibility
> to direct them or to adjust their grievances, or effectively to
> recommend such action, if in connection with the foregoing
> the exercise of such authority is not merely of a routine or
> clerical nature, but requires the use of independent judgment
> [Biddle and Newstrom 1990, pp. 507–8].

Further specifications are found in the 1938 Fair Labor Standards Act, which states that a supervisor is someone who devotes no more than 20 percent of his or her working hours to activities not closely related to managerial work. This law stipulates that the supervisor be paid a salary, regardless of the number of hours worked. Together, these two laws make supervision a bona fide function, an established part of management.

ADMINISTRATIVE DEFINITIONS

Supervision has an administrative dimension that is emphasized in the traditional and legal definitions. Since clinical definitions are the focus of this chapter, it is important to draw a clear distinction between the administrative and clinical domains, as the Association for Counselor Education and Supervision (1989), Falvey (1987), Borders and Leddick (1987), and others have done.

Administrative supervision occurs in most settings, from universities to human services organizations. The administrative supervisor helps the supervisee function more effectively within the organization, with the overall intent of helping the organization run smoothly. Toward this end, the administrative supervisor addresses managerial requirements such as case records, referral procedures, continuity of care, accountability, hiring and firing, and performance evaluations (Abels and Murphy 1981; Hart 1982; Simon 1985; Slavin 1985).

In contrast, clinical supervision is concerned with the actual work of the supervisee in such areas as the counseling relationship, client welfare, clinical assessment and intervention approaches, clinical skills, and prognosis. Hart (1982) summarizes the distinction as follows: "Administrative supervision is aimed at helping the supervisee as part of an organization, and clinical supervision focuses on the development of the supervisee specifically as an interpersonally effective clinician" (p. 13). In other words, clinical supervision attends to the supervisee's professional and personal needs as they directly affect the welfare of the client.

CLINICAL DEFINITIONS

Looking to the mental health fields for guidance, we find many definitions of clinical supervision, each shaped by the theoretical model from which it is derived.

Supervision as Therapy

Some define supervision as a form of therapy, or at least a therapeutic process. For example, Abroms (1977) views supervision and therapy as distinct but parallel processes, the distinction being that supervision is a therapy of the therapy, not of the therapist. Abroms believes that although the supervisor should not become the supervisee's therapist, therapeutic issues can and should be addressed in supervision. That is, if a counselor is experiencing problems that interfere with his or her clinical functioning, such blockages are grist for the supervisory mill. The supervisory milieu is to be a safe sanctuary for the supervisee to explore personal and professional growth issues. In such a milieu, the supervisor's behavior constitutes a compelling model of how a therapy session should be conducted.

Lane (1990, p. 10) defines supervision as "a therapeutic process focusing on the intra- and interpersonal dynamics of the counselor and their relationship with clients, colleagues, supervisors, and significant others." The focus of supervision is on personal and professional growth, transference and countertransference, defenses, analytic processes, and the use of self as an emotional force in therapy. With this definition, the supervisee looks more like a patient than a student. Supervision uses the transference relationship as the principal vehicle to promote the supervisee's growth as a clinician.

Supervision as Education

Others view supervision as more of an educational process—a matter of learning skills and developing professional competence. Bartlett (1983) defines counseling supervision as "an experienced counselor helping a beginning student or less experienced therapist learn counseling by various means" (p. 9). According to Blocher (1983), supervision is "a specialized instructional process in which the supervisor attempts to facilitate the growth of a counselor-in-preparation, using as the primary educational medium the student's interaction with real clients for whose welfare the student has some degree of professional, ethical, and moral responsibility" (p. 27).

There are other variations on these themes:

- Brammer and Wassner (1977, p. 44): "Supervision is the assignment of an experienced person to help a beginning student to learn counseling through the use of the student's own case material."
- Saba and Liddle (1986, p. 111): Family therapy supervision is "the specific development of trainee's therapeutic abilities within the context of treating families."

- Stoltenberg and Delworth (1987, p. 34): "An intensive, interpersonally focussed, one-to-one relationship in which one person is designed to facilitate the development of therapeutic competence in the other person."
- Hart (1982, p. 12): "An ongoing educational process in which one person in the role of supervisor helps another person in the role of the supervisee acquire appropriate professional behavior through an examination of the supervisee's professional activities."

The key elements of Hart's definition, one of the more comprehensive definitions available, are an ongoing relationship between supervisor and supervisee, the addressing of specific behaviors, and the goal of developing a professional role identity.

Perhaps the most ambitious of the educationally oriented definitions comes from the field of social work. Kadushin (1976, p. 20) defines clinical supervision as "an administrative and clinical process designed to facilitate the counselor's ability to deliver the best possible service to clients, both quantitative and qualitative, in accordance with agency policy, procedures, and the context of a positive relationship between counselor and supervisor." This definition is primarily focused on education (skill development) but nevertheless weaves in administrative with clinical themes.

A Composite Definition

Since the Association for Counselor Education and Supervision (ACES) is a trade organization rather than a school of therapy, it has had to adopt a definition broad enough to encompass its diverse membership. Borders and Leddick (1987) stipulate that counselor supervision is performed by experienced, successful counselor-supervisors who are prepared for the task by learning the methodology of supervision. ACES goes on to state that supervision involves facilitating the counselor's personal and professional development as well as promoting counselor competencies for the welfare of the client. Supervisors oversee the counselor's work through a set of activities that include consultation, counseling (if provided for by one's model of supervision), training, instruction, and evaluation. The mention of counseling and personal development makes this definition broad enough to cover the therapeutic as well as educational dimensions of supervision.

TOWARD A WORKING DEFINITION

Taken together, the various definitions indicate that the purpose of supervision is to bring about change in the knowledge, skills, and behavior of another individual, typically one with less training and experience than the supervisor. These definitions have five main components:

1. An experienced supervisor—one who is, at least, more experienced than the supervisee.
2. Actual clients in clinical settings.
3. A paramount concern with the welfare of both the client and supervisee. The number one rule of counseling and of supervision, like that of medicine, is *primum non nocere*—"first, do no harm."
4. Monitoring of the counselor's performance by indirect or direct observation.
5. The goal of changing the counselor's behavior.

The various schools of therapy and counseling differ in the extent to which they demand the shaping of behaviors and even personality to fit that of the supervisor or agency. Some schools disavow any such intention to clone the supervisor, viewing supervision instead as a consultative process, educational in nature. As Part Two will make clear, different practitioners and disciplines also differ as to whether they view supervision as (in addition to skills training) a form of therapy or counseling.

All agree, however, that one does not learn to practice therapy or counseling simply by undergoing therapy or counseling, any more than one learns to perform surgery by being operated on. On the other hand, supervision is something more than counselor education alone. Supervision amounts to the clinical preparation of a counselor for the practice of therapy; as such, it involves transforming principles into practice. In supervision, a successful counselor guides a supervisee's professional development, so that the supervisee acquires essential skills and learns to take independent actions through sound clinical reasoning and judgment. The supervisor helps the counselor fashion a personally integrated therapeutic style that sustains the counselor through a professional lifetime.

Chapter Two

A Working Definition of Supervision

Counselor supervision, however defined, has three main purposes:

1. To nurture the counselor's professional (and, as appropriate, personal) development.
2. To promote the development of specified skills and competencies, so as to bring about measurable outcomes.
3. To raise the level of accountability in counseling services and programs.

These three essential components place skill development in a broader context of professional development. Seen in this broader context, supervision helps the counselor (the most important factor in counseling) understand himself and the process of counseling and master the prerequisite knowledge and skills to perform the tasks required (Wrenn 1962). This lifelong process of professional development involves affirming, internalizing, and living out a professional self-image (Hart and Prince 1970). For alcoholism and drug abuse counselors who do not necessarily have a mental health background and a ready-made professional identity (such as a psychologist or social worker), this self-identification as a professional substance abuse counselor is critical. Counselors must have a strong commitment to the role and a clear perception of their professional responsibilities and functions. It helps, therefore, to have a professional affiliation and to participate in local, state, and national counselor associations. Likewise, counselors must be committed to the goals of the agency in which they work.

Finally, they need to recognize and appreciate the contribution the profession makes to individuals, groups, agencies, and society. Professional accountability begins with a recognition of needs and an understanding of one's own and the profession's impact on those needs.

This expansive vision of counselor development ties together the various definitions presented in Chapter One by showing how a therapy-oriented conception of supervision fits in with a skills-oriented conception. Thus, it points the way to a composite working definition of supervision.

THE BLENDED DEFINITION OF SUPERVISION

The following definition, which encompasses the numerous dimensions and facets of clinical supervision, is the foundation on which the blended model of supervision elaborated in this book will be built:

> Clinical supervision is a disciplined, tutorial process wherein principles are transformed into practical skills, with four overlapping foci: administrative, evaluative, clinical, and supportive.

Let us examine the key words in this definition. First, supervision is *disciplined*. It is regularly scheduled and time limited, with a specific agenda and expectations. Too often these requirements are not present in supervision. Much of what is called supervision is of the "catch you in the hall" variety, crisis focused and random. When asked, "How much time do you spend each week supervising your counselors?" clinical supervisors often answer, "Forty hours a week." This answer clearly fails the first test of supervision. Those who answer in this way probably are providing little structured, scheduled supervision. Effective clinical supervision, in contrast, is disciplined. Counselors are expected to prepare for case presentations and to bring clinical material (notes, audio- or videotapes) to sessions. The supervisor is expected to review the cases to be presented at a session.

Second, supervision is a *tutorial. Merriam-Webster's Collegiate Dictionary,* tenth edition (1988), defines a tutor as "a person charged with the instruction and guidance of another," "a private teacher," "a teacher [giving] individual instruction." A tutorial differs from classroom teaching in that it is learner based. Classroom education, which is necessarily geared to the training needs of all the students, cannot address the specific training needs of each student individually. In contrast, tutorial training involves an individual assessment of progress and an individualized training plan. It begins with what the counselor knows and needs to know to function in specific clinical situations. The content and agenda of the training are derived from observation of the counselor working with clients. Thus, effective clinical supervision requires first-hand oversight of the counselor's practice.

Third, supervision is a *process*, based on a mutually established and agreed-upon relationship of trust and respect. In this sense, the supervisor is a coach, cheerleader, mentor, friend, handholder, educator, and colleague. It is essential that there be cognitive consonance between the supervisor and supervisee. (This point, especially as it pertains to entry-level counselors, takes on special significance in relation to the developmental approach to supervision, as will be made clear in Part Two.) This trusting relationship, which takes time and patience to develop, is essential to the process of supervision.

Finally, *principles* are transformed into *practice*. Most counselors, especially in the alcoholism and drug abuse field, have excellent intuitive skills. They exhibit empathy, genuineness, concreteness, and potency. However, entry-level counselors lack the grounding needed for identifying what they did and why they did it. They have minimal background in conceptualizing treatment plans and justifying specific clinical interventions.

These individuals need concepts or principles on which they can hang their practical skills. They need to learn appropriate rationales for what they do instinctively. This is essentially how adults, as opposed to schoolchildren, learn. They try an intervention that may or may not work. Then they step back and ask, "Why did that work? What went right?" or, "Why didn't that work? What went wrong?" At that point the supervisor introduces a concept, a theory, a principle for intervention that gives the counselor a new perspective on the situation. The counselor tries out the principle, and the next time it works. With practice, it becomes part of the counselor's repertoire.

Thus, a central function of the clinical supervisor is to aid in transforming practice into principle and principle into practice. This "disciplined, tutorial process" involves teaching, mentorship, modeling, and learning. In sum, clinical supervision involves an intensive, evaluative, ongoing, and demanding relationship between two or more persons that encourages both vulnerability and independence (Holloway 1987). It is a working alliance (Bordin 1983) targeted toward goals of mastery of specific skills, a broader scope of concern for the client, awareness of one's own impact on the counseling process, and translation of theory into practice.

THE FOUR FOCI OF SUPERVISION

A clinical supervisor, overseeing the work of a counselor through a range of supervisory activities, is simultaneously an instructor, counselor for the counselor, and evaluator (among other roles). Here is a closer look at the four overlapping foci listed in the definition of supervision: administrative, evaluative, clinical, and supportive.

Administrative

Definitions of clinical supervision often slight the supervisor's administrative functions. That is because most definitions are written for counselors in academic training programs and internships. In the real world of service provision, most clinical supervisors have line responsibility for the functions of their counselors. They structure the counselors' work and evaluate counselors for pay raises, promotions, and certification. In most clinical settings, therefore, the administrative functions of a clinical supervisor must be addressed. In addition to treatment planning and case management, these include planning, organizing, coordinating, and delegating tasks; selecting and assisting staff; and determining clinical and administrative privileges.

To the extent that these functions can be classified as administrative aspects of clinical supervision, they are part of the clinical supervisory training covered in this book. Beyond this clinical and administrative area lies another body of knowledge, administrative supervision. That part of the job, which involves organizational management issues, is the area in which supervisors, especially in the alcoholism and drug abuse field, are least well trained. It would, however, require another book to present it adequately.

Evaluative

In carrying out the evaluative functions of clinical supervision, a supervisor assesses counselor skills, clarifies performance standards, negotiates objectives for learning, and utilizes appropriate sanctions for job performance impairment and skill deficits. Evaluation occurs in two main stages: (1) goal setting (formulating realistic, measurable objectives that make performance review possible) and (2) feedback (providing clear, constructive, humane communication concerning the degree to which goals have been attained). Evaluation is essential if clinical work is to be accountable. There are, however, three main roadblocks to effective evaluation by clinical supervisors: lack of skills in evaluating counselor performance, confusion about the compatibility of supervision and evaluation, and the anxiety-evoking aspects of evaluation.

The typical substance abuse counselor desperately wants feedback on his counseling skills. He wants to ask, "How am I doing?" yet is afraid to hear the answer. The supervisor, meanwhile, typically has little or no training in how to give feedback. Both parties need to understand that evaluation need not evoke fear or anxiety. Evaluation should create positive motivation for growth rather than obstruct improved performance by reducing energy and inhibiting risk taking.

The counselor must be aware of the evaluative procedures and participate in them in conjunction with the supervisor. One way of giving a positive cast to the evaluation process is to make clear that both the supervisor and supervisee are being evaluated. Indeed, criticism of the counselor is implicit criticism of the supervisor's ability to train the counselor in the prerequisite skills. The counselor also has some voice in the evaluation of the quality of supervision received.

Evaluation should be proactive rather than always aimed at correction and punishment. Abraham Maslow is reputed to have said, "If all you have is a hammer, everything starts to look like a nail." Evaluation should not be seen as a hammer. Its goal is to document success in attaining desired objectives and to point the way toward improvement—in other words, to assess the counselor's strengths as well as areas where expansion of knowledge and skills is in order. Thus, it is the responsibility of the clinical supervisor to provide feedback that is constructive, timely, and nonjudgmental. The supervisor looks for opportunities to bestow praise and positive reinforcement while assisting the counselor in making necessary modifications. In the words of *The One Minute Manager* (Blanchard and Johnson 1982), "Catch them doing something right."

Clinical

The clinical, educational, and training functions of supervision include developing counseling knowledge and skills, identifying learning issues and problems, determining counselor strengths and weaknesses, promoting self-awareness and professional and personal growth, and transmitting knowledge for practical use. A clinical supervisor should be a teacher, mentor (not tormentor), trainer, and professional role model.

In this dimension of the supervisor's role, the focus of the supervisory interaction is on the supervisee as a counselor, and the goal of supervision is to instruct. Specifically, the supervisor as instructor evaluates observed clinical interactions, identifies and reinforces appropriate actions by the supervisee, teaches and demonstrates counseling techniques, explains the rationale behind specific strategies and/or interventions, interprets significant events in the counseling process, and confronts the supervisee constructively as needed. The best supervisor teaches by example—not just instructing but modeling clinical competencies.

When I was doing clinical supervision for the U.S. military in Japan, the first counselor I supervised was fresh out of school, up against her first client. The night before, this client had gotten drunk, beaten his wife, and tried to kill himself. The emotional intensity of the client's account was such that I repeatedly had to restrain my impulse to jump in with feedback and recommendations. I sat there saying to myself, "Powell, shut up. Don't say anything. Let her go on with it. Otherwise, you'll intimidate her." Within five or ten minutes, however, I felt I had to say something because the session was going badly, so I stepped in. At the end of the session, recalling that moment, the counselor asked, "How did you know how to do that?" As it turned out, my timely intervention had bonded us together in a productive supervisory relationship. I didn't have to convince her that I had something of value to offer her, because I had demonstrated it.

This is the most effective way to teach: to let the student watch you work. To facilitate such modeling, a clinical supervisor should always have clinical responsibility in one form or another—through private practice, a small caseload in the agency, clinical trouble-shooting with difficult cases, or cofacilitation of a select number of sessions.

This is the consultative function of the supervisor, wherein she is accepted as an authority in her profession, a master clinician who is experienced in performing the counselor's work. In this consultative aspect of the supervisor's clinical role, the focus of the interaction is on the supervisee's client, and the supervisor's purpose is to gather data. In this capacity, the supervisor incorporates case management issues into the supervision. Specifically, the supervisor as consultant solicits supervisee needs, stimulates discussion of clinical problems, encourages the supervisee to devise strategies and interventions, and offers alternative conceptualizations and/or interventions.

The supervisee's development is the joint responsibility of supervisor and counselor, but the primary responsibility is that of the supervisee for his own self-development. The consultant supervisor guides the supervisee in achieving mutually agreed-upon objectives through agreed-upon strategies. The supervisor helps manage the supervisee's anxiety through a contract for learning negotiated by the two parties, which sets realistic limits to tasks and aspirations. Evaluation is conducted as part of this ongoing consultative oversight. Thus, the consultant supervisor combines two seemingly antithetical roles by seeking to create a risk-free, nonthreatening environment for dialogue while evaluating the supervisee's work performance.

Supportive

The supportive functions of clinical supervision include hand-holding, cheerleading, coaching, morale building, burnout prevention, and encouragement of personal growth. In certain respects the supervisor may be said to befriend the supervisee, although the boundaries of the professional situation make a close personal relationship between the two inappropriate.

Particularly for entry-level counselors, the supportive functions of supervision are critical. Counseling is a lonely job. The counselor, once having closed the office door to face the client one on one, is a lone ranger. But even the Lone Ranger had Tonto to turn to for support. To whom can the counselor turn? To whom can the counselor say, "I don't know what I'm doing. Help!" The clinical supervisor fulfills this vital function.

Supervision is not therapy, but the relationship between supervisor and supervisee does have a therapeutic dimension. To suggest what that dimension is, I like to use this saying in my workshops: "Supervision looks like therapy, not because the supervisor is doing therapy but because a therapist is doing supervision." In another clear example of isomorphism, the personality, training, techniques, and style of a therapist carry over into the supervisory role. Although the supervisee is not treated as a patient, the supervisor still sees with the eye of a therapist—one who is sensitive to feelings, perceptive about intrapsychic issues and interpersonal dynamics, and trained in a particular model of therapy. Anything a therapist does may feel more or less like therapy, whereas supervision conducted by, say, an expert in business management might feel quite different.

To the extent that the supervisor does act as a counselor, the focus is on the supervisee as a person, and the supervisor's goal is to facilitate the supervisee's growth in relation to the supervisee's counseling role. Specifically, the supervisor explores the supervisee's feelings during the counseling and supervision sessions (including feelings about specific interventions), provides opportunities for the supervisee to process his or her own affect and/or defenses, facilitates the supervisee's self-exploration, and helps the supervisee identify personal issues and areas for growth.

The supportive functions of counseling lead to a critical boundary issue: up to what point (if at all) is it appropriate for the supervisor to counsel the counselor? Since many of those working in the alcohol and drug abuse field come from a recovery history themselves or are adult children of alcoholic parents (so that in one way or another their own lives have been affected by alcoholism and drug abuse), personal growth and recovery are particularly relevant to the work of the substance abuse counselor. If the supervisor fails to address the counselor's personal-growth issues, the counselor may act out those issues in the clinical setting.

As a rule, the clinical material should be the main focus of supervision. However, when a counselor reveals a personal issue that is impeding the clinical process, the supervisor must see that the counselor gets the support needed to resolve the impasse. The boundary issue is when, where, and how the counseling should be provided. Since that is contingent on the model of supervision being practiced, a full answer will be deferred to Part Two.

However, as a general guideline applicable to most clinical supervisory settings (especially where the supervisor has line authority over the counselor), it is safe to say that the clinical supervisor need not and usually should not provide personal counseling for supervisees. Instead, a referral to the employee assistance program or to an external therapist is appropriate. Such a referral is called for to avoid dual relationships—role conflicts that would compromise the supervisory relationship. In particular, a therapeutic relationship generally involves a degree of dependency that would be out of place in supervision.

SUMMARY

Clinical supervision is a unique and distinctive educational procedure. It is not primarily task oversight, although it includes that component. Neither is it counseling the counselor, although a counselor's conflicts about himself, his vocation, and his work situation may be dealt with or referred out for further counseling. Supervision is not didactic instruction, although substantive content may be conveyed. Nor is it simply practical guidance, although it may contribute to accomplishing this purpose. According to the model developed in this book, clinical supervision is all of the above, blended together into a comprehensive program of structured and unstructured learning and professional and personal growth. It is a method of education designed to permit the integration into practice of self-understanding, relevant theory, substantive knowledge, and functional skills. As such, it enables the supervisee to bridge the gap between vital preparatory learning and actual practice. At the same time, it prepares the supervisee to function as a member of a community of practitioners.

The definition of clinical supervision presented here, with its accompanying descriptions and elaborations, provides essential grounding in supervision. Although the definition provides a point of reference, a concise preview of what is to follow, it remains to be fleshed out in keeping with the model of supervision developed in subsequent chapters. It remains to be fleshed out in another sense as well. This definition anticipates and attempts to incorporate an accelerating pace of change in the field. Supervisors, trainees, and managers will need to develop their own models of supervision in response to the various models described, and the one ultimately synthesized from them, in Part Two. Both in these pages and over time, author and readers together will be working toward a fuller definition of clinical supervision.

Chapter Three

Leadership Principles for Supervisors

The principles and methods of clinical supervision espoused in this book are founded on fundamental concepts of organizational leadership: servant leadership, stakeholders, participatory management, and an effective working environment. The newly emerging team-based organizational structure of corporations is conducive to the implementation of these concepts. Conversely, exercising leadership in the manner described in this chapter can help create an organization well adapted for survival in the new competitive marketplace.

LEADERSHIP, MANAGEMENT, AND SUPERVISION

Leadership is not the same as management, and management is not the same as supervision. Yet it is important for supervisors to realize that they have leadership abilities to discover, develop, and use.

Leadership entails teaching, mentoring, and coaching in the service of a set of core values, such as liberty, justice, equality, honesty, responsibility, fairness, and the honoring of commitments. It transforms people by raising their sights and aspirations to a higher level, thereby engendering a greater sense of purpose. Leadership qualities are present in all persons: parents, teachers, peers, preachers, and clinical supervisors. Whether an individual develops these qualities to the point that she becomes a leader depends on the degree to which she possesses initiative and courage.

Having the position of supervisor does not necessarily make this person a leader. Supervisors do not automatically get respect and acceptance from group members. To earn the leadership of a group and to have a positive influence on the group members, supervisors must exercise specific leadership skills and methods. In the end, the test of a supervisor's leadership qualities is that person's contribution to the group and the resultant organizational change, measured by a growing sense of purpose drawn from collective motives and values.

Leadership abilities differ from those required for management and supervision, as follows:

Leadership Abilities

- To establish trust with co-workers and subordinates.
- To serve as a team leader.
- To define and set departmental and organizational goals and communicate these goals companywide.
- To inspire staff by encouragement and motivation.
- To communicate enthusiasm and capability.
- To keep up staff morale, including one's own.
- To take appropriate risks and to be decisive in action.
- To possess the ability to change in response to the needs of the organization and marketplace.
- To have vision, drive, clear judgment, initiative, poise, and maturity of character.
- To command enthusiasm, loyalty, sincerity, courtesy, and confidence.
- To exercise control through inspiration rather than command.

Management Abilities

- To get work done through staff.
- To make effective use of departmental resources.
- To get results in achieving stated goals and objectives.
- To control through command.
- To identify, analyze, and solve problems.
- To adapt to change and the growing needs of the organization.
- To organize work as needed to get the job done.
- To intervene to bring about positive results.
- To see all aspects of operations.

Supervision Abilities

- To know the responsibilities of staff.
- To communicate clearly these responsibilities to staff.
- To utilize effectively the performance appraisal system to get maximum productivity of staff.
- To write clear job descriptions and quarterly and annual goal and work statements for all staff.
- To manage time effectively for oneself and staff.
- To delegate responsibilities to all staff.
- To promote employees' professional development.

Effective supervisors share a vision for the company. A clearly articulated vision statement answers the question: "Why do we exist?" It is a consciously chosen and precisely formulated direction that uses the talents and abilities of a team, contributes to the successful functioning of the organization, and leads to a sense of fulfillment for team members.

Much of the essence of leadership is summed up by two quotations drawn from widely separated historical moments. Walter Lippmann wrote of Franklin Delano Roosevelt, "The final test of a leader is that he leaves behind him in others the conviction and will to carry on." He does this by helping people grow. The mediocre supervisor tells people what to do, the superior supervisor demonstrates what to do, and the great supervisor inspires people to do what they know should be done. Lao-tsu, in the sixth century B.C., said it this way: "The superior leader gets things done with very little motion. He imparts instruction not through many words but through a few deeds. He keeps informed about everything, but interferes hardly at all. He is a catalyst, and although things would not get done as well if he were not there, when they succeed he takes no credit. Because he takes no credit, credit never leaves him."

THE NEW ORGANIZATIONAL CONTEXT

Until recently, both private- and public-sector organizations were built on a linear, hierarchical, quasi-military structure, with top-down communication and little employee empowerment. In the work environment of postwar America, this structure made sense.

In the late twentieth century, however, a new organizational structure is emerging, based on principles of participatory management, networked communication, and self-directed work teams.

The Command-Control Structure

Previously, a company's organizational chart would have been linear and hierarchical. It would have looked something like Figure 3-1. The old dogma taught that management manages through control and organization while workers work. Companies established hierarchies to make task assignments unambiguous, thereby cutting off contact within the organization according to functions. Information always flowed downward from top management through middle management to line workers, with "stovepipe" thinking (up and down the chain of command). A supervisor working in this traditional structure would manage subordinates through command and control. Within this old organizational chart, the employee saw the goal not as satisfying the customer or improving profits but as climbing up to the top position through empire building.

Figure 3-1. The Command-Control Structure

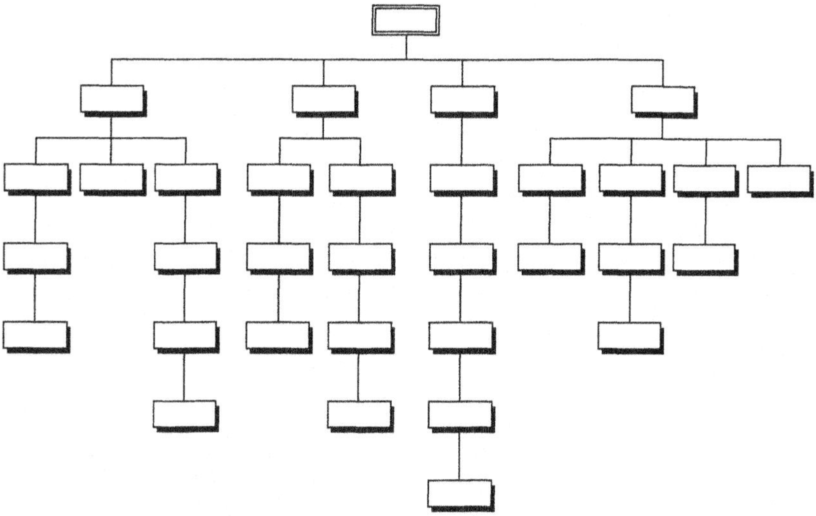

When employees look at a traditional organizational chart, the first thing they see is who is on top and to whom they report. Employees look up and say, "Just tell me what you want," which seems like a reasonable question. However, it is the worst possible question because it means that the person has abdicated all responsibility. It focuses on pleasing the boss (a short-term, individual goal) instead of pleasing the customer (a long-term organizational goal).

The Networked, Team-Based Structure

As American business entered the global marketplace of the 1990s, companies were hungry for new approaches to make them competitive. While the longtime gurus of management theory, Peter Drucker and W. Edwards Deming, celebrated their eightieth and ninetieth birthdays, respectively, the corporate landscape was shifting faster than ever. Increasingly, competition was worldwide, technology was developing at an accelerating pace, and the work force was changing profoundly. These pressures have necessitated fresh approaches.

The solutions being advanced represent a paradigm shift in organizational thinking. A new language for business is emerging in the 1990s with terms such as *learning organization, reengineering, core competencies, organizational architecture,* and *time-based competition.* The primary characteristic of these new organizations is a different way of structuring a company. Business leaders recognize that the line-and-box structure of the past makes less and less sense. A new structure is required to remain competitive in the future, a structure that makes an organization flat (nonhierarchical), focused, fast, friendly, and flexible.

Underlying the new structure is the realization that management must see the big picture, transcend linear thinking, and understand the subtleties of interrelationships. In line with these imperatives, organizational structures are flattened, with functions decentralized. Arrows on organizational charts go in all directions, linking various departments, rather than just up and down. Managers, instead of controlling, direct work flow.

Corporate strategies are based not on products or markets but on skills and knowledge. Jobs are redesigned around outcomes, and not tasks or functions. Core competencies are identified, and companies are organized around what people do best. Time has become the basis for quality, providing an organization a competitive advantage if it can respond faster to the marketplace. The key resource of business is not capital, personnel, or plants but information flow. "Newstreams" that speed up the flow of information are critical if a company is to be fast on its feet to the customer.

Organizations are thinking more broadly about work by creating autonomous work teams and strategic alliances. Smaller is usually better. Bureaucracy and hierarchy are a thing of the past as companies base authority not on position, status, or rank but on persons, with authority flowing from expertise and from relationships. Whereas traditional management is rules oriented, specifying procedures and rewarding adherence to them, post-entrepreneurial management is results oriented, rewarding outcomes and paying people for contributions, regardless of formal position. Bureaucracies operate through formal structures designed to channel and restrict the flow of information. The new, more flexible organizations find opportunities through the expansion of information, by maximizing communication links, coalitions, and alliances.

In today's organization, communication is nonlinear, with networks of information flowing through self-directed work teams (Figure 3-2). When new employees see this open-ended, interconnected chart, they have no idea what is going on, who reports to whom, and who is above or below them in the organization. And that is the point: pigeonholes are obsolete. All employees play a role in customer satisfaction, profitability, and understanding all aspects of operations. Because information needs to flow quickly between customer and company, all employees are encouraged to have direct contact with customers.

In addition to this altered communication flow, the team-based organization operates by means of functional relationships as opposed to traditional departmental or linear relationships. Work is organized by what must be done to meet customer needs. The hub of this organizational structure is customer satisfaction, with customer service as the internal and external governing force (Figure 3-3).

Figure 3-2. The Networked, Team-Based Organization:
Communication Patterns

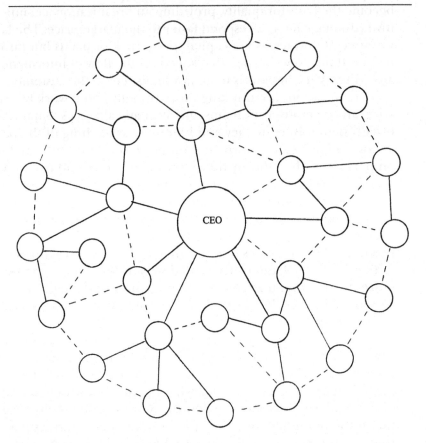

Successful organizations of the future will make decisions based on shared understanding of interrelated functions and patterns of change. This understanding is operationalized by working in teams, with every job function geared toward customer satisfaction and each team having full responsibility for decision making and financial management from the start to the finish of the task. In this new paradigm, management provides vision, values, and mental models. A supervisor must think systematically, looking at underlying structures or systems rather than at particular events as a starting point for change.

Figure 3-3. The Networked, Team-Based Organization: Functional Relationships

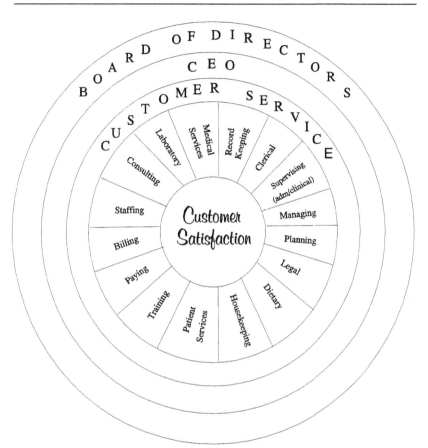

LEADERSHIP QUALITIES IN THE NEW ORGANIZATIONAL CONTEXT

Here are ten principles for exercising leadership in the new organizational context. These are sound for leaders in any type of organization, but they are especially necessary in nonlinear, nonhierarchical organizations:

1. Take full responsibility for decisions you make. Never blame someone else for something that is your fault.

2. Always put the well-being of the people reporting to you above your personal well-being.
3. Always give subordinates full credit for successes.
4. Do not be afraid to take risks when they are in the best interests of the organization or the client.
5. Protect your supervisees, and defend them to senior management when they are unfairly attacked or punished.
6. Take a personal interest in the welfare of your staff.
7. Make decisions promptly. Sometimes decisions must be made without full information. You get paid to make the best decisions you can under the circumstances.
8. Be a teacher. Show someone what to do to make things come out right.
9. Do not play favorites.
10. Do not give orders just to prove who is boss. If you have to prove who is the boss, you are not.

These principles are cornerstones of leadership. All too commonly they are forgotten by aspiring supervisors. In order to practice these principles, a person needs to nurture certain key leadership qualities. These qualities, which largely have to do with caring and a sense of mission, provide an essential foundation for good supervision in the new organizational context.

Good supervision is largely a matter of caring for staff. In the words of Autry (1991, p. 15), "Management is, in fact, a sacred trust in which the well-being of other people is put in your care during most of their waking hours." Being a supervisor means being in relationship with people and having one's own needs inextricably intertwined with theirs. Supervision is not about structures but about people: their needs, concerns, and growth. It involves accepting one's humanness rather than hiding it behind the supervisor mask; attending to one's own life issues such as marriage, childbirth, illness, and death; and supporting others in their life crises. The ultimate goal of leadership is to create a sense of community at work. Ways of demonstrating caring include sending flowers to employees when they or someone in their family is ill, visiting a hospitalized employee, celebrating birthdays and work anniversaries with a card accompanied by a personal note, attending significant events in a staff member's life, such as weddings and funerals, and being available to employees whenever they need to talk.

A supervisor who is to help people grow must have a sense of mission: a belief in her ability to lead, a passion for work, a devotion to people and the agency, and a clear vision of the organization's purpose. A positive vision and sense of purpose demand honesty with self and others. An effective supervisor with strong leadership qualities knows her job. She is technically sound and trusts her skills. She believes she has something to impart to others. She is clinically sound.

Most supervisors have these qualities in varying degrees. The key leadership quality is the ability to bring about a positive change in the lives of those she touches and who touch her. This quality is found in the professor who changes a student's life through thought and inspiration, the manager who believes in the employee when the employee does not believe in himself, the community servant who lives out a life of caring. The mark of leadership is the impression left behind in the lives of those who follow.

SERVANT LEADERSHIP

A fundamental principle of the new organizational structure is bottom-up management, with participation in the decision-making process spread throughout the corporation. To achieve employee involvement and empowerment, the principle of servanthood becomes an essential attribute of leadership for senior managers and line supervisors alike. Greenleaf (1977) asserts that a leader is a servant first; that is the key to the leader's influence. The leader is at the foundation of the enterprise—supporting, not directing, the teams that design and implement the tasks.

Leaders inspire followers in good and bad times and in the short and long term. They acquire followers by serving them. Paradoxical as it seems, true leadership flows from those willing to be led, the followers. The power to lead comes from giving up personal need for power in order to serve the group.

Leadership means going ahead to show the way, venturing creatively, seeing the whole. The leader is not above the others and is not better than the rest but takes up the group's burden (for example, by advocating on behalf of the staff to top management). Max De Pree (1989, p. 3) states, "Leaders bear pain. They do not inflict it." A supervisor stands alongside the supervisees, not obstructing their vision or progress. The leader makes the shared vision clear by standing a step ahead of the followers while standing behind their actions.

In this way, an effective supervisor shares power with the group, guiding them and using the least force required. The danger of being a star is that individual brilliance can outshine the vision, obscuring the mission of the organization. The Tao says, "The best leader is one whose existence is barely known by the people. When a leader's task is completed, the people will say, 'It happened to us naturally.'"

Finally, the servant leader cares for people. People do not care how much the leader knows until they know how much he cares. The servant leader manifests caring by knowing the potential of each of the followers, respecting their powers and skills, and listening to what is in their hearts. People cannot be led where they do not want to go. Business books say that the goal of a leader is to motivate people. However, people cannot be motivated since they are already motivated. The goal of a leader is to identify these motivations and tap into them.

The business of business is a set of relationships that creates value for people, fills their needs, and helps them grow and prosper. Supervisors enter into a covenant with their staff to provide a new reference point for what caring, purposeful, committed people can accomplish together in an institutional setting. De Pree (1989, p. 5) states, "Covenants bind people together and enable them to meet their corporate needs by meeting the needs of one another." This is the essence of a supervisor's servant leadership and the heart of the new organizational context.

A supervisor can apply the principles of servant leadership in a myriad of small ways. For example, when there is photocopying to be done and the secretaries are busy, volunteer to do the copying. Send the staff home an hour early on Friday and cover the phones yourself. Prepare and serve lunch for the staff. If boxes need to be hauled to a car (and if your back can take it), volunteer to help. Notes of praise and thanks to staff for a job well done are acts of thanksgiving and service. At holiday times, remember staff by sending them personal notes. Servanthood is a state of mind. Once a supervisor attains that state, the range of possibilities for servant leadership is unlimited.

STAKEHOLDERS

For whose benefit is a business run? In the old-style organization, it was the investors, the stockholders, who mattered most. The new networked organizations view a broader range of constituents as having an interest, or stake, in their operations. They serve many different individuals and groups, whom we might call *stakeholders,* a term that suggests dynamic interplay between a corporation and the people it serves.

An agency has six major stakeholders: its owners, employees, customers, vendors, competitors, and community. All have some influence over the design and delivery of products or services.

Owners

The agency may be a nonprofit organization, a publicly operated organization, or a privately held corporation. In the case of a nonprofit agency, the members of the board of directors are the stakeholders, with a fiduciary trust on behalf of their state. Whatever the nature of the organization and its ownership, management must serve its stakeholders responsibly through wise stewardship of the funds entrusted to it.

Employees

The employer's responsibilities to employees begin with the obligation to pay each worker a fair wage for services rendered. Recompense includes benefits such as health insurance, pension security, flexibility in task assignments, a clean and safe working environment, and meaningful employment opportunities. Beyond these basic commitments, there are legal and ethical considerations pertaining to labor-management relations, affirmative action, and job security.

There are three ways in which the substance abuse counseling field, along with other mental health fields, often does not serve its employee stakeholders well. First, indiscriminate firings, layoffs, and unfair labor practices have no place in a healthy organization. Just as harmful is the opposite extreme of indulging inadequate job performance in the guise of being nice, patient, kind, and understanding of employees' needs. A supervisor who takes this easy way out is not exercising responsible stewardship. Finally, the field ill serves its employee stakeholders when it pays them inadequately. Agencies must regularly review their salary structures to ensure that employees are being treated fairly.

Customers

The 1990s are ringing with phrases about "staying close to one's customers." Without customers there is no reason for an organization to exist. Indeed, a growing sensitivity to customer input is reflected in the flourishing of market research and public opinion polls. If car buyers want cupholders, the manufacturers find ways to build them in. Politicians, too, have become expert at giving their "customers" what they want.

In the substance abuse and other mental health fields, the customers are the patients served, as well as those who entrust those patients for care, such as employee assistance programs, referral resources, and community agencies. Within an agency, each department has its own internal customers—for example, the finance and accounting department serving the needs of the agency and the housekeeping department serving patient needs. All departments are customers for one another. In this broad sense, customer service is the most critical element in the existence of an agency and should be the supervisor's primary focus. The supervisor should constantly ask, "If the customer knew I was doing this, would he pay for it?" If the answer is no, the supervisor should stop doing it.

Vendors

A health care agency's vendors include suppliers of equipment, paper goods, and housekeeping or dietary services. The new-style organization acknowledges a covenant with vendors that entails a responsibility to pay them promptly, to be clear and open in communications, and to treat them with trust and respect. Agencies are in a partnership with vendors to meet the needs of their mutual customers.

Competitors

Although other companies providing similar services usually are not thought of as stakeholders, the same issues of mutual responsibility carry over to competitive relationships as well. Does an agency refer to competitors in negative terms? How does the company treat competitive intelligence, trade secrets, pricing data, and technical proposals? Books today speak about management as warfare. Although the military metaphor may be relevant in a competitive environment, the tone is unnecessarily adversarial. Even warfare has conventions of combat. It is important to treat competitors with openness and fairness, for the ethical standards an agency maintains toward competitors are a reflection of the way it treats its other stakeholders (such as staff and customers) and, ultimately, itself.

The Community at Large

The notion of community extends to both the local area in which a company does business and the global community. It is increasingly evident that American business must get beyond the minimalist view of communal responsibility it has taken, which has resulted in polluted air, dangerous workplaces, and oil spills.

Although health care agencies serve the community by providing clinical services, their responsibility goes beyond patient care. It also involves programs such as paper recycling or a gift drive for families in need. An agency expresses its stake in the community, as well as the community's stake in the agency, by supporting the local schools, helping to keep the streets safe, and participating in neighborhood improvement programs. Supervisors should encourage employees to be active in their communities and to vote in elections.

These six stakeholders shape the environment in which supervisors work. To be effective in the new organizational structure, a supervisor must balance the interests of all stakeholders. This requirement introduces a new openness to a field where counselors and other professionals heretofore have claimed exclusive knowledge of what constitutes a good treatment program. Organizations formerly characterized by top-down dictation and preaching from certitude must become open and participative, both internally and externally. Success will come to agencies whose actions are guided by core values and produce benefits for each of the various stakeholders. Individuals and groups that come in contact with such agencies will experience interconnectedness, growth, and a realization of their innate potential.

THE NEW WORK ENVIRONMENT

When organizations empower employees to be part of the decision-making process, establish a bottom-up management structure, practice servant leadership, and balance the needs of all stakeholders, they become, in the words of Levering (1988), "great places to work." Although these concepts are relatively new, they have (to a greater or lesser degree) been put into practice by corporations such as Delta Air Lines, Pitney Bowes, Disney, Hewlett-Packard, W. L. Gore and Associates, Quad/Graphics, and Tektronix. Observing the operation of these successful companies, supervisors and managers (indeed, all levels of employees) can discern certain common themes to bring into their own organizations.

Camaraderie

Friendly banter and informal chat should be an accepted part of everyday life at work. In a positive working environment, people enjoy one another's company. There is laughter in the halls. People mix naturally in gathering places such as employee cafeterias. This relaxed attitude toward socializing springs from the relative lack of social hierarchy in good workplaces. Networked companies do not have executive dining rooms, special parking lots, and other executive perks prevalent in top-down organizations. Instead, a social egalitarianism reigns. People work harder in these companies than in the old-style workplaces because they prize a quality job and feel part of the agency's vision and values.

Partying together is a clear sign that this desirable atmosphere has taken hold. At ETP, we liked to find any occasion to party—a holiday, birthdays, pregnancies, work anniversaries, winning a contract. At Halloween, the company president always wore the most outrageous costume. At ETP we had a "Fun Committee" that organized playtime together, sent flowers to sick employees, celebrated birthdays and work anniversaries, and planned annual office picnics and parties. For example, when several employees turned forty at around the same time, the committee organized a "forties party" featuring the vintage rock and roll dear to the hearts of baby boomers. To twist an old slogan, "A company that parties together wins together."

Deemphasis on Politics

Politics are at a minimum in good workplaces. Healthy competition and power struggles are endemic to all organizations, but in an atmosphere of mutual respect and shared goals, they need not lead to mistrust, backbiting, jockeying for position, and sabotage. The key to creating a nonpoliticized environment is a sense of trust, openness, and fairness throughout the company, together with teamwork and cooperation with all stakeholders. People feel less need to play politics when they have meaningful work and a sense of contributing to a whole—that is, to the improvement of the overall quality of life for the stakeholders.

Growth Values

A supervisor should contribute to moving the organization from traditional protection values of safety, ego defense, role playing, superiority to others, control of others, and comfort (avoidance of pain) at all costs to growth values. The values manifested in healthy organizations include truth, spontaneity (risk taking), vulnerability, authentic communications, and connectedness to others. These values, easy to state but hard to live, are essential for an effective supervisor to model.

A key growth value is employee empowerment, giving all staff a voice in their company. Top-down management tells employees what to do. Bottom-up organizations consist of empowered workers

who have a voice in their corporation, including personnel policies and practices, budgeting and pricing, operations, marketing
and sales, and administration. Employee empowerment can be
practiced by forming a team when policies are to be rewritten,
when the health insurance plan is reviewed, when there is a budget crunch. Nothing that may affect employees' lives is kept secret
from them. Employees are kept regularly informed of the company's financial state and given the power to make changes in
operations if necessary. Through employee empowerment, companies can become far greater than the sum of their parts.

How an organization honors its people is another sign of values. In companies that practice growth values, staff members are
publicly praised at meetings. Credit is given to all workers for successes. A supervisor can write "thank you" at the top of a paper
when it is well done. Personnel can be acknowledged as "employee
of the quarter" and "employee of the year." At ETP we arranged
with the landlord to have a parking place outside the entrance with
an "employee of the quarter" sign to recognize valued workers. It
cost the company nothing, and in the middle of a cold New England winter, this parking space became quite prized. New employees were "mugged" at their first staff meeting with a ceremonial
coffee mug and a copy of the ETP values statement, which they
were asked to display in a prominent location in their office. There
are hundreds of ways to honor staff, limited only by a supervisor's
creativity.

Family and Community

Finally, networked environments give people a sense of being part
of a family. This metaphor should not be invoked uncritically,
since people come from different types of families—some healthy,
some unhealthy. In particular, there is no intention here to replicate the traditional patriarchal family structure that business leaders in the past (Henry Ford, for example) have used as a model.
Nonetheless, some people have been blessed by loving, caring
families, and it is these that the new organizational context seeks
to emulate.

The head of a healthy family provides a caring, nurturing environment where people feel valued, and family members do their

part to maintain and reinforce this environment. Individuals feel a long-term commitment to one another. Similarly, the participatory organization is committed to its people and elicits a reciprocal commitment from them. If people perform to standard, there will be work for them. No company can guarantee employees a job for life, but healthy companies care for their people and are dedicated (to the maximum extent possible) to providing meaningful employment in both good and bad times.

In this way, a healthy organization promotes a sense of community around commonly held values. It gives stakeholders a vision for the future and a caring group with which to carry it out. An employee who enters such a work environment feels the sense of connectedness and concern. The supervisor's role is to contribute to this values-driven environment that encourages growth, acceptance, and mutual responsibility.

One sign of this healthy family atmosphere, according to Curran (1983), is shared table time. A family's well-being can be judged just by listening to its dinner conversation. What do the family members talk about? What is the atmosphere around the table? The same is true for companies. How much "table time" do employees spend together? What is discussed? Does the conversation dwell on griping, backstabbing, gossip, and manipulation? Or is it playful, fun, and caring, with a sharing of useful information? Is there laughter in the halls? Do people enjoy one another's company? These are traits of a healthy family or company and, taken together, a theme of organizations built on teams and networks. Creating such an environment for employees is the essence of the supervisory role. Through coaching, cheerleading, modeling supportive relationships, and creating opportunities for people to achieve their goals, supervisors turn organizations into positive workplaces.

At ETP, this proactive supervisory role in the company community was modeled at all management levels, starting at the top. I like to prepare lasagna and invite all staff to sit around together and indulge. Breakfasting individually with personnel was another way to break down barriers—or, better yet, to make sure they do not arise. I will never forget the reaction of a newly hired secretary who, in her first week of work, was served spaghetti by the president. She said, "I can't believe the president cooked lunch for me.

What is it about this place?" This is servanthood, expressed in shared table time.

MAKING IT WORK

The model of clinical supervision espoused in this book is based on the principles of the new work organization: networked systems, servant leadership, participatory management, and stakeholder involvement. The kind of supervisor an individual becomes depends on many variables, especially the model of counseling and supervision he or she chooses from among the models outlined in Part Two. Nonetheless, an essential aspect of an individual's approach to supervision is the principles of leadership to which he adheres.

Supervisors often lament that they cannot apply the principles of leadership presented in this chapter because they work in bureaucratic organizations with self-protective values. To be sure, the health care industry is filled with bureaucratic, top-down hierarchies that stifle growth values and inhibit participatory management. Many agencies are based on the medical model, in which the psychiatrist rules by edict. This is the nature of the health care field, which has lagged behind corporate business in recognizing the value of the new organizational structure.

What can clinical supervisors do in such an organization? First, they must not lose hope. The management principles outlined here are relatively new. Organizations are beginning to understand that to survive in today's competitive environment, they must change the way they do business. The mental health field may be slow in catching on, but there are positive signs of change.

Second, in the 1960s we learned that instead of "cursing the darkness," individuals had a responsibility to "light a candle" in their corner of the world. All the people who work in a organization vote with their feet, their hands, and their voices for the kind of organization it is going to be. A clinical supervisor works in a group, a microcosm of the agency, on which the supervisor can have an impact. A supervisor may not be able to change top-level organizational policy but can begin to change the organizational context by modeling a new standard and process of supervision.

As positive change becomes evident in one corner of the agency, a larger momentum for change may sweep through the whole organization.

Third, supervisors can introduce these concepts to management by demonstrating them in practice as well as by recommending reading and suggesting seminars for senior managers to attend. By modeling the desired behaviors, standing on principles despite management obstacles, and advocating change within an organization, clinical supervisors may well bring about change. And even if change does not occur, these supervisors have provided a model of a healthy organization for tomorrow's generation of supervisors who are in training today.

Chapter Four

Traits of an Effective Clinical Supervisor

How do the principles of servant leadership, mentorship, and participatory management manifest themselves in clinical supervision? What, in the emerging organizational context, qualifies a person to be a clinical supervisor? What are the traits of an effective clinical supervisor? Supervisors in my workshops most often cite the following qualities:

- Clinical knowledge, skills, and professional experience.
- Having been supervised and having had supervision of one's supervision.
- Professional education and training.
- Inheriting the job from someone else and being given the title.
- Good teaching, motivational, and communication skills.
- A desire to pass on knowledge and skills to others (generativity) (Blocher 1983).
- A sense of humor, humility, limits, and balance in life.
- A concerned, sensitive, and caring nature.
- Good helping skills, observation skills, and affective qualities (empathy, respect, concreteness, action orientation, confrontation skills, immediacy) (Blocher 1983; Patterson 1983).
- Openness to fantasy and imagination (Loganbill, Hardy, and Delworth 1982).
- Ability to create a relaxed atmosphere (Bordin 1983).
- Willingness to examine one's own attitudes and biases (Hawthorne 1975).
- Respect among peers and colleagues.

- Willingness to learn from others and introspectiveness.
- Good time management and executive skills.
- Familiarity with legal and ethical issues, policies, and procedures.
- Cognitive and conceptual ability.
- Physical, emotional, and spiritual health, with energy and ambition.
- A serious commitment (Hart 1982) with accompanying enthusiasm.
- Concern for the growth of the supervisee (Hess 1986).
- Concern for the welfare of the client (Bernard 1981; Corey, Corey, and Callahan 1987; Cormier and Bernard 1982).
- A sense of responsibility (Leddick and Dye 1987).
- A capacity for intimacy.
- A nonthreatening, nonauthoritarian, diplomatic manner (Allen, Szollos, and Williams 1986; Worthington, 1984).
- Tolerance, objectivity, fairness, and openness to variety of styles (Stoltenberg, Solomon, and Ogden 1986).
- Ability to convey professional and personal respect for others.
- Ability to advocate effectively on behalf of the counselor, the client, and the agency.
- Survival skills and longevity in the organization.
- Decision-making and problem-solving skills.
- Crisis management skills.

This long list can be summarized simply by a convenient mnemonic for the beginner that captures a good bit of what a supervisor should be: "the four A's of supervision":

Available: open, receptive, trusting, nonthreatening.

Accessible: easy to approach and speak freely with.

Able: having real knowledge and skills to transmit.

Affable: pleasant, friendly, reassuring.

Kaslow (1986b, p. 6) states that a supervisor must be "ethical, well informed, knowledgeable in his/her theoretical orientation, clinically skilled, articulate, empathic, a good listener, gentle, confrontive, accepting, challenging, stimulating, provocative, reassuring, encouraging, possess a good sense of humor, a good sense of timing, be innovative, solid, exciting, laid back—but not all at the same time." A supervisor models excitement, empathy, and curiosity. No one can fake these feelings for long.

At the same time, it is important to distinguish between intrinsic personal qualities and professional skills. Referring to the ten dimensions of effectiveness in interpersonal relations identified by Wolf (1974/1975)—empathy, respect, genuineness, concreteness, confrontation, self-disclosure, immediacy, warmth, potency, and self-actualization—Edelwich and Brodsky (1980, p. 42) comment: "Seen as personality traits, none of these can be taught. Seen as counseling skills, all of them can be taught. That is, one cannot be trained to be empathic, but one can be trained to give empathic responses. One cannot be trained to be warm or to be concrete; one can be trained to manifest warmth or concreteness."

The supervisor should also be able to communicate a coherent model of therapy, articulate a systemic approach to supervision, and show an acceptance of diversity. Together, these attitudes and beliefs form a framework for supervision that establishes a rationale for the supervisor's actions. The supervisor must be able to answer these questions:

1. What do I believe about how change occurs for people?
2. What are the crucial variables in training and supervision?
3. How do I measure success in supervision?
4. How do I contribute to that success?
5. What learning objectives do I have for supervision, and what techniques will I apply to achieve these objectives?

No supervisor is expected to have all this expertise in place on her first day in this role; rather, it takes shape as she gains experience and avails herself of the knowledge the field has to offer. In particular, Part Two of this book will take the reader through the steps of selecting a model and developing a comprehensive personal framework for supervision.

Another way to identify the essential traits of an effective clinical supervisor is to find out how supervisors and counselors alike feel about the adequacy of clinical supervision as it is currently offered. Kadushin (1992) has done this for the field of social work in an article entitled "What's Wrong, What's Right with Social Work Supervision." Kadushin found general agreement between supervisors and supervisees concerning the strengths and weaknesses of supervisors. The greatest perceived strengths of supervisors were their knowledge and experience; their willingness and ability to teach, along with their communication skills; their affective qualities (empathy, respect, relational skills); their listening skills; their sense of fairness; and their being well organized.

When it came to supervisory weaknesses, there was agreement on both sides that the most significant shortcoming was in exercising managerial authority in decision making and giving constructive feedback. This could be termed "managing in the muddle of middleness," a common plight of middle-level supervisors in any occupation. Other shortcomings included an inability to advocate for staff; insufficient time for supervision (case overload); personal characteristics (rigid, unrealistic, impatient, hyperverbal, burned out, overprotective, or too involved with staff); and a lack of supervisory knowledge and skills (the last item was ranked fifth in importance by supervisors, third by supervisees). In these responses the emphasis is on two of the four A's: ability (first and foremost) and accessibility.

It would be useful to have comparable data for the substance abuse field. Meanwhile, any supervisor can replicate this study on an ongoing, informal basis by asking supervisees for feedback ("What could I be doing better?"). Judging from Kadushin's findings, supervisors generally have a good idea of what the answers will be.

THE TWO ESSENTIAL QUALITIES

Kadushin's findings and supervisors' responses point to two qualities that are essential to clinical supervision: sound clinical experience and a passion for counseling. Both might be considered elaborations on *able*, from the four A's.

Clinical Skills and Experience

The first essential qualification of clinical supervisors is to be a good clinician. To supervise effectively, they must believe that they have something of value to impart to others. If they are not accomplished counselors, with confidence in their clinical skill and judgment, they cannot project confidence and efficacy in the supervisory role.

Indeed, in the context of the developmental perspective presented in Chapter Six, it will be clear that a clinical supervisor should be an advanced-level counselor.

Those on whom the title of supervisor is bestowed often feel so overwhelmed by managerial and administrative tasks that they make the mistake of giving up their clinical functions; they stop seeing clients. In so doing, they get too distant from the action, lose their clinical edge, and forfeit their credibility as counselors. No longer can they demonstrate their familiarity with the life of the counselor. Supervisees often remark, "How do *you* know what has to be done? You don't see clients anymore. You don't know what we have to go through." No one can teach what he does not know, and he cannot know what he does not practice. In the words of novelist John le Carré, "The desk is a dangerous place from which to watch the world." Or, as practitioners in the field sometimes say, "Lead with your feet, not just your mouth."

Therefore, all clinical supervisors should retain some form of direct client responsibilities by maintaining a small caseload in the agency, periodically doing intakes, or having a small private practice. Some supervisors occasionally take over a group, but this should be done (if at all) with caution because of the risk of intensified resistance from group members who miss their trusted counselor or the opposite danger of upstaging the counselor, thereby making it more difficult for the counselor to resume leading the group (Edelwich and Brodsky 1992).

Through continued client contact, supervisors keep their clinical edge and credentials. They stay up-to-date on current clinical thinking and retain credibility among supervisees. They should also maintain some form of supervision for both the counseling and supervisory roles. Nothing is more refreshing for an experienced, advanced-level counselor and supervisor than to get a fresh perspective. Finally, if other career avenues are blocked, a supervisor has the security of knowing that he or she can go back to counseling.

Passion for Counseling

Supervisors need a passion for the job. Robert Stuckey, one of my early supervisors, once stated, "No matter how important you become, how many letters you have after your name, how much money you earn, never lose sight of the fact that you are in this field to help the alcoholic or the drug abuser. Once you lose sight of that, you might as well be serving up hamburgers." That is the source of the passion: the desire to help the person needing help and the belief that one can make an impact on people's lives.

Leadership is found in an individual's passion, for when leaders love what they do, they challenge, inspire, enable, model, and encourage. Supervisors who feel passionate about their work inspire counselors to feel the same way. There are many words to describe this emotional energy, words such as *enthusiasm* (*en theos*—"to be one with the energy of the divine"), *desire,* and even *obsession.* One must love and desire one's dream intently if the dream is to come true.

Emotion is energy in motion. To have an impact on staff, a supervisor must exercise that energy, have the courage to act, and live out the passion. Part of the supervisor's role is that of encouragement. When we add *en* to the word *courage* we get *encourage,* which means "to be at one with one's courage." Joseph Campbell called this "following your bliss." Mother Teresa says, "We can do no great things—only small things with great love." That love is the passion that informs the work of the dedicated clinical supervisor.

That this passion can be difficult to maintain is evident from all the attention given to burnout in the helping professions. Sam Keen (1991) writes that the overwhelming problem today is not burnout, an excess of "fire in the belly," but "rust out," a critical shortage of passion for what one does.

The following recommendations for self-interventions can help supervisors maintain passion (see also Edelwich and Brodsky 1980):

1. *Stay focused on the client.* The client is the ultimate raison d'être of all counseling and supervisory activity. I maintain a file of the letters or notes written to me by clients and staff over the years. When I feel tired or burned out, I pull out that file as a reminder of why I do what I do.

2. *Find balance and variety in life.* Peter Drucker, the adviser of Fortune 500 companies, was once asked how one could be a better manager. Drucker replied, "Learn to play the violin." In other words, by taking care of ourselves, by having interests outside of

work, we can maintain a perspective on work so that it is not so consuming and setbacks are not so devastating.

Some of the main ingredients of a balanced life are proper diet, exercise, and sleep, along with family rituals that keep work from disrupting the supervisor's home life. It is helpful to spend time with people who are not in the helping profession. One supervisor reported, "I went mountain climbing this summer, and the people I went with didn't sit around and talk the way we do." For my part, I liked to attend the annual conference of *Inc.* magazine for entrepreneurs. Being in a room with a thousand competent individuals, none of whom works in the substance abuse field, was refreshing and provided balance and variety in my life.

3. *Provide for diversity and fun on the job.* When routine sets in, we become stale. Periodically introducing ambiguity and newness into a workday creates the necessary creative tension that brings about freshness and a desire to change. Everyone needs to take risks, seeking out new challenges and tasks, taking on different kinds of cases, and constantly learning through reading, self-study, and training experiences.

There is also a place for just plain fun on the job. Productive working groups usually are playful as well. In one agency, the staff put on skits dramatizing how they view the clients, and the clients stage their own productions to poke fun at the staff. Another agency posts a "saying of the month"—a quotation from a client or counselor that highlights the poignancy, humor, and hope that attend people's progress toward recovery.

Clinical expertise and a passion for work are the foundations of excellence in clinical supervision. Although not explicitly recognized in credentialing standards for supervisors, they make the difference between merely having the title of supervisor and discharging that responsibility effectively.

LEARNING OBJECTIVES

The standards developed by the Association for Counselor Education and Supervision (Appendix A) are the most universally applicable guidelines for clinical supervisors in the mental health field. To the extent that the alcoholism and drug abuse field has defined the roles of a clinical supervisor, it has done so through the role delineation study of alcoholism and drug abuse supervisors conducted by the Columbia Assessment Service (Appendix B). The task of translating the role delineation study's descriptive statements into standards for credentialing is still in its early stages. In lieu of established learning objectives in the substance abuse field, those used as credentialing requirements by the American Association for Marriage and Family Therapy (AAMFT) will be reviewed here. These are the best-defined standards for supervisors in the mental health professions to date and have some applicability beyond marriage and family therapy. However, since they were not formulated to meet the needs of the alcoholism and drug abuse field, a set of learning objectives specifically designed for this field will be proposed here as well. Additional instruments for assessing a supervisor's training and performance—from the point of view of the supervisor, the supervisor's trainer, or the supervisee—can be found in Appendixes C through E. These instruments can also be used in designing a training program for supervisors.

AAMFT Learning Objectives

AAMFT's learning objectives for certification of clinical supervisors are as follows:

1. The ability to describe models of supervision and to contrast these various models.
2. The ability to articulate one's own personal model of supervision.
3. The ability to relate that model to the supervisor's preferred counseling model (isomorphism).
4. The ability to demonstrate perceptual skills in assessing counselor skills and using feedback with supervisees.
5. The ability to demonstrate conceptual skills in monitoring and evaluating counselor-client relationships.
6. The ability to demonstrate executive skills in structuring supervision using a range of modalities.
7. The ability to demonstrate an awareness and sensitivity to ethical and legal issues, particularly pertaining to clinical functioning and clinical supervisory responsibilities.

8. The ability to convey to others what one has learned from supervision of one's own supervision.

Learning Objectives for Supervisors in the Alcoholism and Drug Abuse Field

The AAMFT standards, being broadly defined, are relevant to supervision in the mental health professions generally. Even so, it would not be appropriate for AAMFT-certified supervisors to receive automatic certification as supervisors in the alcoholism and drug abuse field. This field has its own body of knowledge and practice that needs to be reflected in more specialized standards for supervisors. To meet this need, ETP has written specific learning objectives for the alcoholism and drug abuse field. These can be taken as a good approximation of the credentialing standards currently under development.

At a minimum, a clinical supervisor in the alcoholism and drug abuse field should have competencies in the knowledge and skills required by Birch and Davis (1986). In addition to these core competencies, a substance abuse clinical supervisor must demonstrate proficiency in the following areas:

1. Advanced knowledge in alcoholism and drug abuse, demonstrated by completion of advanced training or academic study in a graduate degree program in the behavioral sciences (social work, psychology, counseling, and so forth), with a concentration in substance abuse.
2. Advanced knowledge of the social and behavioral sciences regarding medical, behavioral, and psychological issues, especially as they relate to substance abuse, demonstrated by advanced training or credentialing in other disciplines (marriage and family counseling, clinical social work, counseling, and so forth), completion of academic study at a graduate level, and/or papers or presentations given at professional meetings.
3. Familiarity with a variety of therapeutic modalities, demonstrated in a statement of therapeutic orientation and case presentation.

4. Operational experience with a variety of treatment approaches used in the alcoholism and drug abuse field, demonstrated in a résumé (work experience section).

5. Familiarity with models of clinical supervision and ability to compare these models, demonstrated by a written statement or oral report.

6. Ability to articulate one's own model of clinical supervision and to relate it to one's model of counseling, demonstrated by a written statement or oral report.

7. Knowledge and skills in clinical supervision, demonstrated by a statement of philosophy of clinical supervision, attendance at training in supervision, and familiarity with a variety of models of supervision. Skills to be demonstrated include familiarity with various methods of oversight and intervention (such as phone-ins, audio- or videotaping, bug-in-the-ear, or one-way mirror).

8. Affective qualities necessary to establish an educational, consultative, supportive, and therapeutic relationship with a supervisee.

9. Ability to deal with a supervisee's psychological and emotional issues, especially with respect to recovery and personal growth processes, as they relate to the supervisee's work, demonstrated by a summary of clinical supervisory sessions and by references attesting to the supervisor's abilities.

10. Advanced skills in the evaluation of supervisees' skills and in the ability to communicate that evaluation to supervisees. Providing criticism in a constructive, educational, and therapeutic manner is an essential skill in supervision. This skill can be demonstrated by examples of clinical supervisory practice (audio- or videotapes, transcripts, and so forth) and by letters of reference from supervisees.

The standards in both lists represent objectives to work toward and directions for learning and growth, not prerequisites for admission to the field. As such, they lay the groundwork for the development of a model of clinical supervision for the alcoholism and drug abuse field. Part Two is designed to help readers fulfill the most ambitious of the learning objectives presented here: formulating an integrated model of counseling and supervision.

Part Two

Models

Chapter Five

Building a Model of Clinical Supervision

Counseling and supervision begin with a model, a plan for where to go, followed by a method, or a path for getting there. The chapters that follow describe in general outline and in historical context the models of supervision associated with several leading schools of therapy, culminating in the blended model developed in Chapter Ten for the alcohol and drug abuse field. These chapters explore the methods employed by practitioners of the various models, methods elaborated on in Part Three as guidelines for supervision under the new blended model.

BLUEPRINT FOR A MODEL

A model of supervision, as practiced by a particular individual under a given set of conditions, requires a more complex representation than any single characterization can provide. Such a model is envisioned here as a series of layers that together depict a unique interaction of principle and circumstance.

In Figure 5-1, one way of diagramming this multilayered structure, the model of supervision is like a pyramid, consisting of the following layers:

Philosophical foundation: an underlying viewpoint about people and how they can change with the help of counseling.

Descriptive dimensions: specific characteristics of therapeutic and supervisory practice that largely follow from the philosophical foundation.

Figure 5-1. A Model of Supervision: Component Layers

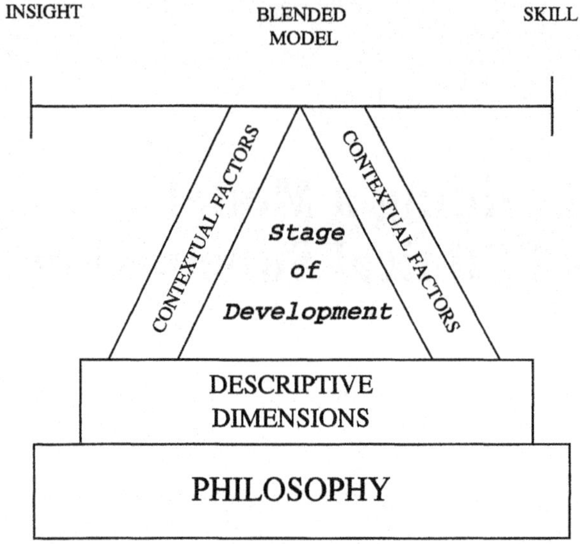

Stage of development: the supervisee's (and supervisor's) level of
training, experience, knowledge, and skill.

Contextual factors: characteristics of the client, counselor, supervisor, and setting that affect the environment of supervision.

As Haley (1976) observed, models of therapy and supervision
fall on a continuum between those that foster a process of insight
and understanding (bringing about attitudinal change) and those
that emphasize didactic skill training (bringing about behavioral
change). This is the fundamental polarity that shapes the practice
of counseling and supervision. Although any model ultimately is
grounded in its philosophical foundation, each successive layer
contributes to adjusting where the pointer falls on the continuum
between insight-oriented and skills-oriented supervision. Thus, one
supervisor, holding to a consistent underlying philosophy, may end
up at somewhat different points on the continuum when working
with different supervisees or in different agency settings.

On the left side of the continuum, counseling is a process of
experimentation, discovery, cognitive and emotional exploration,
and interpretation. The goal of counseling is self-development and

life enrichment for the client. Using his own self-awareness, the counselor assists the client in achieving insight and understanding. Change is spontaneous and unpredictable. The responsibility for change rests with the client, who initiates action; the task of the counselor is supportive, interpretive, and educational. The verbal content of therapy is of primary importance, and insight precedes changes in behavior. In the process, the client may undergo a change in personality.

When this model of therapy is applied to supervision, the supervisor focuses on the verbal content of the therapy. Like counseling, supervision becomes a process of unfolding, uncovering, interpretation, and discovery, focusing on interactions, dynamics, processes, transference, countertransference, and biases. Skill acquisition is secondary to this ongoing exploration. Growth in training is promoted by self-discovery and understanding of feelings, with insight preceding behavioral change. Often the therapist in training is encouraged (even required) to engage in personal therapy as part of the training process.

Supervision under this model progresses spontaneously and somewhat unpredictably, for the responsibility for action rests with the supervisee. The supervisor relies on counselor self-report and indirectly communicated clinical material rather than direct observation of the counselor in action. Insight-oriented supervisors address clinical skills through the unfolding of the supervisee's personal issues. Personality change is a goal of supervision, just as it is a goal of counseling.

On the right side of the continuum, counseling is a process of acquiring new behaviors, with action as the catalyst for change. The goals of counseling are problem resolution, symptom relief, and skill development. Counseling is problem oriented and directive in nature. Change is planned, with the responsibility for the plan resting with the counselor, who knows where to go and when. Thus, the counselor initiates action. Both verbal and nonverbal processes are of primary importance. Self-understanding follows or occurs concurrently with behavioral change and is valued mainly insofar as it reinforces such change.

When this model of counseling is applied to supervision, the focus is on behavioral change and skill acquisition: how to use oneself in counseling to promote behavioral change in the client. Little or no attention is given to dynamic factors such as transference and countertransference or to the counselor's intrapsychic issues. The clinical supervisor's main concern is not why the counselor feels a certain way about a client but how to extinguish any behaviors on the counselor's part that inhibit the change process. The goal is to teach specific skills, and the counselor need learn only as much theory as it takes to be effective. If the counselor's feelings interfere in the process, the supervisor helps the counselor develop the necessary skills to deal with the feelings. Supervision is directive, predictable, planned, and initiated by the supervisor, with routine, direct, structured observation of the counselor in action via phone-ins, one-way mirrors, video- and audiotaping, cofacilitation, and bug-in-the-ear.

These descriptions show an isomorphic relationship between an individual's model of therapy and model of supervision. An isomorph exists when two complex structures are mapped out in such a way that for each part of one structure, there is a corresponding part in the other structure, with the parts playing similar roles in the two structures. Although the context may vary, the structure or form remains the same.

As used here, *isomorphism* means that, within a particular model, counseling and supervision are guided by the same theory and the same principles, so that the counselor-client relationship and the supervisor-supervisee relationship are in many ways parallel. With a supervisor who comes out of a traditional psychodynamic background, supervision will tend to resemble analytically oriented therapy. If the supervisor practices cognitive or behavioral therapy, supervision will take on a very different coloration. This isomorphic relationship holds true, by and large, for each of the models of counseling and supervision presented in the following chapters.

A summary review of those and other models at the end of this chapter will place the blended model of supervision for the alcohol and drug abuse field in historical, theoretical, and methodological context. However, to understand the terms in which the various models are described, a fuller discussion of the component layers that make up any model of supervision (as shown in Figure 5-1) is required.

PHILOSOPHICAL FOUNDATION

Together with some other disciplines, the substance abuse field often turns out clinical technicians with good counseling skills but no theoretical underpinning and little understanding of why they do what they do. Although some models of supervision (as described in Chapters Eight and Nine) largely dismiss philosophical and theoretical issues, both clinical experience and the blended model of supervision developed in this book argue that such narrowness of vision is an unnecessarily high price to pay for technical skills. It is true that some individuals operate quite well on instinct. Nonetheless, it is preferable that counselors and supervisors have some rationale for what they do, since both human behavioral change and counselor development have an inherent complexity that eludes the rote application of techniques.

A model of counseling and supervision is not chosen arbitrarily. It arises from basic beliefs about how we know what we know, what motivates people, and how people change. Given one set of beliefs about human motivation and behavior, a clinician might practice insight-oriented therapy. Given another set of beliefs, she might opt for behavioral skills training. This stratum of fundamental beliefs is represented by the bottom layer of the pyramidal model, the philosophical foundation. In keeping with the principle of isomorphism, these core precepts about the goals, methods, and means of therapy carry over to the theory and practice of clinical supervision. By articulating her assumptions about the nature of therapeutic change and the role of the counselor in that change process (that is, by making an epistemological declaration), the supervisor is also building a framework for training and supervision with clear guiding premises and principles. "This personal framework, with both idiosyncratic and generic aspects, is indispensable in the organization of the supervision context" (Liddle 1988, p. 156). It is the ballast on which the pyramid rests. (Chapter Fourteen provides a detailed questionnaire to help supervisees clarify the philosophical foundations of their personal models of counseling.)

DESCRIPTIVE DIMENSIONS

Bascue and Yalof (1991) identify ten dimensions of theory and practice critical to understanding individual beliefs about therapy and supervision. These essentially represent a detailed breakdown of the philosophical foundation. That is, the specific dimensions might be considered variations of the insight-versus-skills continuum, the basic polarity that underlies them all. At the same time, different models may vary somewhat in their application of core principles to each of these dimensions of theory and practice, or they may develop distinctive approaches to one dimension or another. In any case, the descriptive dimensions provide an invaluable tool for understanding how the foundational beliefs of a model are manifested in practice.

The nine dimensions outlined here are adapted from Bascue and Yalof, with a few modifications. Two of Bascue and Yalof's ten dimensions are omitted: the Developmental dimension, which is given added emphasis here as a separate layer of the pyramidal model, and the Identity dimension, which sets up a distinction between the professional and the technician that does not apply to the substance abuse field. In their place is a ninth dimension created for this book, Strategy. On each of the nine dimensions, the left end of the continuum corresponds roughly to insight-oriented counseling and supervision and the right end to a skills-oriented model.

These dimensions will be used to frame the models of supervision presented in Chapters Seven through Ten, with an X indicating the presumed positioning of the model in question on each of the nine dimensions. For the psychodynamic, skills, and three variants of family therapy models, this will be done only in shorthand form with diagrams since it is not within the scope of this book to analyze these models in depth. Indeed, the interpretations given here are no more than impressionistic, since the Bascue and Yalof scheme is yet to be adopted by the practitioners of the various models, who alone can make an authoritative determination of where their models stand on the various dimensions. Only for the new alcoholism and drug abuse blended model of supervision (Chapter Ten) will elaboration on each of the nine dimensions be provided. These benchmarks can be used not only for understanding where each model appears to fit in the overall scheme but also for developing a unique, personal model of supervision.

Influential

The Influential dimension determines whether a client or supervisee is influenced at an affective or cognitive level. Of course, all counselors and supervisors work on both dimensions, but they vary greatly in the relative importance they attach to feelings and cognitions in bringing about change. On the affective side are psychodynamically oriented practitioners who focus on unconscious emotional forces and the dynamics of the client-counselor-supervisor relationship (Ekstein and Wallerstein 1972; Lane 1990). On the cognitive side are those who teach specific skills and tasks (Boyd 1978; Haley 1976).

Affective	Cognitive
Influential	

Symbolic

The Symbolic dimension deals with whether latent or manifest content is addressed in counseling and supervision. Psychodynamically oriented counselors and supervisors view latent or underlying issues—unconscious conflicts, transference and countertransference, family of origin—as "grist for the supervision mill" (Mueller and Kell 1972). In contrast, those who practice cognitive or behavioral therapy and skills-oriented supervision look mainly at overt, manifest issues (Mead 1990).

Latent	Manifest
Symbolic	

Structural

The Structural dimension describes whether therapy and supervision are spontaneous or planned. In the reactive mode, the therapist (or supervisor) reacts to the material presented by the client (or supervisee). Client-centered therapy ("What do you want to talk about today?") exemplifies the reactive method. With its fluid structure and flexible agendas, it sees change as a function of perception and introspection (Charny 1986). In the proactive mode, the therapist or supervisor sets a preplanned agenda, or curriculum (Worthington, 1987). Behavioral sex therapy ("Do these exercises during the week, and then tell me how you did") exemplifies this highly structured approach to therapy.

Reactive   Proactive

Structural

Replicative

The Replicative dimension refers to the extent to which the supervisor sees observed interactions as representations of isomorphic processes (Kaslow 1986a; Liddle 1988) or as independent of and unrelated to other events. To psychodynamic therapists, a counselor will behave in supervision as the patient does in therapy, thereby replicating the patient's problems (Yalom 1995). Skills-oriented supervisors, on the other hand, may make therapeutic inferences from what occurs in supervision but do not interpret such observed events as parallel to the underlying dynamics. For those at this "discrete" end of the continuum, what the counselor says and does in supervision matters for its own sake, not for its parallels with the counseling relationship or for its revelation of underlying unconscious factors.

Parallel   Discrete

Replicative

Counselor in Treatment

The Counselor in Treatment dimension has to do with whether training and personal therapy are viewed as related or unrelated activities. Obviously, all therapists would see the value of therapy, or else they ought to be in another profession. Indeed, for traditional, analytically oriented psychotherapists, undergoing therapy while in training may be a prerequisite for becoming a therapist. Skills-oriented supervisors impose no such requirement, since they view personal therapy as unrelated to the kind of training they provide. Between these poles are variations of the belief that therapy for the therapist is a personal choice based on specific individual needs.

Related   Unrelated
Counselor in Treatment

Information Gathering

The Information Gathering dimension contrasts indirect methods of obtaining information with direct observation of therapy sessions. The analytically oriented therapist who does not look directly at the patient lying on a couch corresponds to the supervisor who gathers information from indirect sources, such as written transcripts, case notes, or oral presentations alone. Even more indirect is the supervisor's reliance on personal interactions with supervisees as the sole source of information. Here the focus is entirely on the counselor, not the client, with the supervisor making judgments on the basis of subjective impressions of the supervisee's presentation. At the other end of the continuum is the supervisor who directly observes the counselor in action via videotape, one-way mirror, or cofacilitation.

Indirect   Direct
Information Gathering

Jurisdictional

The Jurisdictional dimension concerns who is responsible for client care. Professional discipline plays a role in this dimension. In psychology, for example, the American Psychological Association has assigned the supervisor full legal responsibility for the client and supervisee—an assignment that is reflected in state laws. Other disciplines view the therapist's or supervisor's role as consultative, with less jurisdiction over the client and supervisee. Notwithstanding these variations among professions, recent case law has established that a supervisor, regardless of discipline or philosophy, has vicarious liability for client care. (Vicarious liability means liability for the actions of another person over whom one has authority.) In most teaching and work settings, therefore, jurisdictional responsibility rests with the supervisor, who must do whatever is needed to ensure quality of care, such as observing treatment, reviewing clinical records for accuracy, personally interviewing patients, and dealing with supervisees' psychotherapeutic issues to the extent that they affect the counseling process. Vicarious liability does not stop with the supervisor. It extends up the line to the employing agency, and the supervisor is accountable to the agency as well as to the law.

Therapist	Supervisor

Jurisdictional

Relationship

The Relationship dimension determines whether the counselor (or supervisor) functions in a facilitative or hierarchical role with respect to the client (or supervisee). In any model of therapy or supervision, empathy, respect, and genuineness are core components of the relationship. Beyond these basic affective qualities, the relationship takes on a markedly different character in different schools of therapy. A relatively egalitarian ("facilitative") atmosphere in treatment and supervision is characteristic of insight-oriented and some mixed approaches (Caplan 1970; Carkhuff and Truax 1965). At the other extreme, structural and strategic family therapy training programs establish a hierarchical relationship in which the supervisee is expected to defer to the supervisor's seniority and technical expertise (Haley 1976).

Facilitative	Hierarchical

Relationship

Strategy

The Strategy dimension highlights the teaching of theory versus technique in supervision. Someone who holds (in terms of the Influential dimension) that affect precedes cognition is likely to teach theory in preference to technique. On the other hand, someone who believes that cognition precedes affect is likely to emphasize technique. This continuum is exemplified by the schools of family therapy discussed in Chapter Nine. The insight-oriented models (psychodynamic and Bowenian) deemphasize technique in favor of teaching supervisees to acquire a comprehensive theory of life that organizes their conduct of therapy. In the middle of the continuum, the structural model of Minuchin teaches theory and technique simultaneously. Finally, the strategic model, which is the most skills oriented, attempts to change trainees' interactional sequences with families rather than give trainees a broad theoretical understanding of what they are doing (Haley 1976).

Theory   Technique

Strategy

STAGE OF DEVELOPMENT

Under any model of counseling and supervision, the counselor's level of professional development is a major determinant of supervisory practice. Often, for example, a supervisor may move at least some distance from the right (rote skills training) to the left (mutual exploration and understanding) as a counselor gains experience. To suggest this fine-tuning effect of developmental considerations, the developmental layer is drawn in the form of a pointer in Figure 5-1.

Entire approaches to supervision (most notably that of Stoltenberg and Delworth 1987) have been built around the developmental paradigm. Whether or not the developmental approach to supervision can stand as a model in its own right, it is treated here as an essential layer that all models have in common. Once the foundations of a model have been established, the supervisee's level of development influences how the model is implemented in working with that supervisee. Moreover, the supervisor's own level of development may interact with the supervisee's in a way that further conditions their relationship.

This developmental approach is outlined in Chapter Six. Elaborately worked out by Stoltenberg and Delworth (1987), it is an indispensable adjunct to any of the models that follow, including the alcoholism and drug abuse blended model in Chapter Ten.

CONTEXTUAL FACTORS

When asked how they handle certain types of training situations, clinical supervisors often say, "It depends." On what does it depend? Many situational variables enter into the equation, including client profiles, agency setting and goals, training needs, and credentialing requirements. Most of these variables can be grouped into five categories:

Supervisor: background, training, philosophy, supervisory profile or personality.

Supervisee: formal training and credentials, recovery history, gender, age, race, ethnicity, professional goals.

Client: level of functioning, clinical profile.

Setting: inpatient versus outpatient, type of care (acute, continuing), agency philosophy, organizational climate, sources of funding, budgetary constraints.

Training program affiliation: academic requirements, credentialing or certification programs, internships.

Those factors not encompassed by the philosophical foundation, descriptive dimensions, and developmental stage can best be referred to as contextual factors. A supervisor's sensitivity to this multiplicity of relevant issues plays a considerable role in his or her success as a supervisor. Contextual factors are shown in Figure 5-1 as brackets or sidebars framing the model of supervision. Some of the most important contextual factors will be addressed in Chapter Sixteen.

One crucial cluster of variables that conditions virtually every aspect of supervision addressed in this book grows out of the nature of the work setting. Books on supervision that are written in and for academic training environments do not adequately take into account the practical workaday context of front-line treatment settings: the ever-present administrative requirements, budget compromises, case overloads, and resistant counselors who strain a supervisor's stamina and creativity. Models of supervision rarely survive the rigors of public or private treatment agencies with their purity intact, yet it is in just such agencies that most substance abuse counselors are supervised.

THE BLENDED MODEL IN HISTORICAL PERSPECTIVE

The substance abuse field has not until now had a model of supervision, but it has had a model of counseling that can be understood in the light of its place in the history of the mental health professions. Through the 1950s, psychotherapy was synonymous with the analytically oriented approach of Freud and his numerous offshoots. Since supervision tends to follow therapy in an isomorphic relationship, early models of supervision adopted this psychodynamic emphasis (Eitington 1937; Ekstein and Wallerstein 1972). In the 1960s and 1970s, two other models came to the fore. One was the facilitative, exemplified by Truax and Carkhuff (1967), which was based on Rogers's (1951) client-centered therapy. Therapy and supervision in the facilitative model were less intensively psychodynamic than traditional psychotherapy but nevertheless still preoccupied with mutual exploration, insight, and personal growth. Meanwhile, behavioristic (Horan 1972; Krumboltz 1966) and cognitive (Ellis 1973) therapies made a more radical break with tradition, leading to the skills model of supervision (Ivey and others 1968; Mead 1990). By the 1980s, with the considerable influence achieved by the solution-focused therapy of de Shazer (1988), the task-oriented model of Mead (1990), and the technique-oriented family therapies of Haley (1988) and Minuchin and Fishman (1981), the pendulum had swung to the right side of the continuum.

While the dominant models were moving from one extreme to the other, a variety of models appeared all along the continuum. Caplan (1970) described supervision as a consultative process, a collaborative rather than therapeutic relationship that did not concern itself with intrapsychic issues. Caplan's model might be placed partway toward the skills end of the continuum. In the middle of the continuum was the interpersonal process recall model (Kagan 1975), which combined the stimulus-response scheme of behaviorism with a focus on emotional reactions, interpersonal dynamics, and self-discovery. Closer to the psychodynamic pole was the Mueller and Kell (1972) conflict model, which probed the feelings aroused by the counselor's conflicts with the client, the supervisor, and himself. (These three models are discussed more fully in Powell 1980a.)

Alcohol and drug abuse counseling began in the 1970s, when behaviorism and cognitive therapy were in their ascendancy. Understandably, then, it has featured a strong skills-oriented component, as expressed in the twelve core functions. Very much in the spirit of the 1980s was the Birch and Davis (1986) report, *Development of Model Professional Standards for Counselor Credentialing,* which listed 260 skills for counselors to master. At the same time, this new field was rooted in a tradition of spirituality and the search for self-understanding. Indeed, the twelve steps of Alcoholics Anonymous call for insight as well as skills development. A profession whose counseling practice has always been blended, by virtue of its very origins, offers fertile ground for a blended model of supervision.

Practicing counselors and supervisors, especially those working in agencies characterized by a diverse staff and client population, tend to show discomfort with extreme, dogmatic models and to seek pragmatic alternatives. For this reason as well, the substance abuse counseling field is attuned to the trend within the mental health professions toward blended models of therapy and supervision. Because the pendulum appears to have swung too far toward an exclusively technique- and skill-based approach, there have been attempts since the late 1980s (for example, in the developmental model of Stoltenberg and Delworth 1987) to strike a balance between the two extremes. There is even a new generation of psychoanalytic models with a skills-training component added (Lane 1990).

This historical development is recapitulated in Chapters Seven through Nine, covering the psychodynamic, skills, and family therapy models of supervision. These chapters, skeletal summaries of the models in question, are included to give readers a map of the field, a narrative of its revolution, and some ingredients for building a personal model of supervision. They also show how parts of these models have been synthesized into the alcoholism and drug abuse blended model of supervision (Chapter Ten), which blends elements of insight-oriented and skills-based supervision with a developmental perspective.

One of the learning objectives for clinical supervisors set forth in Chapter Four is to articulate a personal model of supervision. Readers are invited to use the information in this part of the book as material for creating a unique personal synthesis of principle and practice. The true test of a conceptual model of therapy and supervision is that it provides a way of understanding what one is doing and why one is doing it. Another test is whether it actually works with clients and counselors. Does it help supervisees improve their competence? Does it make work more manageable? Does it provide both support and challenge to promote mastery and growth? Does it improve one's effectiveness as a supervisor? Does it meet the expectations of the patient, the counselor, the agency, the credentialing organization, and the training institution? These are some of the criteria by which any model of supervision can be tested in practice.

Chapter Six

A Developmental Approach to Supervision

No matter what model of supervision they choose, supervisors need to take into account the supervisee's level of training, experience, and proficiency. Different supervisory approaches are appropriate for counselors at different stages of professional development. An understanding of the supervisee's developmental needs is an essential part of any model of supervision.

In Figure 5-1, developmental stage is included as the top layer, resting on the philosophical foundations and descriptive features specific to each model. A counselor being trained in a skills-oriented mode might use elementary, "cookbook" techniques at an early stage of development; a counselor learning an insight-oriented approach might concentrate on basic questions of trust and transference and countertransference. Developmental considerations, although manifested differently under the two models, contribute in either case to determining what tasks, methods, and objectives are pursued. Developmental considerations may also influence where a supervisory interaction falls on the continuum from skills to insight, inasmuch as added experience and competence on the counselor's part may set the stage for greater reliance on personal judgment and less on learned techniques.

The same is true for the supervisor. An inexperienced supervisor may revert temporarily to a rote process that he or she has long since outgrown as a counselor. Furthermore, a supervisor at a given developmental stage may work well with a counselor at one developmental stage but not at another. Thus, the developmental perspective can contribute to appropriate matching of supervisors with supervisees.

ROOTS OF THE DEVELOPMENTAL APPROACH

The developmental approach to clinical supervision is based on developmental psychology, which encompasses the description, explanation, and modification of individual behavior across the life span. The individual's past, present, and future potential provide a context for bringing about specific changes in behavior. Factors that contribute to development include heredity, environment, learning process, age, critical periods in the person's life, continuity or discontinuity of development, and structural considerations. The theoretical foundations of developmental psychology can be found in the writings of Baltes, Reese, and Nesselroade (1977), Bruner (1963), Dewey (1963), Gibbs (1977), Kuhn (1978), Loevinger (1977), Miller (1977), Perry (1968), Piaget (1971), and Rest (1973). The most advanced formulations of developmental stage theories currently in use include Alexander and Langer (1990), Colby and Kohlberg (1987), Commons and others (1989), Commons and others (1990), Commons, Richards, and Armon (1984), and Kohlberg (1981, 1984, 1987).

Developmental models of personality have been applied to change theory, to clinical practice (for example, Commons, Demick, and Goldberg, 1995), to alcohol abuse and addiction (Denton and Krebs 1990; Koplowitz 1984), and to counselor training and supervision. This chapter presents a developmental perspective that describes, explains, and predicts changes in supervisees over the course of their training and supervision, as well as the analogous changes observable in supervisors as they gain experience.

DEVELOPMENTAL MODELS OF SUPERVISION: AN OVERVIEW

By the 1980s, developmental models of personality were being incorporated into theories of clinical supervision. Worthington (1987) identified sixteen models of supervision that describe counselor behavior and performance in developmental terms. According to these models, training is tailored to the supervisee's professional and personal development (Alonso 1983; Blocher 1983; Grater 1985; Hart 1982; Heppner and Roehlke 1984; Hess 1986; Sansbury 1982; Stoltenberg 1981; Stoltenberg and Delworth 1987; Wiley and Ray 1986). The centerpiece of all variations of this approach is a self-managed, individualized training plan for each counselor. A historical overview of some of the leading developmental models of supervision follows.

Hogan (1964) outlined the counselor's progression through four stages of development. The first stage is characterized by counselor dependence upon the supervisor. The second stage is defined by autonomy-dependence conflicts with the supervisor. The third stage shows a higher level of counselor self-confidence and autonomy in thought and action. Finally, in the fourth stage the counselor acts as a master clinician with a high degree of personal autonomy, insight, security, and motivation and with an awareness of a continuing need for personal and professional development. For Hogan, the aim of supervision is to foster growth toward independence, moving the trainee from student to colleague to expert.

Littrell, Lee-Bordin, and Lorenz (1979) also specified four stages of development. Stage 1 features a nonjudgmental, supportive supervisory role. The supervisor asks four questions to guide the supervisee: Where are you now? Where do you want to go? How will you get there? How will you know when you have gotten there? Stage 2 shifts to a counseling-therapeutic approach to supervision, addressing thoughts, feelings, and actions that may impede the supervisee's professional performance. In addition, conceptual and clinical skills are taught at this stage. Stage 3 is consultative, with self-evaluation and exploration by the supervisor. This preparation moves the trainee into the fourth stage, that of self-supervision.

Hess (1986) outlined four stages of development: inception (characterized by insecurity, dependency, and inadequacy), skill development (the passage from dependency to autonomy and adequacy), consolidation (self-confidence and a shift from conditional dependence to individuation), and mutuality (a time of creativity and independent practice). Hess also addressed the developmental process of becoming a supervisor. He identified three phases: beginning (when the emphasis is on structuring sessions and learning supervisory techniques), exploration (when the supervisee's learning needs are more important than the supervisor's), and confirmation of the supervisor's identity (characterized by a feeling of confidence about one's knowledge and supervisory skill). These stages of supervisory development prefigure those presented in the last part of this chapter.

Ralph (1980) too saw the supervisory process as having four developmental stages: (1) nondirective expert guidance, (2) adoption of a client/content-centered approach, (3) a relationship-centered approach, and (4) therapist-centered supervision. Ralph thus traced a progression from an expert role for the supervisor to a client-centered/Rogerian orientation, then to an interpersonal focus with a strong therapeutic relationship, and finally to a psychodynamic orientation.

Rice (1986) identified four stages of counselor development: formation (a time of preparation and encounter, when intrapsychic issues are resolved), development (when power and control issues are addressed), stabilization (when the supervisory team members are integrated into a safe and close working relationship), and refreshment (when the supervisory relationship is stabilized, effective, and efficient).

Yogev (1982) presented a three-stage model of role definition, skill acquisition, and solidification and evaluation of practice, primarily geared to first-year graduate students. Yogev's model emphasizes skill development, self-understanding, and an understanding of client problems.

D'Andrea's (1989) developmental model of supervision, termed the person-process model (PPM), postulates three stages, which are adapted from Loevinger's (1976) stages of ego development. Loevinger's first stage, called the preconformist stage, is characterized by impulsiveness and self-protection. The person thinks in simple terms, with marginal problem-solving ability and marked insensitivity to others. He or she is highly impulsive, manipulative, exploitive, and not generally a good team player. To meet the supervisee's needs at this initial stage of professional development, the first component of the PPM focuses on the supervisee as a person. The preconformist supervisee needs one-on-one supervision, with clear expectations, a reward system, and a written supervision contract. D'Andrea calls this the inception stage of supervision; the person establishes confidence and trust, becomes rooted in the work setting, and begins to set goals and objectives for supervision.

Loevinger's second stage of ego development is the conformist stage, characterized by "pleasing" social behavior, cooperativeness, sensitivity to others, a need for acceptance and validation from others, greater openness to criticism, and greater conformity to rules and procedures. The conformist supervisee needs group supervision, verbal feedback by the supervisor, role playing, activities involving teamwork, and less structure than the preconformist. D'Andrea calls this the exploratory stage of supervision; the supervisee acquires a broader professional grounding for skill development, together with a professional sense of autonomy and self-direction and new ways of functioning on the job.

The third and final stage of ego development in Loevinger's scheme, the self-awareness/postconformist stage, is characterized by intellectual maturity, empathy, accurate perceptions and evaluations of others, the ability to use criticism constructively, and a high regard for fairness in relationships. The postconformist is achievement oriented, creative, and self-initiating. With this person, who has higher expectations of supervision as a growth-producing experience, supervision shifts toward consultation, collaboration, increased responsibilities, creativity, leadership training, and peer supervision. D'Andrea refers to this stage as one of consolidation and mutuality, wherein the supervisee develops a clear professional identity, a more sophisticated and effective leadership style, facilitative conditions to realize his own creative potential, and a higher order of competencies. The supervisor becomes a colleague and peer at this stage.

Bradley (1989) defined four finite developmental levels and one open-ended level as part of a continuum of learning. In level 1 a counselor learns entry-level skills and the basic foundational knowledge required of the profession. A level 2 counselor progresses to fully functioning status, with a broader base of competency but a limited repertoire of skills. Most personnel reach these two levels within the first year of counselor practice. In the second year of practice the counselor acquires a refined repertoire of competencies, which Bradley calls level 3. By the third year, the counselor is expected to move into level 4, which involves advanced skills and some supervisory responsibilities. Beyond level 4 is an open-ended, continual process of professional development.

Loganbill, Hardy, and Delworth (1982) specified three stages of trainee development—stagnation, confusion, and integration—that provide a framework for eight content issues to be addressed in supervision: competence, emotional awareness, autonomy, theoretical identity, respect for individual differences, purpose and direction, personal motivation, and professional ethics. The authors describe the process by which a trainee cycles and recycles through the various domains of learning. In so doing, they outline four supervisory functions: monitoring client welfare, enhancing growth through the stages of development, promoting transitions from stage to stage, and evaluating the counselor.

In this scheme, stage 1 represents naive unawareness; stage 2 consists of a sense of instability, disorganization, conflict, and fluctuations; and stage 3 is characterized by a sense of integration, reorganization, flexibility, security, and a new conceptual understanding. The task of the supervisor is to guide the supervisee in the formation of attitudes about oneself, the world, the supervisor, and the quest for values in counseling. Loganbill, Hardy, and Delworth also address supervisor variables; potency (a term made familiar to the alcoholism and drug abuse field by Wolf (1974/ 1975), genuineness, optimism, courage, sense of humor, sense of time as a gift, capacity of intimacy, openness to fantasy and imagery, and capacity for respect and consideration.

Hess (1986) has classified several of these models, along with several others, and their stages of supervisee development in terms of his own four stages of development (inception, skill development, consolidation, and mutuality). Table 6-1 presents his classification (Hess 1986, p. 54).

Empirical evidence of the validity of developmental models of supervision can be found in the following reports: Heppner and Roehlke (1984), Hill, Charles, and Reed (1981), McNeill, Stoltenberg, and Pierce (1985), Miars and others (1983), Reising and Daniels (1983), and Worthington (1984). Many key concepts of developmental theories of supervision are supported by these

Table 6-1. Hess's Classification of Developmental Models of Supervision

| | Supervisee Stages | | | |
	A: Inception	B: Skill Development	C: Consolidation	D: Mutuality
Hogan (1964)	1. Insecurity-dependency	2. Dependency-autonomy	3. Self-confidence	4. Creativity
Delaney (1972)	1. Initial session 2. Facilitation of supervision relationship	3. Goal identification and strategy selection 4. Strategies-instructions, remodeling and reinforcement 5. Termination and follow-up		
Gaoni and Newmann (1974)	1. Pupil	2. Apprentice	3. Therapeutic personality	4. Mutual consultation
Yogev (1982)	1. Role definition	2. Skill acquisition	3. Solidification and evaluation of practice	
Loganbill, Hardy, and Delworth (1982)	1. Stagnation	2. Confusion	3. Integration	
Blount and Glenwick (1982)	1. Adequacy-inadequacy	2. Dependency versus autonomy	3. Conditional dependency versus individualism	4. Independent practice and collegial consultation

Note: Letters A, B, C, and D refer to the author's putative stages; the numbers in the body of the table refer to the particular theorist's stages.

Source: Reprinted by permission from Hess (1986), p. 54, ©1986 by Haworth Press, Inc.

research findings. As supervision progresses, supervisees report increasing levels of self-awareness and counseling skills, reduced dependence on the supervisor, and greater autonomy in counseling.

STOLTENBERG AND DELWORTH'S INTEGRATED DEVELOPMENTAL APPROACH

As Hess's summary makes clear, there are common themes running through the various developmental models. None of those models, however, is a fully adequate vehicle for presenting and implementing a developmental model of supervision. Most of them were originally proposed in brief articles; they tend to be insufficiently developed or leave out essential components of a model of supervision (for example, treatment or training issues).

These deficiencies are remedied by Stoltenberg and Delworth's (1987) integrated developmental model for supervision (IDM), which synthesizes the common elements of previous models into a comprehensive, well-elaborated whole. Integrating theory, practice, and research, the IDM defines the purpose of supervision, outlines its characteristics, and explains how it brings about change. Its starting point is Loganbill, Hardy, and Delworth's (1982, p. 14) definition of supervision as "an intensive, interpersonally focused, one-to-one relationship in which one person is designated to facilitate the development of therapeutic competence in the other person." This model calibrates the developmental levels of both counselors and supervisors according to three basic structures:

1. *Autonomy,* which deals with dependence on authority figures, the ability to make independent decisions, the degree of supervision required, and self-confidence.
2. *Self- and other awareness,* which deals with the cognitive and affective components of focus on self and others; fears, anxieties, and uncertainties; and how certain behaviors affect the client and others.
3. *Motivation,* which deals with the understanding of the role of the counselor and the process of counseling, the desire to help people, and the learning of idiosyncratic strengths and weaknesses.

In each stage of development, Stoltenberg and Delworth trace the counselor's progress in terms of the three structures within eight competency domains, which are roughly comparable to the twelve core functions identified by the alcoholism and drug abuse field:

Stoltenberg and Delworth's Domains	Twelve Core Functions
Intervention skills	Screening
Assessment techniques	Assessment
Interpersonal assessment	Orientation
Client conceptualization	Intake
Individual differences	Counseling
Theoretical orientation	Treatment planning
Treatment goals and plans	Crisis intervention
Professional ethics	Client education
	Referral
	Report and record keeping
	Consultation with other professionals in regard to client treatment/services
	Case management

Writing for the mental health professions generally, Stoltenberg and Delworth envision a relatively orderly and, by and large, planned sequence of development in the various domains, even if development does not necessarily occur at the same rate in all domains. An individual's development, however uneven, is fairly linear and can be mapped in terms of certain predictable plateaus. Such a pathway is feasible in a structured learning environment such as a university-based training program, where course work precedes field internships and where clinical responsibilities are assigned in graded sequence. In a psychology or social work degree program, for example, entry-level clinicians may be assigned to assist in leading groups rather than be primary group leaders.

In alcohol and drug abuse counseling, on the other hand, there is relatively little school-based training; counselors at all levels of education, training, and experience are thrown immediately into work situations and given major clinical responsibilities in a number of domains simultaneously. Training takes place mainly on the job, and development occurs most rapidly in the areas where the counselor (out of necessity) gets the most practice. Under these conditions, it is impossible to prescribe or predict a counselor's developmental path with any precision. Instead, the supervisor must monitor closely the specific developmental path of each counselor to make sure that the individual has the training, instruction, and feedback needed to perform the required tasks. That is part of the special challenge of supervision in the substance abuse field.

Although the application of Stoltenberg and Delworth's model to the substance abuse field thus diverges somewhat from the other mental health professions, the model's descriptions of the three levels of counselor development apply equally well here. As in the earlier developmental models of supervision, these levels are loosely based on the stages of human development. The level 1 counselor can be thought of (professionally) as a child—dependent, curious, innocent, uninhibited, egocentric, enthusiastic, easily frustrated, demanding of attention. In level 2, the counselor enters into a professional adolescence—insecure, self-conscious, judgmental, rebellious, desirous of autonomy, and confused about identity. The level 3 counselor emerges as a mature professional—emotionally secure, self-aware, internally motivated, responsible, caring, goal oriented, flexible in methods, respectful of limits, and able to tolerate frustration and delay gratification.

An adult, of course, is not necessarily a perfectly developed human being. Professionally, as in the rest of life, the developmental process is not guaranteed to be smooth, linear, and complete. How quickly a counselor moves through the developmental stages depends on aptitude as well as on individual growth and personal issues. Age, gender, ethnicity, and experience as a counselor also play a role in development. There are stages within stages of counselor development, just as a child of two is quite different from a child of ten, or a thirteen-year-old from an eighteen-year-old adolescent. Thus, the general characterizations of the three stages can be further qualified to describe substages.

Finally, as in all other areas of life, two steps forward may be followed by one step back. According to Stoltenberg and Delworth (1987, p. 36), "While we view the levels as representing irreversible structural change, the model allows for brief regressions while trainees are faced with new or ambiguous tasks." Disappointing clinical outcomes and disruptive interpersonal conflicts can also contribute to regressions. How brief such a period of regression will be is contingent on the counselor's personal integration, health, and work reassignment.

It is difficult to generalize about counselor behavior because a number of variables influence the counselor's development at all stages. It is unlikely that a counselor will be at level 2 in all domains or for any sustained period of time. Rather, the counselor should be viewed as in a constant state of flux and growth. He may advance or retreat within the various domains throughout his development. To claim that "all level 2 counselors are like this" is inaccurate and unfair. It is wise to say instead, "This counselor is like this today. He may be like that tomorrow."

Levels of Counselor Development

Level 1

Level 1 (entry-level) counselors differ from other counselors with respect to their ego strength, work experiences, affective qualities, and helping skills. Typically, they have not come to terms with their personality characteristics as these affect their practice, and in many cases their recovery experiences loom large in their backgrounds. It is a truism that people enter the helping professions because they want to help others. In the alcohol and drug abuse field, this ethical commitment often is reinforced by personal or family experiences with substance abuse. Such experiences, while contributing to a deeper understanding and dedication, can generate countertransference issues that are worked through only as they unfold in the realities of practice.

Edelwich and Brodsky (1980) have described in detail the enthusiasm with which entry-level counselors begin their careers. This mission to save the world is the source of much creative energy and caring. Unfortunately, enthusiasm may be followed by disappointed expectations, the first step on the path to counselor burnout. Part of the supervisor's responsibility, then, is to help level 1 counselors manage their enthusiasm and moderate their expectations.

Structures. With respect to the basic structural issues identified by Stoltenberg and Delworth—autonomy, self- and other awareness, and motivation—level 1 counselors exhibit the following characteristics:

1. *Highly dependent on others.* Level 1 counselors imitate their mentors and expect to be given the "right" answers by their supervisors. They overaccommodate to the recommendations of the supervisor, whom they look upon as the all-knowing expert. As a result, they employ cookbook solutions to clinical issues and adopt a mechanistic counseling style.

2. *Lacking in self- and other awareness.* Instead of being self-aware, they are self-conscious. They tend to focus intensely on themselves, with the world revolving around their needs. They have a relatively low self-concept and lack confidence in their clinical repertoire. As much as they want to ask, "How am I doing?" they worry about evaluations. The process of being videotaped, audiotaped, or observed is unnerving. Videotaping, in particular, arouses intense anxiety in entry-level counselors (Duval and Wicklund 1972).

3. *Categorical in their thinking.* Their understanding of individual clients is rigid and stereotyped, with one- and two-word descriptors and minimal conceptualizations. Anecdotes substitute for analysis.

4. *Highly motivated and committed to work.* Driven by a combination of idealism, unrealistic expectations about outcomes, and anxiety about their competence, they are determined to do a good job.

Description. Lacking confidence in their ability to make appropriate interventions, level 1 counselors are plagued by feelings of anxiety and apprehension. They are driven by the desire to "do it right," as if the correct intervention could be chosen without full understanding of the client's issues. A counselor exposed to a particular therapy model will tend to overuse that model. For example, the counselor may decide that every client needs "reality therapy." "This is how I learned to do it in school, and this is how I'm going to do it," runs the train of thought. The counselor avoids other methods of intervention, even when suggested by the supervisor. This myopia is not necessarily counterproductive at this early developmental stage because it gives the counselor a basis for action. Using the model gives the counselor a sense of potency: the model works, and the counselor is able to bring about change in clients.

Some counselors join the "fad of the month" club, counseling by best-seller or bumper sticker. Their orientation is whatever is in the latest book they have read. This "radical eclecticism" is based not on any theoretical understanding but on a kind of primitive empiricism. The counselor will cling rigidly to one model until it fails to work consistently. When it does not work, the supervisee is ready to learn more from the supervisor, on whom he is highly dependent. This process, however haphazard and inefficient, represents the way inexperienced counselors typically open themselves up to new approaches. Once they have broadened their horizons, level 1 counselors prefer shared clinical experiences, positive feedback, modeling by the supervisor, and readings suggested by the staff (Worthington and Roehlke 1979). They are interested in building rapport with their supervisors and peers.

In the experience of the Clinical Preceptorship Program, level 1 alcoholism and drug abuse counselors are especially in need of supervisory assistance in the appropriate use of confrontation and self-disclosure (Powell 1980a). At one extreme, they confront and disclose in an overly directive, intrusive manner. "Listen, this is the way *I* did it in my recovery, and this is the way you'll do it, too." At the other extreme, they act as if the client were too fragile to be confronted. Operating from this "spun glass theory of the mind," which holds that clients will break at the slightest touch, entry-level counselors fear the slightest deviation from the textbook in the way they approach clients.

Training in basic assessment skills is also necessary for entry-level counselors, given their tendency toward categorical thinking. In the absence of sensitive assessment skills, level 1 counselors project their own experiences onto others. Everyone reminds them of what they looked like in their drinking phase. Beyond that, they must rely heavily on supervisors to categorize clients and conceptualize problems, because their own conceptual frameworks are still undeveloped.

Level 1 counselors tend to formulate clinical concepts on the basis of a single aspect of a client's history. They practice by for-

mulas such as, "All clients in early recovery are . . ." Grand conclusions are based on minimal information and fragments of a
complete clinical picture, such as client statements taken out of
context. Bits of data are selected because they fit into the counselor's theoretical orientation rather than because they illuminate
the case. Conceptualizations are simple and unidimensional: the
client is "sociopathic," "borderline," or "codependent." Level 1
counselors are especially susceptible to sweeping generalizations,
such as the fashionable claim that 95 percent of all clients are
codependent; the rest are in denial. They are not well attuned to
clinically relevant contextual variations, such as gender, racial,
ethnic, and cultural differences. Clearly, level 1 counselors can
benefit from strong supervisory guidance in learning to collect a
broad range of relevant information and integrate it into a theoretical framework through sound conceptualizations and treatment planning.

Beginning counselors do not know how to formulate sound
treatment plans. They cannot visualize and articulate the therapeutic process from intake through intervention to termination.
"Often beginning trainees are satisfied if they can get their clients
to talk for most of a session and seem unable to devise a plan for
dealing with the client's concerns" (Stoltenberg and Delworth 1987,
p. 58). Level 1 counselors' treatment plans are brief, anecdotal, and
untranslatable into specific interventions and techniques. Long-
term treatment goals are unclear. Short-term objectives for counseling are unrelated to an overall treatment strategy.

Finally, entry-level counselors recite ethical and professional
guidelines by the book, with little understanding of the practical
implications of the standards and little experience with their application. They have not integrated ethical standards into their clinical practice. When problems occur, they feel stuck, caught in an
apparent ethical dilemma that the supervisor may be asked to step
in and resolve. The characteristics typical of level 1 counselors are
summarized in Table 6-2.

Most research on counselor development has involved entry-
level counselors because they are an easy population to access and
an interesting one to study. Their initial skill development and
knowledge acquisition lend themselves well to research (Hogan
1964; McNeill, Stoltenberg, and Pierce 1985; Miars and others 1983;

Table 6-2. Level 1 Counselor Characteristics

Focused on basic skills

Motivated by anxiety, enthusiastic

Emulates a role model

Articulates one-word descriptors, categorical thinking

Learns "right way," cookbook answers

Is highly dependent, with a self-focus

Has difficulty conceptualizing

Lacks self-awareness

Does not know what he or she does not know

Overuses a model, tunnel vision

Has difficulty confronting and self-disclosing

Uses anecdotal conceptualization

Makes categorical statements

Has a limited idea of treatment planning

Lacks integrated ethics

Raphael 1982; Stoltenberg 1981; Stoltenberg, Pierce, and McNeill 1987; Stoltenberg, Solomon, and Ogden 1986; Wiley 1982).

Supervisory Environment. The optimal learning environment for level 1 counselors is one that encourages autonomy while providing instruction, support, and modeling within a structured atmosphere. Entry-level counselors need the structure to modulate their anxiety and their high motivation. The supervisor should provide the support the counselor needs to function without frustrating the counselor's need for growth and autonomy. Supervisors, especially those who are not themselves recovering or who have limited experience with substance abuse, should be prepared for challenges to their credentials and expertise. Such challenges notwithstanding, the supervisor must provide the counselor with positive feedback, sandwiching recommendations for improvement between slices of praise and encouragement.

As in the medical precept *primum non nocere* ("first, do no harm") the primary responsibility of the supervisor is to protect client needs at all times. The supervisor must reconcile this duty with that of encouraging risk taking by the counselor who is moving toward autonomy. This is done (as discussed in Chapter Twelve) by watching the supervisee in action via videotapes, co-facilitation, or one-way mirrors, as well as by conducting simulations, group case presentations, and role playing. The supervisor should use a variety of tools to help the counselor assimilate and categorize information into sound treatment plans and conceptualizations. Simple, time-effective ways of summarizing these data can keep the counselor from drowning in anecdotal information.

To facilitate growth, the supervisor should introduce the counselor to ambiguity and conflict. This ambiguity must be challenging but not disabling. Disequilibrium should be introduced periodically. The key is to find the right balance between support and uncertainty, autonomy and dependence. As the counselor gains confidence and feels more secure, the initial dependency on the supervisor will subside.

Finally, the supervisor working with a level 1 counselor should take into account the supervisee's learning style. Some learn by doing and should be given more independent study and readings; others learn vicariously, by osmosis, and benefit from directive skill building and modeling by the supervisor. Learning style also is influenced by three other variables: conceptual skills, locus of control, and oral versus written processing.

Stoltenberg and Delworth show that consideration of the trainee's conceptual level helps to create an appropriate supervisory environment. With counselors who have relatively low conceptual skills, more structure is needed to facilitate learning. For those with higher conceptual skills, the structure that is useful early on to clarify the supervisory process is rapidly outgrown as the trainee learns and integrates information.

Supervisees with internal locus of control (those who see themselves making things happen) can learn by processing information and drawing their own conclusions inductively. Trainees with external locus of control (those who see external forces in control of events) prefer direct feedback and guidance, since they need to have conclusions drawn for them deductively (Bernstein and LeComte 1979; Handley 1982).

Finally, some supervisees learn best from written information, while others learn best through conversation and discussion. Those who learn through reading should be provided with homework assignments and literature to read. Oral processors should have opportunities to discuss cases with colleagues and peers to assimilate the information learned. (Supervision issues are summarized in Table 6-3.)

The transition from level 1 to level 2 is not always a clear, linear process. Individual differences, setting and client variables, and training requirements affect the transition. At the end of level 1, the trainee is less anxious but still too unaware, rigid, and dependent to be an effective therapist. Although she feels more secure, she still has the limited insight characteristic of level 1. She does not know how much she still does not know. For this reason, the most effective way to aid counselors through the transition process is by using "affective confrontations focusing on the trainee's awareness of self and client. These interventions may take the form of process comments by the supervisor, highlighting important

Table 6-3. Level 1 Counselor Supervision Issues

Expose to numerous orientations

Be sensitive to trainee anxiety

Promote autonomy

Encourage risk-taking

Promote exposure to models

Introduce ambiguity

Balance support with uncertainty

Use role play, application, presentations

Help to conceptualize

Address strengths first

Do not take too much control

Be aware of trainee learning styles

    Active versus vicarious

    Locus of control

    Conceptual levels

    Oral versus written processors

son struggling to attain professional maturity by becoming more fully socialized and gaining emotional control.

With a more difficult caseload than the beginner's, level 2 counselors do not have the easy successes they may have had before. The straightforward interventions that previously sufficed are inadequate for the more complex situations counselors confront at level 2. As a result, their motivation fluctuates between the zeal they displayed at level 1 and discouragement, even despair, about their future in the profession. Whereas level 1 counselors do not know what they do not know, level 2 counselors are more aware of their deficits but do not know what to do about them. Compounding the frustration and anxiety they feel is the impact of an inadequate income. The counselor's low pay, acceptable in the context of the beginner's zeal for counseling, is no longer acceptable when work becomes frustrating (Edelwich and Brodsky 1980). Feeling stalemated, counselors may consider leaving the field or may create emotional distance between themselves and their work through attendance problems, inattention to tasks, tardiness with clients, or becoming more academic or research oriented. Overall, level 2 counselors have a more realistic awareness of themselves and the world of work. Their awareness is not necessarily helpful, however, inasmuch as they lack the skills to resolve their work problems. They feel frustrated and stuck.

Level 2 counselors are less narcissistic and more client focused than level 1 counselors. Indeed, they can become too client focused, empathizing excessively with the client. Peabody and Gelso (1982) call this reaction "extreme countertransference," and Hoffman (1984) terms it an "emotional contagion." It leads the counselor to be either enmeshed with or emotionally distanced from the client, both countertherapeutic reactions. In this context, issues of isomorphism become critical for the level 2 counselor.

Level 2 counselors generally move away from a strict adherence to a particular theoretical orientation. They are beginning to be able to personalize their own model of counseling and are becoming skilled in using a variety of orientations with particular clients. What they lack is an understanding of what to use in a given circumstance—and why. They may have difficulty justifying their approach to a particular case and the specific interventions employed (Heppner and Roehlke 1984). A counselor who shows this deficiency probably has not integrated his skills into a theoretical orientation. He wants to learn and integrate new techniques and skills, which is best done at this stage on the counselor's own initiative rather than at the supervisor's instruction. Thus, a major goal of supervision for level 2 counselors is to reinforce the developmental gains made to date while strengthening the counselor's ability to conceptualize cases and to strengthen overall clinical skills.

While more aware of the client's needs, the level 2 counselor is not yet sure how to respond to the client and, frustrated, responds in an idiosyncratic manner. Level 2 counselors are better able to conceptualize and articulate clinical issues and have more sophisticated assessment skills than level 1 counselors. They are more conversant with the *Diagnostic and Statistical Manual* (third edition, revised) of the American Psychiatric Association (*DSM-III-R*, soon to be *DSM-IV*), although they are not always clear as to the ramifications of their use of diagnostic classifications. Moreover, they are generally unable to tie their diagnoses to specific treatment planning goals and interventions.

Level 2 counselors are more aware of gender and cultural variants, although there remains a tendency to make stereotypical judgments, such as "All blacks are like that," or "That is typical female client behavior." According to Stoltenberg and Delworth (1987, p. 77), "The domain of individual differences is one where often the most productive work at level 2 is done. The trainee is now deeply aware of individual differences and, even if confused and vacillating, has greater openness to seeing and understanding the varieties of human experience."

Finally, level 2 counselors have a more complex understanding of professional ethics. They realize that ethical standards do not fit into neatly wrapped boxes as the level 1 counselor imagines. Because of a tendency to overaccommodate to the client, the counselor at level 2 may uncritically take the side of the client against the agency in an ethical dilemma. This way of reacting may put the supervisee and supervisor in conflict with each other (Reising and Daniels 1983). (Table 6-4 summarizes level 2 counselor characteristics.)

Table 6-4. Level 2 Counselor Characteristics

Focuses more on client

Exhibits greater awareness, frustration, confusion

May not look as advanced as level 1

Shows uncertainty and lingering idealism

Loses motivation after difficult clients

Has dependency/autonomy conflicts with supervisor

Is less imitative, more self-assertive

Is less inclined to ask for recommendations

Better articulates client classifications

Evidences greater cultural awareness

Uses more eclectic theory

Uses better-formed ethics

Supervisory Environment. Supervisors must take into account the differences between level 1 and level 2 counselors and alter their supervisory approaches accordingly. Whereas level 1 counselors need structure, support, and specific instruction, level 2 counselors need an environment that promotes greater autonomy with moderate (low-normative) structure through support, limited instruction, and ambivalence clarification. Supervision at this stage provides a transparent safety net, giving counselors the courage to venture out with the knowledge that someone is there to catch them should they fall. The supervisor uses less didactic methods and offers more modeling opportunities. Counselors need to be given the tools to fix what is broken themselves.

Level 2 counselors need to be given a caseload balanced between challenging, difficult cases and opportunities for success. A counselor who is given only tough cases may experience frustration and conclude that he cannot do anything right. At the other extreme, a counselor who is given only straightforward cases may suffer from arrested professional growth. To the extent that counselors select their own cases, supervisors should pay attention to their choices. Does a counselor seek only clients with whom she can be successful, or is she reaching too far beyond her abilities?

The counselor may resist presenting cases with which she is having difficulty because she wants to look competent in the eyes of her colleagues and supervisor. Yet she needs to be encouraged to work through difficult cases, for that is where real professional growth and job satisfaction lie.

Notwithstanding the counselor's need to function more autonomously in level 2, supervisory oversight continues after cases are assigned. For the sake of the client as well as the counselor, the supervisor must not abandon the counselor but must monitor the counselor's performance, which may still be uneven. Level 2 counselors need freedom to move across all domains (Rabinowitz, Heppner, and Roehlke 1985). Less is riding on the specific interventions of supervisors at level 2 than at level 1, since counselors are no longer either insisting on cookbook instructions or reacting with heightened anxiety to perceived reprimands. Since level 2 counselors have built up a reserve of ego strength in their professional role, the supervisor can feel freer to point out discrepancies in a counselor's work. It is permissible to create dissonance for the supervisee, provided that the person can integrate the information and that it does not create too much disequilibrium.

On the other side of the coin, knowing that level 2 counselors are not inclined to take the supervisor's word as gospel, supervisors must be prepared to take challenges to their knowledge and authority in stride. Supervisors who feel secure in their own clinical skills will be comfortable stepping down from the pedestal of expertise to hear and respond to challenges from counselors. For the secure supervisor, such challenges are an opportunity for growth.

Hill, Charles, and Reed (1981) found that entry-level counselors believed their supervisors knew almost everything. Over time, they could allow their supervisors to be more human and could recognize more realistically the limitations of the supervisors' knowledge and judgments. This mature understanding of the supervisor is not, however, arrived at by a smooth, linear path. Instead, level 2 brings sharp oscillations in the counselor's opinion of the supervisor. When the counselor views the supervisor as incompetent, as many teenagers view their parents, the supervisor must realize that in time the counselor will develop a more realistic perception of the supervisor's skills. Mark Twain wrote how as a teenager he thought his parents knew nothing. He was amazed how much they learned by the time he was twenty-one!

If level 1 counselors are characterized by bursts of vertical growth, level 2 counselors trace a more jagged developmental path. They progress in a cyclical rather than a linear fashion, regressing at times to earlier developmental issues. A level 2 counselor may even look less secure and developed than a level 1 counselor. The supervisor should validate this process, reassuring counselors that periods of frustration, anxiety, and regression are not uncommon. This validation gives the counselor permission to be "normal." That, then, is the task of the supervisor: to guide the counselor through the rocky roads of adolescence into maturity.

Level 2 counselors present numerous challenges that make the supervisor's job interesting and rewarding as well as frustrating. The nature of the challenges varies with the model of supervision used. If it is a therapy-oriented model, the supervisor must maintain clear boundaries; the temptation to counsel arises more insistently in level 2. At another level altogether, supervisors of level 2 counselors need a good sense of humor to be able to laugh at themselves and at times even the counselors. Supervisees at level 2 can be difficult to work with but also very gratifying in the end. There is great joy in seeing an adolescent mature into adulthood— in seeing a rough-edged counselor develop into a finished professional. The counselor's frustrations will lessen as he or she matures into level 3. Fortunately, most counselors either quickly outgrow their adolescence and move on to level 3 or leave the counseling field. Few stay stuck at level 2; the frustration is too great. (Table 6-5 summarizes the supervision issues.)

Level 3

If level 2 counselors are in the trials and tribulations period of development, level 3 counselors can enjoy the calm after the storm. To adapt the terms coined by Yalom (1995) with reference to the developmental stages of therapy groups, we can describe level 1 of counselor development as *forming*, level 2 as *storming*, and level 3 as *norming*. For the experienced counselor, norming involves establishing one's own therapy model and normalizing that approach in a range of clinical situations. Motivation stabilizes in level 3, and

Table 6-5. Level 2 Counselor Supervision Issues

Understand that counselor is less technique oriented

Realize counselor is ready for confrontation and needs to learn alternatives

Be prepared for challenges to supervisor competence

Focus on transference

Develop consultative supervision

Encourage independence

Realize the counselor knows something is wrong but lacks skills to fix it

Provide blend of clients

Recognize need for convincing rationale

Distinguish clearly between supervision and therapy

---

a sense of autonomy and interdependence replaces the internal conflicts of the level 2 counselor. Level 3 counselors show stable performance in all domains. With exposure to a broader range of clients, these mature counselors can adapt to a variety of contextual issues. Their "motivation is less likely to be adversely affected when the therapist is confronted with a client with whom successful work is improbable" (Stoltenberg and Delworth 1987, p. 40).

These are the adults of counseling, and just as adulthood is the longest phase of a normal life span, so is level 3 in the normal career span. Once the basic skills are acquired, counselors continue to mature throughout their professional years. Theirs is a lifelong pilgrimage of development (Powell 2003).

Structures. In terms of Stoltenberg and Delworth's three basic structures, following are the salient characteristics of level 3 counselors:

1. *Securely autonomous.* Level 3 counselors are secure enough to form interdependent relationships with supervisors and colleagues. While functioning autonomously in most clinical activities, they can support or rely on other staff members as appropriate.
2. *Aware and accepting of self and others.* Level 3 counselors have a mature awareness of their own strengths and limitations, together with a realistic confidence in their capacity to grow in

their weaker areas. Similarly, they can empathize with a client while maintaining sufficient objectivity to process the interaction. As a result, they can make therapeutic use of their own and the client's reactions. Their greater awareness of others also enables them to have more collegial, mutually supportive relationships with supervisors.

3. *Stably motivated.* Level 3 counselors' motivation is steady, consistent, realistic, and balanced. They know they cannot save the world, yet they maintain enthusiasm for the work. They can "check their egos at the door" when entering the office and not take their caseload home with them after hours. Although doubts remain, level 3 counselors are not immobilized by them. Instead, they show "commitment in the face of doubt" (Reising and Daniels 1983, p. 241).

Description. Level 3 counselors exhibit increased self-awareness, self-confidence, and emotional security on the job. They are highly differentiated personally and professionally and are forging their own unique professional identities. Moreover, level 3 counselors have a realistic sense of the boundaries and limits of counseling. As a result, they are better able to live with ambiguity and doubt.

Having arrived at a balanced perspective about their work, counselors can now begin to sort out the motivations that brought them into the field. Loganbill, Hardy, and Delworth (1982) list six general motivating factors that influence people to enter the helping professions: intimacy, power, financial success, personal growth, intellectual stimulation, and altruism. Added to these are the recovering person's zeal to help others in their recovery. It would be highly desirable for counselors at all stages of development to understand these motivations and their impact on clinical work. However, level 1 counselors are not yet in a position to develop and apply such insight. Level 2 counselors sometimes can begin to do so, but this stormy period of development usually is not conducive to detached self-examination. It is in level 3 that counselors become sufficiently calm, reflective, and receptive to acknowledge their motivations, work through the clinical implications, and channel them constructively. Supervisory guidance is crucial in confronting these issues (Hill, Charles, and Reed 1981; McNeill, Stoltenberg, and Pierce 1985; Reising and Daniels 1983).

When it comes to theoretical orientation, level 3 counselors have developed beyond both random eclecticism (that is, grasping for expedient, ad hoc solutions) and the strict, dogmatic adherence to one theory or approach. When they describe their therapy model as eclectic, they usually mean that although they have grounded themselves in a particular counseling model, they draw from a variety of models as appropriate for the client in a specific context. Instead of grasping for pat answers, they creatively adapt general approaches to individual client variables.

A firm but flexible theoretical orientation makes for a clear relationship among concepts, treatment goals, and techniques. Level 3 counselors use treatment plans as linchpins that tie together their assessments, conceptualizations, and specific clinical interventions. These treatment plans are focused, coherent, and finely tuned documents that serve as reliable road maps for the clinician.

Level 3 counselors are highly proficient in counseling techniques. They can experiment with various approaches, switching tracks easily when one path to a clinical goal is blocked. They thoroughly understand the process of interviewing, diagnosis, and assessment and seek training when they find themselves deficient in some area. Having left behind the stereotypical thinking and categorical judgments typical of level 1, they realize that each client is unique. Moreover, they are able to understand that uniqueness in terms of a wide range of variables, such as age, gender, ethnicity, and diagnostic category. This focused understanding allows for improved clinical conceptualization and articulation of treatment goals.

Level 3 counselors have a seasoned understanding of professional ethics. They no longer expect to find textbook answers to ethical dilemmas, for they have learned from experience that reality eludes neat classifications and frustrates ethical complacency. For example, properly supervised counselors at all levels learn to delineate and respect the boundary between having countertransferential feelings toward clients and acting out sexually with clients. By the time they reach level 3, most counselors have internalized that distinction to the point where they are much less uncomfortable when sexual attractions arise and are better able to turn those feelings to therapeutic and educational gain. They can then begin to address the many ambiguous questions or gray zones that arise in this area, such as whether former clients are always and forever off limits for personal relationships (Edelwich and Brodsky 1991). (These ethical complexities will be discussed further in Chapters Twelve and Fifteen.)

Training and supervision continue for level 3 counselors throughout their professional lives, evolving from mentorship to a dialogue more closely resembling consultation and collegial support. Even within this optimistic, forward-looking framework, however, supervisors must exercise caution, for a counselor may be a pseudo–level 3, giving the impression of professional maturity by escaping the outward turmoil of level 2. Stoltenberg and Delworth (1987, p. 103) describe one such case as follows: "While firmly planted in the rigid and dualistic ground of Level 1, the supervisee achieved a more sophisticated way of articulating client concerns and the process of therapy." Individuals such as this may be difficult to identify.

Furthermore, supervisors need to watch for counselors who have not reached the same level of development in all domains. For example, a counselor may be skilled in assessment but weak in group counseling. Supervisors must be careful not to allow a halo effect to create a false impression of mastery in all domains.

Finally, a level 3 counselor may regress temporarily to an earlier stage of development because of the work environment, caseloads, personal stressors, agency policies and procedures, and any number of other situational variables. Given appropriate interventions (self-initiated, supervisory, or institutional) and the absence of severe, intractable problems, the counselor will likely rebound quickly and return to level 3 functioning. Realistically, however, counselors and supervisors alike should be made aware that repeated experiences of the burnout cycle (from enthusiasm to stagnation to frustration) are a normal part of professional life. Interventions should be designed to prevent the descent into the fourth stage of long-term apathy (Edelwich and Brodsky 1980). (Table 6-6 summarizes level 3 counselor characteristics.)

Supervisory Environment. If the watchword for supervisors of level 1 counselors is patience, and for level 2 flexibility, for level 3 it is wisdom. While modeling an understanding of self and of the realities

Table 6-6. Level 3 Counselor Characteristics

Has deeper client understanding

Understands limits, not disabled by doubt

Is consistently motivated over time

Is forging own therapeutic style

Displays increasing autonomy

Is stable in six factors

    Intimacy

    Power

    Financial concerns

    Personal growth

    Intellectual abilities

    Altruism

Is nondefensive

Displays appropriate use of self

Is able to switch tracks

Pigeonholes clients less often

Accepts supervisor of different orientation

Can move smoothly from assessment to conceptualization to intervention

Displays broad ethical perspectives

---

of clinical practice, the supervisor guides the supervisee toward mastery and integration of all domains, from assessment to treatment to aftercare. The supervisor needs wisdom in confronting the counselor at the right time and in the right way, balancing remarks that are supportive, facilitative, exploratory, and confrontive. Catalytic remarks by the supervisor are especially beneficial in that they promote self-exploration, leading to incremental learning and further conceptual development.

Being more secure in their theoretical orientation, level 3 counselors can accept supervisors of differing orientations. They value dialogue, diversity, and discovery. At the same time, they need experienced supervisors who have something to teach them. At this stage of development, a counselor is looking for a supervisor who can command respect, broaden horizons, and offer relevant guidance in challenging situations. In terms of the developmental scheme for supervisors presented in the next section, level 3 counselors need to be supervised by level 3 supervisors. Otherwise, the counselor may accommodate to the supervisor's modest expectations, thereby missing opportunities for growth, or look elsewhere for instruction and stimulation.

Level 3 counselors will likely undergo career transitions. Having reached a high level of sophistication and professionalism, they are ripe for recruitment by other agencies or promotion within their agency. Indeed, they will likely move into supervisory roles themselves. It is important for level 3 counselors to reach closure on their own issues in supervision lest they act out their unfinished business with their supervisees.

Self-disclosure on the supervisor's part is more appropriate with level 3 counselors than with level 1 and 2 counselors. Level 1 counselors tend to be uncomfortable hearing self-disclosures from their supervisors. Level 2 counselors may see supervisory self-disclosure either as condescending or as compromising the supervisor's authority, thereby giving the supervisee the upper hand. Level 3 counselors, with their greater awareness of self and others, are less reactive and more amenable to supervisory self-disclosure. Altogether, supervising level 3 counselors is a highly rewarding experience, if one can let go of one's own ego needs and allow counselors to grow at their own pace and manner. (Table 6-7 summarizes level 3 supervision issues.)

Levels of Supervisor Development

Stoltenberg and Delworth's model lays out three developmental levels for supervisors that parallel those for counselors. The analogy with the developmental path from childhood through adolescence to adulthood applies here as well. Specifying and describing these three stages of supervisory development is useful not only for supervisor training and evaluation but also for matching supervisors with supervisees.

Supervisors, like counselors, operate in numerous domains and fill a variety of roles: teacher, coach, cheerleader, consultant, evaluator, administrator, role model, and mentor (at times even

Table 6-7. Level 3 Counselor Supervision Issues

Requires level 3 counselor/supervisor

Use a client-centered approach

Be a supportive colleague/friend, reality tester, sharer of experiences

Use wisdom as a guide

Stimulate and challenge the counselor

Use catalytic interventions

Use self-disclosure when helpful

tormentor). More advanced supervisors can move nimbly among these roles, depending on the needs of the supervisee. Entry-level supervisors, like entry-level counselors, have one or two techniques that they use and overuse. As they grow in experience and proficiency, they acquire many more tools to select from—more tactics and strategies to use as appropriate. As with level 1 versus level 3 counselors, it is like the difference between a farm team pitcher in baseball who can throw only one good pitch, regardless of the batter, and a major league pitcher at the top of his form who can vary the pitch with the batter.

Of course, a clinical supervisor should be a skilled counselor. It is assumed that a candidate for supervisory responsibilities is already a level 3 counselor. However, since supervision is a distinct discipline with its own requisite skills and proficiencies, an advanced counselor may be a beginning or intermediate-level supervisor. Guidelines for assessing one's own or another person's level of development as a supervisor can be found in Appendixes A through F.

Level 1

Level 1 supervisors are characterized by anxiety and naiveté. They aim to say the right things, to have the right answers, to supervise by cookbook. They tend to be mechanistic in their style, playing out the expert role. They seek help frequently from their supervisors and draw upon their own experiences in supervision. Excited by the challenge of their new tasks, they are highly motivated; trainee success is very important to them. Because of their strongly felt need to succeed, together with their overinvestment in the supervisee's adopting their model of counseling, entry-level supervisors require structure in their supervision.

Assuming that a level 1 supervisor is an advanced counselor, he can be of help to level 1 counselors, who stand to learn much from a sound clinician. However, level 1 supervisors are not a good match for level 2 counselors, who are primed to challenge the supervisor's authority. For the level 1 supervisor, insecure in his own theoretical approach to supervision, a challenging counselor can be quite threatening. Such challenges push the supervisor toward professional maturity. Meanwhile, however, according to Stoltenberg and Delworth (1987, p. 156), "There is just no feasible way for the Level 1 supervisor to deal with the conflict and confusion of a Level 2 trainee. What often happens is that both parties wait out the period of supervision, and little of consequence occurs." Both adopt the government employee's rule of survival: "Go along to get along." (See Table 6-8.)

Level 2

Level 2 supervisors are characterized by confusion, conflict, and frustration. They realize that supervision is more complex than they imagined. It is no longer the great adventure and ennobling experience they originally thought it was. The additional income likely does not compensate for the added responsibilities, hours worked, and frustrations. As a result, objectivity, together with the supervisor's sense of purpose, may be lost. Motivation may vary from session to session. "There is a tendency to 'go on one's own' in supervising, with occasional lapses into dependency on a trusted

Table 6-8. Level 1 Supervisor Characteristics

Displays a mechanistic approach

Plays a strong expert role

Depends on own supervisor

Is highly motivated

Is moderately to highly structured

Is invested in trainee's adopting one's own model

Has trouble with level 2 counselors

supervisor, or colleague" (Stoltenberg and Delworth 1987, p. 156). Level 2 supervisors may withdraw from staff interactions, blaming the administration or the counselors for their frustration.

Fortunately, supervisors do not stay in this stage for long. They either grow up or get out. In most cases, they have the insight and self-awareness to become senior-level supervisors, especially when they are given appropriate and consistent training experiences (such as cosupervision, a valuable way to learn techniques and feel more secure about skills). However, "adolescent" supervisors can hide out in their role long enough to grow into level 3 supervisors.

Level 2 supervisors are a poor match for adolescent and senior-level counselors. They work best with entry-level staff who can gain from the supervisor's clinical experience without challenging the supervisor's authority. However, level 2 supervisors and level 2 counselors can work together provided that they share their vulnerabilities and needs for growth in an atmosphere of honesty. (See Table 6-9.)

Level 3

The majority of supervisors go on to function stably and autonomously at level 3, with consistent motivation and with little need for oversight of their supervision. These supervisors are capable of honest self-appraisal and are relatively experienced in all domains. They can supervise counselors at all levels of development, although (depending on their model of counseling and other factors) they generally prefer working with counselors at one or another level. (See Table 6-10.)

Assessing a Supervisor's Developmental Level

A supervisor's level of professional development can be assessed through supervisee evaluations of her supervision (Appendix E), her own supervisor's evaluation (Appendix F), self-assessment instruments (Appendixes C and D), and a review of the following questions:

1. What is the supervisor's level of development as a counselor (level 1, 2, or 3)?

Table 6-9. Level 2 Supervisor Characteristics

Displays confusion, conflict issues

Sees supervision/counseling as more complex, multidimensional

Has fluctuating motivation, especially when supervisory functions are not rewarded

Focuses on supervisee

Loses objectivity

Blames supervisee for supervisor's problems

Works best with level 1 counselors, okay with level 2 counselors

Table 6-10. Level 3 Supervisor Characteristics

Functions autonomously

Displays self- and supervisee awareness

Differentiates boundaries/roles

Able to supervise at all times

Prefers to work with certain level of counselor

2. What is her supervisory training experience, including both didactic and experiential training (Appendix C)?

3. What has been the individual's experience as a supervisor and supervisee, including the amount and type of supervision received (both as counselor and as supervisor) and provided to supervisees?

4. How does the person function in the three structures— autonomy/dependence, self- and other awareness, and motivation—as related to the supervisory role?

APPLICATION OF THE DEVELOPMENTAL PERSPECTIVE

Counselors grow and adapt over time, from the naiveté of level 1, to the tenuous clinical self-confidence of level 2, to the realistic self-appraisal and mastery of level 3. Supervisors must adapt to the changing supervisee. Supervisors must carefully assess the counselor's level of functioning and provide information and guidance relevant to a counselor at that level. In this process supervisors, too, are growing. It is essential for them to learn to assess their own developmental level as a supervisor as well as that of the supervisors they administer or employ.

This developmental perspective underlies all the models of supervision presented in the following chapters, including the new model developed in Chapter Ten for the alcohol and drug abuse field. It is like a colored lens through which each model is to be viewed. No matter what the model of therapy and supervision—skills oriented or dynamically oriented—the developmental stage of clinicians and supervisors must be taken into account.

Chapter Seven

The Psychodynamic Model

The psychodynamic model of supervision, for decades the cornerstone of the field, is reemerging after having fallen out of favor a generation earlier. Its changing fortunes have been linked with those of the psychodynamic school of psychotherapy, since models of supervision follow in the wake of the corresponding models of therapy or counseling. Necessary as it has been to balance the psychodynamic perspective with one that emphasizes skills training, it would be shortsighted to discount a model that has done so much to shape the practice of counseling and supervision. To the extent that we need to know about the dynamics of the counselor-client relationship, beginning with the selection of clients and continuing throughout the therapeutic interaction, it is to the psychodynamic model that we must turn.

The term *psychodynamic,* as used here, encompasses both the psychotherapeutic and psychoanalytic models of supervision, which are essentially similar despite significant shades of difference. The psychodynamic model regards supervision as a therapeutic process focusing on the intrapersonal and interpersonal dynamics of the counselor in relation to clients, colleagues, supervisors, and significant others. Its goal is dynamic awareness, which includes understanding dynamic contingencies (past learning experiences that reassert themselves in present situations), observing changes in the dynamic, and making therapeutic use of the dynamic in counseling. For psychodynamically oriented supervisors, the primary objective of supervision is not to teach techniques. Rather, it is to refine the supervisee's mode of listening and bring about the internalization of a particular attitude about therapy—one that entails a sensitivity to transference, countertransference, drives, and defense mechanisms.

Underlying this model is the assumption that there are structural and dynamic similarities between therapy and supervision, linking the counselor, patient, and supervisor in an isomorphic relationship—that is, a complex set of interactions with parallel dynamics. What a person experiences in one relationship, the person tends to experience in other relationships as well (Gediman and Wolkenfeld 1980). The interpretation of this parallel process as it works itself out between client and counselor and between counselor and supervisor is central to supervision in the psychodynamic model. In the interpretation of this dynamic, primary process (the manifest, observable content of the interaction) is considered merely an expression of secondary process (the less obvious, latent meaning). What is said and done is just a starting point for uncovering the underlying experience (Wilner 1990).

The psychodynamic model addresses questions that are central to the practice of clinical supervision—questions without which a comprehensive model of supervision would be incomplete, such as the following:

- What are the emotional and personality conflicts that contribute to supervisee resistance (for example, the wish to please the supervisor or an avoidance of aggressive or sexual material)?
- How should the supervisor deal with these conflicts?
- Should unresolved intrapsychic conflicts be permitted to intrude on the supervisory process?
- How much should the supervisee's dynamics be discussed in supervision?
- Where does one draw the line between supervision and therapy?
- Is it within the scope of the supervisor's role to recommend personal therapy for the supervisee?

PSYCHODYNAMICALLY ORIENTED DEFINITIONS OF SUPERVISION

Lebovici (1970) defines supervision as the development of a relationship between two persons that deals with transference displacement. The supervisory relationship, thus conceived, addresses personality characteristics of the supervisor and the supervisee and the interactions between the two. Emch (1955) defines supervision as an "experience overtly taking place between two people" that deals with who else is (figuratively) in the room at the time and what else is occurring overtly or covertly in the interaction (p. 299). Psychopathology may manifest itself in supervision, evoking a range of feelings and reactions from the supervisor-therapist.

With this emphasis on personalities and their interaction, clinical supervision from a psychodynamic perspective is a dynamic process much like therapy. In line with this parallel, Fleming and Benedek (1966) emphasize the role of the supervisor in creating a "learning alliance"—a climate of trust and cooperation, free from neurotic conflicts, that makes learning possible (Cherniss and Egnatios 1977; Friedlander and Ward 1984; Levenson 1984; Rosenblatt and Mayer 1975).

The psychoanalytic model of supervision examines a variety of intrapsychic issues as essential to supervision. The supervisory interchange reawakens oedipal and narcissistic conflicts in both supervisee and supervisor. These neurotic conflicts are acted out in supervision as the supervisee filters out information about clients for fear of disappointing the supervisor. The supervisor, feeling competitive with the supervisee, may inject aggressive or conflictual content into the supervision sessions (Searles 1965).

Parallel Process in Supervision

Psychodynamic approaches to supervision have greatly influenced the thinking even of nonpsychodynamic theorists and practitioners. For example, there is a general awareness of parallel process in supervision. Supervisors and their supervisees are trained to observe and take into account the parallel reenactments of significant psychic events that regularly occur. Parallel process, then, is a central feature of supervision. Gediman and Wolkenfeld (1980) state that parallel reenactments are multidimensional, ubiquitous, and inevitable in supervision, encompassing the full range of neuroses.

Wolkenfeld (1990) sees supervision as a process of ever-increasing refinement of the supervisee's psychoanalytic mode of listening, the internalization of the "psychoanalytic attitude." Through listening, musing, suspension of judgment, tolerance for ambiguity, and rejection of illusion, the analyst grows and matures. Parallel processes are the reenactments of this listening, with the supervisee as the primary focus of the client-supervisee-supervisor triad. "More students lean towards a confessional approach than an educational one in the supervisory experience" (Schwartz 1990, p. 89).

Self-Exploration in Supervision

Other psychodynamic supervisors postulate the importance of counselors' understanding of their own dynamics and their ability to use the self as a major emotional force in therapy. For Newirth (1990), for example, supervision involves the creation of a holding environment, continual growth on the counselor's part, and the development of the self and interpersonal relations. For Singer (1990), supervision is the playing field on which the pulse of counseling is taken, with the social and interpersonal realities of counseling as grist for the mill in the supervisory relationship. Even so, the supervisor's area of concern is limited to the counselor's countertransferential reactions toward the client (Issacharoff 1982).

To understand any model of supervision, it is necessary to understand its philosophical underpinnings—in the case of the psychodynamic model, an ambitious undertaking. Caruth (1990), for example, incorporates such arcane psychoanalytic concepts as "the dyadic pre-oedipal area of narcissistic vulnerability" and "oedipal issues" in relation to "triadic aspects" and "overlapping triangles." These parallel processes, which raise issues of matching and mismatching in the counseling relationship, are played out in the supervisee's desire to "cure" himself so as to achieve an analytic identity (Oberman 1990). Understandably, supervisors will differ as to their willingness to learn and apply this dense terminology.

The mystification to which psychoanalytic theory lends itself has contributed to the rejection of this model in favor of a skills-oriented approach to supervision. The substance abuse field has been particularly scornful of psychodynamic therapists for their failure to treat alcohol and drug addiction as a primary disease, which many counselors see as enabling drinking behavior. Valid as this criticism may be, the psychodynamic model raises important questions that must be addressed.

METHODS IN PSYCHODYNAMIC SUPERVISION

The primary methods of observation in the psychodynamic model of supervision are nondirective, such as process notes, verbatim reports, and oral presentations by the supervisee. Dynamic insight is critical to the learning process. It involves an incorporation of self into the supervisory interchange for the purpose of gaining insight into client and counselor behavior, feelings, attitudes, and reactions. Caligor, Bromberg, and Meltzer (1984), Fleming and Benedek (1966), Kris (1956), and Lane (1985) have made clear that the extent to which supervision resembles therapy depends on the supervisee's needs. Other psychodynamic theorists, placing far less emphasis on personal therapy in supervision, concentrate on presenting ideas, strengthening the student's understanding of the therapeutic process, and fostering empathy (Schwartz 1990).

In the initial stage of supervision, the supervisor explores the expectations, hopes, fears, and anxieties in the supervisor-supervisee relationship. The focus is interpersonal and intrapsychic, with the counselor learning to explore the dynamics of the counseling experience through modeling tapes and structured exercises. As supervision progresses, the focus shifts to using the supervisory exchange as a therapeutic tool in clinical work and developing the counselor's own style through self-exploration and insight.

SELECTION OF PATIENTS FOR SUPERVISION

The psychodynamic model sheds useful light on the selection of patients for and by supervisees. If parallel processes are critical to supervision, if isomorphism characterizes the supervisory interaction, then patient selection requires careful consideration. Furthermore, since entry-level counselors are expected to treat a broad range of patients, the question of patient selection raises fundamental ethical and legal issues. Each patient brings a new set of variables and unique problems that must be taken into account in designing supervision programs, especially for the level 1 counselor. Supervisors must also be prepared to monitor, explore, and correct the favoritism counselors often show toward preferred patients.

Patient selection has received little attention in the literature aside from broad generalizations about its importance. Except in the psychoanalytic literature, there has been little research on the influence of specific client characteristics on supervision (Ekstein and Wallerstein 1972; Fleming 1967). This scholarly silence may reflect widespread resistance in the mental health professions to acknowledging the existence of bias in patient selection and identifying the factors underlying it. Supervisors may be hesitant to admit that unconditional positive regard and acceptance of all patients are easier said than practiced. Moreover, to address this issue may call attention to the difficulties posed in measuring therapeutic success. If the dependent variables that define a good outcome cannot easily be specified, how can the impact of an independent variable such as patient selection criteria be evaluated?

In addition, an examination of patient selection bias would raise the issue of countertransference, which is ignored by models of supervision concerned primarily with developing technicians. Addressing this issue, it is feared, might allow for regression to past conflicts. Supervisors and supervisees alike may be understandably resistant to recognizing personal issues that affect client outcome. "As supervisees might want to preserve their secret source of control, and supervisors might not want to admit a situation that seems to undermine their control, writers might avoid attending to such charged process issues in the supervisory dyad" (Searles 1965, p. 591).

In particular, there is the highly charged issue of selective attention to preferred clients. Research has shown that counselors typically spend more time with clients who are of the opposite gender, young, attractive, verbal, intelligent, and successful (Schofield 1964). These patients remain longer in treatment (Garfield 1986; Imber, Nash, and Stone 1955; Lorr, Katz, and Rubenstein 1958). When supervisees are permitted to select patients for supervision, as they often are, they tend to favor younger and more "successful" clients (Burgoyne and others 1976; Greenberg 1980; Steinhelber and others 1984; Wagner 1957). In these studies, patients under medication were less likely to be selected as supervision clients. Intensive "supervision was more likely to be given to patients with a diagnosis of personality disorder, neurosis, and transient situational reaction, and low supervision to those with psychotic affective disorders, schizophrenia, and borderline personalities" (Lane

1990, p. 16). Other determinant variables included social class and potential for premature treatment termination. Counselors want to look good for their supervisors, so they will select less problematic patients with a better prognosis.

Key patient variables affecting supervision—age, socio-economic status, diagnosis, education, sex, race, personality traits, attitude toward counseling, psychological mindedness, birth order, and transference factors—have been explored. These variables must be correlated with counselor variables such as personality attributes, therapeutic skill, motivation, developmental level, attitude toward therapy and supervision, independence/dependence, theoretical and philosophical frame of reference, locus of control, fragility, sensitivity to criticism, self-confidence, ability to handle aggression and confrontation, and awareness of self and others. Further research is needed on these and other such variables as they affect patient selection by counselors, patient outcome, and criteria for patient-counselor matching by supervisors.

COUNSELOR DEVELOPMENT FROM A PSYCHODYNAMIC PERSPECTIVE

The development of a therapist has been analyzed at length in the psychodynamic literature, with parallels drawn to a person's growth from childhood to adulthood. Chazan (1990) and Winnicott (1971) postulate three phases of discovery, which they describe as follows.

Phase 1: Childhood

In the first phase, supervision is likened to the mother-child relationship. At birth, the child separates from the biological inner space of the mother and enters an external reality that is shared with her. Play becomes the universal form of communication, moving both mother and child toward growth and health. Similarly, a supervisor creates space for the "child" supervisee to play—a home base for exploration and experimentation. Personal and professional identities are fused during a close bonding process.

In this childhood phase, the supervisee and supervisor question whether they will like, understand, trust, and appreciate each other. They want to see whether they can reveal their doubts openly and, ultimately, whether they can work together. Paradigms from the past influence the resolution of these questions, as transference conditions this orientation to the supervisory process. Mahler, Pine, and Bergman (1975) call this phase of supervision "twinning." When this interpersonal space has been demarcated, so that the possibility for further growth is opened up for the novice therapist, the supervisory relationship enters the structure-building phase.

Phase 2: Adolescence

In the structure-building phase, according to Mahler, Pine, and Bergman, the supervisor functions as an alter ego, strengthening the supervisee's feelings of competence through shared understanding. The conviction that "we are alike" begins to form. Confidence builds as the supervisee's narcissistic issues facilitate growth, and the supervisee feels free to venture and experiment with new approaches. The supervisor's role now becomes that of a nondirective guide and motivator for further exploration. Work and play are integrated through interlocking space in the supervisory relationship.

In this phase the supervisee alternates between exploration into new areas and retreating to the safety of "home." Through this process, the supervisee develops his own therapeutic model. Differences of opinion, disappointments, tests of strength, and power struggles are to be expected. Resistance to change and growth is not necessarily a negative factor at this stage, for it is an expression of growing pains. It is crucial that the supervisor deal with these blockages with tact, empathy, tolerance, and support. Narcissistic domination must be avoided. Authority should not be imposed on the supervisee unless absolutely necessary for the client's well-being.

Signs of growth at this stage include assimilation of criticism, a lack of strong and disabling negative backlash in response to feedback, a better understanding of feelings, a freeing of energies for creative renewal, fewer "hurts" in therapy, and a consistency of understanding and movement toward the final phase of supervision, that of reunion.

Phase 3: Adulthood

Chazan points to Erikson's (1959) adult ego development phase with terms such as *intimacy, generativity,* and *integrity.* Ego functioning in adulthood is free from conflicts. Values develop that stay with the person for a lifetime. There is a mutual interdependence between young and old, built on a foundation of basic universal values such as faith, hope, love, peace, respect, and harmony. Along with this mutuality with others comes a dependable inner experience of well-being. This is analogous to the final stage of supervision, in which the supervisee settles into his own professional identity, becomes a colleague of the supervisor, and assumes the role of supervisor for others. "Struggles and expressions of difference now take the form of organizational forums, intellectual debates, and political issues. The space has widened beyond the dyad to an ongoing reaching out beyond and within the self to the definition of boundaries of professional identity" (Chazan 1990, p. 28).

Not surprisingly, these three phases envisioned by psychodynamic theorists roughly parallel Stoltenberg and Delworth's (1987) three developmental levels. The added contribution of the psychodynamic model is to conceive of these stages in dynamic terms, based primarily on issues of narcissism and oedipal development. Superego development is critical to this process, as the supervisee acts out the developmental issues occurring elsewhere in life. Similarly, ego and id interpretation are seen as essential components of supervision. All of these analytic dimensions are manifested in the countertransference, which is the key to the supervisee's unresolved personal conflicts. Figure 7-1 shows an interpretation of what the descriptive dimensions might be for the psychodynamic model of supervision.

CURRENT DIRECTIONS IN PSYCHODYNAMICALLY ORIENTED SUPERVISION

During the second half of the twentieth century, psychoanalytic supervision has moved from the classic approach of Freud, who called supervision "superego training," to a questioning of whether

Figure 7-1. Descriptive Dimensions: Psychodynamic Model

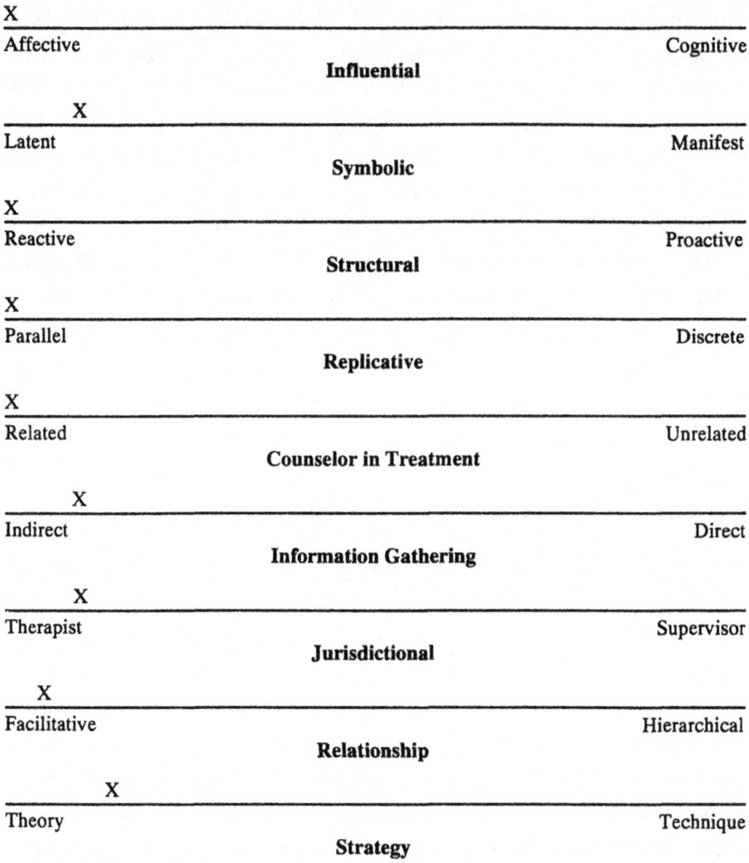

Left Pole	Dimension	Right Pole
X		
Affective	Influential	Cognitive
X		
Latent	Symbolic	Manifest
X		
Reactive	Structural	Proactive
X		
Parallel	Replicative	Discrete
X		
Related	Counselor in Treatment	Unrelated
X		
Indirect	Information Gathering	Direct
X		
Therapist	Jurisdictional	Supervisor
X		
Facilitative	Relationship	Hierarchical
X		
Theory	Strategy	Technique

supervision is therapeutic or didactic, treatment or training. Psychodynamic supervision generally has moved toward a consultative approach, with Ekstein (1960) viewing supervision as largely a matter of demonstrating techniques and Lesser (1983) emphasizing the modeling of behavior as opposed to the analysis of countertransference.

As the psychodynamic model evolves, it retains its distinctive emphasis on the theory of the psyche and the analysis of countertransference and interpersonal interactions (Fiscalini 1985; Issacharoff 1982). Interpretation of intrapsychic issues is still grist for the supervisor's mill. In today's more narrowly focused psycho-dynamic model, however, such interpretation is limited to the supervisee's emotional reactions to the patient, as opposed to other figures in the supervisee's life. Now, when the discussion spills over into the supervisee's own intrapsychic conflicts, the supervisor is likely to refer the supervisee to a therapist. Differences do remain among psychodynamically oriented practitioners with respect to the boundary between supervision and therapy. Some view the two as intertwined, whereas others treat them as separate processes. Increasingly, the latter view has prevailed, allowing the supervisor to concentrate on technical difficulties in therapy, while the super-visee's analyst or therapist addresses the countertransference and other intrapsychic material.

It was in the 1960s and 1970s, when behavioral methods were in the ascendancy and the psychodynamic model under attack, that the latter preserved its relevance by incorporating a practical, skills-training dimension, as in the psychobehavioral model of Boyd, Nutter, and Overcash (1974). Such hybrid models have sought to integrate insight-oriented and behavioral approaches by helping the supervisee gain self-awareness for the purpose of modifying maladaptive clinical behaviors and acquiring effective counseling skills. The supervisor explores the intrapersonal and interpersonal dynamics of clinical and supervisory situations so as to devise strategies for bringing about change for the client.

The most influential of these syntheses has been Carkhuff's experiential-didactic approach (Carkhuff 1969; Carkhuff and Truax, 1965). Based on Carl Rogers's client-centered therapy, it sets a collegial tone for the supervisory relationship. On the relation-ship dimension it falls at the facilitative rather than hierarchical end. Carkhuff conceives of supervision as a therapeutic process for shaping the counselor's personality and behavior. Counseling skills are taught in an atmosphere of freedom and openness in which the counselor's feelings are nurtured. In this way, the relationship with the supervisor becomes a basis for understanding and mod-eling. Carkhuff's approach (described more fully in Powell 1980a) has been the most successful bridge between the psychodynamic model of supervision and the skills model presented in the fol-lowing chapter.

Figure 7-2. Descriptive Dimensions: Carkhuff's Experiential-Didactic Model

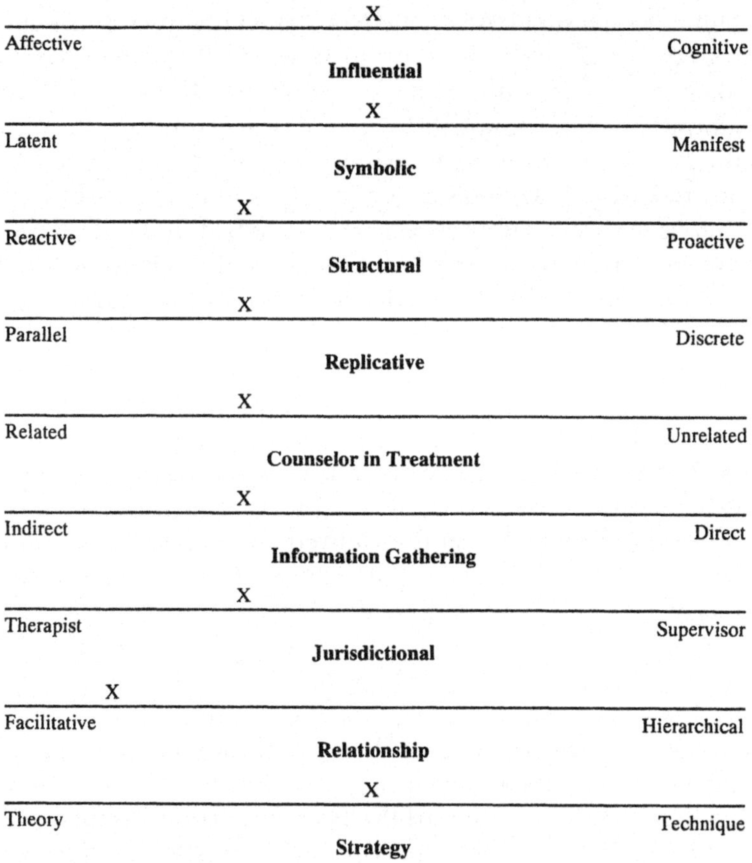

	X	
Affective		Cognitive
	Influential	
	X	
Latent		Manifest
	Symbolic	
	X	
Reactive		Proactive
	Structural	
	X	
Parallel		Discrete
	Replicative	
	X	
Related		Unrelated
	Counselor in Treatment	
	X	
Indirect		Direct
	Information Gathering	
	X	
Therapist		Supervisor
	Jurisdictional	
	X	
Facilitative		Hierarchical
	Relationship	
	X	
Theory		Technique
	Strategy	

The current revival of interest in the psychodynamic model was made possible by its accommodation to the need for behavioral skills training. The more balanced model that resulted from this evolution could be taken seriously as speaking to today's needs. At the same time, while the psychodynamic model was shedding its classical rigidity, there was a growing recognition in the mental health disciplines that the pendulum had swung too far in the behavioristic direction. Theorists and practitioners were ready for a new look at the intrapsychic issues they had disregarded for a generation. Thus, the blending of dynamic and skills approaches is an idea whose time has come. It is also an underlying principle of the model of supervision for the alcohol and drug abuse field that will be presented in Chapter Ten. Figure 7-2 shows an interpretation of what the descriptive dimensions might be for the Carkhuff experiential-didactic model of supervision.

| The Skills Model

The skills model of supervision is based on the behavioral counselor education model of Delaney (1969), Hackney and Nye (1973), Jakubowski-Spector, Dustin, and George (1971), and Krumboltz (1966). A corollary of the behavioral model of therapy that rose to predominance in the 1960s and 1970s, skills-oriented supervision has exerted a correspondingly large influence in its domain. It forms the basis of much of the work done in substance abuse counselor training, sex therapy supervision, family therapy training, and numerous other disciplines.

BASIC TENETS

The skills model has three basic tenets:

1. *Counselors must learn the appropriate skills and extinguish inappropriate behaviors.* Counselor performance is a function of learning skills and developing clinical competency as opposed to personality exploration and adjustment, which may or may not be related to clinical demands. Thus, the skills model allows for a developmental perspective, but it is a question of skills development, not personality development.
2. *Supervision assists counselors in developing and assimilating specific skills.* These skills are required to perform the tasks and assume the roles inherent in the job description.
3. *Counselor knowledge and skills should be formulated in behavioral terms,* as is the case with Birch and Davis's (1986) core competencies in the alcoholism and drug abuse field. The principles of learning theory should be applied to training counselors in these behaviorally based skills.

Skills-oriented supervision is a process of learning core competencies and refining these skills for the betterment of the client. The focus of supervision is on the individually assessed needs of the supervisee, specified in terms of the knowledge and skills required to perform the tasks of a counselor. "Generally speaking the minimal broad goal of any supervisee would be a level of skill functioning representing the competent performance of the counselor's role and function: beyond this minimal level the goal would be a level of functioning above the present performance yet within realistic expectation" (Bradley 1989, pp. 126–127). The welfare of the client is always protected in this skill acquisition process, as it must be in any other model of supervision.

METHODS OF SUPERVISION

The following methods are employed in the skills model.

1. *Establishing a relationship between supervisee and supervisor is a dynamic component of the learning process.* This relationship, however, does not have the same character and function as it does in the psychodynamic model. Instead of serving as a springboard for personal and professional growth, the supervisory relationship exists to facilitate learning and skill development by both didactic instruction and modeling behaviors.

2. *Supervision begins by asking what one needs to learn to be an effective counselor.* What does the counselor know? What can she do? What skills are necessary to perform as a counselor? What must be learned to acquire the core competencies? What is the most efficient means of learning these skills? Whether one uses the twelve core functions of the alcoholism and drug abuse field or the Borders and Leddick (1987) skills profile, the challenge of supervision is to translate the requisite skills into discrete items to be taught to the supervisee.

3. *The next step is to set realistic, measurable, and timely supervision goals that enhance the supervisee's motivation.* From these mutually agreed upon goals, a supervisory strategy is developed that includes effective strategies for reaching these goals, the counselor's preferred learning modes (inductive versus deductive, visual versus auditory), and the resources needed to achieve the goals (facilities, materials, observation tools, and so forth).

4. *Modeling and reinforcement are basic tools of the skills model.* The supervisor models the behavior for the purpose of skill acquisition. The modeling is not one-sided, however, since passive observation alone is not sufficient. Rather, the counselor must demonstrate the skill to the supervisor to ensure that the acquisition process is effective.

5. *Skills monitoring is an ongoing process that helps the counselor identify appropriate professional performance.* Together with a positive model of counseling, supervision should provide the counselor with accurate feedback on skill development and performance.

6. *Role-playing and simulation techniques are used.* Role playing is the participatory dramatization of a contrived situation for the purpose of altering behavior. Simulation recreates a specific clinical situation (Carlson 1980; Spivack 1972; Ward and others 1985).

7. *Microtraining breaks down a specific skill into well-defined, measurable categories, enabling the counselor to acquire skills in small steps* (Baker and others 1983, 1985; Ivey and others 1968). In microtraining, a counselor simulates a clinical situation, which is videotaped. The performance is evaluated by the supervisor, who provides feedback about the counselor's skills. The feedback takes the form of discrimination training, which identifies what the counselor was observed to do on the tape. The supervisee then demonstrates the skill again on videotape. Microtraining concentrates on one skill at a time. Once this skill is documented, the counselor moves on to the next increment of learning until the core competencies are mastered.

8. *Other behaviorally based techniques contribute to skills training as well.* These include self-management methods (Boyd and LaFleur 1974; Kahn 1976; Keller and Protinsky 1986; Tennyson and Strom 1986), overt and covert stimulus control (Beck 1976; Ellis 1973; Mahoney and Thoresen 1974), and cue-controlled relaxation training (Russell and Wise 1976; Sanchez-Craig 1976).

9. *What the counselor learns in one context is generalized to other contexts.* "If you used that technique with this client," the supervisor asks, "in what other situations might this skill be appropriate?"

THE TASK-ORIENTED MODEL

The task-oriented model of supervision is the most well-defined and articulated variant of the skills model. Developed by Mead at

Brigham Young University, task-oriented supervision draws from behavioral models as well as from the computer sciences (Mead and Crane 1978). Behavioral variables are manipulated to influence the outcome of supervision and thereby control the actions of the supervisee and supervisor. By reinforcing the variables of counselor behavior, task-oriented supervisors believe they can train more effective counselors.

According to Mead, the task-oriented model is uniquely able to guide the work of supervisors of varying degrees of sophistication and different (if any) theoretical models. The coherence it offers is less crucial in academic institutions, where counselor training tends to be closely tied to a particular theoretical model. In the world of work, however, theoretical purism usually is unattainable. Agencies employ supervisors who may be clinically competent but who likely have had little opportunity to conceptualize their specific clinical model. This is certainly true in most alcoholism and drug abuse treatment centers in the United States, which, despite the unique brand of counseling they practice, do not uniformly apply any underlying model of counseling and supervision. Instead, eclecticism reigns. As a result, counselors are exposed to a variety of clinical models at different stages of their development. The task-oriented model provides a framework that gives supervisors, regardless of their counseling model or supervisory sophistication, a coherent foundation for their efforts.

The task-oriented model identifies categories of necessary tasks, derived from computer science (in particular, expert systems), that are not theory specific. These task requirements apply across the board, regardless of whether one is psychodynamic, behavioral, or skill based in orientation. They constitute general procedures that all supervisors must perform. These tasks give rise to a basic, albeit crude, description of the supervisory process, defined by Mead (1990, p. 17) as "an experienced therapist safeguarding the welfare of clients by monitoring a less experienced therapist's performance with the clients in a clinical setting with the intent to change the therapist's behavior to resemble that of an experienced expert therapist." Several key words in this definition (*monitoring, intent to change, resemble*) indicate that supervision in the task-oriented model, as in other skills-training models, amounts to a process of shaping behaviors.

Mead (1990) defines an expert clinician as a person "who has mastered most of the technical skills and who has developed an integrated personal clinical model of therapy" (p. 18). This definition allows for diversity of clinical models but subjects them to reasoned, objective, critical examination. Mead's expert therapist-supervisor is not merely a technician who teaches certain discrete clinical skills that he or she has mastered. On the contrary, the expert must have a clearly articulated model of counseling drawn from a number of sources and integrated into a consistent approach. The experienced supervisor, as envisioned by computer modeling of expert systems, makes use of theory to determine what information is to be collected, how that information is processed and organized, and how it is used to formulate treatment plans.

The task-oriented model also postulates a dimension of supervision that is independent of whatever therapeutic model the supervisor espouses. It is this dimension that allows the supervisor to function effectively regardless of therapeutic orientation. If the goal of supervision is, as Mead claims, to change the behavior of the supervisee so that it resembles that of the supervisor, a task-oriented model of supervision works regardless of whom the supervisee is to resemble. It works by arranging experiences and interventions. Task-oriented supervision involves modeling, programmed interventions, and feedback into the therapeutic process. In all cases it entails direct observation of the therapist, using live material for supervision. In this model, according to Mead (1990, p. 20), "Supervision is, first and last, an activity that is designed to change [a] therapist's interaction with clients in clinical sessions in such a way that the therapist's interaction is therapeutic for the clients."

Task-oriented supervision brings the promise of coherence to the chaos of the eclectic work setting. However, there is reason to question Mead's sweeping claim of its universal applicability. The direct observation of therapy sessions that Mead requires is not employed by some other models of supervision, such as the Bowen and Whitaker variants of family therapy (see Chapter Nine). Also, there are models (in particular the psychoanalytic) in which the content of training resists being broken down into discrete tasks. How is a supervisor to reduce "learning the analytic attitude" to a set of tasks? Task-oriented supervision, then, may best be thought of not as the neutral framework for all other models that Mead presents it to be but as a worthy model in its own right, some of whose features can be generalized to structure the work done under other models.

Systems of Supervision

Although Mead's definition forms an excellent foundation for a model of supervision, it does not yet delineate a fully developed model. To complete the description of the model, we must examine three distinct levels, or systems, of interaction: the counselor-client level, the supervisor-counselor level, and the supervisor-counselor-client level (Breunlin, Liddle, and Schwartz 1988; Tomm and Wright 1982). Each level is characterized by its own distinctive tasks. The only way to identify all the necessary tasks involved in supervision is to break them down level by level. (Mead's levels are not to be confused with the developmental levels described in Chapter Six, just as his systems are not to be confused with family systems as described in Chapter Nine. The terminology used here is Mead's own and does not carry over to any other models of supervision.)

In terms of the Relationship dimension, Mead structures the three levels hierarchically. That is, what goes on at level 3 (the supervisor level) overrules what goes on at level 2 (the counselor level). The supervisor is always in charge. This view of the supervisory relationship would, of course, be disputed by psychodynamic theorists, as well as by Bowenian family therapists, who conceive of supervision as a person-to-person relationship in which teaching and learning are mutual and reciprocal.

The hierarchical organization of the three levels of supervision does not, however, make for a linear sequence of steps or procedures. Instead, overlapping processes occur simultaneously, and the three levels of concern come in and out of focus in a cyclical pattern. This continuous looping-back process, the continual flow and movement from one level to another, resembles the mathematical and computer models developed from the science of chaos (Gleick 1987). Just when an issue seems to be focused at the client level, a therapist-level issue interposes itself. Mead diagrams his conception of the three levels running parallel to and interacting with one another (Figure 8-1). Although derived from representations of chaos, this process need not be unmanageably chaotic in practice, for there is a natural progression through the three levels that the supervisor can anticipate.

The role of the supervisor is to understand these patterns of action, to foresee the probabilities of various events, and to predict clinical outcomes and changes in counselor and client behaviors. The supervisor should be active at the three levels of the process by asking the supervisee how he conceptualizes the case, what additional information is needed, and how to derive that information. By reviewing the steps in the process outlined by the counselor, the supervisor evaluates the counselor's clinical reasoning and conceptual skills and suggests the alternative procedures to follow.

Client Level

Figure 8-1 traces the client's progress through counseling, irrespective of the model of therapy used. Each client comes to counseling with a set of goals he or she hopes to achieve. Although these may not be well formulated in the client's mind, the client generally expects to leave feeling better than before. Level 1 on the diagram shows the sequence of events by which therapy aims to help the client bring about this outcome.

The supervisor uses client information to aid the counselor in structuring the therapy process by observing the client-counselor interactions and determining the client tasks the counselor needs to work on to move therapy ahead. The supervisor learns the counselor's goals and objectives as they relate to the client level and proposes action that is congruent with the tasks to be accomplished.

Counselor Level

Counselors come to supervision with a broad range of personal and professional experiences. Similarities between the client's and counselor's histories, especially in the alcoholism and drug abuse field, may need to be explored. Additionally, it is important for the supervisor and counselor to be aware of relevant aspects of their respective histories. A primary task of the supervisor (especially when supervising recovering alcoholics or addicts who seek to work in the substance abuse field) is to clarify for the supervisee her readiness to assume the counselor's role in the light of that personal and professional history. The supervisor, who in the task-oriented model

Figure 8-1. Task-Oriented Model of Supervision

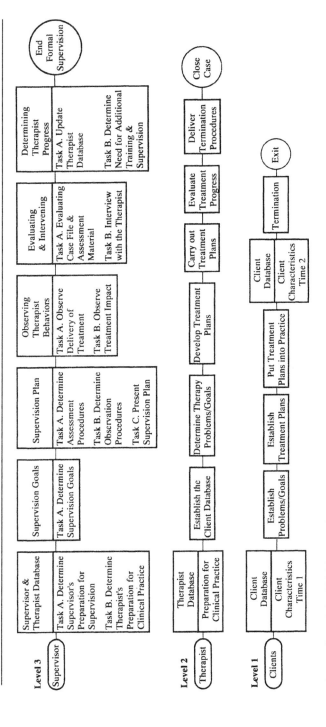

Level 3

Supervisor

Supervisor & Therapist Database	Supervision Goals	Supervision Plan	Observing Therapist Behaviors	Evaluating & Intervening	Determining Therapist Progress	End Formal Supervision
Task A. Determine Supervisor's Preparation for Supervision	Task A. Determine Supervision Goals	Task A. Determine Assessment Procedures	Task A. Observe Delivery of Treatment	Task A. Evaluating Case File & Assessment Material	Task A. Update Therapist Database	
Task B. Determine Therapist's Preparation for Clinical Practice		Task B. Determine Observation Procedures	Task B. Observe Treatment Impact	Task B. Interview with the Therapist	Task B. Determine Need for Additional Training & Supervision	
		Task C. Present Supervision Plan				

Level 2

Therapist

Therapist Database	Establish the Client Database	Determine Therapy Problems/Goals	Develop Treatment Plans	Carry out Treatment Plans	Evaluate Treatment Progress	Deliver Termination Procedures	Close Case
Preparation for Clinical Practice							

Level 1

Clients

Client Database	Establish Problems/Goals	Establish Treatment Plans	Put Treatment Plans into Practice	Client Database	Termination	Exit
Client Characteristics Time 1				Client Characteristics Time 2		

Source: Copyright 1990 from *Effective Supervision: A Task-Oriented Model for the Mental Health Professions* by D. E. Mead. Reproduced by permission of Routledge/Taylor & Francis Books, Inc.

does not give clinicians personal counseling, needs to direct the counselor toward resources that will help resolve disruptive personal and professional issues.

The task-oriented model of supervision assumes a commonality of counseling skills, although these may be carried out differently in accordance with different therapeutic models. These basic skills are analogous to the twelve core functions of the alcoholism and drug abuse field. In the task-oriented model, the core knowledge and skills required to perform clinical tasks are reviewed and assessed at the counselor level of supervision. The supervisor monitors the counselor's demonstrated abilities and intervenes as needed to support and correct what the counselor is doing. "By identifying the tasks that are causing difficulty, the supervisor will be in a position to offer interventions that may help the therapist improve her or his clinical skills" (Mead 1990, p. 27).

Supervisor Level

Level 3 of Figure 8-1 outlines the tasks minimally required of a supervisor in order to train and monitor counselors—again, according to Mead, under any theoretical model. First, the supervisor must assess the counselor's readiness for clinical work based on the stage of development the counselor has reached. Readiness involves technical skills as well as the ability to differentiate oneself from others.

Before cases are assigned to the counselor, the supervisor determines with the counselor the goals of supervision. A contract is established outlining expectations, outcomes, evaluation and intervention methods, and administrative and executive issues such as scheduling, absenteeism, and sanctions for unfulfilled expectations. (Further information on supervisory contracts is provided in Chapter Eleven.)

Once goals are set, the supervisor establishes how the counselor will be observed and how feedback will be given. The supervisor then observes the counselor in action, assesses skills, and gives feedback. This cycle is repeated throughout the supervision process. After several cycles of observation, assessment, and feedback, the supervisor conveys an overall evaluation of the counselor's skill and competency levels and recommends further training and supervision as needed. Self-education and self-supervision are expected to play a growing part in this ongoing learning process.

The Preparation of a Supervisor

The task-oriented model is unusual, if not unique, in the attention it pays to the preparation of supervisors. That is one of the major strengths of this model. Every supervisor comes to the task with a personal and professional history and a model of therapy. However, as Mead rightly insists, supervisors still need training in a number of areas:

- The technical skills of supervision.
- Conceptual skills in formulating client, counselor, and supervisor issues.
- Background on the theories and models of supervision.
- Familiarity with ethical and legal concerns, especially as they relate to supervision.
- Developing an integrated model of supervision derived from their professional and personal experiences, their model of therapy, and their interpersonal style. This model must be contextualized in terms of the setting in which the supervisor functions, the culture of the agency, the types of clients served, and the treatment model used.

These requirements roughly parallel the learning objectives for supervisors developed by the family therapy and substance abuse fields, which are listed in Chapter Four.

An assessment must be made of the readiness of the supervisor to conduct supervision. The mental health field has debated whether this readiness is determined by the supervisor's ability to have an impact on the client or on the counselor (Goodyear and Bradley 1983; Hansen, Pound, and Petro 1976). The task-oriented model sees both levels of assessment as necessary. Thus, Mead (1990, p. 30) asks, "Did the therapist's performance in sessions with clients change as a result of the supervisor's interventions?" The assessment continues with questions such as the following: Was this change a result of the in-session interventions of the supervisor

Figure 8-2. Descriptive Dimensions: Skills Model

		X
Affective		Cognitive
	Influential	
		X
Latent		Manifest
	Symbolic	
		X
Reactive		Proactive
	Structural	
		X
Parallel		Discrete
	Replicative	
		X
Related		Unrelated
	Counselor in Treatment	
		X
Indirect		Direct
	Information Gathering	
		X
Therapist		Supervisor
	Jurisdictional	
		X
Facilitative		Hierarchical
	Relationship	
		X
Theory		Technique
	Strategy	

or out-of-session interventions? Have there been changes in the counselor's and supervisor's skills over time? Client self-reports can be used in determining changes in the counselor's behavior, which may be attributable to interventions by the supervisor.

The task-oriented model of supervision, as a prominent exemplar of the skills model, contributes a distinctive viewpoint on supervision. It provides the methodology needed to establish a therapist database, to set goals for supervision, to develop a supervision plan, to observe therapists at work, to assess therapists' skills, to intervene in therapy when needed, and to determine therapists' progress. The task-oriented model offers a generic framework for understanding important aspects of the supervisory process, regardless of therapeutic model or supervisory orientation. After all, supervisors must learn skills under any model. One way of learning general skills, as Mead shows, is by learning specific tasks, even if those are not always the particular tasks Mead prescribes.

Overall, the skills model of supervision has reinforced the behavioral approach to therapy as a necessary counterweight to the mental health profession's early emphasis on psychodynamic theorizing and insight-oriented therapy. In particular, a skills-oriented approach has greatly influenced the training of family therapists. Figure 8-2 shows an interpretation of what the descriptive dimensions might be for the skills model of supervision.

Chapter Nine

Family Therapy Models

As part of its emphasis on clinical training, family therapy has devoted far more attention to developing models of supervision than any other mental health profession. In earlier decades, training in family therapy was "a fairly homogeneous concept, modest in scope and influence and characterized by the clinical wizardry of the 'Great Originals' rather than by clearly articulated curricula and objectives" (Liddle 1988, p. 3). Since the 1980s, however, this field has seen an intensification of interest in training and supervision. In this respect, the Commission on Supervision and Training of the American Association for Marriage and Family Therapy (AAMFT) has assumed the leadership of the entire mental health field. AAMFT has created a specialty of supervision with its own mission, content, methods, and credentialing process. Its certification criteria were presented in Chapter Four as model learning objectives for supervisors in other disciplines as well.

The AAMFT's efforts notwithstanding, it has been impossible in practice to establish one model of supervision for family therapists because there is no one model of family therapy. The proliferation of distinctive schools of family therapy prompted Minuchin and Fishman (1981, p. 9) to write, "The field of family therapy is full of clinicians who change chairs a la Minuchin, give directions a la Haley, do primary process a la Whitaker, offer paradoxes in Italian, tie people with ropes a la Satir, add a pinch of ethics a la Nagy, encourage cathartic crying a la Paul, review a tape of the session with the family a la Alger, and sometimes manage to combine all of these methods in one session." Today there are family therapy supervision models that are structural (Minuchin), functional (Haley), systemic (Liddle), Milanian (Palazzoli), Bowenian

(Bowen), and psychodynamic (Nichols), among others. These models are diverse and heterogeneous, each with its own character and approach. Moreover, they are often context bound; their implementation depends on the chemistry generated by a charismatic leader in a particular setting. It is said, for example, that the only person practicing the "Minuchin model" is Minuchin himself; everything else done in his name is a variant or offshoot.

Even so, there can be discerned within family therapy a continuum of approaches similar to that found in the mental health field as a whole. These approaches range from the theory-oriented, facilitative supervisory methods of Bowen and Nichols to the technique-driven, hierarchical methods of Haley and (to a lesser degree) Minuchin. Seen in this light, family therapy looks like the mental health field in microcosm. To indicate the range of approaches within family therapy, I have included descriptive dimensions for the Bowenian model as well as the structural (Minuchin) and functional-strategic (Haley) models at the end of this chapter (Figures 9-1 through 9-3). These models are not all equally influential. The schools associated with Minuchin and Haley have generated considerably more writing on training and supervision than other models (for example, Framo, Bowen, Whitaker) that may be equally important in day-to-day clinical practice. As a result, the former models have had a much larger impact on family therapy supervision and for that reason are highlighted in this chapter.

SYSTEMS THEORY

Granted the intimidating heterogeneity of this field, it is remarkable that most schools of family therapy have a common frame of reference—indeed, a common philosophical foundation—in systems theory. Systems theory, which has dominated the thinking of family therapy, has had a profound impact on clinical training and supervision (Bernstein and LeComte 1979; Blocher, Dustin, and Dugan 1971; Canada and Lynch 1975; Horan 1972; Saylor 1976; Thoresen 1969). AAMFT has incorporated systems models into its supervision guidelines, and the Association for Counselor Education and Supervision (1989) has recommended that all supervisors be trained in the systems model of supervision.

The systems model of supervision is defined as the application of systems technology to the process of supervision. Systems technology is "a disciplined way of analyzing as precisely as possible an existing situation by determining the nature of the elements which combine and relate to make the situation what it is, establishing the interrelationships among the elements, and synthesizing a new whole to provide means of optimizing system outcomes" (Ryan and Zeran 1972, p. 13). In systems theory, the primary focus is on this larger whole, or system, which is defined as "an integrated and related set of components (subsystems) organized for the purpose of obtaining a specific objective" (Horan 1972, p. 162). The key word here is *subsystems*—the interrelated components that make up the larger whole. Family system theory, which sees the family as a system composed of networks of relationships among family members, characterizes the supervisory process in the same complex terms. By working with the counselor to keep this big picture always in view, the supervisor seeks to "elicit the creative, innovative, and problem-solving potentials of the counselor and supervisor" (Bradley 1989, p. 231).

Blocher, Dustin, and Dugan (1971, p. 3) describe the advantages of this complex model for therapeutic problem solving:

> [A systems approach] offers us a way of focusing on the larger-picture: the total environment that impinges upon any single individual or group. It enables us to identify the key variables and factors at work within a total process. In doing this, it enables us to specify the outputs or outcomes that we expect or desire from a given process and conceptualize the needed inputs or interventions that will be needed to produce those ends.

By analyzing the entire interrelated system of family interactions, the counselor can determine at what particular point(s) in the system a decisive intervention can occur—that is, what parts of the system need to be changed to bring about changes in the whole.

This approach to therapy and supervision brings to bear complex and sophisticated models of communication and learning theory, involving systems analysis, diagnostics of breakdowns in communication, synthesis (the establishment of relationships between previously unrelated parts combined into a new whole), and flowchart modeling. It imports so much technology from outside the clinical professions that an attempt such as Ryan's (1969) to describe the functions of a counselor in systems terms—such as designing and pilot-testing a counseling prototype—sounds more like the process of producing an airplane. But it is just such rigor, in the hands of experienced clinicians and supervisors, that has produced remarkable therapeutic results.

Let us say that a counselor is working with a family experiencing problems of communication between the parents and a teenage son. The first step in the counseling process using a systems approach is to study the family's environment (social, cultural, economic, and political conditions). The counselor defines the problem situation and identifies specific instances of communication breakdown within the family system. She then describes the problem situation and analyzes when, where, and why the communication breakdown occurs, the elements and process variables, and the key relationship issues in that breakdown. Next, the counselor establishes a plan of action to resolve this systemic communication problem, determining the limitations and constraints that affect problem resolution. A prototype for change is established: the family constructs, with the help of the counselor, specific scenarios in which communication can be improved. During the counseling process, the constructive communication patterns are modeled and reassessed, and a systems change is recommended: whenever a specific barrier to communication occurs, the family will resolve the problem by following the prototype model. The systemic changes are reevaluated and the problem behavior eventually eliminated from the family communication patterns.

Family systems theory underlies most models of supervision used in family therapy. Two of these models, the structural and strategic, have shaped the landscape of family therapy training and supervision for more than a decade.

STRUCTURAL SUPERVISION

Minuchin's structural model, which he originated at the Philadelphia Child Guidance Clinic, has been modified by many practitioners, including Minuchin himself. Even Minuchin's own writings offer no authoritative version of structural supervision, only successive approximations. In fact, there may not be a structural way of doing supervision that can be generally applied—only the idiosyncratic expressions of Minuchin's genius around some paradigmatic core.

Supervision in the structural model of family therapy is based on the structural theory of the family, which examines the organizational structure of a family as the primary source of the family's problems. Whereas the systemic approach to family therapy looks at the effect of a presenting symptom (such as alcohol abuse) on the family system, structural family therapy comes at the problem from the opposite direction, looking first for structural problems in the family system that interfere with a clear flow of information and decision making. These include space configurations such as closeness-distance between family members, inclusion-exclusion of individuals, fluid-rigid boundaries, and hierarchical arrangements. Thus, if boundaries are too rigid or too fluid and unclear, or if lines of authority and responsibility are left ambiguous, miscommunication and conflict may occur. For example, a family may not have established clear norms about how they communicate and make decisions about money matters.

By helping the family discover these missing or flawed patterns in its internal ecosystem, the structural therapist allows the family to become its own healer. The therapist creates healing scenarios to mobilize the internal resources of family members and to help overcome inertia and resistance. In the process, the therapist constantly changes his or her stance, oscillating between the role of the objective, removed observer and that of a direct, intensely involved participant in the process. Through this movement, which is both structural and physical, the therapist models the change process for the family.

Training in the structural model is skills oriented but not as rigidly so as in the functional-strategic model. "Training in family therapy should . . . be a way of teaching techniques whose essence is to be mastered, then forgotten. . . . The goal is to transcend technique" (Minuchin and Fishman 1981, p. 1). Although structural family therapy does not concern itself with the counselor's intrapsychic issues, it is process oriented in its attention to client-counselor dynamics. The counselor is not just a technician but a personal presence, a therapist. Since the structural model calls for a creative use of oneself in therapeutic spontaneity, the training of a family therapist might be thought of as a process of planned spontaneity. Training ingrains techniques in the clinician so that he or she ultimately will be able to respond to the client in a free-flowing, unrehearsed manner.

The structural model has a place for theory as well as technique. Even with Minuchin's admonition that supervisees should not be "taught to the head," there are large doses of theory, especially for the beginning counselor. There is a spiral pattern of learning, driven not by "how-to" but by "what-for" questions that help trainees see the structures underlying the family situations presented to them. Trainees are taught to elicit information about the family context, to use visual aids such as family mapping, and to depict complex interaction patterns metaphorically.

In this way, the supervisee simultaneously processes two sets of information in supervision: data about the dynamics of human change (theory) and specific operations of the therapeutic experience (technique). According to Minuchin and Fishman (1981, p. 5), "The methodology of teaching the difficult art of family therapy has to be harmonious with both the concepts and the practices taught." Thus, theoretical constructs about family systems and methods of change are learned deductively. The spontaneous skills of the therapist are learned inductively, by a graded process of observation and practice.

In Minuchin's view, a supervisor cannot ask the supervisee to describe the phenomenological events he is experiencing, for the supervisee cannot articulate what he does not yet know. Nor is the beginning trainee yet able to role-play his position in the family system. Giving the supervisee insight into himself is neither necessary nor sufficient to train a spontaneous therapist. Inductive methods of teaching are more effective.

In the first phase of induction, supervisees watch the supervisor work, all the while identifying observed techniques and analyzing videotapes of sessions. Through observation they are taught to "use themselves" in therapy and to develop and monitor their own therapeutic style. They learn how to alternate between supportive gestures and a "kick in the seat of the pants," expressed through gestures, body postures, movement of chairs, and concrete metaphors. These tactics, while occurring spontaneously, become the foundation on which supervisees construct their own theoretical models.

This phase of supervision is followed by live observation (using the one-way mirror) and videotaped sessions. The supervisor may intervene in a session by asking the supervisee to come behind the mirror, by stepping into the room and speaking with the supervisee, or by phoning in advice. Other supervisees observe from behind the mirror. All sessions are videotaped and reviewed, and a picture of the supervisee's style of therapy emerges. The supervisor prescribes measures to expand the supervisee's skills and to nurture the supervisee's individualized therapeutic style. Since there is no one correct way of counseling, education means drawing out the supervisee's own way of doing therapy. "Every therapist needs certain specific skills in order to achieve the goals of family transformation, but each therapist has a different way of using himself in implementing these techniques" (Minuchin and Fishman 1981, pp. 8–9).

On our descriptive dimensions, the supervisory relationship in structural family therapy stands somewhere between the hierarchical and facilitative extremes. Indeed, over time there is less emphasis on direct observation as the supervisee achieves a spontaneous integration of theory and technique. With enough practice from which to generalize, each therapist builds a foundation of applied theory tested by experience.

These techniques of supervision are intended for professional therapists with prior training and experience who want to learn family therapy as an additional specialty. Family therapy training is not appropriate for counselors without professional degrees, who require a more intensive training format. Moreover, for the beginning therapist who lacks a foundation of theory and technique, a heterogeneous approach to training may lead to undisciplined eclecticism. These cautionary points of Minuchin's are especially applicable to the alcoholism and drug abuse counselor. Figure 9-1 shows an interpretation of what the descriptive dimensions might be for the structural model of supervision.

Figure 9-1. Descriptive Dimensions: Structural Model

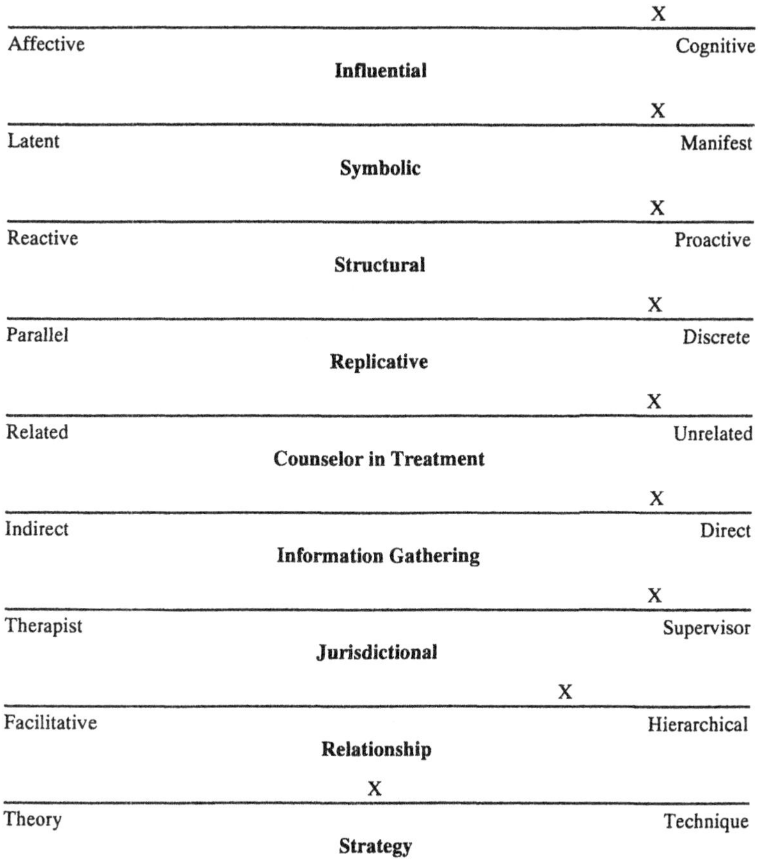

	X	
Affective		Cognitive
	Influential	
	X	
Latent		Manifest
	Symbolic	
	X	
Reactive		Proactive
	Structural	
	X	
Parallel		Discrete
	Replicative	
	X	
Related		Unrelated
	Counselor in Treatment	
	X	
Indirect		Direct
	Information Gathering	
	X	
Therapist		Supervisor
	Jurisdictional	
	X	
Facilitative		Hierarchical
	Relationship	
	X	
Theory		Technique
	Strategy	

STRATEGIC SUPERVISION

At the behavioristic, skills-oriented end of the continuum, Jay Haley established the school of strategic family therapy, in which therapy is brief and problem focused, with planned sessions and an active counselor. Whereas Minuchin's method looks at structural relationships within the family, Haley's looks for strategies, functions, and meanings in family interactions. For example, a violent twelve-year-old boy has been referred to a family therapist along with his mother and father. In a structural model, the therapist deals with the closeness, distance, and boundaries between the parents and the son, together with the family's hierarchical arrangements, in order to resolve the family's organizational flaws ("The parents' avoidance of conflict is crippling their parenting of the son"). In a strategic model, the therapist generates new strategies and skills for the family to resolve the problem behaviors, focusing on the function of the symptom ("Joey's temper tantrums distract his parents from their marital conflict").

Strategic family therapy is pragmatic and outcome oriented. In a typical example of isomorphism, supervision and training in this model have the same character. For Haley, a counselor needs to be educated as a people changer, for the true test of the success of a clinical supervisor is in the outcome of the actual counseling session. The goal of training is to produce successful therapists, not self-actualized ones. In this respect, Haley (1976, pp. 178–179) throws down the gauntlet to the rest of the field: "There does not appear to be a single research study showing that a therapist who has had therapy himself, or understands his involvement with his personal family, has a better outcome in his therapy." He adds, "My own experience has been that the more personal therapy trainees have had, the more difficult they are to teach. They become so preoccupied with themselves that clients have trouble getting their attention" (Haley 1988, p. 361).

Haley (1976) stresses that change should be planned, not spontaneous. He views therapy as a process of action to cause change as opposed to understanding as a catalyst for change. Since the strategic model is highly directive, training in this model is also directive. Therapists learn by doing, with interventions to effect change. A hallmark of strategic therapy is its insistence on direct observation of the supervisee's practice in live sessions. While a therapist is working in front of the mirror, the observer-therapists behind the mirror receive instruction from the supervisor, who teaches at a meta-level through phone-ins to the supervisee in the counseling room as well as the supervisees behind the mirror. From that vantage point the supervisor gives specific tasks to practice, such as, "The next time the client says this, this is what I want you to say." Technical skills are taught with a view toward the development of a conceptual framework, giving the supervisee a method of thinking and not a model of therapy.

For Haley, both therapy and training are problem oriented rather than method oriented. A supervisor watches the counselor work, determines his knowledge and skill levels, observes his deficits, selects clients to operationalize the skill-building process, and again observes the counselor in action, addressing the problems that occur. This intensive monitoring requires considerable flexibility on the part of the supervisor in providing the trainee with a variety of clinical contexts. Moreover, the supervisor must constantly check the outcomes to see if the desired skills have been acquired, for the method used is secondary to the pragmatic goal of resolving the problem. Technique for its own sake is as useless as theory for its own sake; the only measure of success is behavioral change.

Thus, strategic family therapy training is a process of skill building, with theory secondary to process and form following function. Learning does not occur by talking about it. It does not even occur by watching someone else do it, although such observation is valuable at certain points in training. Therapy is a personal experience, and one needs to experience the process of doing therapy oneself. "Ideally, [the trainee] learns to do therapy by doing it while guided by a supervisor at the moment the therapy is happening" (Haley 1988, p. 362). Practice makes perfect, or at least success, as one learns the desired clinical behavior well enough to generalize it appropriately to other situations. Haley believes that a counselor should develop a clear ideology after rather than during the training. This does not mean that Haley is antitheory. Therapists should think through what they are doing and be able to explain their actions. Conceptual development is important; however, skill learning comes first.

In summary, Haley is critical of training institutions that emphasize personal problems of the therapist at the expense of skill building for change, that use the supervisee groups for group therapy, that have only one class of clients available for the supervisee to work with, and that place too much emphasis on diagnostic skills. He especially disdains inpatient settings characterized by social control, overdiagnosis, and "impermeable walls." How well Haley would work in the alcoholism and drug abuse field, with its emphasis on residential rehabilitation programs, is questionable. However, the cost controls and questions of efficacy that are forcing the substance abuse field to reconsider this model may well move it in Haley's direction.

Haley thinks that a positive training experience includes the use of one-way mirrors to observe therapists in supervision, routine videotaping sessions, interviewing whole families, teaching a variety of problem-oriented techniques, and paying attention to the specific outcomes as opposed to simply the process of therapy.

Since the ground rules for supervision should be clear, Haley recommends the following contract:

- The supervisor will intervene reluctantly and only when essential, preferring phone-ins to bug-in-the-ear. Haley does not find it effective for the supervisor to sit in the room, since it involves the supervisor directly in the therapy process and prevents private communication between the supervisor and supervisee.
- The supervisor will offer only one concise, brief idea at a time instead of a series of suggestions.
- If more involved recommendations are necessary, the supervisee will be called out of the room to talk with the supervisor.
- The supervisor and supervisee will discuss the strategy for the case prior to the counseling session to reduce the number of interventions during the session.
- All suggestions are only suggestions. The therapist has the responsibility to guide the session as he deems appropriate. However, if a supervisor tells a counselor he must do something, that is to be considered a directive. Since the supervisor has clinical responsibility for the client, she must always retain the authority to direct a session should she think it necessary. Obviously, directives are to be used sparingly and only for the protection of the patient or when a session has become countertherapeutic or destructive. The supervisor must protect the client from counselor incompetence or from intrusion into private areas that are beyond the realm of the therapist.
- Group training, using observation from behind the mirror, will be used when possible because it is the most efficient way to train therapists.

Figure 9-2. Descriptive Dimensions: Strategic Model

		X	
Affective			Cognitive
	Influential		
		X	
Latent			Manifest
	Symbolic		
		X	
Reactive			Proactive
	Structural		
		X	
Parallel			Discrete
	Replicative		
		X	
Related			Unrelated
	Counselor in Treatment		
		X	
Indirect			Direct
	Information Gathering		
		X	
Therapist			Supervisor
	Jurisdictional		
		X	
Facilitative			Hierarchical
	Relationship		
		X	
Theory			Technique
	Strategy		

Figure 9-2 shows an interpretation of what the descriptive dimensions might be for the strategic model of supervision.

THE CONTRIBUTION OF FAMILY THERAPY TO SUPERVISION

Family therapy encompasses a diverse set of models offering a wide range of approaches to counseling and supervision (Liddle, Breunlin, and Schwartz 1988). However, the dominant structural and strategic schools, by establishing a number of training institutes and by generating an extensive body of literature on supervision, have set the tone for training and supervision in family therapy. In so doing, they have moved the entire mental health field in the direction of a skills-oriented approach. The alcohol and drug abuse field, which came into being when the Minuchin and Haley models were at the height of their influence, has felt that influence keenly. The structural and strategic schools have laid the groundwork for a generation of models that will follow, modify, develop, or react against their precepts but cannot ignore them.

As an example of the range of models that make up the field of family therapy, Figure 9-3 shows an interpretation of what the descriptive dimensions might be for the Bowenian model of supervision.

Figure 9-3. Descriptive Dimensions: Bowenian Model

X		
Affective		Cognitive
	Influential	
X		
Latent		Manifest
	Symbolic	
X		
Reactive		Proactive
	Structural	
X		
Parallel		Discrete
	Replicative	
X (Family of Origin)		
Related		Unrelated
	Counselor in Treatment	
X		
Indirect		Direct
	Information Gathering	
X		
Therapist		Supervisor
	Jurisdictional	
X		
Facilitative		Hierarchical
	Relationship	
X		
Theory		Technique
	Strategy	

Chapter Ten

A Blended Model of Clinical Supervision for the Alcoholism and Drug Abuse Field

Although alcohol and drug abuse has plagued civilization for millennia and the treatment of substance abuse has matured for over half a century, it is still a relatively young discipline. Alcoholism and drug abuse counseling as a distinct, recognized profession came into being only in the 1970s. In its brief life to date, it has incorporated models of therapy by osmosis rather than by design. The twelve core functions of alcoholism and drug abuse counseling do not even constitute a method of counseling, let alone a model with philosophical underpinnings, although they are often misconstrued as such by practitioners. Rather, they are tasks performed by counselors in pursuit of a method.

Traditionally antischolastic, this field sorely needs literature on models of treatment. At present, practitioners must glean material from a limited number of sources, none of them definitive. To find the dominant models of treatment in the field, one must review (as I do in this chapter) the Minnesota model of recovery, together with one of its central components, the twelve steps of Alcoholics Anonymous. These models, which are the basis of most treatment programs, blend insight-oriented change with specific behavioral principles for the purpose of helping the individual recover from alcoholism or drug abuse. Rather than attempt to define a model of therapy for the alcoholism and drug abuse field

(an ambitious task best left to those managing treatment programs), this chapter will take as its starting point the currently
dominant models of recovery, the Minnesota and twelve-step models. These are not, of course, the only possible approaches to the
treatment of alcoholics and drug abusers. As the field develops,
other models will be utilized as well, and the model of supervision
will evolve (or new models will come into being) around those new
approaches to therapy.

For now, though, this chapter describes a model of supervision
consistent with current practice in the field. I call it a *blended model*
because, like alcoholism and drug abuse treatment itself, the supervisor process blends insight-oriented with skills-oriented approaches.

WHAT IS SUBSTANCE ABUSE?

The unique, defining attributes of a problem must be understood
before a model of therapy for it can be conceptualized. The following, therefore, is a brief overview of the diagnosis and treatment
of alcoholism and drug abuse.

Diagnostic Definitions

The *Diagnostic and Statistical Manual,* third edition, revised (*DSM-
III-R*), of the American Psychiatric Association defines alcohol and
drug dependency as impaired control of substance use and continued substance use in spite of adverse consequences. Dependence usually includes the development of tolerance (a user must
increase the dosage to maintain the same effects) and the development of withdrawal symptoms upon discontinuation or dosage
reduction. In order to meet the diagnostic criteria for psychoactive
substance dependence, some of the cognitive, behavioral, and/or
physiological symptoms resulting from use of the chemical must
persist for at least one month or occur repeatedly over a longer
period of time. Symptoms associated with psychoactive substance–
induced intoxication, according to *DSM-III-R*, include personality
and mood disturbances, mood lability, suspiciousness, and violent
behavior.

DSM-III-R also has a residual diagnostic category for maladaptive behavior resulting from psychoactive substance use but not

meeting the diagnostic criteria for psychoactive substance dependence: psychoactive substance use disorders. The maladaptive behavior may be either continued substance use despite occupational, psychological, or physical problems or recurrent use in physically hazardous situations.

The fourth edition, *DSM-IV,* has broadened the concept of *substance* by changing the name of the relevant section from "Psychoactive Substance Use Disorders" to "Substance-Related Disorders." By so doing, it has taken the position that although most substance-induced disorders result from the intentional use of a substance, "some substance-induced conditions occur as a result of unintentional exposure to substances or as a side effect of a medication. Such cases would be classified using one of the 'Other (or Unknown) Substance-Related Disorders' categories" (p. E1). Also, *DSM-IV* places dependence, abuse, intoxication, and withdrawal syndromes together in a reformulated "Substance Use Disorders" section. Other substance-induced disorders are distributed among other sections containing those disorders with which they share phenomenology.

Unique Characteristics

Costs
Substance abuse has persisted throughout history. It affects every aspect of life, from the inner-city streets to the workplace to highways. The total economic costs of alcohol and drug abuse to American society are in the hundreds of billions of dollars. A significant proportion of these costs is in the form of escalating health care costs.

Denial
Denial is a principal attribute of the problem. Often the first step in treatment is to convince the sick person that he is sick. A fundamental premise of the Minnesota model is that treatment may entail educating the person to accept something he does not yet see.

Lack of a Consistent Pattern
There is no one single type of alcoholic, and there is no consistent pattern of abuse found in all abusers. Some drink daily; some are

episodic or binge drinkers. There are differences in drinking patterns with different choices of beverage. Alcohol abusers can and do drink anything—beer, wine, spirits, bay rum, liquified shoe polish (a beverage of choice of youth in the former Soviet Union), and anything else that contains alcohol. Quantity of consumption is also unclear as an indicator; some drink large quantities daily, while others drink relatively little.

Deleterious Consequences

One common denominator for most abusers is the effect their substance abuse has on their lives. Identifying the consequences of the abuse is a better indicator of the problem than patterns of drinking, beverage preferences, or consumption rates. Substance abuse shows up early in blackouts, strained personal relationships, impaired job performance, legal problems (drunken driving, financial liabilities), and impaired health. Other indicators include preoccupation with drinking, occasional loss of control, decreased social contacts, and emotional mood swings.

Not all of these indicators apply to everyone. One encompassing definition is that alcoholic or drug abusers "cannot consistently control their drinking [or drug taking] over time, and . . . cannot guarantee their personal and social behavior once they start to drink [or take drugs]" (Wallace 1985, p. 10).

Pervasive Effects

Substance abuse affects every major area of a person's life—physical, psychological, social, and spiritual.

Physical

Alcohol and drug abuse can lead to a range of medical problems— such as liver disease, severe inflammation of the pancreas, hypertension and other cardiac risk factors, brain damage, and sexual dysfunction—that can affect most or all of a person's bodily systems. In order to understand the physiological effects of alcohol and drugs, researchers have turned their attention to brain chemistry, in particular the neurotransmitters (serotonin, noradrenaline, acetaldehyde), the family of brain chemicals called tetrahydroisoquinolines (TIQs).

Psychological

Alcohol and drug abuse either precede or are caused by psychological factors, such as depression, anxieties, fears, resentments, anger, self-pity, lack of self-confidence, loneliness, and a whole range of emotional consequences. Although there is much controversy about whether the substance abuse causes the emotional problems or vice versa, the association is in any case clear, and the question of first cause becomes less important once the vicious cycle has begun.

Social

Alcohol and drug abuse are associated with antisocial attitudes and behavior and adjustment problems, including pessimism about life, withdrawal from social contacts, marital and family problems, work-related difficulties, and legal and financial problems.

Spiritual

For many abusers, life is meaningless, devoid of purpose, and futile. They feel hopelessness, sorrow, dread, emptiness, despair, and a loss of will. Their lives are bereft of joy, wholeness, hope, and fulfillment.

A Primary Problem

For years psychotherapists have looked at substance abuse as a symptom secondary to a family systems issue, impaired oedipal development, mental illness, and so forth. Mental health professionals have dealt with substance abuse as if it were a kind of behavior that would disappear with treatment of the primary problem through psychotherapy, medication, family therapy, or some other modality. On the contrary, according to the Minnesota model and the alcoholism treatment field, alcoholism is a primary disease and not a symptom of some other underlying disorder. Certainly, alcoholism manifests itself in other problems and affects all aspects of a person's life and social environment. Depression, family systems issues, and early childhood development factors are all aspects of the illness. Put simply, however, an alcoholic is an alcoholic because he drinks too much.

That is not to deny that some alcoholics and drug abusers are also depressive, schizophrenic, phobic, or any other psychiatric designation. The substance abuse field has come to acknowledge that many of the clients it treats have dual diagnoses. The first step in treatment, however, usually is to stop the abuse pattern. After a period of abstinence from abusive use of chemicals, other psychiatric problems that may be affecting the individual, especially if there is a biological or chemical impairment, can be assessed. The person's recovery might then involve dealing with other forms of compulsive behavior as well, such as obsessional love relationships, gambling, workaholism, sexual compulsivity, or excessive dependency on others.

Substance abuse is a family problem with genetic or historical roots in the abuser's past. Studies have shown that alcoholics tend to come from alcoholic homes or at least homes that were abusive in some way. Nonetheless, families do not cause substance abuse and are not to blame for its appearance in certain family members. Family systems issues do contribute to and exacerbate the abuse problems; conversely, alcoholism and drug abuse cause problems affecting all aspects of family life: marital discord, inner withdrawal from the relationship, acting out, overcontrolling behavior, verbal and physical attacks, and protection of the abuser. Denial is pervasive in an addictive home.

According to the currently dominant paradigm in the field, however, changing the family system or structure will not, by itself, arrest the alcoholic behavior. The first step is to stop the drinking; then the family dynamics can be addressed. Stopping the drinking entails cutting through the denial of all parties, not placing or accepting blame, accepting the problem in their lives, seeking out help from others, surrendering to the obsessions that drive the family (as the recovering alcoholic surrenders to her inability to control her drinking), and having family members individually learn to accept responsibility for themselves. This substance abuse–centered approach to family dynamics is that of the alcoholism and drug abuse treatment field and is not practiced by any orthodox school of family therapy.

Treatment

Alcoholism and drug abuse treatment in America has become a big business, with inpatient and outpatient centers proliferating. The future of this business is uncertain, however, as managed care and increasing constraints on reimbursement threaten to turn the once sacrosanct twenty-eight-day residential treatment program into an extinct species. There will, of course, continue to be a great need for treatment services, but the need must be met by agencies that can adapt to changing conditions by providing the services more efficiently and effectively.

In 1990 there were approximately 7,000 substance abuse treatment programs in the United States. Most of these programs are built upon the Minnesota model of recovery and AA's twelve-step program. They generally agree on the following critical goals for addiction treatment:

- Detoxification.
- Dealing with patient denial through information and confrontation.
- Overcoming guilt, shame, self-blame, and other destructive emotions.
- Establishing a healthy life-style and behaviors that make it possible to maintain sobriety.
- Aftercare in a program of self-help and/or ongoing therapy.

THE TWELVE STEPS OF RECOVERY

The twelve-step movement has been called "the greatest social movement of the twentieth century" (Naisbitt and Aburdene 1990). By 1992 there were approximately 250 self-help program throughout the world based on the twelve-step principles and tens of thousands of AA meetings worldwide. In the twelve-step approach, two primary goals—acceptance and surrender—form the basis for early recovery from alcoholism or addiction.

Acceptance is the breakdown of the illusion that through willpower alone one can limit or control substance use. It means acknowledging that one suffers from a chronic and progressive illness, that one's life has become unmanageable as a result of alcohol and/or drugs, that one has lost the ability to control this substance use effectively through willpower alone, and that the only alternative is complete abstinence from the use of alcohol and drugs.

Surrender involves a reaching out for help beyond oneself by admitting the reality of the loss of control and acknowledging that there is hope for recovery (sustained sobriety). Surrender also involves faith in a higher power and the fellowship of addicts who have been able to sustain their sobriety. The best chance for success, according to this viewpoint, is to live the twelve steps and become actively involved in a twelve-step fellowship.

The specific objectives for recovery in twelve-step programs can be divided into six dimensions:

1. *Cognitive* objectives mean that abusers must understand how substance abuse has affected their life, how denial and rationalizations contribute to continued drinking or drug use despite negative consequences, and how the negative consequences are connected with the alcohol or drug abuse.
2. *Emotional* objectives include the need to acknowledge feelings such as anger, resentment, loneliness, and shame and to understand how these emotions can lead to substance use and abuse. Also, the abuser needs to deal with these emotions in a way that minimizes the risk of relapse.
3. *Relationship* objectives include understanding that substance abuse affects relationships with people and that significant others have "enabled" substance abuse by helping one obtain the substance or by minimizing the negative consequences of its use.
4. *Behavioral* objectives include understanding how substance abuse affects everything one does and that fellowship of AA or other self-help programs provides a resource for changing addictive habits.
5. *Social* objectives include the need to participate in a self-help program, to form a relationship with a sponsor, to seek meetings within the fellowship as the urge to drink or use drugs presents itself, and to reevaluate relationships with enablers and others.
6. *Spiritual* objectives include the need to experience hope that the addiction can be arrested, to believe and trust in a power greater than oneself, to acknowledge one's own character

defects and the harm one's actions have caused, and to heal the shame, guilt, and negative emotions one carries by sharing a searching moral inventory with another trusted individual.

Several assumptions, explicit and implicit, underlie the twelve-step model of recovery and its professional application in the Minnesota model of treatment. According to these assumptions, addiction is a chronic, progressive disease with predictable symptoms and course. Willpower alone is insufficient to overcome the problem, for the abuser is powerless to deal with the addiction and his life has become unmanageable. He has permanently lost control over the problem. He is an addict and will always be an addict since substance abuse affects body, mind, and spirit. The only alternative to addiction is total and lifelong abstinence from alcohol and drugs; even one drink or use of a substance can trigger the craving and lead to a renewed cycle of abuse. This translates into the goal of resisting the urge to take a drink or drug "one day at a time." To accomplish this, faith in a power greater than oneself gives strength and hope.

These assumptions are validated not by scientific research but by the experience of those who have benefited from the twelve-step philosophy. Their validity is being held up to searching scrutiny, which is likely to spur the development of alternative models of recovery for those who do not subscribe to the twelve steps (Fingarette 1988; Katz and Liu 1991; Peele 1995; Peele, Brodsky, and Arnold 1991; Trimpey 1992).

THE MINNESOTA MODEL OF TREATMENT

The Minnesota model of recovery, which originated with the founding of three treatment centers for alcoholism in the late 1940s and early 1950s, is a comprehensive, multiprofessional, abstinence-oriented approach to the treatment of addictions based on twelve-step principles. It espouses a disease concept of drug and alcohol dependency, with the promise of recovery, not cure, for those who adhere to it. There are four key elements in the Minnesota model philosophy.

First is the conviction that addicts can change their beliefs, attitudes, and behaviors. Proponents of the model claim that the likelihood of a successful outcome does not depend on initial motivation, since the program's interventions are effective in breaking down resistance and denial.

Second is the concept of alcoholism or addiction as a primary, chronic, multifaceted disease characterized by loss of control with regard to the substance or object of addiction. *Multifaceted* refers to the physical, psychological, social, and spiritual dimensions listed above.

Third, both long- and short-term treatment goals are specified. The two long-term goals are abstinence from alcohol and all other drugs of abuse and a better life-style characterized by improved mental health and emotional adjustment. In other words, abstinence alone does not necessarily define a successful outcome. Four short-term goals of treatment facilitate achievement of the long-term goals:

1. To help the chemically dependent person recognize the illness and its implications for his or her life.
2. To help the person admit that he or she needs help and concentrate on living a constructive life in the face of an illness that cannot be cured.
3. To help the person identify what behaviors need to be changed so as to live with the illness in a positive, constructive manner.
4. To help the person translate that understanding into action by developing a new life-style.

Fourth, the principles of AA and Narcotics Anonymous (NA) are fundamental to recovery. They emphasize confession (steps 1–3), reconstruction of self (steps 4–11), and helping others (step 12). These principles involve three core objectives: growth of spiritual awareness, recognition of choice and personal responsibility, and acceptance of peer relationships. The resources for recovery lie primarily within the chemically dependent person. Treatment offers the opportunity to discover and use these innate resources, to create a therapeutic atmosphere conducive to change, and to provide the professional support and guidance necessary to achieve recovery goals.

The Minnesota model offers assessment-to-aftercare treatment, which usually includes regular attendance at AA or NA. This comprehensive, interdisciplinary program encompasses information and referral, diagnosis, detoxification, primary care, a therapeutic community, residential intermediate care, outpatient treatment, and aftercare services. The program has twelve standard components:

1. Group therapy.
2. Lectures.
3. Multiprofessional staff.
4. Recovering alcoholics or addicts as counselors.
5. Therapeutic milieu.
6. Work assignments.
7. Family counseling.
8. AA attendance.
9. Daily reading groups.
10. Life-history taking (usually by keeping a diary).
11. Twelve-step work.
12. Recreational and physical activity.

There appears to be considerable uniformity in philosophy and practice among the facilities espousing the Minnesota model, which constitute a considerable percentage of the treatment programs in America. The Minnesota model has shaped the field of alcoholism and drug abuse treatment for four decades; elements of it are incorporated in virtually all treatment programs for addictions in the United States. Therefore, the philosophical foundation of a model of treatment and supervision for the alcoholism and drug abuse field must, at least for the present, have at its core the key premises of the Minnesota model.

PHILOSOPHICAL FOUNDATION OF THE BLENDED MODEL

The philosophical foundation of a model of therapy and supervision consists of a set of assumptions about how people can be motivated to change. The following assumptions constitute the underlying philosophy of the alcoholism and drug abuse blended model of supervision.

1. *People have the ability to bring about change in their lives with the assistance of a guide.* People seeking help, whether they are alcoholic

patients desiring to recover or supervisees wishing to grow professionally and personally, come with both an openness to growth and a resistance to change. In other words, they have the insight and ability to change despite their denial of the realities of their personal or professional lives. Thus, whoever is guiding an individual through a change process must blend insight with specific behavioral skills to effect growth. This is especially applicable to the alcoholic patient who lives in denial of his disease even while he desperately wants to stop the pain. Similarly, the supervisee simultaneously craves and fears learning and growth. The guide needs to work with both the desire for and the resistance to change.

2. *People do not always know what is best for them, for they may be blinded by their resistance to and denial of the issues.* The role of the therapist or supervisor is to amplify the change process so as to help the person find solutions to her problems. The guide shows the way out of the problems into recovery and growth by sharing his personal experiences with recovery or by deploying skills acquired in professional training. A supervisor guides the supervisee through what he knows and does not know by providing a training road map that can be used as needed when the trainee gets lost. In either case, the guide does not allow the individual to wander lost in the darkness until he finds his own way out. Nor does he dictate precisely where and when to turn, for to do so disregards the first precept: that the individual has within herself the capacity to change with guidance. Even when she is confronting denial and resistance, guidance must be offered in a spirit of respect for the person's integrity and autonomy.

3. *The key to growth is to blend insight and behavioral change in the right amounts at the appropriate time.* Too much insight can lead to "analysis paralysis," whereby the person loses her ability to act. At the other extreme, too much behavioral change can flood the individual with skills that she cannot possibly apply all at once. AA uses the expressions "one step at a time" and "one day at a time," which are applicable to both the alcoholic in recovery and the supervisee in training. As the individual progresses, the rate of insight or behavioral change can accelerate, since the individual has a foundation for growth and greater conceptual skills. Moreover, sometimes one must act first and analyze later. AA says, "Fake

it until you make it," meaning that one first brings about a specific behavioral change and only later gains insight into the meaning of that action.

As these mottos suggest, alcoholism and drug abuse treatment based on the twelve-step model has always offered a natural blend of insight with behavioral change. Trying to stay sober "one day at a time" is quite behavioral, and doing "90 meetings in 90 days" is about as concretely behavioral as one can get. Yet a recovering abuser also gains insight into herself and how alcohol has affected her life, especially by taking the fourth step of making a searching and fearless moral inventory and the eleventh step of growing spiritually.

In supervision, the goal of the blended model is to promote both behavioral change (skill acquisition) and affective growth, especially as personal recovery issues may interfere with the counseling process. Insight and behavioral change are blended by the supervisor in a manner appropriate for the setting, the stage of development of the supervisee, and the model of treatment espoused.

4. *Change is constant and inevitable.* People will change despite the obstacles they face. When a habitual response pattern is thrown off course, when a fortuitous event intervenes to stimulate self-questioning, a moment of openness occurs that can start the momentum for positive change. Therapists and supervisors must look for these windows of opportunity. Alcoholism and drug abuse counselors talk about "hitting bottom," "moving up the bottom," or "getting them when they are ready"—phrases that refer to a disruption of ingrained patterns that allows the guide to bring about change. In supervision these are the teaching moments. Rapid change is possible, but generally growth is progressive. Indeed, dramatic breakthroughs are often simply the crystallization, or visible manifestation, of a long period of preparatory development. There is a ripple effect to change, a snowballing. The key to being an effective change agent is to know what is possible and when to find the crack and "open up the closing" while the opportunity is there, one step at a time. This is the art of clinical supervision: reinforcing the inevitability of change in a progressive, developmental manner, depending on the stage of growth of the supervisee.

5. *In supervision as in therapy, the guide concentrates on what is changeable.* The serenity prayer used by AA states this concept in spiritual language: "God grant me the serenity to accept the things I cannot change, the courage to change the things I can, and the wisdom to know the difference." An effective therapist or supervisor addresses only the areas the person can change, avoiding characterological issues that may not be changeable. If change is inevitable, then the key is to know when these moments of readiness occur and to capitalize on them. Someone who at first does not succeed in bringing about change may need to change his definition of what would constitute success within a given time frame. In supervision, the solution-focused techniques outlined in Chapter Fourteen speak to the need to address changeable behaviors and to work toward solutions rather than dwell on problems.

6. *It is not necessary to know a great deal about the cause or function of a manifest problem to resolve it.* Often therapy and supervision are problem saturated; all one sees is what is going wrong—and where and how and when. If one knew everything about one's problem, inside and out, would one be any healthier or more effective? Not necessarily. In AA the expression KISS applies here: "Keep It Simple, Stupid," or "Keep It Simple, Supervisor." For too many years therapists sat with alcoholics gaining great insights into why they were alcoholic. This gave the alcoholic yet another excuse to continue drinking (for example, "If you had my wife, you'd be a drunk, too!"). The field has since learned that the first step is to accept powerlessness over the problem and to surrender to the solutions that inevitably follow. The key, as always, is the blending of insight into self with behavioral change.

In supervision, the first step is to teach demonstrable skills, particularly for the entry-level counselor with limited formal academic background. The twelve core functions must be taught during the internship and initial certification process, and the counselor's performance must be monitored according to those manifest criteria. Latent content, unless it clearly detracts from the counselor's effectiveness, is not relevant.

7. *There are many correct ways to view the world.* Guides do not know all the routes to change and should not impose rigid dogmatisms and hierarchies by insisting, "Do as I say, for I know the

path of recovery or growth for you." Effective guides listen to the individual and share his hope, strength, and experience. There being many right paths to growth, guides seek to amplify what the individual has already discovered about himself and guide him in discovering new ways of thinking and new solutions. The change agent does not sit back while the person wanders about blindly but builds on the person's innate abilities by pointing him in the direction of growth.

The guide draws out the person's natural curiosity, asking, "What do you think? How do you want to change? What do you see happening in this process?" The guide then intervenes in these events, offering alternatives and options for change. Accumulation of knowledge alone does not bring about change, and knowledge does not by itself make an effective counselor or supervisor. Effectiveness is the timely blending of insight, guidance, and skill development that brings about lasting change.

DESCRIPTIVE DIMENSIONS

The descriptive dimensions adapted from Bascue and Yalof (1991), with the modifications noted in Chapter Five, will be used here to frame the blended model of supervision for the alcoholism and drug abuse field. Where this model falls on the continuum for each descriptive dimension is largely determined by the model's philosophical underpinnings. In addition, where clinicians find themselves on each dimension in an actual clinical situation depends on the developmental stage of the supervisee (and, perhaps, of the client and supervisor as well). Thus, as shown on the following page, the designation on the continuum may move from right to left on the basis of developmental considerations. Contextual issues also contribute to defining one's approach to a particular supervisee.

Taken together, the descriptive dimensions fill out the picture of the alcoholism and drug abuse blended model of supervision with a more textured image, just as they do in the case of other established models or an individual's personal model. They serve as a conceptual framework for specifying beliefs and practices essential to the practice of therapy and supervision.

Influential

It is the premise of the alcoholism and drug abuse blended model of therapy and supervision that clients and supervisees are influenced both affectively and behaviorally, depending on the individual's stage of development, needs, and cognitive abilities, as well as contextual variables. Following the developmental stages for alcoholism and drug abuse counselors and depending on the prior personal and professional experiences of the counselor, the approach of supervision will vary in its emphasis on cognitive relative to affective issues:

Level 3	Level 2	Level 1
Affective		Cognitive

Influential

Level 1 counselors with limited formal academic training will look for cookbook answers, basic helping skills to assist them in their early work with clients. At that level, a supervisor will address the basics of the twelve core functions and the learning of basic helping skills (for example, attending, paraphrasing, summarizing, reflecting feelings, probing, confrontation, and self-disclosure) as well as basic helping qualities (empathy, genuineness, concreteness, immediacy, and potency).

As the counselor progresses, the supervisor will address more theoretical issues and deal with affective (countertransferential) concerns in counseling. This is not a sequential, linear process. An AODA (alcohol and other drugs of abuse) supervisor may need to alternate between affective and cognitive issues at any stage of the counselor's development, depending on the presenting concerns. For example, a level 1 counselor may have personal preoccupations interfering with clinical functioning, requiring the supervisor to deal with these concerns earlier in the process than usual. Given the tendency of the AODA field to attract people with their own history of recovery from substance abuse or other associated problems, such as codependency, the supervisor must attend to both cognitive and affective issues at all stages of counselor development. It is the skillful supervisor who knows which side of the continuum to address with a particular counselor at any given moment.

Symbolic

The AODA blended model emphasizes primarily manifest content, viewing the unconscious material as interesting but nonessential to bringing about the desired behavioral changes in clients and supervisees:

X

| Latent | Manifest |

Symbolic

The counselor should be less concerned with historical information, particularly in early growth stages, than with skill acquisition and overt behavioral and cognitive issues. This is especially true in a service agency where a supervisor is in direct reporting line with a supervisee, so that role confusion and a dual relationship may arise if the supervisor becomes the counselor's counselor. To deal with latent content issues that are rooted in the counselor's past, the supervisor should refer the counselor to the organization's employee assistance program or other external resources for help.

Structural

The alcoholism and drug abuse field tends to be more structured than spontaneous, especially in early stages of recovery and counselor development. Counseling begins by helping the client discover concrete behaviors he can practice to stay sober one day at a time. Similarly, supervision of the level 1 counselor involves teaching the twelve core functions, with highly specific learning goals and explicit supervisory activities. ETP developed a structured internship curriculum that provided the counselor and supervisor with specific learning objectives and knowledge and skills to be addressed in the first year or two of the counselor's development, leading up to certification as an alcoholism and drug abuse counselor.

As the recovering individual grows, the focus moves to a more flexible agenda reflective of the person's capacity for introspection and insight, and the counselor moves from a structured internship period to a more consultative and collegial supervision. Not only does the degree of structure change from proactive to reactive, but the locus of control also shifts over time to more self-directed instruction. The counselor has increasing responsibility for directing the course of instruction and supervision (for example, by raising concerns about burnout or ongoing professional growth):

Level 3	Level 2	Level 1
Reactive		Proactive

Structural

Replicative

The AODA blended model acknowledges the replicative nature of events in both counseling and supervision. Counselors do behave in supervision in a manner parallel to clients in therapy, and isomorphism is central to the clinical and supervisory processes. However, in the AODA model, the supervisor will rarely address the unconscious identification or other psychodynamic factors underlying the counselor's actions and attitudes, except as these issues interfere with clinical functioning. In agency settings (where most alcoholism and drug abuse counselors work), the danger of role conflicts and dual relationships makes it inadvisable for the supervisor to cross over the imaginary line between skill building and providing therapy for the therapist. The focus must always be on helping the counselor be a more effective clinician (as opposed to a more functional individual). If replicative issues continue to intrude on the therapeutic process, the supervisor should refer the counselor for external assistance. Thus, although this model acknowledges the existence of parallel processes influencing counseling and supervision, it chooses for pragmatic and ethical reasons to treat these as discrete entities outside the supervisory process.

	X
Parallel	Discrete

Replicative

Counselor in Treatment

The AODA blended model does not view therapy as an essential ingredient in the counselor's supervision and holds it to be inappropriate for the supervisor to provide such therapy. However, since many professionals in the field come from either a recovery background or analogous life experiences (such as living in a family dominated by addictive behaviors), it is important that they engage or have engaged in whatever program of personal recovery is needed to ensure that those issues do not intrude into clinical practice. This recovery program is external to the supervisory process and not mandated by the supervisor, who deals directly only with questions of job performance.

If a counselor comes with a history of recovery from alcoholism or drug abuse, the supervisor should remind the counselor to continue with the program of recovery, such as regular attendance at self-help meetings. It is ironic that a profession that knows so much about relapse prevention for patients fails to address in supervision concerns about a supervisee's potential relapse. (This question will be discussed further in Chapter Sixteen.)

If a counselor has had other life experiences that may be interfering with clinical functioning, such as sexual abuse, incest, codependency, or growing up in an alcoholic home, the supervisor should point out how these issues appear to be presenting themselves in the counselor's work and refer the counselor out for help. Thus, while recognizing that these personal therapeutic issues can be central to a counselor's functioning, the AODA blended model treats them as structurally unrelated to training and supervision.

	X	
Related		Unrelated

Counselor in Treatment

Information Gathering

The AODA blended model emphasizes direct observation of counselors, especially in the early and middle stages of development (levels 1 and 2). Since specific skills (twelve core functions) are to be learned, it is essential that the supervisor directly observe the counselor in action so as to determine the training needs of each individual. Indirect methods may be used as the focus shifts toward more symbolic and replicative issues, once the counselor's basic helping skills have matured. As the counselor grows in the three developmental structures (motivation, self- and other awareness, and autonomy-independence), the supervisor is able to address more insight-oriented issues, thus bringing to bear more indirect methods of information gathering:

Level 3	Level 2	Level 1
Indirect		Direct

Information Gathering

Contextual issues must also be considered. More than in any other field, a supervisor of alcoholism and drug abuse counselors must take into account setting and client variables, such as concerns about confidentiality in an employee assistance program or detoxification setting, that might interfere with direct information gathering.

Jurisdictional

The AODA blended model sees jurisdiction over the client and supervisee as resting ultimately with the supervisor, who cannot escape the legal and ethical implications of practice:

	X
Therapist	Supervisor

Jurisdictional

In clinical practice the buck stops with the person likely to be sued, which can be the counselor, the supervisor, or the employing agency and those responsible for its management. (Often the broad net of litigation sweeps in all of the above.) There is a dual liability on the part of the counselor and the supervisor, but the supervisor, representing the agency, is often the first target of litigation. In any case, an agency can never exempt itself from jurisdictional responsibility and liability.

Relationship

The AODA blended model leans more toward nonhierarchical relationships, although the type of relationship formed in counseling or supervision is contingent on setting variables, treatment approaches, and client factors. For example, in a therapeutic community (TC) the program is likely to have a strong directive component. Experience is valued and confers power. Thus, in the early stages of recovery in a TC, the client will be told what to do and when to do it. As a patient stays sober in the TC, the program becomes far less directive and less hierarchical. The supervisory relationship likewise becomes less hierarchical as the counselor gains experience, moving toward the facilitative end for the level 3 counselor. In a less directive setting such as an outpatient program, on the other hand, treatment will likely be less structured, more consultative, and more facilitative from the outset, with staff acting as coaches to the client, although again this will vary with the stage of treatment. In such settings, and especially in a private practice where clients have a longer period of sobriety, supervision is likely to be more consultative, facilitative, and unstructured.

Level 3	Level 2	Level 1
Facilitative		Hierarchical
	Relationship	

Strategy

The AODA blended model provides for the teaching of technique and theory either simultaneously or in alternation, depending on the level of development of the individual supervisee. Initially the supervisor should teach the twelve core functions and the basic helping skills. These techniques form the foundation upon which a counselor's developing model of counseling will be based. As the counselor matures, larger doses of theory can be taught, producing these conceptual pegs on which the counselor can hang his techniques:

Level 3	Level 2	Level 1
Theory		Technique
	Strategy	

The AODA field offers a unique opportunity for counselors to specialize in alcoholism and drug abuse counseling after formal academic training or years of clinical experience in another discipline, such as psychology or marriage and family therapy. The individual who takes this path needs less emphasis on initial training in the twelve core functions or the theory of counseling and greater emphasis on the model of recovery and the intervention techniques unique to this field. Developmental factors along with prior training and clinical experiences must be taken into account.

These nine dimensions constitute the conceptual framework that largely defines the AODA blended model of supervision, which incorporates elements of skill-based supervision with insight-oriented approaches. A supervisor working within the model can move back and forth along the various descriptive continua depending on the counselor's stage of development. Thus, supervision can be either structured and hierarchical or unstructured and facilitative, depending on the supervisee's needs and stage of development. Much like therapy with alcoholics and drug abusers, the blended model of supervision incorporates cognitive and affective influence, direct and indirect observation of a counselor in action, and theory and technique. It acknowledges the relevance of parallel process in counseling and supervision but elects to have such issues addressed outside the supervisory context.

Most important, just as in counseling alcohol- and drug-abusing clients, an AODA supervisor should integrate behavioral training with a deeper understanding of all aspects of the disease, including psychological and spiritual dimensions. If the fourth step of AA is to take a searching self-inventory, a counselor in supervision in the AODA field should likewise be encouraged to engage in a personal moral inventory and spiritual search.

Thus, the blended model of supervision takes its character from the model of counseling practiced in this field. It benefits as well from the models of counseling and supervision developed by the older mental health professions, from which it draws a variety of principles and techniques.

THE NEW BLENDED MODEL OF CLINICAL SUPERVISION

Lily Tomlin once said, "I've always wanted to be somebody. Now I see I should have been more specific." As I look at the blended model of clinical supervision that I developed in the early 1990s, I see that perhaps I should have been more specific. Indeed, the dearth of literature on clinical supervision in this field continues. Despite the expansion of psychotherapeutic approaches and theories and, in turn, supervision approaches in the mental health field in the past thirty years, the substance abuse field has done little exploration of supervisory models and theories. Programs such as the Clinical Preceptorship Program and the Wisconsin Training Program have developed training approaches based upon the International Certification & Reciprocity Consortium (IC&RC) Role Delineation Study (1992). However, hardly any writing has been done on theoretical models for supervision in the substance abuse field, other than the discussion of the blended model.

During the 1990s there were significant changes both in substance abuse treatment and in the health care delivery system. One of the most significant, although subtle, changes in physical and behavioral health treatment has been a further incorporation of spiritual issues into therapy. A new form of the blended model of clinical supervision is required to meet the changing demands of the substance abuse field. The new blended model incorporates issues related to spirituality and therapy. The new blended model also incorporates research findings on what brings about change in people, such as the groundbreaking work of Hubble, Duncan, and Miller in *The Heart and Soul of Change* (1999).

Psychological Foundations

We begin with the psychological underpinnings of the new blended model. Researchers have identified the following "Big Four," the primary factors that affect change.

Extratherapeutic Factors

Extratherapeutic factors account for 40 percent of the change that occurs in treatment. They consist of the individual's strengths, the supportive elements in her environment, her stage of readiness for change, her faith and persistence, and even chance events such as a job change. These are all factors related to the client and not the actions of the therapist.

For too long we have believed that change is the result of some magical cure or words uttered by a skilled expert or clinician, leaving out the client's role in the change process. Conventional wisdom held that when treatment succeeded, it was because of the therapist's actions, but when therapy failed, it was the client's fault: the client was unmotivated, in denial, too sick, or resistant. Actually, research indicates that if change occurs, it is the client who is the magician, who has utilized her unique powers for healing and change. The therapist or supervisor sets the stage and assists in safeguarding the conditions under which the client's magic can operate.

Other extratherapeutic factors affecting treatment are the presence of an underlying personality disorder, the length of time the addiction has persisted, and the client's sense of faith, personal responsibility, and persistence. High-remission disorders, such as depression, anxiety, phobias, obsessive-compulsive disorder, and addictions, may also be factors. Central are the client's strengths and even fortuitous events. Key to treatment outcome is identification not only of what the client needs but also of what the client already has in her life that can help her to reach her goals (see, for example, Peele, Brodsky, and Arnold 1991). Trainees ask, "How do you motivate clients?" and "How do you motivate resistant supervisees?" The fact is you cannot motivate anyone because everyone is already motivated by something. Your task is to find out what motivates each person. Alfred Adler said, "I am fully convinced that no matter what I might be able to say . . . the client can learn nothing from me that he, as the sufferer, does not understand better" (Ansbacher and Ansbacher 1956, p. 336).

Relationship Factors

Relationship factors are the single most significant issues in therapy outcome, accounting for 30 percent of the change. Carl Rogers knew a long time ago that the affective qualities of the therapist influence treatment outcome. We now know that the factors affecting the effectiveness of therapy include caring, empathy, warmth, acceptance, mutual affirmation, and encouragement of risk taking. It appears that different types of clients react differently to the various therapeutic interventions, whose impact is mediated by various client factors. Key, though, is whether the client feels the therapist's compassion, caring, warmth, accurate empathy, congruence, positive regard, genuineness, and acceptance. Conversely, when clients are pulled into hostile exchanges, arguments, or inappropriate confrontations, they resist change. We blame such reactions on client resistance, lack of motivation, or denial when, in fact, the therapist has established a defensive, hostile, and confrontive environment, diminishing the probability of change. A basic rule is that people change when they are moving toward you, not away from you. And most important, it is not the therapist's perception of the relationship that brings about change; it is what the client feels about the quality of the therapeutic relationship.

The nonspecific therapist factors affecting the outcome are the therapist's personality and the therapist's providing a time and safe place to talk, being a good listener, understanding the needs of the client, offering opportunities for self-help, and providing coaching and teaching. With experience and training, counselors can learn to better understand the client's experiences.

What does not work in treatment is attributing failure to the client through words such as, "He's not ready for treatment." Also, it does not work to argue with the client; to be hostile, passive, or defensive; to ignore the client's feelings; to have negative confrontations; or to offer mechanical responses. A widespread trend in treatment that does not seem to work is a strict adherence to the medical model of therapy, wherein the counselor views the client's problem as an illness and prescribes a solution for it.

Given these findings, supervisors should be alert to warning signs of compassion fatigue, whereby the counselor who feels overstressed may become critical, confrontive, attacking, and even abusive. A counselor in this state may ignore the client's feelings and offer mechanical responses.

Placebo Factors

Placebos—such as hope and expectancy—account for 15 percent of the change in therapy. Hope is the way people think about the possibility of attaining their goals and is a common factor in all change. The client contributes to the placebo effect when he has a sense of optimism, an expectancy of self-healing and self-efficacy, and a belief that he can successfully perform a behavior. The opposite of placebo (a Latin term meaning, "I shall please") is nocebo ("I shall harm"), the lack of hope in a positive outcome. Expectancy research has clearly shown that clients model their therapists' patterns of thinking. When we as therapists stop believing that our clients can succeed in their recovery, the clients sense this and in turn lose hope.

Substance abuse is a disease of relapse and recidivism. A cardiologist does not give up on her client because he fails to exercise or to maintain a healthy diet. Alcohol and drug abuse counselors, however, have subtle and not so subtle ways of conveying disappointment and discouragement with client behavior. By so doing, they diminish a client's sense of hope. One of the easiest and most effective things a therapist can do is to continue to encourage clients with words such as, "I know you can do this. You have done it before. Keep it up." Therapists can contribute to the placebo effect by offering support, mutual agreement, partnership, empathic communication, clear expectations, and empowerment.

The first stage of treatment of substance abusers is that of discovery, which involves instilling a sense of hope, discovering that change is possible. Recovery happens after the initial placebo effects are realized. It is important for a counselor to enter into the client's subjective world and the personal meaning of his symptoms. Counselors need to offer a holding environment where hope grows through involving the client in healing rituals, presenting a positive orientation to the future, and highlighting the client's sense of personal control. Research clearly shows that the stronger the alliance between client and caregiver, the more powerful the placebo effect. Likewise, the stronger the alliance, the better the outcome (Hubble, Duncan, and Miller 1999).

Technique Factors

Technique factors account for only 15 percent of therapeutic change. After years of emphasis on learning skills and techniques in therapy, the data indicate that they all have similar outcomes. Technique is important in history taking, maintaining confidentiality, adhering to legal and ethical standards, accurate patient placement, and so forth. Technique is what we use until the real supervisor or therapist shows up. We need to learn technique, master technique, then transcend technique.

This does not mean technique is unimportant. Instead, counselors need to find a model that fits the client and reflects the common factors that bring about change in any therapy. The counselor needs to match her interventions to the client's stage of change. To isolate specific techniques without greater attention to the basic skills is a misguided if not completely illusory approach (Hubble, Duncan, and Miller 1999).

What Counselors Need to Learn in Supervision

The implications of these findings about how people change are dramatic and far-reaching for training and clinical supervision. In place of the usual focus on teaching skills and techniques, we need to emphasize the following:

- Counselors need training in attuning themselves to the client's feelings, establishing rapport, and demonstrating caring, compassion, and empathy.
- Counselors need to find a collaborative instead of a combative metaphor for treatment. Counselors must learn the subtle interpersonal aspects of the therapeutic relationship.
- Counselors need to learn how to develop and monitor the therapeutic alliance, how to assess when there are difficulties with that alliance, and how to repair alliance ruptures. The therapeutic alliance is fundamental to the change process.
- Counselors must be familiar with social support networks, community services, and family and community resources, in order to marshal and enhance the potential for success.
- Counselors must not accept the conventional wisdom that when treatment does not meet the desired outcome it is the client's fault. They must avoid blaming the client's defensiveness, narcissism, borderline personality disorder, codependency, irrational thinking, or projection and not allege denial or resistance to treatment. Conversely, counselors must understand that if there is any magic in treatment, it is the magic brought by the client and not the counselor.
- Counselors need to promote the client's sense of personal control and empowerment. Counselors need to encourage clients to see their own gains, always conveying positive expectations and hope, always expecting clients to get better, always helping clients to find their own solutions.

- Counselors need to learn to focus on the future and on the client's ability to overcome the past. Far too often in the addiction field, we predict relapse and failure instead of the possibility of success. Even when relapse does occur, counselors must maintain the attitude that the client can and will find solutions that work.

- Given the realities of third-party payment, counselors need training in intervention with clients who need fewer than ten sessions. Often simply scheduling an appointment begins the change process. Although 20 to 30 percent of clients (those with multifaceted, more intensive problems) need treatment for more than twenty-five sessions, counselors need to be adept at working with short-term as well as long-term clients and at knowing the difference between them.

- Counselors need to establish the affective qualities essential for counseling before they are taught diagnostics by their supervisors. This is not to say that diagnostics are unimportant but that counselors need to be taught in a way that helps them avoid making premature assessments and quick value judgments about clients.

- Counselors need to be able to adapt their relationship to different clients and their needs. The most important question a counselor can ever ask a client is, "What do you want?" followed by, "How can I help you get there?"

- The earlier change happens in treatment, the more likely will be a positive outcome. Counselors need to remember this fact and realize it is not the therapist that makes the client work but the client that makes the therapist work.

New Descriptive Dimensions

Central to the 1993 blended model are the nine dimensions that define the nature of supervision, taking into account the three levels of counselor development described in Chapter Six. The new blended model adds the following four descriptive dimensions to those presented previously. The added dimensions are, collectively, explained in detail in the following section, which outlines the principles of contemplative supervision. Like the earlier diagrams, the diagrams that follow refer to the three levels of counselor development.

The Journey Dimension

Is supervision primarily a process of deepening (going downward and inward for reflection and introspection) or developing (growing upward and outward in professional development)?

Level 3	Level 2	Level 1
Deepening		Developing

The Internalization Dimension

Does the supervisor seek to aid the supervisee in developing wisdom and integrating therapeutic behaviors and attitudes or to isolate external philosophies through a compartmentalization process?

Level 3	Level 2	Level 1
Integration of Wisdom		Compartmentalization of External Philosophies

The Listening Dimension

How does the supervisor listen—with the head or the heart?

Level 3	Level 2	Level 1
Listening with the Heart		Listening with the Head

The Questioning Dimension

Does the supervisor pose questions or answers?

Level 3	Level 2	Level 1
Questions		Answers

The new dimensions take into account the four common factors affecting change, building especially on the strength of the therapeutic alliance and the extratherapeutic factors pertaining to the client or supervisee. They (particularly the dimension of listening with the heart) point to a collaborative model of supervision. These dimensions provide a means to further describe one's approach to and model of supervision.

Spiritual and Contemplative Foundations

Plato said, "The greatest mistake in the treatment of disease is that there are physicians for the body and physicians for the soul, although the two cannot be separated." With this preface, we will explore the spiritual dimensions of clinical supervision.

The new blended model of clinical supervision integrates spiritual aspects of change. The term coined for the integration of spirituality is *contemplative supervision.* This integration is based on the data cited earlier on how and why people change, what people want in therapy and supervision, and what truly is important in treating the client. It draws upon the foundational work of authors such as Carl Jung, Gordon Allport, Abraham Maslow, M. Scott Peck, Sam Keen, Irvin Yalom, Thomas Moore, Jerry May, Mary Pipher, and Ken Wilbur and upon transpersonal psychology. It also incorporates the spiritual principles of twelve-step programs. Indeed, addressing spiritual aspects of counseling and supervision may reflect the growing maturity of the psychotherapy field as it seeks a holistic approach to healing the mind and body and spirit.

To some, discussing spirituality as a factor in counseling and supervision may seem strange, not typical subject matter for a textbook on clinical supervision. However, from the evidence of my practice and the resonance of supervisors in my training classes to spiritual aspects of therapy and supervision—an informal, empirical test—spirituality is clearly an essential part of the change process for clients and supervisees. Thus, the new blended model reflects what is already occurring in the clinical practice of many counselors and supervisors.

Why is this the case? Paradoxically, the practical constraints on counseling and supervision today put a premium on the intensity of the exchange. In an outcome-driven, evidence-based, brief therapy world, there is less time to establish a therapeutic alliance, the single most important factor in bringing about change in a counseling or supervisory relationship. Hence, in a world with less time to talk, fewer communication exchanges, and an urgent need to establish rapport quickly, contemplative counseling and supervision are all the more essential. Because the obstacles to establishing a therapeutic alliance are greater today, concentrated attention needs to be given to listening, rapport, and relationship building.

Finally, as stated in Chapter Seven, there is an isomorphic, parallel process in supervision, as the supervisor models a valid counseling modality. If contemplative approaches in counseling are important, it is essential that the clinical supervisor model such an approach for counselors.

Contemplative supervision reduces the supervisor's need to be the expert, to have all the answers for the counselor. It empowers counselors to find their own answers and approaches. It is a commitment to healing by enhancing the isomorphic relationship between counselor and supervisor and between counselor and client. It models a healthy therapeutic alliance that puts counseling and supervision in a larger, more global context and promotes dialogue as one realizes that one's life is not just about oneself but part of the larger human story.

Traditional supervision addressed the efficiency of functioning, how one should live. The contemplative approach looks at a dynamic process, what one wants to see occur in therapy and supervision. Fundamental to this process is the integration of body, mind, and spirit, always seeking to accommodate the supervisee's state of readiness for change. The key to outcome in supervision is to identify not what the person needs but what she already has to work with and for her.

The Principles of Contemplative Supervision

We begin with the basic question, What is health? Although seemingly an elementary question, it is essential to understanding what we are trying to accomplish as health care providers. Health is when the mind is present in the heart, when mind, body, and spirit are integrated, when an individual is at peace with his mind, body, and spirit, even if one of those elements is experiencing pain or suffering. Jean Vanier said, "To be human is to accept ourselves just as we are, with our own history, and to accept others as they are.

To accept history as it is and to work, without fear, to greater openness, understanding and love of others—searching for truth" (Vanier 1998, p. 15).

Do not seek to offer answers. Too often supervisors feel the need to be the expert. Instead of offering answers, offer mystery, compassion, wonder, openness, simple presence, and waiting alongside the person. Much of life cannot be explained, only experienced. Instead of offering answers, create a sacred space for the work to be done by encouraging and allowing intuitive connection so that there is room for experience and expression.

In 1999 I helped Kosovar refugees living in Bosnia just after the war in Kosovo. In a camp housing 1,200 Kosovar refugees, there was an eighty-four-year-old man, Alji, whose farm had been burned to the ground and who had lost thirty family members: his wife, all of his siblings, all of his children, and most of his grandchildren. Nothing in my years of counseling offered me any words or answers to give him. All I could do was hold his hand, and we cried together. I am not suggesting that supervisors hold supervisees' hands and that they weep together, at least not literally. But the key to change is simple presence, compassion, and love. Supervisors often worry about what words to say or what the correct therapeutic answer is. If one is present in one's heart, the words will emerge from a source deep within oneself. Supervisors need to trust that presence and be always anchored in their caring and compassion for the person sitting in front of them.

The root of a Latin word meaning "to listen" (*audire*) is the same as the root of a Latin word meaning "to obey" (*oboedire*): "to give as a gift." Contemplative listening is hearing without an agenda, without a compulsion to help, by abandoning one's desire to be wise, comforting, and knowledgeable. Contemplative listening is being receptive to visual, auditory, kinesthetic, and intuitive cues.

Contemplative listening allows one to see the world, as Buddhists say, through beginner's eyes, to be open and receptive to life's hidden meanings. This aids in finding meaning and purpose in life, in being mindful of the present moment, fully attentive to the meta-messages in communication. It is a way of seeking further collaboration and compassion in the supervisory system.

Supervision is as much about love as it is about skill. Expertise cures, but healing comes from the sharing of experiences and wounds. The appropriate use of self-disclosure needs to be taught. This does not mean always telling one's own stories and oozing all over with one's own wounds. It does mean being present in love, allowing the still, small voice within the supervisor to emerge, trusting that voice, and sharing experience whenever appropriate. Compassion in supervision is the tender opening of the heart to the affect of others, being present with love. It requires a quiet mind, free of the baggage of distorted desires, focusing not on the outcome but on the journey.

Before every session, one should take a moment to remember one's humanity. By doing so, one sees there is nothing a client has experienced that a therapist cannot share. Before a supervision session, a supervisor should ask himself, "What's the rush? What are the storms in life that I am trying to weather? What do I need to do to overcome these storms at this present moment? How do I regain inner control?"

The most important phrases a supervisor can learn are "I don't know" and "I could be wrong." Often an unanswered question is a fine traveling companion. If counseling is about intimacy, at the heart of intimacy is vulnerability. This involves letting the question be something to ponder, searching for meaning as opposed to getting involved in a potential power struggle. Change is always about the degree of connectedness between individuals, not about one person having the answers for another. Supervision is about the quality of attention given. Our greatest gift to others is our wholeness, and that may mean at times to let the question be.

A contemplative supervisor begins with a nonjudgmental, authentic presence, teaching through being, in an accepting attitude that promotes empathy and understanding. He begins with openness and a willingness to understand the supervisee's emotional, psychological, physical, social, and spiritual dimensions as they have an impact on health. When a supervisor is open to and compassionate with the supervisee, the two of them are more present to each other's hearts. Supervisees don't care how much a supervisor knows until they know how much he cares.

A contemplative supervisor roots wisdom in the full cooperation of all ways of knowing: observation, logical inference, behavioral learning (affective and physical), and intuition. The goal of supervision should not be the separate autonomy of the individual

self but the realization of one's essential rootedness in and relatedness to something broader than the self. It requires a willing surrender to otherness and not willful mastery of the situation. The
greatest gift to give a supervisee is wholeness, the integration of
body, mind, and spirit.

Growth is paradoxical. Sometimes less is more. People grow
through what they let go as opposed to what they gain. Supervisors
must seek transformation of self and others, not simply behavioral
change. Transformation occurs through the process of letting go
of pain, for unless one transforms one's pain, one transmits it in
behavior toward oneself and others.

Supervisors need to learn and be comfortable with silence in
supervision, trusting that there is a power at work within the supervisee and within the space between supervisor and supervisee that
brings about change. A contemplative supervisor begins the session in silence, leaving space for the unique spirit of the individual before her to emerge. A skilled supervisor seeks stillness within
herself and the environment in which she works, allowing the
unseen to sing softly to itself. A skilled supervisor trusts that something is at work at all times, promoting change, especially in
silence.

Contemplative supervision requires learning how to manage
and value emotions (anxieties, fears, anger, and sadness) and being
open to the wisdom, lessons, and potential of emotions to aid the
present relational dynamics (triadic aspects of the supervisor, counselor, and client).

One must ask oneself, "To what am I attached today that might
get in the way of my listening and showing compassion? What is
my meaning and purpose? What keeps me going day-to-day? Why
do I do what I do? What am I searching for today? How do I want
to be remembered as a person, a counselor, and a professional?
What is waiting to happen in my life right now? What would be
unlived if it all ended today?" Rumi, the thirteenth-century Sufi
master, said, "Let yourself be silently drawn by the pull of what you
truly love." What do you love today? What gives you significance in
life (Powell 2003)?

To develop the skills of contemplative listening, one needs to
have one's own spiritual practice that includes the process of

deeper listening. Supervisors cannot take someone to a place they themselves have not been. One should ask oneself, "What are the quiet, contemplative times in life when I listen to my heart?"

Contemplative supervisors need to explore their own spiritual journey through stillness, meditation, and reflection. There are many training programs for contemplative listening, such as those presented by the Shalem Institute for Spiritual Formation, Spiritual Directors International, organizations that offer Buddhist meditation, and other groups. On this journey, it is advisable to have a guide to support the process of contemplative listening.

Contemplative listening involves storytelling and metaphors as ways of unraveling truth. Through stories, a supervisor is able to search and find meaning in despair and gather in the vicissitudes of others without imposing his or her will.

Martin Buber, the philosopher and theologian, spoke of the I-Thou relationship that is central to contemplative listening. By serving the Thou of another, a supervisor is able to transcend self and find a generous, reflective relationship. When listening to another, a supervisor can realize she is now in an encounter with a unique person, Thou; with that realization the supervisor and supervisee can go to places the two have never been.

The contemplative supervisor is open and passionate about exploring existential questions. He is courageous in opening the discussion with others and demonstrating wisdom in understanding how to help the counselor integrate the insights gained and move forward.

The contemplative supervisor does not use the relationship to pursue her own spiritual agenda, that is, to push a particular religious belief system, structure, or self-help orientation. One cannot teach others to be spiritual, because they already are.

Conclusion

The new blended model is much like life: a work in progress, always seeking to reflect the deeper movement within. Supervisors need to grow by exploring these deeper, contemplative dimensions rooted in spiritual truths, together with the science of what brings about change—physically, socially, emotionally, and spiritually.

Part Three

Methods

Chapter Eleven

Establishing a Supervisory Contract

The methods of supervision practiced under the blended model follow from the general characteristics of the model, as well as from the nature of substance abuse counseling and the conditions under which it is typically practiced (in particular, the nonacademic agency setting and the varied backgrounds of the staff, many of whom lack formal training). These dictate an emphasis on basic skills, clearly defined responsibilities, and pragmatic use of resources.

The first task in supervision is to establish an oral or, preferably, written behavioral contract with the supervisee that provides realistic accountability for both parties and manages the counselor's anxiety by limiting his tasks and responsibilities. If the contract involves renegotiating an existing relationship, the supervisee may be uncomfortable with the added formality it introduces. To minimize this discomfort, the supervisor might say something like, "Given this particular situation with its demands and possibilities, given who you are and who I am, and given the time and resources available, how can we work out a plan for this learning process that will take into account all these factors?"

Any possible ambiguity about the supervisor's role should be resolved at the outset. Is this a directing supervisor, who has line authority over the supervisee, or a consulting supervisor, who acts as colleague, coach, cheerleader, and consultant? The former model is more common in service agencies, the latter in private practice and academic institutions. In an agency such as a substance abuse treatment center, a supervisor who is not the counselor's immediate superior in the chain of command may nonetheless have the authority to make binding recommendations and give performance evaluations that affect the counselor's standing in the agency. This element of power changes the nature of the supervisory contract as well as the tenor of the supervisory relationship. On the other hand, when the supervisor is well respected in the field or has formal qualifications far exceeding those of the supervisee, it may be hard to hear the supervisor speaking simply as an experienced clinician who is trying to be helpful.

In the initial sessions, a number of tasks essential to any teaching relationship must be accomplished:

1. Establishing a working relationship, which includes laying a groundwork of trust and respect.
2. Assessing the counselor's clinical knowledge and skills, prior experiences, and training needs.
3. Agreeing to a behavioral contract setting the ground rules for the supervisory sessions, thereby introducing the counselor to issues such as confidentiality, dual relationships, informed consent, and administrative requirements.
4. Setting learning goals for the supervision in the form of a supervision training plan or individual development plan (IDP).

While fulfilling the more formal requirements listed under points 2 through 4, it is easy to overlook the less tangible effort required under point 1: establishing respect and trust. From the beginning, the supervisor must demonstrate positive regard for the supervisee's prior learning and work experiences. In the alcoholism and drug abuse field, it is equally important to respect the person's prior life experiences, since the person may come with a recovery history in place of formal academic training. The supervisor should show sincere interest in the supervisee's previous experiences in supervision, preferred counseling approach, and preferred supervision and learning style.

Contrary to the dogma of some books on management, a supervisor cannot motivate anyone. People are already motivated. Everyone has desires and interests. A key to being an effective supervisor is to find out what motivates an employee. Who is this counselor? What motivates her? What does she do for fun after work? What does she lose sleep over at 2:00 A.M.? What are her personal needs and concerns? How and to what extent can these needs be met in the workplace? Is there a danger that they may impede her work? With these questions comes a reciprocal opportunity for the supervisee to learn something about the supervisor. To create a spirit of mutuality as well as to let the supervisee know what to expect, the supervisor should share what he or she brings to the field, in terms of past experience and orientation.

AGENDA FOR THE INITIAL SESSION

The following list specifies the issues to be addressed in the first supervisory session. It is essential that goals and objectives for supervision, as well as expectations and deliverables, be established at the outset.

I. Introduction of supervisor and supervisee(s)
   A. Supervisee's description of personal counseling experience and background
      1. Types of experience
      2. Settings worked
      3. Influences of these experiences on current counseling philosophy and orientation
      4. Motivations for becoming a counselor and for undertaking the training/employment
   B. Supervisor's reciprocal description of background
      1. Relating the supervisor's experiences to those of the supervisee
      2. Demonstrating the supervisor's qualifications for being a supervisor
II. Presentation of specific requirements of supervision
   A. Meeting time and place (duration, frequency)
   B. Observation procedures and requirements, including those pertaining to taping
      1. Releases required
      2. Number of tapes required
      3. Tape review procedures
      4. Variety of tapes (different clients, phases of care)
      5. Write-ups expected (format)

6. Cofacilitation procedures
7. One-way mirror procedures
8. Process notes, verbatims
9. Confidentiality restrictions

C. Evaluation procedures
   1. Acknowledgment of supervisee anxiety and fears about observation and evaluation
   2. Presentation of evaluation criteria and methodology
   3. Feedback from supervisee regarding evaluation
   4. Agreement on type and frequency of evaluation
   5. Site visits by field supervisors, if relevant

D. Individual development plan (IDP)

III. Anticipated structure and process of supervision
   A. Teaching mode to be employed
   B. Supervisory process issues
   C. Boundaries of supervision versus therapy
   D. Clarification of any other supervisory relationships
   E. Group supervision issues, if applicable
   F. Resources available, reading assignments, homework
   G. Supervisee's and supervisor's expectations, desired outcomes
   H. Plans for next session, first quarter of training/supervision
      1. Time/scheduling
      2. Arrangements for taping, observation, write-ups
      3. Time management, scheduling, cancellation procedures, administrative tasks, job requirements, filings, confidentiality of information
   I. Ethical, legal, and professional requirements

IV. Behavioral contracting
   A. Establishment of a behavioral contract between supervisor and supervisee
   B. Criteria for evaluation of outcomes of behavioral contract and outcome measurements
   C. Rewards and reinforcements for fulfillment of behavioral contract
   D. Sanctions for noncompliance with behavioral contract
   E. Criteria for supervisee progress, including skills and knowledge gain, behavioral changes, expectations of level of change, developmental expectations

F. Obstacles to progress: lack of time, fear of success, fear of failure, performance anxiety, resource limitations

G. Progress review

GETTING TO KNOW THE SUPERVISEE

The supervisor's next task is to establish a database on the counselor so as to determine the counselor's readiness for practice and professional needs. A productive supervisor-counselor working relationship is grounded in a clear understanding of the goals of supervision and a clearly worked out supervision plan. Such a plan presupposes an accurate assessment of the counselor's knowledge and skills—the level of professional development the counselor has attained. This ongoing assessment is described in detail in Chapter Thirteen. In the meantime, even to begin the supervisory relationship, a preliminary assessment of the counselor is required. This assessment has several facets.

Knowledge and Skills

How prepared is the counselor to perform specific clinical tasks? How able is she to articulate a theoretical model of counseling? How skillful is she in interacting with clients? Does the supervisee have the skills to fulfill the responsibilities demanded by the job in question, as well as the qualities and resources needed to strengthen those skills? Several instruments have been developed to assess counselor skills (Borders and Leddick 1987; Mead 1990; Shaw and Dobson 1988; Stoltenberg and Delworth 1987). The Barrett-Lennard Relationship Inventory (1964) and the evaluation form in Appendix F also measure counselor skills.

Learning Style

The supervisor should assess the counselor's learning style (as described in Chapter Six). Does the counselor learn by doing (active) or by osmosis (vicarious)? Is this a person with internal locus of control, who can process information and draw conclusions inductively, or one with external locus of control, who needs more direct feedback and guidance? Is the counselor an oral processor, who benefits most from discussions, or a written processor, who can make good use of reading materials?

Conceptual Skills

What hypotheses are formed by the counselor from the information gathered? What treatment plans follow from those hypotheses? Here the supervisor is assessing the counselor's technical skills for organizing data into a coherent treatment plan linked with specific clinical interventions. The most effective way for the supervisor to assess the counselor's conceptual skills is to have the counselor present cases. Several instruments have been developed to assess counselors' conceptual skills: the Oetting-Michaels Anchored Ratings for Therapists (Michaels 1982), the Intentions List (Hill and O'Grady 1985), the Clinical Assessment Questionnaire (Holloway and Wolleat 1980), and the Written Treatment Planning Simulation (Butcher, Scofield, and Baker 1985).

Suitability for Work Setting

The supervisor must assess not only the counselor's general clinical skills but also the counselor's ability to meet the specific requirements of the work setting. How good is the match between the person and the milieu? To make this judgment, the supervisor must list the range of problems the counselor may encounter, the types of cases that occur most frequently, and the specific skills needed to do the job. This job-specific assessment is reinforced on an ongoing basis by asking the counselor to present for supervision a broad spectrum of cases (for example, both men and women, both more healthy and less healthy individuals) rather than just the ones in which the counselor appears most expert. By utilizing this technique of supervision, the supervisor also acts to strengthen the counselor's general skills and to broaden the range of jobs for which the counselor will be qualified.

Motivation

To what extent is the counselor motivated by values (for example, helping others) and to what extent by needs (for example, healing personal wounds)? Has the counselor's own history been characterized primarily by positive or negative reinforcers? Is the counselor at high risk for burnout? What are the counselor's fears, anxieties, and stressors with regard to the job? A number of tools have been developed to assess counselor motivation: the Environment Scale (Wiley 1982), the Reising and Daniels (1983) Counselor Development Questionnaire, the Worthington and Roehlke (1979) Supervision Questionnaire, and the Supervisor Perception Form (Heppner and Roehlke 1984).

This initial phase of supervision, the contracting period, customarily lasts for two to three sessions. At its completion, the supervisor is ready to move into the next phase, establishing the goals of supervision.

GOALS OF SUPERVISION

Goal setting is essential to the supervision process. It gives the supervisor and supervisee a shared vision, specific steps for realizing that vision, and benchmarks for evaluation. Goals for supervision should be in writing and should be agreed upon by the supervisor and supervisee. They should have the following components:

1. A clearly stated, attainable, specific, measurable, and observable outcome.
2. Specific action steps to bring about the outcome.
3. Specific procedures to evaluate the outcome (Mager 1972; Borders and Leddick 1987).

A supervisor and supervisee may determine, for example, that the supervisee needs to improve on his intake skills, specifically assessment and diagnosis. The goals set for the next year will be for the counselor to increase his knowledge and use of *DSM-IV,* to be familiar with its diagnostic axes, and to meet a professional standard of accuracy in assessments and client conceptualizations, as determined by the supervisor. The supervisor will measure the attainment of these goals by observing a series of intakes done by the supervisee and reviewing the diagnoses and rationales. To aid the counselor in reaching the goals, the supervisor will provide reading material and didactic presentations on *DSM-IV* for staff, will allow the counselor to observe the supervisor doing intakes, and will give the counselor feedback on particular clinical cases. If necessary, the supervisor will require the counselor to conduct a variety of intakes on various *DSM-IV* diagnostic categories and axes. This is an example of clearly stated goals, specific action planning, and specific evaluation mechanisms.

Goals should be reviewed regularly by the supervisor and supervisee and revised to remove anything that is not attainable. These goals are called key results areas (KRAs)—measurable outcomes that will determine if supervision is successful. After the list has been reviewed by both parties, they should ask, "If the counselor achieved these things, would he have achieved the goals of his position? How will one know if one has achieved those goals? What will be different in one's action?"

The goals established by the supervisor and supervisee may differ for a number of reasons. First, they may vary due to different experiences of counseling and supervision, especially when the counselor's developmental level is factored into the equation. Level 1 counselors want support and technical assistance with cases. Their goal may be to get approval along with "cookbook" learning. The supervisor may be more interested in teaching tactics and strategies to help the counselor learn to use empirical data to conceptualize and build a detailed treatment plan.

Level 2 counselors may seek to leave behind the familiar methods they have learned and try new theories, while still struggling with feelings of inadequacy. Supervisors may encourage their counselors to confront the confusion and frustration they feel when letting go of methods they have come to believe work with everyone all of the time.

Level 3 counselors may gravitate to unexamined eclecticism, which leaves them still unable to articulate why they use a given technique with a particular client. The supervisor may push the counselor to clarify this eclecticism and to formulate a personal counseling model as an integrated, coherent whole.

Another source of contention in goal setting is divergent philosophical allegiances. Some of the most difficult struggles in the supervisory relationship occur when the supervisor and supervisee are working from different paradigms of human behavior. Similar conflicts occur as a result of conflicting institutional goals. For example, the goals established by counselor certification boards may be different from those of a supervisor who, as a certified marriage and family therapist, works under a compatible but different set of guidelines. Training institutions, too, may impose goals on the supervisee that do not concern the agency or the supervisor. The converse is also true: the agency may maintain standards of practice or a philosophy of treatment that the training organization does not. These are among the reasons why one of the first tasks in supervision is to identify and state the goals of supervision.

THE INDIVIDUAL DEVELOPMENT PLAN

After goals have been set, a plan of action, the individual development plan (IDP), is formulated. This detailed plan for supervision includes timelines for change and methods by which the supervisee will acquire the agreed-upon knowledge and skills. As a guide in creating an IDP, Greenberg (1980) and Loganbill, Hardy, and Delworth (1982) have established goals for counselors at various stages of their development. (See Appendix G for guidance in formulating an IDP based specifically on the twelve core functions.) The IDP should include the following components:

1. *Expectations for supervision.* Under this heading is included the model of therapy to be taught and its philosophical basis. The plan should specify the number and types of patients to be seen by the supervisee, the number and duration of supervision sessions, and the techniques and interventions to be used. Contingencies should also be specified, such as what to do in case of emergencies (personal or clinical), how fees are to be handled (if applicable), whether site visits are to be conducted (when, by whom, for what purpose), and other administrative details. The type and frequency of evaluations should be part of this written plan as well. The boundaries of confidentiality should be stated, reaffirming the code of ethics of the profession together with any applicable laws. Grievance procedures are to be included, should there be major differences of opinion between the supervisor and supervisee.

2. *The counselor's experience and readiness for the position.* What is the counselor's base of knowledge and experience? How well

prepared is he for the job tasks? What are his strengths and areas for growth?

3. *Procedures to be used to observe the counselor in practice.* The methods of observation used will depend on the customary practices of the agency, the training requirements of the profession and/or the training institution, the counselor's skill levels, the availability of technical equipment, the client base, the potential need to intervene in treatment, and the availability and preferences of the supervisor. The possible impact of observation on the client must always be taken into account. The IDP should specify both the preparation expected of the supervisee prior to each observation and the procedure to be followed by the supervisor and supervisee after the observation. For example, will the supervisor and supervisee meet immediately after the observed session? If so, for how long? Who else might be involved in the debriefing? How will audio and video material be processed? Are both parties expected to review the material prior to the supervision session? If so, how long before the session will the tapes be made available to the supervisor?

4. *Procedures to be used to determine the counselor's reasoning, conceptualization, and decision-making skills.* The IDP should state how the supervisor will assess the counselor's clinical reasoning, including task selection, identification of variables critical to the case (as opposed to insufficient or unnecessary variables), predictions for outcome, strategies and hypotheses, and diagnosis and prognosis. The counselor's ability to formulate a treatment plan with appropriate clinical interventions will be part of this assessment.

5. *Procedures to be used to evaluate the counselor.* Evaluation procedures include the number, frequency, and types of assessments (oral, written, formal testing) and who will make them. What feedback process between the counselor and evaluator(s) is provided for? What will be the outcome of the evaluations? What sanctions may be used, and how will recommendations for change be implemented?

6. *Procedures to be used to intervene to help the counselor achieve supervision goals.* Finally, the procedures for supervisory intervention will be specified in the IDP. The supervisor may intervene by phone-ins, cofacilitation, role playing, call-outs during a session, or bug-in-the-ear. Since the fidelity of the supervisor's information

about the counselor depends on the method of observation, it is recommended that the IDP provide for as much direct observation of clinical practice as is feasible under the circumstances. Although there will be situations in which it is contraindicated, live observation (supplemented when possible by an audiotaped or videotaped record for later review) is desirable in most cases. (Further discussion of the advantages and disadvantages of the various methods of observation and intervention can be found in the following chapter.)

Determining the progress of the counselor in meeting the supervision goals and following the IDP is critical. Counselor performance must be evaluated on a regular basis through self-report, reviews by other supervisees, client ratings (if appropriate), counselor ratings of the supervisor and the supervisory process, and the supervisor's rating of the counselor. (These modes of evaluation will be discussed in Chapter Thirteen.)

ASSESSING THE LEARNING ENVIRONMENT OF SUPERVISION

The supervisory contract and the IDP, together with the overall atmosphere of the agency, create an environment for supervision. The following questions identify the components of the optimal learning environment for supervision and assess the dynamics of the supervisory learning process. Supervisors can use these questions to assess their supervisees' learning environment at the time of the initial contract and on an ongoing basis.

1. Is there sufficient challenge in the learning environment to keep the supervisee motivated?
2. Is the theoretical or philosophical dissonance between supervisor and supervisee manageable enough to maintain proper motivation for the supervisee?
3. Does the supervisee have the knowledge and skills sufficient to begin this process and to meet the demands of the task?
4. Does the supervisee have sufficient personal development, self-esteem, and sense of self-worth to progress through this process and separate himself from professional success or failure?

5. What is the supervisee's investment in the learning process?
6. Does the supervisee possess (or manifest) the basic affective qualities needed for counseling, such as empathy, warmth, genuineness, concreteness, and potency?
7. Is the amount of support available to the supervisee sufficient and proportional to the challenge of supervision and learning?
8. Are the goals and means of supervision clear and understood by all parties involved?
9. Are the evaluation criteria realistic, measurable, attainable, accurate, relevant, and clearly understood?
10. To what extent can the supervisee process feedback?
11. Is the supervisory environment such that risk taking can be attempted, with sufficient safety protection for the counselor to try out new skills and behaviors?
12. To what extent does the supervisor help the supervisee integrate new techniques and skills for the supervisee's professional growth, sense of identity, autonomy, and maturity?
13. Is there a basis for terminating the supervision at the appropriate time, delineating further concerns and avenues to address these issues?

Once the supervisory environment has been established and assessed, the actual process of supervision can begin. The following chapters present methods and guidelines for implementing the supervisory contract and the supervision plan.

Chapter Twelve

Basic Supervisory Techniques

The blended model of clinical supervision for the alcoholism and drug abuse field employs a variety of methods and techniques consistent with the assumptions and principles of the model. These techniques begin with the context of supervision and come full circle to its content. First, it is necessary to set the scene by addressing the mundane questions of scheduling, budgeting, personnel allocation, and agency policies. After these structural questions have been resolved, the day-to-day techniques of supervision take shape: how the counselor's work is observed, how case material is presented, and how the supervisor intervenes to redirect the counselor's efforts. Finally, there is the content of supervision, the essential issues to be covered in the supervisory dialogue.

THE CONTEXT OF SUPERVISION

A model of supervision is practiced not in a vacuum but in a particular context. In allocating time for the supervision of staff, the unique conditions, limitations, and requirements of the agency must be taken into account. How many counselors report to a supervisor? How many hours in a counselor's workweek should be devoted to supervision? Are there any guidelines as to how much supervision a counselor should receive? How does one arrange one's schedule to allow for supervision time? How does one adapt to having more counselors to supervise? Finally, how much supervisory responsibility is too much for one person?

Determining Supervision Time

Case law has established that it is an agency's responsibility to make a "reasonable effort" to supervise its staff. What is "reasonable," however, given the unique circumstances and constraints of each agency? A rule is that for every 20 hours of direct client contact, a counselor should receive 1 hour of clinical supervision. In most work settings, this translates into a full-time workload. Most counselors spend about 20 hours a week in individual and/or group counseling, intakes, and family work. They will likely spend 15 additional hours on case management, follow-up, staff meetings, and other management and administrative tasks. (Center for Substance Abuse Treatment data indicate the average alcohol and drug abuse counselor spends 20 percent of his time doing paperwork [Center for Substance Abuse Treatment 2003].) Another rule of management is that approximately 10 to 12 percent of a workweek (4 to 5 hours) will be spent on vacation, sick days, and holiday time. The 20 direct client hours, 15 hours of management time, and 4 to 5 hours of G & A (general and administrative) time add up to the usual 40-hour workweek. Situations will vary, of course, and the amount of direct client contact will be less clear in a residential setting where counselors are interacting with clients most of the day. However, since 20 hours of actual counseling time per week is a good estimate for most agencies, everyone who provides direct counseling services should receive at least 1 hour of supervision per week. This rule holds regardless of the counselor's length of service or professional standing, although more experienced clinicians will often receive peer or collegial supervision.

The mandated hour can be spent in individual and/or small-group supervision. It is recommended that the small groups average four to six members to allow time for presentations by all group members. Individual sessions should run approximately 1 hour and small-group supervision 1 to 1½ hours. These numbers translate into formulas for allocating supervisory time, depending on the number of counselors reporting to a supervisor.

Managing the Supervisory Workload

If a supervisor is responsible for one to five counselors (a typical staff size), the supervisor may do up to 5 hours per week of individual supervision, 1½ hours per week of small-group supervision, or some combination of the two. With one to three counselors, the supervisor can easily see each counselor individually once a week. With five counselors, the supervisor may choose to conduct a small-group session weekly for all five while supervising each counselor individually every other week, for a total of 3½ to 4½ hours of supervision.

In addition, the supervisor will need to spend time observing the counselor in action—at a minimum 1 hour to 1½ hours per week observing each counselor who will present at supervision. Built into this observation time is preparation time (for example, to review the videotape of the observed session). Thus, an additional 3 to 4½ hours are added for observation and/or preparation time, for a total of 6½ to 9 hours per week of supervisory activity—a manageable workload for most supervisors. In addition, the supervisor will likely be carrying a caseload, be responsible for other management tasks, participate in various meetings, and occasionally even take some time off.

If a supervisor oversees the work of six to ten counselors, the situation becomes more complex. It is recommended that the supervisor hold two small-group sessions per week with four to six counselors per group, for a total of 3 hours of group supervision per week. In addition, the supervisor should see supervisees individually every other week, adding up to 5 more hours of supervision per week. This totals 8 hours of supervision time. Finally, the supervisor should observe the counselors in action, requiring 5 to 8 hours of observation and preparation time. A supervisor may not be able to observe all of the counselors who are presenting in supervision (individual and group) each week.

This number of 13 to 16 hours weekly is still manageable, although it takes up a larger portion of the supervisor's time. A supervisor may observe part rather than all of a counseling session, review only key segments of a videotaped session, or not observe all of the presenting counselors each week. One good videotape from a prior session may last for weeks of supervision.

When a person supervises more than eleven counselors, other methods of supervision become necessary. A supervisor usually needs to concentrate on small-group supervision, taking 4½ hours for three groups and an equal amount of observation time, for a total of 9 hours of supervision. In addition, the supervisor must allocate some time for individual supervision for counselors with special needs and, especially, for entry-level staff. These adaptations keep the supervisor's load down to approximately 12 to 15 hours of supervision per week. Another approach is to set up peer small-group supervision, allowing the supervisor to provide individual supervision for those in need. A variation is to ask a level 3 counselor on staff to conduct the small-group supervision sessions and to oversee the work of level 1 counselors. The supervisor is then free to supervise the senior counselor's supervision. Although difficult to manage, the task of supervising eleven to fifteen counselors can be accomplished with some creative juggling.

It is rarely possible to supervise more than fifteen counselors without suffering an unacceptable level of personal stress or deviation from professional standards. In this case peer small-group supervision is the primary option available. Designating a senior counselor as supervisor will be a necessity. Management must be informed of the obstacles to making a reasonable effort to supervise and of the legal liability that may result from having too many counselors report to one supervisor.

Other than in such extreme conditions, however, through a combination of individual and small-group supervision, with a proportionate amount of direct observation time, most staffing patterns allow for a reasonable effort at supervision, so that the agency can maintain standards. As the field evolves, supervisors may be able to increase their effectiveness through further innovation and flexibility—for example, by challenging the ritual of the "50-minute hour" for all activities derived from psychotherapy. Perhaps some supervisory functions can be discharged just as adequately and more efficiently in 30-minute blocks.

Finally, two of the adaptations to contextual pressures recommended here, group supervision and peer supervision, can themselves be looked at as special contexts of supervision.

METHODS OF OBSERVATION

If the supervisor is to have a consistent, accurate picture of the counselor, frequent observation of the counselor over an extended period of time is essential. Traditionally, supervisors have most often employed indirect methods of observation, such as case notes, process recordings, and verbatims, but these are no longer recommended. Process notes present an obstacle for individuals who have difficulty articulating their thoughts in writing. In any case, counselors' accounts of sessions, oral or written, are so conditioned by biases and distortions (whether conscious or unconscious) that the information presented to the supervisor must be considered unreliable. It is ex post facto supervision.

Since the fidelity of the information the supervisor receives is greatly enhanced by directly observing the counselor at work, this approach has become a cornerstone of the alcoholism and drug abuse blended model of supervision. Live observation is recommended wherever possible, although it is time consuming and requires a postsession debriefing. Live observation combined with taping offers the ideal mix; the supervisor's first-hand observation is reinforced by a record of the session that the supervisor and supervisee can review together.

Supervisors today have at their disposal a variety of high-tech aids: audiotapes, videotapes, one-way mirrors, bug-in-the-ear, telephones in the counseling room, interactive video, and video-based training. The most familiar of these techniques, audiotaping, is inexpensive and convenient but loses the nonverbal communication between counselor and client that reveals so much about transference, countertransference, and even possible misconduct. The use of more powerful, up-to-date tools is therefore desirable.

The choice of methods and techniques in any given situation will depend on the need for fidelity of information, the availability of technical equipment, the ability to intervene, the immediacy of the supervisory debriefings, and the counselor's skill level. Pragmatic considerations such as these have limited the use of one-way mirrors, bug-in-the-ear, and phone-ins in the alcoholism and drug abuse field. While briefly considering these techniques, therefore, this section will emphasize two other modes that are more commonly used and are highly recommended: videotaping and cofacilitation.

Videotape Supervision

Nichols, Nichols, and Hardy (1990) did a revealing study of how supervision in family therapy changed between 1976 and 1986. In

1976, the most common way of obtaining information was through process notes, used by 40.1 percent of the respondents in the study as their primary method of supervision. In 1986 only 20.1 percent used process notes as their primary method. While the proportion of supervisors relying mainly on this indirect method thus dropped by half, the percentage using live observation as their primary method quadrupled from 6.2 percent in 1976 to 25.7 percent in 1986. While audiotaping as a primary method declined from 28.8 percent in 1976 to 22.4 percent in 1986, videotaping rose from 5.1 percent to 13.7 percent. These findings are consistent with the growing influence of skills-oriented models of supervision (such as Haley's and Minuchin's in family therapy).

If the same study were to be conducted again, the figure for videotape supervision would likely increase even more significantly, given the relatively inexpensive portable video cameras that have come on the market since 1986. Video cameras are increasingly commonplace in professional settings, and videotape supervision (VTS) has become a primary method of supervision, especially in marriage and family counseling (Berger and Dammann 1982; Breunlin and others 1988; Kramer and Reitz 1980; Liddle, Breunlin, and Schwartz 1988; Whiffen and Byng-Hall 1982). It is likely to become the dominant supervisory mechanism in the mental health field.

Videotape supervision is easy, accessible, and relatively inexpensive. It is also a complex tool, the most powerful and dynamic available to supervisors, and one that can be challenging, threatening, anxiety producing, and (as one counselor put it) "humbling." Supervisors need training in how to use VTS effectively: how to maximize its technical capability, minimize its pitfalls, and make it serve the purposes of good supervision. This training is far more than simply learning to turn on the equipment and point the camera.

Early writings on VTS were based on psychodynamic theory (Berger 1978) and emphasized such concerns as internal process, therapist self-awareness, flexibility, and congruence (Kramer and Reitz 1980). In keeping with the blended model, in which these therapeutic dynamics are balanced by the necessities of practical skills training, the following are proposed as the next generation of ideas governing the use of VTS.

1. *Clear goals must be set to determine why, when, and how VTS will be conducted.* Too often supervision consists of watching long, uninterrupted segments of the tape, with little direction or purpose. A 1-hour videotaped session, with segments carefully selected for viewing, will last for hours of supervision if used in the context of a detailed training plan. The therapeutic tasks assigned and the videotapes recorded should be derived from the IDP. Whenever possible, both the supervisee and supervisor should review tape segments for selection prior to the supervision session. Segment numbers read off the counter on the videotape machine will enable the supervisor to home in on the desired segments instead of letting the tape drone on. Brief vignettes relevant to the supervision goals should be selected. The discussion that follows the viewing of the tape needs to be clearly focused.

2. *Interactive processes recorded on tape should be contextualized.* That is, they should be related to the actual counseling session, its goals, and the memories of the session. For example, if a counselor makes a clinical intervention during a session, the context of that intervention should be explored. The supervisor should never take anything the counselor says or does out of context. Thus, the counselor should be asked to comment on the video segment before the supervisor does, to provide a contextual backdrop for the interventions. By taking this precaution, the supervisor will also have an opportunity to assess the counselor's cognitive and conceptual abilities. If the supervisor comments first, the counselor may simply parrot back what he thinks his mentor wants to hear, instead of thinking for himself and expressing his own ideas.

3. *Tape segments should be selected for review because they provide teaching moments, not pretexts for scoring critical points.* Some supervisors sit in supervision with the videotape in one hand and a list of counter numbers in the other, waiting to pounce on every error or shortcoming preserved on the tape. Because videotapes mercilessly expose all mistakes and blemishes, a supervisor must take care to use VTS not as a weapon but as a constructive tool for learning. To keep the focus on constructive teaching, it helps to have the supervisee preselect segments of taped sessions for review. (Of course, the supervisor is still free to review and comment on the rest of the tape.)

4. *The supervisor should provide gradual feedback, not a litany of judgments.* Allow time between segments to discuss and assimilate

issues. "Moderate discrepancies between goals and observations of performance are optimal for learning. If there is no discrepancy, then there is no challenge for learning. Large discrepancies lead to unfavorable self-evaluations, which in turn produce intense therapist discomfort and increase arousal" (Breunlin and others 1988, p. 202).

Some ground rules are necessary for using VTS. First, signed releases must be obtained from patients prior to taping. It is generally recommended that upon admission to the treatment program, the patient be informed that videotaping will occur and asked to sign a release at that time. The release should specify that the tape will be used exclusively for training purposes and will be reviewed only by the counselor, supervisor, and other supervisees in group supervision.

Second, on the day prior to the taping, the counselor should inform the patient(s) that videotaping is planned for the next session. Patients should be given the opportunity to state that they do not wish to have the session taped. A patient who intends to discuss sensitive information at the next session may not want that disclosure to be videotaped. The patient has this prerogative, which counselors and supervisors must respect.

Permission is more likely to be granted if the request is made in a sensitive and appropriate manner. As Edelwich and Brodsky (1992, p. 165) comment in the context of group counseling:

> If the leader says, "They're making me do this, but you don't have to do it if you don't want to," permission may well be denied. The leader stands a much better chance of success by presenting the request in this way: "Hey, I really need this for me. This is just for me and my supervisor to look at, and I really need your help with this." Group members tend to respond positively to such an appeal.

It should be added that "patient resistance" to videotaping is usually a projection of the counselor's resistance.

Finally, risk-management considerations in today's litigious climate necessitate that tapes be erased after the training session(s) for which they are made. Videotapes of counseling sessions are admissible as evidence in court, just like any other clinical record.

It is not enough just to tape over the session with new material. A magnetic tape eraser should be used to ensure that no residue of the previous taping remains. This is not a special liability that attaches to VTS so much as an extension and reminder of the sensitive nature of all clinical records.

VTS offers nearly unlimited potential for the creative imagination:

- A supervisor might run the tape in fast forward to convey a heightened image of the counselor's and client's body movements.
- The supervisor and supervisee might turn down the audio and try to fill in what is being said on the basis of nonverbal cues. Conversely, they might just listen to the audio and try to imagine the participants' expressions and movements.
- The supervisor, while reviewing the tape prior to the supervision session, might do a voice-over, dubbing questions for the supervisee onto the tape.

By allowing for flexible exploration, VTS can greatly enhance the effectiveness and job satisfaction of supervisor and supervisee alike.

Cofacilitation

Cofacilitation, along with the one-way mirror, is one of the live-observation techniques that are supplanting the indirect methods of information gathering previously relied on by supervisors (Nichols, Nichols, and Hardy 1990). It is by far the most commonly used method of observation in the alcoholism and drug abuse field. For the purposes of this book, cofacilitation means having a supervisor sit in on an actual counseling session with the supervisee(s) for the duration of the session. In one-way mirror supervision, the session is observed by the supervisor and perhaps other supervisees, who are not visible to the participants. A videotape may also be used behind the mirror to record the session. This combination of mirror and videotaping may be the best of both worlds; it allows for unobtrusive observation of a session, immediate feedback to other supervisees, and a record of the session to review subsequently in supervision. However, since one-way mirrors are not often available in alcoholism and drug abuse treatment agencies, cofacilitation is the more practical way of achieving the direct observation of counselors emphasized by the blended model.

Even assuming the availability of the one-way mirror, I have found cofacilitation more effective for several reasons. First, it allows the supervisor to get a true understanding of the counselor in action. By experiencing the session, the supervisor can gauge the feelings aroused. Second, cofacilitation gives the supervisor an opportunity to model counseling techniques during an actual session, thus serving as role model for both counselor and clients. Third, should a session become countertherapeutic or destructive to the client, the supervisor can intervene for the well-being of the client. Fourth, counselors often state that they feel supported when a supervisor joins a session. Live supervision is more than supervision; it is teamwork that requires flexibility, role acceptance, and confidence on the part of the supervisor and supervisee.

Cofacilitation also has its disadvantages. First, it is time consuming. With another hour of processing added to each hour of live observation, most supervisors can do no more than 1 or 2 hours of cofacilitation per week, or one session monthly with each counselor in a normal workload. Second, it is obtrusive and alters the dynamics of counseling. Patients may put on their best behavior in the presence of the supervisor. Any form of direct observation provides only a snapshot of a fluid situation; however, if it is done regularly, an accurate picture of a counselor's knowledge and skills eventually will emerge. Third, cofacilitation can be anxiety provoking because, as with videotaping, the counselor has nowhere to hide. Fourth, if the session is not videotaped, there is no record of the session to review later with the counselor. Finally, a supervisor who is not careful to stay in role may usurp the leadership of the session, thereby undercutting the credibility and authority of the counselor.

Taking these factors together, the advantages far outweigh the disadvantages. All of the rules stated for appropriate use of videotaping apply to cofacilitation as well, especially with regard to confidentiality, informing clients of the intended change in procedure and obtaining their prior consent, and making the cofacilitation as unobtrusive as possible. As with videotaping or any other form of direct observation, the client has the prerogative of deciding that cofacilitation would be intrusive, although persistent refusal of permission should be made a therapeutic issue. Here are several guidelines for conducting cofacilitation.

1. *The supervisor should sit in the group or beside the counselor in an individual counseling session.* Sitting outside the circle undermines the human connection between the supervisor and the participants by giving the impression that the supervisor is conducting an inspection. Also, it makes it more awkward for the supervisor to intervene, since the supervisor has not been part of the process until then.

2. *The supervisor should begin the session with a pledge of confidentiality.* It must be made clear that whatever is discussed in the session stays there, except to the extent that it is reviewed by the supervisor and supervisee(s) for training purposes only. No one else will have access to it. At some agencies all clients routinely recite a confidentiality pledge at the beginning of each group session.

3. *As preparation, the supervisor and supervisee should briefly discuss the background of the session, the salient issues in the therapy or group, and plans for the season.* The role of the supervisor should be clearly agreed upon by the counselor(s) and the supervisor prior to the session. Minuchin recommends that the supervisor and supervisee conduct a few practice walkthroughs—scenarios in which the supervisor might intervene. Since supervision demands quick decisions as to when such intervention is needed, prior discussion will make the interventions less of a surprise for both parties. There may be opportunities where, even though the counselor is not in error, the supervisor sees a chance to move the process of training or therapy along by intervening. To the extent that these moments can be anticipated, they should be scripted before the session. For example, a counselor may be doing an excellent job helping a family negotiate a curfew with a teenager when the supervisor hears a remark by a sibling as signaling a significant change of subject, focusing the issue back on the sibling and away from the teenager negotiating the curfew. Should the counselor miss this shift, the supervisor might intervene to reframe the session.

4. *The supervisor should take notes during the session as a means of recalling key issues to be discussed in supervision.* Over the years I have taught myself to take notes inconspicuously, without looking down at the page on which I am writing, so that I can maintain eye

contact with the group. (Of course, afterward, I cannot always read what I have written.)

5. *The supervisor's interventions during the session should be limited to no more than three to four comments.* Otherwise the supervisor risks disrupting the flow of interaction and taking control of the session. There is nothing sacred about the limit of three to four comments; it is simply a guideline that forces the supervisor to be mindful of his role and the problems of exceeding it. Supervisory interventions should occur only when the supervisor sees an opportunity to model a skill for the counselor, when the group is far afield of its goals, or when the session has become countertherapeutic or destructive.

6. *Feedback should be given to the counselor(s) as soon as possible after the session.* This recommendation holds true for all observation techniques, but it is especially important to use the data from a co-facilitated session while it is still fresh in the minds of the supervisor and counselor. Ideally, the supervisor and supervisee should meet privately immediately afterward, outline the key points for discussion, and (if time does not permit having that discussion right then) agree on the agenda for their next supervision session.

7. *If (as is often the case) a group session is led by two counselors, the supervisor should meet with the two supervisees jointly.* Dealing with cotherapists together in supervision avoids triangulation of communication and allows the supervisees to address cocounseling dynamics. The only situations in which it may not be advisable to do so are when one counselor needs individual supervision for serious deficiencies or when there is sufficient conflict between the cotherapists to make joint supervision counterproductive. Although these recommendations regarding cocounseling apply to any form of supervisory observation, they are especially relevant to cofacilitation because of the immediacy of this technique.

8. *Cofacilitation should be used in conjunction with videotaping whenever possible.* This pairing supplements live observation with a record of the session to review in supervision.

One-Way Mirror

The one-way mirror—or, as it has been called, "supervision through the looking glass"—has been used in the training of therapists for many years, especially in the structural and strategic models of family therapy. It is not readily available in most alcoholism and drug abuse agencies, however, perhaps because of the cost of installation, but more likely because its rationale and modus operandi have never been established in the training of substance abuse counselors.

When a mirror is available, other supervisees may be asked to observe a counseling session with a supervisor, either behind the mirror or on a television screen that can reproduce with close-ups and at different angles the view from behind the mirror. When this method of training is employed, it should be made clear to all observers prior to the counseling session that silence behind the mirror is expected, with a limited number of comments between supervisor and supervisees. The observers should take notes and save their talking for the group supervision session that follows.

There are several reasons for this policy. First, when the observers are seated directly behind the mirror (assuming there is no soundproof barrier), silence is necessary to avoid distracting the counselor and client(s). Second, when supervisees talk, they are not observing, even if they are discussing the session observed. Third, if the supervisor is not careful about what is said concerning the observed counselor during the session, such loose talk can turn into an inadvertently destructive form of casual feedback. "The simplest and most innocuous remarks can be repeated to the performing supervisee by the observing supervisees and can be misinterpreted" (Munson 1983, p. 236).

The supervisor must be alert for competition between the observing and observed supervisees. The observed supervisee, anxious under the close scrutiny of peers, may not perform well during the session. It is the supervisor's responsibility to protect the well-being of the observed supervisee. On the other side of the mirror, for a generation of supervisees raised on television and used to today's fast-paced learning media, sitting still and silent (sometimes in cramped, darkened quarters) can be deadening. Some may sit mesmerized and spaced out; others may be swept away by the drama of the session. The supervisor is the drama's director, organizing the action on both sides of the mirror while simultaneously initiating the responses to the counselor and engaging the observing supervisees' attention with apt observations.

Nonetheless, the supervisee, rather than expecting the supervisor to be brilliant and prepossessing, should engage her own imagination and knowledge in the observation process.

One technique I find effective is to do a sociogram of a group counseling session, mapping where the interactions and interchanges occur (Figure 12-1). These maps can provide a graphic portrayal of the communication flow and group dynamics. Arrows from one group member to another indicate an exchange. Hatch marks are used to indicate the number of interactions between group members. An arrow that goes both ways indicates a dialogue between members. If an arrow goes from one member into the center of the group, it indicates a comment to the group as a whole. Gender issues in a group can also be mapped, as the chart reveals when and how men and women interact. Although a sociogram may be prepared in conjunction with videotape or even cofacilitation, it is especially suitable for mirror supervision, where the supervisor has the opportunity and time to draw out the map during the session, filling in the sociogram as the drama unfolds. (See Appendix H for further guidance on using the sociogram.)

Counselors should have the experience of observing live supervision behind the mirror before they themselves are observed in this manner. Since mirror supervision is an evaluation of both the treatment and the counselor, it is essential to establish some degree of comfort before putting the supervisee in front of the mirror. Mirror supervision, when conducted in a sensitive, positive manner, can promote confidence and foster autonomy in the counselor. On the other hand, when the mirror (like videotape) is used to be punitive or overly confrontive, it becomes a destructive weapon. The keys to the effective use of the mirror are the quality of the relationship between supervisor and supervisee(s), the intent of the observation, the skills of the supervisor in using the medium, creativity in using the technique, and the confidence of all parties in the value of observation.

Bug-in-the-Ear and Phone-Ins

A bug-in-the-ear is the use of a transmitter from behind the mirror and an earpiece in the counselor's ear to convey messages from the supervisor regarding the session. A variation is the phone-in,

Figure 12-1. Supervision Sociogram

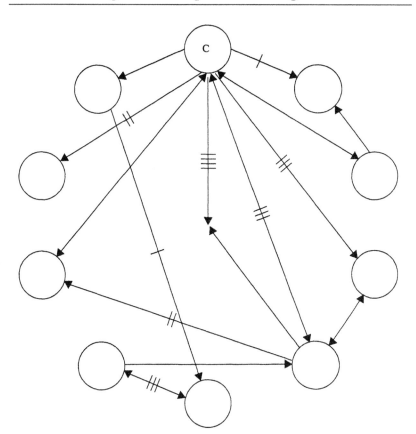

whereby a supervisor sitting behind the mirror calls into the counseling room and gives instructions to the counselor to redirect the
session. These powerful tools are used extensively for the kind of
directive intervention practiced in structural and strategic family
therapy training.

The use of these aids requires planning, training, and practice.
They cannot be used for all cases or all supervision. A careful selection of tools, tailored to the needs of each supervisee, is necessary.
Moreover, when using the bug-in-the-ear or phone-in, the supervisor needs to be aware of its impact on the counselor. If the supervisor is too active and intrusive, the counselor may feel confused,

frustrated, and thrown off course. Here are some counselors' comments about how they have experienced this kind of supervision:

- "I lost my train of thought."
- "It was hard to keep my focus on the client."
- "It's awkward, because the client knows who's calling."
- "One time I got so frustrated that I said, 'Here, you tell *him*,' and handed the phone to the client!"

To reduce distraction, a supervisor should limit the number of interventions, especially when phoning in. When giving prescriptive feedback, the supervisor should skillfully craft the directives, limiting them to "must-do" comments and avoiding the tendency to volunteer interesting but noncritical feedback on the spot. Afterward, the supervisor should solicit feedback from the supervisee about the extent of her involvement during the counseling session.

Given the typical profiles of alcoholism and drug abuse counselors and the practical problems of using these sophisticated tools in work (as opposed to academic) settings, phone-ins and bug-in-the-ear are not encouraged in the blended model of supervision. The technology is usually not available, and relatively few people in this field have had training or experience in the use of these techniques.

SPECIAL SUPERVISORY ENVIRONMENTS

Supervision does not always take the form of a one-to-one exchange between a counselor and a supervisor with greater experience and professional training. Two useful variations that fill out the picture of the supervisory environment are peer supervision and group supervision.

Peer Supervision

Peer supervision, the "poor man's learning environment," is an efficient means of providing feedback to counselors. It is best done in small groups of two to six people, with counselors engaged in individual and/or small-group supervision of one another, using all of the techniques and methods of observation that a master supervisor would use. Despite the absence of the master clinician's depth of experience and learning, this adaptation offers counselors an inexpensive means of growth and input.

Peer supervision is infrequently utilized, and little research has been done to study how—and how well—it works. It is not a substitute for a master's-level supervisor working with a less experienced counselor but a means of supplementing the efforts of overworked supervisors. Some observers have suggested that peer supervision can be harmful, with little quality control to safeguard the welfare of the client. These concerns can be addressed with frequent and intensive peer review, a format that involves observation of one another's work, and proper training of counselors before they take the job.

The key to making peer supervision effective is to structure the training with clear, measurable learning objectives. Counselor self-awareness and self-monitoring should be promoted. For peer supervision to work, a climate of openness and trust must be established among supervisees. Like any other method, peer supervision has limitations. It is not recommended for counselors with significant skill deficiencies or extreme defensiveness. Inexperienced, overzealous staff may seek to impose philosophical conformity in the guise of professional standards. For more skilled staff, peer supervision may not give the counselor the depth of experience and wisdom needed for further professional growth. However, for learning core competencies, such as the twelve core functions of the alcoholism and drug abuse counselor, peer supervision can be an efficient and effective tool.

Peer supervision assumes some degree of equality among the participants, who can then function as colleagues, and is best done by professionals at level 3, either in combination with or in lieu of individual supervision. It is highly rewarding to work with a peer to resolve difficult clinical cases and to find support and challenge from a colleague. Peers in supervision should understand each other's caseloads and clinical dilemmas while contributing different perspectives, interests, and expertise. In peer supervision, all participants are responsible for sharing and discussing issues in a spirit of equality. This mutuality is difficult to achieve in the hierarchical, title-conscious world of work. Peer supervision practiced by true colleagues who can set aside their power and status concerns confers an additional dimension of professionalism on each participant.

Group Supervision

Group clinic supervision is a frequently used format (Holloway and Johnson 1985) and an effective method for exploration, trust building, and personal and interpersonal growth. Group supervision is defined as a format in which a supervisor oversees a trainee's professional development in a group of supervisee peers. The recommended group size is four to six persons, which allows for frequent case presentations by each group member. If the group is much larger and if one clinician presents a case at each session, it will be two to three months between presentations for each counselor, too infrequent to provide consistent growth opportunities. With four to six counselors, each counselor can present a case every other month—an ideal situation, especially when combined with individual supervision sessions.

Group supervision differs from supervision on a one-on-one basis in the same way that group therapy differs from individual therapy. Group supervision involves two or more individuals who see themselves bonded together with a common focus and goals and who are interdependent in pursuit of learning and goal attainment. The supervisor facilitates the development of knowledge and skills and addresses interpersonal dynamics of the supervisees (Holloway and Johnson 1985). In the 1960s and early 1970s, interpersonal process group supervision was prevalent. In the 1990s skills-oriented, case presentation–based approaches are more commonly used. Attention is focused on the case presentation, enriched by didactic material and group dynamics.

There are four goals of group supervision: skills development, personal growth and integration, mastery, and evaluation. Skills development is generally the primary goal of supervision groups, although dynamically oriented supervision groups may also seek intrapsychic and interpersonal insight. Experiential group practices may be used to promote personal growth. The group is an effective method for learning because it is a microcosm of real life

(Edelwich and Brodsky 1992). Group process, as applied to group supervision, facilitates exploration, openness, and responsibility and is an ideal vehicle to promote risk taking (Sansbury 1982).

The benefits of group supervision include the following:

1. It provides a cost-effective way of supervising more people in the same time.
2. It offers each counselor a reality testing of her perceptions through peer validation.
3. Learning is enhanced by the diversity of people in the group. The range of learning opportunities is exponentially expanded by the number of group members (up to the desired limit of four to six members).
4. Group supervision creates a working alliance among counselors that engenders a sense of psychological safety and reduces self-defeating behaviors.
5. Group dynamics and group process facilitate learning by setting up a microcosm of the larger social environment. Each group member's style of interaction will inevitably appear in the group transactions. Given enough time, every person in group supervision will become himself, will interact with the group members as he interacts with others in the social and clinical spheres, and will create in the group the same interpersonal universe he inhabits elsewhere. Through this revelatory process, group members (guided by the supervisor) learn to model acceptable behavior in an accepting group context.
6. Group participation gives counselors a sense of commonality with others in place of isolation and alienation. They find that their worries, fears, frustrations, temptations, and ambivalences, rather than being unique, are shared by others. This awareness is especially beneficial to the level 1 counselor.
7. Group disclosure enhances the potential for self-disclosure and confrontation, thus creating opportunities for growth.
8. Empathy and sharing of interests are available to a greater extent than in individual supervision.
9. If a group works together over time, personal growth on the part of individual members can be reinforced positively by the group.

10. Alternative clinical approaches and methods of helping are available to a far greater extent than a single supervisor can offer. As a result, group members acquire a broader perspective on counseling styles.
11. The potential for critical feedback is greatly expanded.

Although there is little research or writing on group supervision, there is a broad body of theory and practice concerning group therapy, which may be adapted for group supervision as well (Holloway and Johnson 1985; Yalom 1995). The rich body of knowledge available on group theory and group dynamics is applicable to the process of group supervision. It is not necessary, however, to plumb the depths of psychodynamic group therapy to meet the more limited, practical needs of counseling and supervision in the alcoholism and drug abuse field. Edelwich and Brodsky (1992) offer a rigorous but straightforward approach to group process, developed in the substance abuse counseling milieu but applicable to problem solving and decision making in any personal or professional sphere, which relies on modeling and experiential learning rather than didactic education. When even this streamlined, practical version of group process is unworkable (for example, in a group of more than eight or ten members), a more explicitly didactic approach may be called for.

Group supervision should use the energy of the group to foster growth. The group can be therapeutic in spirit even though it does not undertake to do therapy. Individual therapeutic change can occur and can be promoted in a group supervision session. The primary goal is to provide an "intensive group experience, the expression and integration of affect, and the recognition of here-and-now process" (Yalom 1995, p. 527). In group supervision, counselors learn to trust one another as well as their own intuitions and to model behaviors desired in counseling. They learn the presentation of data from their feelings and experience, the appropriate use of self-disclosure, and the boundaries of interaction.

Group supervision encompasses a number of group processes that occur in all types of interactive groups: cohesiveness, a sense of "we-ness," a shared frame of reference, tolerance of diverse opinions, and movement toward common goals. Group norms are established, including mutual expectations and agreed-upon guidelines for acceptable conduct within the group. The task of a supervisor, like any process group leader, is to help the group identify its norms and to model appropriate qualities, behaviors, and skills. Among other things, the supervisor models genuineness, trustworthiness, responsibility, respect and concern for others, empathic responses, and appropriate confrontation and self-disclosure (Edelwich and Brodsky 1992; Hayes 1980). Emotional immediacy establishes an environment in which feelings can be expressed. (How fully they are expressed depends on the model from which the supervisor is working.) Validation of group members' concerns and feedback from each member are essential elements of group supervision. Problem solving is another group function in which active participation of all members is sought. "The full exploration of alternatives by the group is likely to lead to a more effective solution than one offered by single members or even the leader" (Bradley 1989, p. 407).

Leadership skills are explored in group through modeling and simulation exercises. Leadership is exercised not only by the nominal group leader, the supervisor, but by all group members, and encompasses the whole range of their initiatives and responses. Rather than direct the group discussion, the supervisor establishes a climate for exchange and risk taking. The supervisor guides the group process by moving the group through its administrative tasks, facilitating appropriate discussion, and keeping the group focused. She thus models group leadership skills that the counselors can use in their own therapy groups.

Self-disclosure is modeled by both the supervisor and group members. Appropriate self-disclosure entails full respect for supervisees' rights and group norms. Group roles are another essential process in group supervision as supervisees have the opportunity to act out various roles. This can be a powerful learning experience for counselors (Savickas, Marquart, and Supinski 1986; Stenack and Dye 1982).

In agencies with multidisciplinary staffs, supervision groups should be intradisciplinary; if the various professions work together with clients in interdisciplinary teams, supervision groups may reflect that mix of disciplines. Within the counseling profession, the best developmental mix for group supervision includes level 1 and 2 supervisees together with some level 3 staff. Group discussion should address the developmental needs of supervisees.

Sansbury (1982) applies a developmental perspective to group supervision. With level 1 counselors, the group addresses specific interventions, with emphasis on specific case-oriented information, suggestions, and feedback. As the supervisees grow and develop (level 2), the group addresses individual supervisees' affective responses as those feelings pertain to clients. Finally, at the fullest stage of development (level 3), group supervision deals with the group's interactions so as to facilitate supervisee exploration, openness, and responsibility.

Stoltenberg and Delworth (1987) state that the group will determine its own agenda, depending on the developmental levels of the supervisees. Generally, level 1 group supervision sessions are more structured; level 2 groups, given a minimum threshold of trust and openness, focus on affective responses and the fluctuating motivations of supervisees. Level 3 supervisees are more likely to exchange ideas about client conceptualizations and interventions.

The primary difficulty with group supervision from a developmental perspective is how to meet the different needs of each supervisee. A mixture of the three approaches identified by Sansbury seems appropriate unless all of the supervisees are functioning at the same developmental level (an unlikely scenario in most agencies). When a range of approaches is used in group supervision, supervisees are given a more rounded and complete understanding of group process, one that allows for peer supervision and support to occur.

Group supervision has come to be recognized as an efficient and effective means of providing supervision and a unique and special opportunity for counselor development and learning. Further study is needed, however, on the use of group supervision methods in both teaching settings and service agencies, so that the field will not simply be extracting issues from group therapy and applying them on faith to group supervisory experiences.

An interesting adaptation of the traditional group supervision model has evolved from the proliferation of therapeutic teams in the family therapy field (Cade, Speed, and Seligman 1986). In these teams, three or four therapists regularly work together, often with more disturbed and difficult individuals and families. One or two therapists work in the therapy room while the other team members observe from behind the one-way mirror. A variety of intervention techniques is used. Advice is given either by telephone or by calling the therapist out of the room. This model, which builds on both peer and group supervision, can be called a peer team approach to supervision.

CASE PRESENTATIONS

An important but little discussed aspect of supervision is case presentation methodology. Both direct and indirect methods of observation are predicated on the ability of the counselor to review pertinent case information with the supervisor and other supervisees. A prescribed format for case presentations is recommended. One of my most valuable learning experiences early in my career was that of presenting at rounds before a critical, demanding supervisor who insisted that cases be presented exactly as he directed. The discipline he taught the counselors lives on in my clinical practice long afterward.

The case presentation format should be built around problem- and solution-oriented questions to be answered and should move from client information to dynamics, prognosis, and treatment plan. There are many stock presentation formats that can be used for guidance (see Appendix I for a sample form). Still, it is best for each agency to design its own format based on its unique reporting and administrative requirements and teaching methods. Counselors should be instructed on how to follow this format.

Supervisors should be alert for several common distractions that can undermine the case presentation procedure:

1. Too many presentations in too short a time frame.
2. Focusing on a specific problem instead of giving a case overview.
3. Anecdotal material that is not conceptualized by the counselor.
4. Supervisee dynamics that interfere with free and open discussion of the case.
5. Expectations for interventions beyond the capabilities of the counselor.

The second and third of these hazards are addressed in the discussion below on case conceptualization.

Counselor anxiety about presenting a case can also be distracting. This anxiety can be reduced by having the supervisor present a case first, allowing the supervisee time to prepare for the presentation, and giving the supervisee a prescribed, written format to follow. If the format is clear, organized, and focused, it will help to lessen supervisee anxiety about the case presentation procedure.

CASE CONCEPTUALIZATION

In the blended model of supervision for the alcoholism and drug abuse field, the principal tasks of the supervisor are to observe the counselor's actions, determine their impact on the client, assess the counselor's clinical reasoning process, and help the counselor improve treatment delivery (Mead 1990; Wetchler, Piercy, and Sprenkle 1989). How does the counselor decide how to act toward clients? What affective, behavioral, and cognitive responses does the counselor attend to, and why? What is the counselor's clinical reasoning concerning the client-counselor interaction? What inferences and hypotheses has the counselor formed about a case, and how are his interventions tied to this conceptualization? At a broader level, how does the counselor deal with internal inconsistencies in his own behavior? How is this behavior related to his personal theoretical model? How is it integrated into his personal style?

Case presentation offers one of the main opportunities to make these assessments of the counselor's clinical thinking and overall clinical personality. Clinical reasoning skills will be demonstrated in a case presentation, since the counselor must reason out what the issues are in order to present a case. The substance abuse field has not given adequate attention in supervision to the conceptual and clinical reasoning skills of the supervisee. This may be due, in part, to the nonacademic orientations of the field's early clinicians. Yet this is an area where supervisory guidance is crucial. Entry-level counselors tend to give heavily anecdotal case presentations ("He said . . . ; I said . . ."). They have difficulty abstracting the underlying issues from this specific content. Their intuitive responses are often sound, but they do not know how to build from their insights a specific, well-elaborated, and well-documented conceptualization of the case. An essential task of supervision, therefore, is to teach counselors the skill of turning unorganized data into themes and concepts. This conceptualization process links assessment, diagnosis, treatment planning, and intervention. It translates psychosocial information into treatment goals, which generate specific therapeutic actions.

According to the definition given in Chapter Two, clinical supervision is a process whereby principles are transformed into practical skills. Case conceptualization is perhaps the quintessential example of this aspect of supervision. The supervisor is giving counselors concepts and principles on which to hang their intuitive responses and practical skills. The literature on counseling and supervision offers little in the way of codified knowledge about this sensitive learning process, although Loganbill and Stoltenberg's (1983) case conceptualization format is a useful tool for supervisors. It is an evolving, somewhat ad hoc process, an ebb and flow of action and reflection. In developing a clinical repertoire, the counselor moves back and forth between the practical plane of trial and error and the conceptual plane of organizing hypotheses and interpreting feedback. It is on the latter plane that the supervisor steps in, offering general principles that make sense of particular outcomes.

ROLE PLAYING, ROLE MODELING, AND DEMONSTRATION

Three additional teaching techniques in supervision are role playing, role modeling, and demonstration. These techniques add to the supervisor's flexibility and confidence in handling a diverse mix of counselors and situations, with the effect of increasing the value of supervisory training for supervisees.

Role Playing

Role playing is the acting out of parts in an unrehearsed drama. It is an alternative to observing a clinician in an actual counseling session. A role play may be overt—all participants know all the information and instructions—or covert—some information is withheld from some participants. The situation dramatized may be contrived or simulate an actual client and counseling situation.

Role playing is ideal for practicing skills. It is the teaching method of choice when the supervisor wants to simulate real-life situations while retaining control over the drama and avoiding intruding into an actual counseling session that may prove volatile, unpredictable, and therefore unsatisfactory as a learning environment. Role playing would be appropriate, for example, if an inexperienced counselor needed assistance in working with a client newly referred by an employee assistance program. Since it would be intrusive to use a direct method of observation such as cofacilitation with a new client, the supervisor might set up a simulated session for the counselor.

Role playing provides an opportunity to learn by doing, to practice behavior in a safe environment, and to receive helpful feedback on skills that are usually practiced behind closed doors. It also enables nonparticipants to learn by observation. It is, however, a high-risk technique for supervisors and counselors because it requires active participation and is somewhat unpredictable. Like other methods of observation, it may heighten fear, anxiety, and a preoccupation with "doing it right." It may generate hostility and decrease trust between supervisor and counselors. Boundaries must be monitored carefully, since people may unconsciously select roles that allow them to act out their own issues. The emotional intensity of the role play may then spill over into the participants' interactions in "real life." On more than one occasion I have seen counselors show personal hostility toward one of their peers following a role play in which that person had simulated an aggressive, abusive client.

To fulfill its purpose, role playing requires a clear and realistic scenario, reflecting as closely as possible the types of situations counselors will come across in their work. A counselor may act out either the client or counselor role. Processing a role play—debriefing the participants afterward to get them out of role—is a vital component of the technique. The first steps are to elicit the participants' feelings and reactions to the experience, so as to reduce the emotional energy that has been generated, and to give feedback on alternative behaviors. It is useful to end the role play with a summary statement of the concepts learned from it.

Role Modeling

Role modeling means learning by watching an expert perform the task to be learned. Although there is no immediate opportunity to practice the skill as demonstrated, the counselor can draw on the role-modeling experience later. Learning is reinforced if the counselor and supervisor discuss the skills in question immediately after the expert has modeled them. Role modeling can also be done on tape, thus allowing for immediate feedback and discussion among viewers.

Role modeling is the teaching method of choice when a skill can better be illustrated by seeing an expert performing it than by reading or talking about it. The advantages of role modeling are that many counselors can observe a model simultaneously; they can see how experts practice the skill and imitate the role model at a later time, especially if the learning experience has been reinforced by a discussion. The disadvantages are that it is a passive learning experience and that counselors often do not have an immediate opportunity to practice the skill.

The components of a successful role-modeling experience include an expert role model, a clear understanding of the purpose of the experience, and a follow-up discussion led by the supervisor or expert. A good role-modeling experience requires advance preparation on the part of both supervisor and counselors, who should discuss what they will be looking for. Videotaping should be arranged if possible.

Demonstration

Demonstration, a presentation by an expert that displays and explains a procedure, followed by opportunities to discuss and practice the skills, is the teaching method of choice when the supervisor wants to teach new skills and procedures that are observable. It is important that the number of learners be kept small, so as to provide individualized supervision when they are practicing the skill.

A demonstration is an active learning experience that combines the explanatory value of a lecture with hands-on practice in a safe environment, and it offers immediate feedback from an expert. It can be used with only a small number of learners at a time and can be costly and time consuming.

A good demonstration presents an observable procedure; provides a clear, organized, step-by-step explanation of the procedure; uses real-life situations; and provides a safe, comfortable environment for learning. Like role playing or role modeling, a good demonstration requires advance preparation, including a knowledge of the learners' skills, a clear purpose for the demonstration, and an outline detailing each step. Afterward, each participant should be given an opportunity to practice the skill followed by feedback on her proficiency.

FEEDBACK AND INTERVENTION

After reviewing the counselor's clinical reasoning process, the supervisor gives the counselor feedback concerning his learning needs. *Feedback* here means responding—in whatever way the supervisor chooses—to the data presented. Unlike a quarterly or semiannual performance review, this day-to-day feedback is not primarily evaluative; rather, it is supportive and pragmatic, designed to bring about a positive change in the professional life of the counselor.

Supervisors often mistakenly think they are not doing their job unless they say something critical at every session. That is counterproductive. Although there are times to be critical, the skillful, experienced supervisor is more concerned to provide ongoing encouragement and coaching, so as to help the counselor find his own path through any difficulties. In formulating feedback, the supervisor asks, "How can I help this counselor change so that he can better help these clients?"

The supervisor must work to make the counselor self-observing, self-correcting, self-reinforcing, and self-soothing. Toward those ends, the supervisor should challenge rather than confront as much as possible, stimulating the counselor to discover the discrepancies between what he is doing and what he wants to achieve. The supervisor should challenge the counselor to review his therapy goals and how he intends to attain those goals. Mead (1990), drawing upon Borders and Leddick (1987), suggests that "effective challenges (a) are tentative, such as 'Could it be that . . .'; (b) include expressions of care and respect; (c) are tied to reinforcement for steps which have already been successfully accomplished; and (d) are specific and concrete behaviors and are controlling variables, rather than therapist traits" (p. 113).

In determining the threshold for supervisory intervention, the key issue is to safeguard the welfare of the clients. Mead (1990, p. 114) provides a framework for deciding when and how decisively to intervene:

> To perform a supervision triage the supervisor places the therapist's erroneous treatment delivery or reciprocal acts into one of three categories: 1) those therapist behaviors that require immediate intervention—by the supervisor with the therapist—for the welfare of the client; 2) those therapist behaviors that require supervisory intervention with the therapist but that have a low probability of doing harm to the clients unless repeated or continued over several sessions; and 3) those therapist behaviors that could use supervisory intervention to tune up some theoretical or technical point but that will not lead to any foreseeable harm to the clients.

Immediate intervention is dictated when the supervisor's ethical and legal responsibilities come into play.

The gradations of response Mead outlines are encompassed by five types of supervisory intervention that cover most of the variations of tone and content used by supervisors in giving feedback to counselors.

1. *Facilitative.* Using client-centered models, a supervisor facilitates discussion by asking nondirective questions, such as, "How do you feel about that comment?" "What did you see happening at that moment?" "Tell me more about that response." "How did you feel about the way the session went?" Facilitative responses move the discussion along without providing direction or confrontation. They are nonthreatening and probably represent the most common type of supervisory response.

2. *Confrontive.* Confrontive responses by the supervisor address a specific action or behavior on the part of the counselor and

require the counselor to answer a question about it—for example, "I saw this going on in the session. Did you notice it? If not, what got in your way?" Another example is, "Why did you say that? It did not seem to work. I know you are aware of group dynamics, so why did you make that response?" Confrontive responses can be given in a supportive and helpful manner or can put the counselor on the defensive.

3. *Conceptual.* A conceptual response contributes new information and a different way of visualizing the case—for example, "There seems to be some transference going on in this session. Let's talk about how transference affects the session." In group counseling, a conceptual response might sound like this: "If you recall from Yalom, this group appears to be at an early stage of development. Let's review early-stage issues and how you can get past this impasse." Conceptual responses are educational and instructional.

4. *Prescriptive.* Prescriptive responses, heard most frequently in skills-oriented models of supervision, direct (or strongly encourage) the counselor to respond in a particular manner the next time a certain set of circumstances occurs. A supervisor who is responding prescriptively might say, "The next time the client says this, I want you to respond in this manner, to say that . . ." Prescriptive responses are most often associated with bug-in-the-ear and phone-in supervision, with the supervisor using the immediacy of the medium to redirect the counseling session.

5. *Catalytic.* A catalytic response moves the process along by asking provocative or what-if questions—for example, "Do you think this session might have gone differently if you had said this?" "If you made this one change in your procedure, what do you think might happen?" "What if you got up and changed chairs?" With a catalytic response, the supervisor provokes the counselor to take a different perspective or adopt a different paradigm. Whereas prescriptive responses might be most helpful for level 1 counselors, level 3 counselors can benefit greatly from catalytic remarks, which promote self-exploration, conceptualization, and more inclusive integration of methods.

With experience, a skillful supervisor masters all five types of response, using each when appropriate. The blended model of supervision calls for an evenly balanced repertoire of responses, with any of the five types available depending on the needs of the counselor at the time. Overuse of any one response will limit the richness of the supervisory process.

THE CONTENT OF SUPERVISION

Now that the contexts and processes of supervision have been established, the content of supervision can be considered. What do the supervisor and supervisee talk about? What skills, procedures, and potential problems are monitored and processed? The content of supervision will, of course, vary depending on the discipline and developmental stage of the supervisee, setting variables, and client characteristics. Nonetheless, several main themes or content areas of supervision can be identified.

The Twelve Core Functions

The alcoholism and drug abuse field's twelve core functions constitute a general framework of areas in which a counselor should be proficient. These areas are:

- Screening
- Intake
- Orientation
- Assessment
- Counseling (individual, family, and group)
- Case management
- Treatment planning
- Consultation
- Crisis intervention
- Client education
- Referral
- Report and record keeping

These basic requirements undoubtedly will be expanded in the coming years. Areas of competence that may be added include professional ethics, supervision, dual diagnosis, incest, codependency, addictions other than alcohol and drugs (for example, sexual addiction), and working with incarcerated and HIV-positive individuals.

Whatever expanded list of core functions is adopted, it is clear that more will be demanded of counselors in the alcoholism and drug abuse field.

Affective Qualities

Clinical supervision is also concerned with the affective qualities a counselor should possess. These qualities include the following:

- Empathy
- Unconditional positive regard
- Genuineness
- Respect

- Potency (ability to serve as a catalytic agent for change)
- Immediacy
- Concreteness
- Congruence

Generally, alcoholism and drug abuse counselors show good affective qualities from the outset, even before they gain experience and professional training. Although not everyone necessarily comes by these qualities naturally, people can be trained to manifest them in a professional context.

Helping Skills

Superimposed on the counselor's affective qualities are a set of more focused and directed helping skills (NIAAA 1978). These tools of the trade, which are more obviously acquired through training than are the affective qualities, are typically broken down into eight categories:

- Attending
- Paraphrasing
- Probing
- Reflection of feelings

- Summarizing
- Confrontation
- Self-disclosure
- Interpreting

Substance abuse counselors usually are good at attending (listening closely and respectfully) and paraphrasing. However, entry-level counselors may need to work on some of the more sophisticated skills. They often engage in inappropriate confrontation and self-disclosure. When it comes to probing they tend to get in over their heads because they do not have a clear enough idea of what to ask.

Other subjects that fall within the scope of clinical supervision include communication skills, significant transitions in the counseling process (eye contact, speech patterns, signs of resistance or openness), client thought processes such as denial and perseveration, latent content and unconscious material (at least in some therapeutic models), ways of expressing and dealing with anxiety (humor, game playing, seduction), client motivators, differential diagnosis, and termination. Detailed discussions of these processes can be found in the literature on counseling and therapy.

Transference and Countertransference

A major focus of discussion in supervision is transference and countertransference. Transference is defined as an irrational attitude manifested by a patient toward the counselor or others in a way that is not evoked by the realities of the present but is instead derived from the patient's relationship with someone else (past or present). The patient may see the counselor as a parent, a spouse, a sibling, a friend, or a competitor; as an authority figure, a withholding figure, or a sexual figure. Countertransference, the mirror image of transference, is the counselor's tendency to project similarly unresolved issues onto the patient. Transference and countertransference may occur isomorphically in supervision, where issues parallel to those in the counseling relationship may be acted out.

Transference occurs in most relationships and may be provoked by the most incidental and innocuous aspect of a person's appearance or demeanor, let alone the highly charged dynamics of the counseling situation. Issues of transference and countertransference should be dealt with routinely in supervision in terms of their impact on the counseling process. In the blended model, however, the supervisor does not enter into a therapeutic dialogue with the counselor about the origins of the transferential issues between counselor and supervisor.

Supervision should stimulate counselors' awareness of the transferential reactions that may arise even from the way they choose to decorate their offices. For example, the credentials on the wall project an image of competence and expertise, one that may touch off personal reactions in some clients. What messages are conveyed to a client when a therapist displays a picture of a spouse and children in the office? How does a gay client relate to these images? a single client who has never had children? a client whose early life experiences contrast painfully with the idealized happy family shown in the photograph? How does the counselor dress? What message does a beard convey? How do age and gender affect transference?

There is no prescription for personal appearance or office decor that comes out of these questions. Surely it is advisable not to flaunt one's life-style (heterosexual or homosexual, single or married) in front of clients, and cultural sensitivity in a counselor's or agency's self-presentation is recommended. In one agency that frequently had Vietnam veterans among its clients, the staff put up a picture of the Vietnam Memorial in Washington. When this gesture proved more distracting than alliance building, the staff took the picture down. Nonetheless, unpredictable transference reactions will occur in any case, and the supervisor's aim should be to have counselors consider these dynamics and use them to therapeutic advantage.

The quintessential example of transference from my practice occurred when a woman whom I had been counseling for six months came in and announced that she had been having sexual fantasies about me. She said that if we did not have sex right then and there, on the floor of the office that evening (the evening sessions may have contributed to stimulating the transference), she would kill herself. I resolved this issue by having her recall and relate her sexual fantasies as vividly as she wanted (which was quite vividly) while I wrote them down as she stated them. At the end of the session, I handed her the piece of paper on which I had been writing and told her, "You can have your fantasies back now and do with them whatever you desire." It worked. She was able to deal with her sexual issues without having to feel mentally exposed.

Experienced supervisors are accustomed to helping counselors deal with the transferential feelings of clients. Countertransference can be a more difficult problem, for the counselor's feelings toward clients may stem from longstanding intrapsychic issues, which in the blended model are not to be addressed in supervision. For example, a counselor had a strong emotional reaction to a female alcoholic client who was the same age as the counselor's mother had been when she died of alcoholism. It is appropriate to acknowledge and briefly process such a reaction in supervision as long as the counselor can then relate to the client therapeutically. If deep-seated intrapsychic issues emerge from such a countertransferential reaction, the counselor should be referred to an external therapist.

Not all emotional reactions to clients are countertransferential, and not all countertransferential reactions are harmful. There are times when revulsion from a client's behavior is simply an expression of normal human values and standards. No matter how much training and experience I have, I will still have strong reactions to the behavior of child sexual abusers. There is no reason to be uncomfortable with such normal personal reactions as long as they do not get in the way of discharging professional responsibilities toward the client (Edelwich and Brodsky 1991). Even from a therapeutic point of view, there are times when it is appropriate to be angry at a client—by saying, for example, "What you're doing is really unacceptable. I can't approve of this kind of behavior."

The key to maintaining effectiveness is to separate the client's issues from the counselor's. The counselor, with the supervisor's assistance, needs to differentiate between healthy personal or therapeutic responses to clients and unhealthy responses arising from the counselor's own unresolved conflicts. Moreover, feelings (countertransferential as well as transferential) are an indispensable therapeutic instrument. If the counselor feels alone and alienated when talking with a client, what does that say about the client's social relationships? If the counselor feels angry, offended, or sexually stimulated in a client's presence, does that give a clue to the emotional tone of the client's interactions with people and to the reactions the client typically engenders in others?

Physical Contact and Sexual Misconduct

Physical contact in counseling is a special supervisory concern in the alcoholism and drug abuse field. One study found that 59 percent of all counselors engage in hugging, kissing, and affectionate touch with their clients. The substance abuse field in particular is very touch oriented. Group counseling sessions routinely end in embraces, with the group members standing around the room, arm in arm, saying the serenity prayer. What is the effect of this ritual on the gay client or on the incest survivor who feels forced by peer pressure to do something that may feel intensely uncomfortable? Once past the clear principle that it is unethical for a clinician to have sexual relations with a client, the boundaries between appropriate and inappropriate behavior begin to blur.

To clarify the boundaries, I have found two simple guidelines helpful. First, physical contact with a client is justified only if it is therapeutically supportive. As Silverstein (1977) aptly puts it, when a counselor touches *every* client—male and female, young and old, gay and straight, attractive and unattractive—in the same way, he will know that the touching is therapeutic rather than self-gratifying. A counselor who differentiates between clients on the basis of any of these factors should question in supervision how his own needs may be compromising the therapeutic value of the touching. Second, nothing is to be done in private that cannot be done in public. If a counselor is uncomfortable touching a client in the hallway or with the office door open, she should question what meaning the touch has for her that would cause her to be embarrassed to be observed by a colleague. The supervisor's role is to see that these questions are actively engaged rather than evaded in an atmosphere of indulgence. A supervisor must be ready to ask, "Why did you hug that patient? What did it mean to you?"

How can a supervisor monitor counselors' countertransference feelings and, if possible, prevent those feelings from being acted out in damaging or unethical ways? In this crucial dimension of quality control, risk management, and good clinical care, four tools of the trade are indispensable:

1. Close supervision to maintain reasonable oversight and vigilance, especially when there is reason to suspect misconduct or countertherapeutic activity.
2. Thorough, high-quality training of personnel to resolve potential countertransference issues as fully as possible before the counselor assumes responsibility for client care.

3. A limited intake questionnaire to minimize opportunities for counselor voyeurism and exploitation. (The basic rule of thumb is, "Do not ask the client the question unless you are going to deal with it in counseling." Of course, a full psychosocial intake may be required, with questions about incest and sexual adjustment, even if the treatment program will not deal with these issues directly. However, the supervisor must monitor the intake process for possible abuses.)
4. Heightened counselor self-awareness gained prior to training, while in training, and through ongoing clinical supervision.

Detailed guidelines and case examples covering the range of issues growing out of client-counselor sexual dynamics are found in Edelwich and Brodsky (1991). In their analysis, overt sexual misconduct is the visible culmination of a long progression of unspoken vulnerabilities, incitements, opportunities, and escalating boundary violations (see also Strasburger, Jorgenson, and Sutherland 1992). Although most clinicians do not act out sexually with clients, their discomfort with sexualized transference and countertransference can impair their effectiveness and increase job stress. Edelwich and Brodsky show how counselors can validate their personal feelings toward clients without compromising professional or ethical standards. They also outline the professional sanctions, civil liabilities, and (in some states) criminal prosecutions that individuals and agencies may incur as a result of sexual misconduct by therapists, and they explore the evolving ethical and legal debate over boundary issues such as sexual relationships with former clients.

Ultimately, the content of supervision is to be derived from an accurate and thorough needs assessment of each counselor's knowledge and skills, her developmental stage and career goals, and the needs of the agency and clients. The individual development plan forms the basis for the content of supervision.

| **Evaluation and Feedback**

One focus of the definition of clinical supervision in the blended model is evaluation of the counselor's knowledge and skills. The supervisor must regularly determine the counselor's progress in meeting the objectives set forth in the individual development plan. This assessment is part of a broader evaluation of the counselor's suitability for the field and professional potential.

Evaluation is often uncomfortable for both supervisor and counselor. Most supervisors have had little or no training in personnel performance appraisal or in giving critical feedback to staff. Moreover, the unconditional positive regard that therapists are supposed to have for clients can get in the way of giving negative feedback. These reactions must be overcome, since accurate assessment of the counselor is essential if the supervisor is to provide the appropriate environment for growth and learning. Therefore, it is necessary to have a standardized, objective format for evaluation and feedback.

Supervision is an inherently evaluative process (Loganbill, Hardy, and Delworth 1982) that nonetheless builds on a collaborative relationship between counselor and supervisor. Ongoing feedback is an essential part of that relationship. In addition to the nonevaluative (supportive and corrective) feedback described in the previous chapter, there is also evaluative feedback. A climate conducive to such feedback should be established at the outset of supervision, with the supervisor stating the purpose of the assessment and the methods of evaluation. Feedback should be presented in a nonthreatening manner. Supervisors must realize, too, that an assessment of a counselor is also an indirect assessment of how well the supervisor has selected and trained staff members. Therefore, forms for supervisor as well as counselor evaluation and self-evaluation are provided in the appendixes.

The corporate or agency culture will determine how feedback is viewed by supervisor and supervisee. Feedback need not have a negative connotation. Even in its evaluative function, it should not be construed primarily as a statement of what was done rightly or wrongly. Rather, it is a skills-building process, emphasizing growth and development. Assessment is an integral aspect of the movement of a counselor from skill to skill, toward a desired end state of competency. "One does not accuse a child of inadequacy because he or she is not yet an adult" (Stoltenberg and Delworth 1987, p. 123). One's stage of development is a reflection of time more than of inadequacy or incompetence.

DETERMINING SKILL LEVELS

The developmental approach to supervision provides a valuable framework for determining counselors' knowledge and skills at each stage of their growth and development. The following rules can guide supervisors in assessing the developmental levels of counselors:

1. A supervisor should not assume a developmental level based on the counselor's experience and training. Although experience and training do contribute to skill development, they do not reliably indicate skill levels. Experience is at best a crude measurement of a counselor's development (McNeill, Stoltenberg, and Pierce 1985).
2. A supervisor should not assess counselors simply on the basis of initial impressions. Clinical impressions, sound as they may be, are not infallible. Objective measurements provide a necessary corrective.
3. A supervisor should not determine developmental levels simply on the basis of performance in one or two domains. A counselor may be excellent in intake or assessment, but that does not necessarily mean that he or she is proficient in all domains. Counselors must be assessed in all core functions, domains, and structures.

Several sources of information are available concerning a counselor's level of development: assessments by former supervisors, measurements administered by the current supervisor, counselor self-assessments, client ratings, and work samples. Used in isolation, none of these instruments is sufficient. In combination, they give the supervisor a reliable and well-rounded picture of the counselor's development.

Former Supervisor Assessments

In academic settings, supervisors may utilize the assessments of previous academic supervisors. In service agencies, however, these prior assessments generally are not accessible, given the constraints on information dissemination and the confidentiality of work records. Furthermore, this second-hand information may be biased, incomplete, or irrelevant to a different work setting. A former supervisor's judgments may be misleading insofar as they are based on a therapeutic model or programmatic structure different from that found in the current setting. Therefore, second-hand reports on clinical development are not particularly reliable for the next supervisor except as a baseline for future assessments and a reflection point to review with the supervisee. They are most useful as a teaching and learning tool when used in conjunction with current supervisory impressions.

Competency Assessments

The primary mode of evaluation on which supervisors must rely is behavioral observation. More objective criteria, such as time spent with clients, client retention, and client outcomes, have some limited value in pinpointing issues for resolution, but because they are subject to many contextual influences, they are crude, inaccurate indicators of counselors' skill levels. There is no substitute, then, for watching the counselor in action. Although behavioral assessments are still subjective, one can stand on one's own (as opposed to a former supervisor's) observations. Moreover, the fact that behavioral observations are subjective does not mean they are not classifiable or measurable. As used in supervision, behavioral observations entail the classification of discrete behaviors into categories or, in the case of the alcoholism and drug abuse counselor, core competencies. A number of preexisting categorization schemes are available for use by supervisors (Amidon 1965; Blumberg 1970; Carkhuff 1969; Flanders 1970; Hill 1965; Holloway 1982; Holloway and Wampold 1983; Ivey 1971).

These classifications all have problems inherent in subjective observations. In one way or another, all are incomplete. Some measure the frequency of clinical responses; some observe only verbal responses, leaving out nonverbal cues; some are biased toward a primary model of counseling. Most are time consuming to implement and must be adapted to the treatment setting and training model of the supervisor. The behaviors they measure must be observed and observable. Finally, all rely primarily on behavioral observation by a supervisor. Technology such as interactive computer-based training (CBT) may aid in shortening the observation time or in the coding and analysis of observed behaviors. The substance abuse field is held back from adopting this technology only by time constraints, limited financial resources for developing these systems, and the Luddite ("technopeasant") attitudes of clinicians and supervisors who feel threatened and intimidated by high-tech tools.

Whatever the mode of observation (videotape, one-way mirror, sitting in, bug-in-the-ear, phone-in), a supervisor's observing a session changes the flow of it. A supervisor is simply getting a snapshot of a counselor in action on a particular day, a snapshot distorted by the counselor's and client's need to perform for the supervisor: counselors want to perform well for the boss, and clients want their counselor to look good (or bad, depending on the nature of the transference). What the supervisor sees, therefore, is an aberration from or (at best) approximation of the counseling process. Given this limitation, it is still a useful snapshot. Moreover, this observation bias can in part be overcome by observing so frequently and from so many angles that there are enough snapshots together to form a more complete picture of the counselor.

Counselor Self-Assessments

Self-assessments, predicated on the assumption that counselors have insight into their own behavior, are a useful tool in evaluating counselors' knowledge and skills. However, such self-measurements must be interpreted in the light of the degree of insight and functioning of the counselor in all three domains, given the counselor's stage of development. Level 1 and 2 counselors, who lack thoroughgoing self-awareness, may be limited in their ability to measure their own performance. Supervisors must take such self-measurements not as an accurate, objective measure of counselors' clinical skills but as a statement about counselors' perceptions and feelings, especially their anxiety levels. These data contribute a valuable piece to the assessment puzzle as long as they are used in combination with other modes of evaluation.

As with supervisory assessment, standard instruments have been developed for supervisee self-measurement (Friedlander and Ward 1984; Heppner and Roehlke, 1984; McNeill, Stoltenberg, and Pierce 1985; Reising and Daniels 1983; Stoltenberg, Pierce, and McNeill 1987; Worthington 1984; Zucker and Worthington 1986). These instruments must be adapted to fit a particular treatment setting, model of counseling, and client population.

Perhaps the largest biasing factor to be taken into account in interpreting counselor self-reports is supervisee anxiety, which generates irrational thoughts about one's competence. For counselor assessments to have maximum utility for both evaluative and remedial purposes, the sources of the anxiety must be addressed.

Client Assessments

Client assessments of counseling services are another source of input for a supervisor. They elicit the client's level of satisfaction, which may be expressed in terms of perceptions of the counselor. More than likely, they reflect the client's opinion about how effective or how agreeable the therapy has been. If, for example, the client does not like the confrontive approach of the agency or the counselor, this dislike will find its way into the assessment form. But if the client has been able to hide out for the duration of the group sessions, this "positive outcome" may condition the assessment.

My personal experience leads me to take a guarded view of the reliability of client assessments. There have been days when I felt

I did a terrible job, only to have the client come back the next week and rave about the session. On other occasions, when I have been appropriately confrontive, the client will have hated that session. Thus, client assessments are as much a reflection of how the client feels on a particular day as of the counselor's competence.

Nonetheless, as part of a comprehensive approach to counselor evaluation, client assessments fill out one more piece of the puzzle. Instruments designed for this purpose must, of course, be tailored to the settings and situations in which they are used, including the clients' presenting problems.

Work Samples

Work samples—such as treatment plans, process notes, reports, verbatims, progress notes, written and oral conceptualizations, and aftercare plans—are pictures of the counselor's work. Written statements may be as much a reflection of writing skills as of conceptual skills. It is necessary to separate a counselor's ability to write and to verbalize from the ability to counsel.

Summary

Counselor assessment is an ongoing process requiring frequent observation and feedback. Evaluative information must be derived from many sources, situations, and angles of perception and counselors assessed across all domains and structures. A combination of objective and subjective instruments should be used, and these should be quantified as much as possible. Specific forms for assessment should be developed by each agency, addressing the core competencies unique to that facility.

The ambiguities of counselor assessment reflect the state of the art of evaluation, which has not found ways to quantify and measure counseling skills in all situations and with all kinds of clients. The mechanisms of evaluation yield only approximations of the counselor's skills. Therefore, the evaluative role of the supervisor remains critical. The supervisor must synthesize information derived from observation of clinical performance; review of work samples; input (as appropriate) from the counselor, clients, and former supervisors; and a sound job performance appraisal system. As with other tasks requiring human judgment, advances in technology, however useful in streamlining the mechanical components of decision making, will never remove the essential element of subjectivity.

When the appraisal is completed, the supervisor's job has just begun. The supervisor must now be able to communicate this appraisal to the counselor and work with the counselor to improve performance. If the assessment process seems difficult, that of conveying the necessary feedback is even more complex, requiring the artistry of a skilled supervisor.

DEALING WITH ANXIETY

The first step in this delicate communication is to acknowledge and confront the endemic anxiety (on both sides) that threatens this phase of the supervisor-supervisee relationship. The necessity for evaluation challenges the relationship because it accentuates the different roles of the supervisor and supervisee, increases the social distance between them, demands the exercise of authority, and may lead to the expression of negative judgments and negative feelings. In this highly charged atmosphere, the supervisor struggles with the necessity of making subjective appraisals and the difficulty of finding meaningful, personal language in which to express these appraisals.

Supervisor Anxiety

People usually do not go into the counseling profession because they want to evaluate others critically; rather, they want to be warm, empathic helpers. When they become supervisors, they typically are uncomfortable in the evaluative role, for which they have little or no training. "I've never supervised anyone before!" they may complain. This can be a disruptive issue for level 1 supervisors, who may have difficulty shifting gears into their new role and may experience stress in reviewing the work of former peers (Hart 1982; Hess 1986). They may fear being found incompetent in their new role, and this fear of evaluation may intensify the conflict they feel about evaluating others. In addition, they may realize that a negative evaluation of a counselor implicitly calls into question their own adequacy as a supervisor.

A supervisor may manifest this anxiety by being overly supportive or overly distant, inappropriately confrontive or hesitant to confront. Anxiety may also be expressed in a demanding, rigid attitude toward counselors. The supervisor may set unrealistic goals and expectations for staff. Even as level 1 counselors act out their anxiety about the tasks of counseling, so does a supervisor new to that role.

A supervisor's anxiety may also be rooted in what motivated her to take the job. She may have wanted to be loved, admired, sought after, validated, or even feared. When these desired outcomes do not occur, the supervisor may act out the resulting stress in the supervisory relationship. For a supervisor to evaluate staff, she must deal with her own anxiety in the roles of supervisor and, especially, evaluator.

Short of the kind of processing she may need to do with her own supervisor or (in greater depth) with her own therapist, the supervisor can use the simple technique of disarming the issue with the counselor at the beginning of their relationship. The supervisor can say, "I don't like to do it, but every so often I have to step out of my normal role and fulfill my administrative responsibility by doing your job performance evaluation." Both parties can take this opportunity to verbalize their feelings of anxiety. The supervisor can then reassure the counselor (and herself) by describing the day-to-day feedback process that, if carried out properly, can make the annual performance review little more than a formality. If ongoing feedback is reinforced by quarterly benchmark reviews, there will be few surprises at the end of the year. By anticipating this sequence of events, the supervisor has acted to alleviate her own anxiety and the counselor's at the same time.

Supervisee Anxiety

While the supervisor is dealing with her own anxious feelings, she must attend to the stress and anxiety of the supervisee as well. A counselor's anxiety may be caused by a number of factors, including job-related concerns, career issues, knowledge and skill deficits, and disruptive personal problems. Several major sources of anxiety are as follows:

- *Beginner's quandary,* or fear of the unknown—of what might happen in supervision.
- *Spun glass theory of the mind.* Level 1 counselors tend to have a "spun glass" concept of people; they think of their clients as delicate objects that one must be very careful about touching for fear they will break. "What if I say the wrong thing? Will I hurt the client?" Eventually counselors learn that people are relatively sturdy and do not break quite so easily.
- *Performance and approval anxiety.* "I want to be the perfect counselor, the outstanding student. I want the supervisor to think well of me." Concerns such as these can motivate outstanding performance, but when they are taken to an extreme or coupled with severe insecurity (together with lack of self-insight), they can lead to silence and hesitation on the part of the counselor, excessive intellectualization, anger and aggression acted out toward the client, or premature termination of sessions.
- *Dominance anxiety.* This form of anxiety arises when one finds oneself in a variety of roles with respect to the same individual(s), so that being in a position of power in one respect (for example, supervisor versus supervisee) may make it possible to exercise power in other respects as well. On both sides of the power inequality, dominance anxiety may involve a cluster of concerns about emotional dominance, dual relationships, sexuality, attraction, and harassment (Rozsnafszky 1979).

Counselors voice, suppress, or act out anxiety about a number of concerns:

"Am I a good counselor?"

"Will I succeed on this case?"

"Will I be admired for my skills?"

"Will my 'bad' treatment be discovered?"

"Will my negative attitudes toward patients be found out?"

"Will my being bored and useless as a counselor be discovered?" ("I'm not helping this patient, and that's going to be found out.")

"Will my jealousy about a patient's wealth or position be evident?"

"Is the counseling really doing anything?"

They typically wrestle with these thoughts:

"I can't stand seeing this client. I hate him. But I shouldn't have feelings like that if I really want to be a counselor."

"It's amazing, but I can't remember the name of this patient from session to session."

"This family makes me crawl. What if they knew I can't stand my patient?"

"I am very frightened that the patient may flake out."

"I feel so responsible for this family, for their health, and for what happens to them in counseling."

"What if I'm not really helping but hurting them?"

"I'm ashamed to admit it, but I'm in love with this patient. I even get sexually aroused during a session when she talks about intimate matters."

"I wish they'd cancel, and for that matter, I wish all of my patients would cancel today. They are such a drain."

All therapists, at some point in their careers, have these feelings, questions, and anxieties. Sometimes these feelings intrude quite often. The supervisor should first reassure the counselor that the feelings are normal and do not in themselves reflect badly on the counselor's professionalism or compromise the counselor's work (Edelwich and Brodsky 1980, 1991). Identifying and expressing these feelings is a positive step.

Anxiety Management

Having laid this groundwork, the supervisor can employ a technique called anxiety management, based on the work of Dodge (1982), which utilizes a rational-emotive approach. Anxiety management consists of the following steps:

1. The supervisor identifies the supervisee's anxious behaviors, such as rationalization, discussing tangential issues, showing anger and aggression, judgmental behavior, blaming statements, or using anxiety as a defense. For example, the supervisee may have said, "I can't do that. I'm too nervous. The clients are too anxious about taping. It violates confidentiality." The supervisor asks the supervisee to consider the implications of such a statement.

2. The supervisee recognizes the cognitive pattern and explores the needs it expresses, such as performance demands and the need for approval: "I need to be a good counselor. If I'm not perfect, I'm a failure." Or, "I need my supervisor's approval for what I do."

3. The supervisor challenges the irrational beliefs with questions such as, "How bad will it really be if I don't get what I want?" or, "Where is the evidence that you must always be competent here—that you cannot fail at times?"

4. The supervisor and supervisee construct rational and logical thoughts related to the anxiety or anger. They do this with statements such as: "Yes, you want to be a skilled clinician, but at times you will need help from others. It is okay to ask for that help. It is not a weakness." Or, "Why should you always have to act the way I want you to? Can your style be different from mine and still be okay?"

5. The supervisee agrees to take a behavioral risk and try out the supervisor's logical arguments. The supervisee may say something like this: "I want to get this task accomplished in counseling, and this is what I'll do to get there, even if it feels a little unfamiliar or uncomfortable." Eventually the supervisee is able to present the case with little anxiety, once the sources of the anxiety have been addressed in a rational manner.

Another technique is to ask the supervisee to write down the name of each client and state what aspect of each case worries him. The supervisor will then have the necessary data to explore the sources of the anxiety and to apply the rational-emotive approach.

Above all, it is important for the supervisor to confront the anxiety and to give the supervisee permission to acknowledge and work through feelings. If the anxiety becomes immobilizing, the supervisor must intervene for the sake of the patient and refer the counselor for help in overcoming these fears.

STANDARDS OF EVALUATION: OVERCOMING BIAS

Supervisors tend to favor one person over another, one trait over another, or one way of doing things over another for reasons that have nothing to do with professional standards. Consciously or otherwise, their judgments may be colored by some systematic perceptual bias. Such idiosyncratic bias is referred to as the halo effect. A number of factors contribute to the halo effect:

- *Recency.* Supervisors tend to remember what happened last week, not six months ago. A positive recent memory may distort the supervisor's feedback in favor of the staff member. If the memory is negative, the supervisor may "gunnysack" the staff member's activities in negative terms. Either way, the supervisor is being shortsighted.
- *Overemphasis,* or placing too much weight on one factor, good or bad. The supervisor locks onto a mental image of a person and fixates on that idea.
- *Unforgivingness.* An unforgiving supervisor does not acknowledge improvement in an employee's performance; the employee can never overcome his or her past record.
- *Prejudice.* Prejudice is an uncomfortable notion for helping professionals, who are trained to have unconditional positive regard for everyone. Yet all supervisors bring their preferences and prejudices to the counseling room. Prejudice allows a supervisor to obscure a staff member's good works with unrelated and unjust attributions.
- *Favoritism.* Supervisors have their favorites among the staff. Individuals become favorites by virtue of their likeability, attractiveness, ingratiating behavior, or other factors.
- *Grouping,* or putting all employees with a particular designation into the same evaluative category, usually substandard: "All social workers are . . ." "All recovering counselors are . . ."
- *Indiscrimination,* or being either too approving or too critical with employees. Either everyone gets a good rating, or no one does.

- *Stereotyping,* or basing judgments on preconceived notions about race, gender, religion, ethnicity, age, national origin, sexual preference, or marital status.

To minimize the halo effect, a supervisor should use standardized rating scales for all employees. All successful appraisal systems are based on clearly defined—and explicitly articulated and communicated—standards and expectations of performance. One such system makes use of behaviorally anchored rating scales (BARS), which are descriptions of desired behaviors in clear, measurable terms. BARS specify the level and standard of performance sought in an objective, impersonal manner.

Specification is relatively simple in the case of clerical or assembly-line work—for example, How many typos are acceptable in a letter? What is the quota of acceptable defects in a manufactured product? It becomes more difficult to develop clear, measurable objectives for white-collar work, and the same is true for clinical functions. Nonetheless, supervisors can and should design BARS for counseling skills, as appropriate for the particular clinical situation and the counselor's developmental needs. The possibilities are limitless; some examples are as follows:

"During the next counseling session, you will make two confrontive interventions."

"At the next group counseling session, whenever a member goes into a monologue, you will involve other members of the group instead of responding directly in a one-on-one dialogue."

"During the group session you will make at least four positively reinforcing comments."

"Make eye contact with your cofacilitator, and have an interchange with her that contributes effectively to the group process. Practice that skill at least three times in group."

"For the next month, see if you can have your *DSM-IV* diagnoses agree with your supervisor's diagnoses 80 percent of the time."

The alcoholism and drug abuse field has led other disciplines in operationalizing its component skills through the task analysis and core competencies outlined in Birch and Davis (1986) and mandated by the counselor certification process. The field's twelve core functions are to be used as guidelines for goal setting in supervision, which is formalized in the individual development plan. The formulation of goals in terms of key results areas (KRAs) ensures concreteness, measurability, and accountability. These initial goals, subject to ongoing revision as the supervisor observes the supervisee at work, are then translated into specific behavioral objectives, or BARS. They are also the basis of the criteria used in the counselor's quarterly or annual performance appraisal, which in turn generates new goals and new arrangements for supervisory support and follow-up. At each stage, the supervisee should be actively involved in the evaluation, doing self-ratings on the same scales used by the supervisor and then comparing notes.

Table 13-1 shows an example of how supervision goals can be broken down into measurable terms for purposes of evaluation. (See Appendix G for guidance in formulating training goals based on the twelve core functions for the IDP.)

Table 13-1. Sample of Supervision Goals

Core Skill	Specific Skill Area	Supervisor Rating	Supervisee Rating
Group Counseling	Ability to terminate a group counseling session, ensuring closure of issues discussed for all group members	3	4
	Ability to conduct a task-oriented group session dealing with denial	2	3
	Ability to introduce new group members effectively into an open-ended group, reducing anxiety and mistrust for all members		
Family Counseling	Ability to conduct a thorough family intake, deriving sufficient data to write a treatment plan	2	3
	Ability to identify structural flaws in a family system	1	1

GUIDELINES FOR USEFUL FEEDBACK

Even the most sensitive appraisal is of little use if it is not sensitively communicated. Conveying feedback so that a particular supervisee can best hear it is a skill that supervisors acquire with experience. Such experience can, however, be distilled into guidelines for general use. Feedback is appropriately given when it has the following characteristics:

- Solicited rather than imposed.
- Timely rather than remote.
- Serving both the giver and the receiver.
- Presented so that it can be heard correctly.
- Given to be helpful rather than aggressive or accusatory.
- Descriptive rather than judgmental.
- Specific rather than general.
- Concrete rather than abstract.
- Direct rather than oblique.
- Directed toward changeable behavior.
- Not overloaded with information
- Not used as a disciplinary weapon.
- Confirmed with the group (in group supervision).

When counselors are asked what aspects of supervisory feedback they have found most helpful, they often mention the following:

- "Chunking" (breaking down information into manageable bites).
- Nonthreatening but thought-provoking questions.
- Self-reference (sharing one's own experiences in concrete terms).
- Support and encouragement.
- Suggested alternatives.

Two other characteristics of effective feedback—sandwiching and soliciting reciprocal feedback—are sufficiently important to merit some elaboration.

Sandwiching

An invaluable feedback technique for supervisors is sandwiching: positioning unfavorable comments between the slices of favorable comments. For example, a supervisor might say, "I'm pleased with the way you conducted group last week. You have made considerable improvement in your group processing skills. I think we still need to work on your use of confrontation in group. I'd like to work on these skills in our next supervisory sessions. I feel sure you can improve in this area, as you have in so many areas in the past. Your attitude toward skill development is outstanding. I really like your desire to learn."

Sandwiching sensitive feedback begins with recognition of work well done, goes on to discuss any unsatisfactory areas of performance, and ends with a summary of favorable and unfavorable performance. It is consistent with Blanchard and Johnson's (1982) maxim, "Catch them doing something right." Although some criticize the technique as simplistic and transparent, it enables supervisors to give constructive guidance to supervisees who might otherwise feel too threatened to hear what they are being told. Like all other such techniques, sandwiching should be used selectively, depending on the personalities and learning styles of supervisees. Some counselors can be hit over the head with criticism, which rolls off their backs instead of leaving them demoralized. Others require that feedback be administered especially sensitively. For these individuals, especially, sandwiching should be used routinely.

Soliciting Reciprocal Feedback

Trust is a two-way street. Counselors will be more open to hearing feedback from the supervisor if the supervisor is open to their feedback as well. It makes a big difference when the supervisor asks, "How am I doing? What could I be doing better?" After all, one's supervisees are among one's stakeholders, and one needs to know whether one is giving them the tools and resources they need to do the job. Asking for feedback reinforces the message that supervision is a collaborative learning process. As one supervisor put it,

"Just as when I was a counselor, I have to be always teachable, always willing to learn more."

Finally, two apt quotations sum up the constructive spirit in which effective feedback is offered. It is reported that Abraham Maslow once said, "If the only tool you have is a hammer, everything starts to look like a nail." In other words, the effective supervisor is interested not in being critical for its own sake but in providing tools for improvement. Along the same lines, Covey (1992) has written, "The challenge is to be a light, not a judge; to be a model, not a critic."

COUNSELING INDIVIDUALS OUT OF THE PROFESSION

With the help of the standards set by the agency, the supervisor must determine the level of competence sufficient to permit a counselor to practice and whether a supervisee has achieved that level of competence. If not, can the counselor be expected to reach that level in a reasonable amount of time? What resources will need to be expended to bring about that result?

At times this assessment may entail counseling the counselor out of the profession. ACES (1989) states the issue very clearly:

> Supervisors in training programs and agencies, through continual student or supervisee evaluation, must be aware of any personal or professional limitations of the students or supervisees which could impede future professional performance. Supervisors have the responsibility for recommending remedial assistance to the student or supervisee and for screening from the program or agency those persons who are unable to provide competent service [pp. 3–4].

This difficult gatekeeping function goes with the territory of being a supervisor. Agencies should formulate a policy for dismissal of clinicians on the basis of incompetence as well as ethical and legal violations. Sanctions for noncompliance with learning goals must be understood by the supervisee, with sufficient time allowed to remedy the problem after notice has been given. Eventually the supervisor may need to inform some individuals that they are not suited for this job and should find work elsewhere, perhaps in another profession.

Any awkwardness the supervisor may experience in terminating a counselor is likely to be magnified if the supervisor has not been trained in job performance appraisal and documentation. Most supervisors, afflicted with the clinician's disdain for paperwork, do not adequately document job performance, including performance problems. When it comes time to terminate an individual, they find themselves constrained from acting because they lack the necessary supporting materials.

Unethical or illegal conduct, on the other hand, calls for direct action. Such behavior, depending on the severity of the infraction, may constitute grounds for immediate dismissal. The code of ethics of the counselor's discipline, together with the agency regulations, governs this decision.

INSTRUMENTS FOR COUNSELOR ASSESSMENT

Stoltenberg and Delworth (1987, pp. 183ff.) summarize the range of instruments available as of that date for evaluating counselors (and supervisors as well). Included here is a comprehensive counselor evaluation form synthesized from a number of sources, preceded by a preparatory exercise for supervisors concerning the evaluation process. In addition, Appendix J contains forms developed by the American Association for Marriage and Family Therapy (AAMFT) for counselor assessment. An agency should adapt these forms to its philosophy of treatment, model of therapy, core competencies, and individualized administrative requirements. These forms illustrate the range of possibilities for the counselor assessment process.

Appraisal of Employee Performance

Before undertaking a performance evaluation, it is helpful for supervisors to assess their readiness to conduct such evaluations. Supervisors may feel uncomfortable both about assuming the role of evaluator and about the personnel performance appraisal system, especially if the evaluations affect merit increases or changes in rates of compensation. The following items enable supervisors to examine their attitudes toward the evaluation and job performance review process. The supervisor should respond yes or no to each item and indicate the actions needed to bring about any necessary improvements. There is no scoring for this instrument, which is simply a checklist for the supervisor's personal use.

1. Is my attitude about the evaluation process focused on how the counselor can improve his or her performance so as to match the job requirements?
2. Do I exercise care in separating the discussion of the employee's appraisal rating from any talk, or consideration, of money?
3. Can I rate the employee on a behaviorally oriented anchoring rating scale?
4. Do I make a conscious effort to apply the same standards to all supervisees, so that my ratings are consistent from employee to employee?
5. Do I maintain a file of critical incidents or specific and representative examples of each employee's behavior so as to support the appraisals I make?
6. Do I adequately document job performance issues and leave a paper trail to back up my performance evaluations?
7. Do I guard against the halo effect, which discriminates for or against a person on the basis of a single incident or trait?
8. Do I properly prepare for and conduct appraisal interviews by ensuring privacy, sufficient time, emphasis on job standards, credit where it is due, mutual examination of the facts supported by critical incidents, focus on the future, and a sharing on my part of responsibility for the individual's performance?
9. Do I establish a positive, constructive atmosphere during the evaluation process so that the employee feels safe?
10. Am I willing to listen to an employee's rebuttal of my evaluation and to change the ratings if the argument is sound?
11. Is my treatment of supervisees confidential with respect to their peers?
12. Do I strictly observe legal regulations as they affect the performance appraisal evaluations?
13. Do I show ongoing interest in and evaluation of the individual's performance, so that my appraisal is not a one-time event?
14. Do I actively assist the employee in overcoming specific weaknesses and in developing desirable skills?

15. Do I thoughtfully examine conditions beyond an employee's control that may be contributing to substandard performance: a poor skills-job match, inadequate training, workgroup pressure, physical or emotional problems, inadequate supervision, or technical problems in the process or procedures?

Counselor Competency Evaluation

In addition to the Birch and Davis (1986) competencies, which can be used as a guide for knowledge and skills assessment, following is a summary of areas to cover in the supervisory evaluation process. All items must be applied in a manner consistent with the counselor's theoretical frame of reference. (These counselor competencies were adapted from a number of sources, including Bradley 1989; Kaslow 1986a; and Stoltenberg and Delworth 1987.)

Personal Characteristics

1. People-oriented. Counselor appropriately displays affective qualities of empathy, respect, genuineness, concreteness, and potency.
2. Fallibility. Counselor recognizes that she is not free from making errors.
3. Personal problems. Counselor's personal problems are kept out of the counseling session.
4. Modeling. Counselor models appropriate cognitive and affective qualities during the counseling session.
5. Nondefensive. Counselor gives and receives feedback to and from clients, peers, and supervisor without making excuses or justifications.

Philosophical Foundations

1. Evaluation. Counselor can describe the cognitive, behavioral, and affective changes occurring in counseling.
2. Diagnosis. Counselor can identify maladaptive behaviors.
3. Theory. Counselor can articulate his or her assumptions about human behavior, including empirical findings.
4. Prioritizing. Counselor is able to decide which problems to address in counseling.

5. Interpretation. Counselor is able to provide the client with explanations for behaviors, cognitions, and feelings.
6. Prognosis. Counselor makes an assessment of the client's potential for successful treatment.
7. Interactions. Counselor describes clinical interactions.
8. Defense mechanisms. Counselor is aware of client defenses, the purposes they serve, and how to help the client substitute more adaptive mechanisms.
9. Catharsis. Counselor understands and utilizes the process of catharsis, as appropriate.
10. Natural consequences. Counselor understands the concept of environmental manipulation and natural consequences of behaviors.
11. Test selection. Counselor selects appropriate testing procedures.
12. Inference. Counselor explains client behaviors and their impact on the counseling process.

Communications

1. Open-ended questions. Counselor asks open-ended questions.
2. Minimal verbal response. Counselor uses minimal verbal responses efficiently without interrupting the client's verbal discourse or thought process.
3. Language. Counselor uses terminology that is understandable to the client.
4. Clarification. Counselor has the client clarify vague or ambiguous expressions.
5. Paraphrasing. Counselor restates in fewer words the client's responses, without changing the meaning.
6. Summarizing. Counselor combines two or more responses into a general statement.
7. Restatement. Counselor conveys to the client that a response was understood by restating in nearly exact wording what the client verbalized.
8. Empathy. Counselor responds with expression of feelings at a deeper level than the client was able to express.
9. Reflection of feelings. Counselor reflects the client's affective state.

10. Perceptions. Counselor names client perceptions.
11. Confrontation. Counselor confronts the client with possible consequences of his or her behaviors.
12. Probing. Counselor derives relevant and essential information from the client in a nonthreatening manner.
13. Disapproval. Counselor makes statements that disapprove of client behaviors, feelings, or cognitions when these are destructive to the client and others.
14. Advice giving. Counselor shares advice that might be helpful to the client.

Counseling Skills

1. Voice. Counselor's tone of voice and rate of speech are appropriate.
2. Eye contact. Counselor attends to the client through comfortable eye contact.
3. Initial contact. Counselor greets client in warm, accepting manner.
4. Activity level. Counselor maintains appropriate activity throughout the interview.
5. Physiological response. Counselor's posture, facial expressions, and gestures are natural and congruent with the session.
6. Counselor self-disclosure. Counselor shares personal information appropriate to the session to facilitate client progress.
7. Silence. Counselor uses silence therapeutically.
8. Objectivity. Counselor does not impose his or her values on the counseling session, except as may be therapeutically beneficial.
9. Probing. Counselor pursues therapeutically beneficial areas.
10. Resistance. Counselor is able to work with client resistance for therapeutic gain.
11. Verbosity. Counselor speaks when appropriate and necessary, not interrupting client or verbally dominating the session.
12. Transference. Counselor works with feelings about the counselor imposed by the client from other spheres.
13. Countertransference. Counselor is aware of and processes his or her feelings and issues about the client.
14. Manipulation. Counselor recognizes client attempts to manipulate the counselor.

15. Contextual factors. Counselor explores factors influencing the process, such as socioeconomic, cultural, ethnic, racial, gender, and other personal factors.
16. Dependency. Counselor encourages client independence by not accepting responsibility for the client's behaviors, cognitions, or feelings.
17. Theory. Counselor works with the client from at least two models of counseling.
18. Implementation. Counselor helps the client put into action an appropriate course of recovery.
19. Distortions. Counselor explains client's perceptual distortions.
20. Motivation. Counselor confronts client motivation issues.
21. Case history taking. Counselor obtains and records client information in developing a treatment plan.
22. Insight. Counselor helps the client gain insight into his or her actions along various domains: cognitive, behavioral, affective, and spiritual.
23. Structure. Counselor structures sessions to provide continuity of services.
24. Inconsistencies. Counselor identifies and explains client's contradictions.
25. Reframing. Counselor appropriately redirects the process.
26. Goal setting. Counselor establishes with the client short- and long-term goals that are consistent with the client's potential.
27. Reinforcement. Counselor identifies reinforcers to facilitate client progress.
28. Flexibility. Counselor adapts goals as changes occur in the counseling process.
29. Behavioral change. Counselor develops plans to measure the client's behavioral change.
30. Strategy. Counselor has a course of action consistent with counseling model.
31. Termination. Counselor is able to end sessions in a manner that is therapeutically beneficial to the client, resolving client's periodic desire for premature termination.
32. Emergencies. Counselor handles emergencies appropriately.
33. Periodic evaluation. Counselor assesses progress toward goals with the client.

34. Fantasy. Counselor uses imagination to gain insight.
35. Homework. Counselor assigns client work to be done outside the counseling hours.
36. Problem solving. Counselor helps client learn ways to resolve problems as they arise.
37. Test interpretation. Counselor interprets tests, as appropriate.
38. Role playing. Counselor helps client grow by role-playing issues.
39. Desensitization. Counselor applies behavioral techniques to reduce client anxiety.
40. Dreams. Counselor helps client work through dreams, if appropriate.
41. Contracts. Counselor makes contractual agreements with client for achieving counseling goals.

Adjunctive Activity

1. Case notes. Counselor communicates clearly and concisely in writing ongoing case issues.
2. Staffing. Counselor staffs a case as needed, to achieve the client's goals and to optimize prognosis.
3. Test administration. Counselor administers tests as appropriate.
4. Diagnosis. Counselor identifies client issues according to *DSM-IV,* if appropriate.
5. Appointments. Counselor sets and adheres to appointment schedule and is punctual in meeting appointments.
6. Informs. Counselor provides the client and the agency with the pertinent information concerning the case.
7. Organized. Counselor organizes his or her workday within time frames and limitations.
8. Attire. Counselor's attire is appropriate to the client population and agency setting.
9. Responsibilities. Counselor understands roles in agency and in counseling and supervisory relationships.
10. Atmosphere. Counselor sets an office atmosphere that is therapeutically beneficial, consistent with the approach of the agency, and physically and psychologically comfortable for the client.

11. Cancellations. Counselor notifies the client as promptly as possible regarding appointment cancellations.
12. Competency. Counselor acts only in those areas in which he or she is competent and does not go beyond his or her abilities.

Ethical Standards

1. Professionalism. Counselor acts in a manner that is consistent with the standards of the profession.
2. Ethics. Counselor adheres to ethical codes.
3. Confidentiality. Counselor adheres to standards of confidentiality.
4. Legal. Counselor adheres to legal requirements and is knowledgeable about professional reporting.

INSTRUMENTS FOR SUPERVISOR ASSESSMENT

An evaluation of a counselor is, implicitly, an evaluation of the counselor's supervisor as well, for the supervisor bears a major share of responsibility for the counselor's selection, training, education, support, and monitoring. In addition to the core competencies and task definitions for clinical supervisors that are reviewed in detail in Appendixes A and B, the appendixes include a variety of instruments for self-assessment of a supervisor's preparation and readiness for the job (Appendixes C and D), evaluation of the supervisor by the supervisee (Appendix E), and evaluation of the counselor by his or her supervisor (Appendix F). The appendixes also contain forms for an individual development plan (Appendix G), a suggested outline for case presentations (Appendix I), and counselor assessment forms (Appendix J).

Provision for assessment of the supervisor by the supervisee is especially crucial, all the more so because it is often overlooked. A supervisor's expressed willingness to be evaluated by supervisees tells them that she does not ask staff members to undergo anything that she herself will not undergo. Reciprocal evaluation of the supervisor by supervisees not only provides valuable feedback for the supervisor; it also creates an atmosphere of trust, mutuality, and good faith. In addition, it gives counselors a sense of responsibility and involvement in the design and development of supervision.

Chapter Fourteen

Innovative Techniques in Supervision

New techniques are constantly being developed that can serve valuable ancillary functions. There is no limit to the creativity that the well-informed, well-rounded supervisor can bring to bear in synthesizing a supple clinical repertoire from diverse sources. For example, paradoxical techniques are powerful tools in the hands of a skilled supervisor, as are anecdotes and teaching tales. Milton Erickson's use of indirect suggestions in therapy has been adapted for supervision by clinicians of the strategic school. The founder of the strategic school, Jay Haley, uses an indirect teaching technique whereby the supervisor provides a "worse" alternative for the therapist. A level 1 counselor, for example, may be quite anxious about being supervised in front of a one-way mirror. The supervisor tells the counselor that the case he will confront will be so difficult that he will not have a chance to be nervous about the supervision. The alternative provided here is that the clients will give the counselor more to worry about than the supervisor will. This is an indirect way to alleviate a counselor's anxiety.

This chapter examines several innovative techniques that work well in conjunction with the blended model of supervision for the alcoholism and drug abuse field: a questionnaire that elicits the philosophical foundations to which a counselor subscribes, effective questions, solution-focused supervision, and in vivo supervision. The first two of these are derived from my own work, the last two from the work of others. The chapter concludes with guidelines for making the transition to the supervisory role and inoculating oneself against supervisor burnout.

PHILOSOPHY AS MATERIAL FOR SUPERVISION

Amid all the detailed process issues discussed in supervision, the counselor's philosophy of treatment can easily be overlooked. That is a short-sighted omission, for a set of core beliefs about how people operate and how people change forms the foundation of an individual's model of therapy and supervision. What is the counselor's view of humankind? his anthropology? epistemology? What is the counselor's cosmology? Does it envision a safe, positive world where people strive to do their best, to be self-actualized? Or is it a malevolent world where evil prevails and people struggle with their innate tendencies to do wrong? More specifically (but still in the realm of philosophy), what is the counselor's therapeutic orientation, and what boundaries in therapy does it dictate? These are central issues for supervision. The clinical supervisor must ensure that they are not obscured by the demands of the caseload and the need for training in specific technical skills.

To facilitate discussion of these larger issues in supervision, a questionnaire was designed as an adjunct to small-group clinical supervision sessions. Supervisors have found it a valuable tool in helping counselors articulate their concepts of humanity's place in the universe, their philosophy of counseling, and their understanding of how change takes place in counseling. The questionnaire is administered to supervisees and key questions selected by the supervisor for discussion at group supervisory sessions. The discussion of a question may take an hour or may last for weeks of supervisory sessions. A question may also be used to spin off into other related areas.

The questionnaire is best used in conjunction with clinical cases for illustration and discussion. For example, question 5 ("A counselor should not personalize his or her office with photos of family, souvenirs, mementos, and so forth") raises important issues about transference. How does the counselor wish to portray himself to clients? What transferential images occur when a counselor has a picture of her husband and children on her desk? How will a gay client or an unmarried client without children relate to the photos? There are no right or wrong answers here, only grist for the supervisory mill.

Question 20 ("Whatever direction a client chooses to move in [short of murder, suicide, and the like] should be satisfactory to the counselor") raises interesting dilemmas about structure and direction in counseling. Are there ever situations in which a counselor should direct the client away from particular behaviors? How does the counselor present these directives? How does the counselor confront the client's maladaptive behaviors?

Finally, the answer to question 40 may seem obvious, but is it always clear when a counselor should and should not see the client's family? at what stage of treatment? What family issues should be addressed, and when? For example, an alcoholic at an early stage of recovery perhaps should have his spouse in the family treatment program, but should family therapy be conducted in the first month of sobriety? How about sexual counseling with the couple in early sobriety? What sexual issues should or should not be addressed at this stage? These questions can provide hours of stimulating discussion and case illustrations.

The questionnaire consists of fifty-four questions, with the following rating scale:

1 = disagree very much

2 = disagree quite a bit

3 = disagree mildly

4 = disagree a little

5 = agree a little

6 = agree mildly

7 = agree quite a bit

8 = agree very much

The questions can be modified to fit the agency's needs, the duration of supervision, the number of supervisees, or the staff's training needs.

Philosophy of Counseling	*Rating*
1. A counselor should have long-range goals for his or her clients.	_____

Philosophy of Counseling	*Rating*

2. Some emotional involvement with clients is inevitable.   _____

3. There may be unconscious motives, but they play a minor role in a person's daily behavior or in shaping his or her life.   _____

4. A wise counselor advises the client about the best way of coping with a life situation.   _____

5. A counselor should not personalize his or her office with photos of the family, souvenirs, mementos, and so forth.   _____

6. With proper timing a counselor should usually analyze client resistance for the client.   _____

7. It is often good counseling to urge the client strongly to try out certain behaviors that are initially frightening.   _____

8. Whatever the intensity of a client's expression, counseling is most effective when the counselor feels detached, objective, and impersonal.   _____

9. It is necessary for clients to learn how early childhood experiences have left a mark on them.   _____

10. Counselors should make an overall treatment plan for each case.   _____

11. It is all right for a counselor and client to have coffee or other refreshments together during the counseling hour.   _____

12. Counselors should introduce topics during the session whenever they need discussion.   _____

13. The most important learning in counseling is verbal and conceptual in nature.   _____

14. The most important results of counseling are the new ideas and ways of thinking about himself or herself that a client achieves.   _____

15. It is important for a client to be helped to make a social adjustment.   _____

Philosophy of Counseling	*Rating*

16. A counselor can help a client more if the counselor has met and mastered problems similar to the client's. _____

17. When a client relates a dream in counseling, the counselor should try to help him or her understand its meaning. _____

18. The most important factors in successful counseling are professional training and expert use of therapeutic techniques. _____

19. Understanding why one does things is the most effective factor in changing one's behavior. _____

20. Whatever direction a client chooses to move in (short of murder, suicide, and the like) should be satisfactory to the counselor. _____

21. The more effective counselor does things during the hour for which he has no reasoned basis, merely a feeling he is right _____.

22. It is rarely helpful for a counselor to formulate for himself the psychodynamics of the counselor-client relationship. _____

23. The counselor should point out connections between the client's behaviors and attitudes—both those expressed in counseling and those described from present and past situations. _____

24. A counselor should not have any physical contact with a client (other than an occasional handshake). _____

25. The most beneficial outcome of counseling is for a client to learn the reasons for his or her behavior. _____

26. It is acceptable to interrupt a client while he or she is talking in order to make a comment. _____

27. It is all right to address clients by their first names. _____

28. It is all right to discuss politics, movies, weather, current events, sports, or philosophy with a client during the hour. _____

Philosophy of Counseling	*Rating*

29. A counselor should assume different roles with different clients. _____

30. The most important results of counseling are the new feelings and emotions clients come to experience. _____

31. A thorough case history and a proper diagnosis are very important to treating a case effectively. _____

32. In counseling, a client learns mostly through the affective and unverbalized relationship between himself or herself and the counselor. _____

33. It is important to interpret symptomatic behavior, such as slips of the tongue and mannerisms. _____

34. Deliberately expressing approval of desirable client behavior is not a good therapeutic policy. _____

35. The counselor's personality is more important to the outcome of care than the client's personality issues. _____

36. With most clients, it is important to lead the interview into fruitful areas of discussion. _____

37. It is very important for the counselor to conceptualize how the client is relating to him or her. _____

38. A counselor should spontaneously express his or her thoughts about the relationship during the hour. _____

39. For a client to improve his or her current way of life, he or she must come to understand early childhood relationships. _____

40. It is rarely wise to see other members of the client's family. _____

41. If a client is very critical or appreciative of a counselor, it should not change the counselor's feelings toward the client in any way. _____

42. It is possible to make sense of a client's behavior without assuming motives of which he or she is unaware. _____

Philosophy of Counseling	*Rating*

43. The goals of counseling should be set only by the client. _____

44. In counseling, the counselor should act reserved, uninvolved, and impersonal. _____

45. It is unwise for a counselor's remarks and reactions to a client to be unplanned, spontaneous, not thought through. _____

46. A good counselor interprets the client's behavior, in the sense of telling its real significance or meanings of which the client is unaware. _____

47. It is important to analyze the transference reactions to the client. _____

48. A counselor who is emotionally involved with a case is defeating his or her own purpose. _____

49. The best counselors are fairly passive and silent during the therapy hour. _____

50. It is usually all right to have a telephone conversation with a client even when there is no pressing issue. _____

51. A counselor must feel warm toward a client if he or she is to help him or her. _____

52. A counselor should avoid asking probing questions. _____

53. A counselor should never show anger toward a client. _____

54. It is all right for a counselor to walk about the room during the counseling hour. _____

This questionnaire can be the basis for an extended discussion of a counselor's approach to treatment, philosophy of change, the role of the counselor in the change process, and styles of clinical intervention. Used in this way, the questionnaire is an invaluable learning tool, aiding in the development of theoretical constructs. The theory that emerges from this exercise requires terminology (defined words with which to specify observations) and a formulation of a chain of causal hypotheses. In the process, the counselor's implicit theory of personality becomes explicit, so that the counselor can describe and explain different individual personalities as they are and how they came about.

EFFECTIVE QUESTIONS

A supervision session is a natural place to apply the technique of asking effective questions (EQs). Effective questions are open-ended, asking "what" and "how" instead of trying to pin down "why" answers. By always giving the supervisee credit for answering, correctly or incorrectly, the supervisor helps the supervisee feel valued and empowered. The following is a potpourri of EQs as applied to supervision:

"What have you accomplished so far that you are most pleased with?"

"How would you like this case to proceed?"

"What kind of support do you need from me to ensure success?"

"What do you need to get to where you want to be?"

"What were you able to do today that you have not been able to do in the past?"

"What allowed you to do it that way this time?" [or, "What got in the way of your doing it that way this time?"]

"What did you learn that can be used elsewhere, at other times?"

"How does that fit in with what else you have learned?"

"In what way will that allow you to do it even better tomorrow?"

"What are you doing that is already working well?"

There is no limit to the EQs supervisors can come up with. For example, a real teaser along these lines is, "If you were not a counselor, what would you want to do in that situation?" This kind of question can create some emotional (and even cognitive) clarity by putting the counselor in touch with a range of reactions normally ruled out by the constraints of the counselor's role. The counselor would not, of course, act on the impulse to throw the client out of the room, but it can be helpful to acknowledge the feeling of wanting to do so. Moreover, this reaching out for a broader range of responses may generate creative solutions that can appropriately be applied in counseling.

SOLUTION-FOCUSED SUPERVISION

A technique that incorporates effective questions designed to break through counseling dilemmas is solution-focused supervision, derived from the solution-focused counseling developed by de Shazer (1988). A premise of the blended model of supervision for the alcoholism and drug abuse field is that the supervisee has the inner capacity to change his practice, with guidance from the supervisor. In other words, the supervisee can find his own solutions to problems with direction and refocusing by a guide and mentor. This is also the premise on which the solution-focused model of counseling and supervision is based.

De Shazer begins therapy by focusing on solutions, not problems: "People often find it difficult to stop trying to solve a problem because 'deep down' they (we) stick to thinking that an explanation is both realizable and indispensable if a problem is to be really resolved" (de Shazer 1988, p. 10). Thus, therapists and supervisors frequently miss solutions because they are too busy searching for explanations, not realizing that the solution itself is the best explanation. AA uses a variation of this concept expressed in the phrase, "Fake it until you make it." Similarly, behavioral therapists have clients practice new behaviors that may not at first feel natural, so that they can experience the rewards and thereby come to feel that the new behaviors are part of them. In other words, focus on the solution, and the problem will take care of itself.

Insight-oriented therapists begin by having the client describe in detail the complaint, the presenting problem, which is then explored in depth. For de Shazer, by contrast, the focus shifts to solutions immediately after the presentation of the problem. The first step is to search for exceptions to the problem—times when it did not occur. "No matter how much the client tells the therapist about the complaint, the conversation will be brought back to when it is that the complaint does not happen" (de Shazer 1988, p. 51).

The therapist then asks the client to describe a vision of the future when the problem will be resolved. How will things be different? How will the client act differently when there is no problem?

This is followed by suggested action steps to turn that vision into the reality of a solution. It cannot be that simple, some say. What if it does not work? De Shazer's solution is just to do something else. Change is a process of trial and error. People find solutions to problems by both deliberate and spontaneous goal setting followed by action (see also Peele, Brodsky, and Arnold 1991).

The solution-focused techniques outlined below, drawn from de Shazer's model of counseling and Thomas's (1992) related work on clinical supervision, are easily incorporated into the blended model of supervision. As in alcoholism and drug abuse treatment, the supervisor seeks to blend behavioral change with insight. The emphasis, however, is on insight that contributes directly to solutions to problems, not on insight for its own sake. Thus, solution-focused supervision more closely parallels the practical than the spiritual side of substance abuse counseling.

Socializing

The first task of the supervisor is to find areas of success for the counselor in each hour of therapy. One should never ask a question that brings a "failure" answer into the supervision session. A supervisor exerts influence not by issuing directives but by co-opting the supervisee into finding the solutions. This is best done by asking positive questions such as:

"How have you been successful in the past with this type of client?"

"Even in a bad session, what were the good moments?"

"What are your good feelings about this session?"

"What do you do well in this type of group?"

"What models do you like to use?"

"What brings you success with this client?"

This application of effective questions puts the supervisee at ease and minimizes power issues and distancing between supervisor and supervisee.

Saliency

Next, the supervisor elicits the supervisee's viewpoint on the agenda for supervision by asking, "What is the most important thing I need to know about your practice? What is important to you?" These questions are in stark contrast to the stereotypical supervisory attitude of, "I know what is important for you to learn." After asking what other issues the supervisee thinks are important to talk about, the supervisor should allow time for the supervisee to ponder the question, which amounts to asking the supervisee to trust the supervisor's openness to honest input. Trust does not come automatically with supervisory status, especially when the supervisor is in a position of power. Trust is earned over time by demonstrating respect and by staying focused on the solution: "You do well with what kinds of problems? Tell me what you do well." A supervisee who continues to bring up problems should be diverted from this problem focus. "I'm kind of slow here," says the supervisor. "I'd like to hear just what you do well."

Boundary Profiling

When the counselor has a persistent feeling of frustration about a particular problem, the supervisor can ask, "When was this less of a problem for you?" "When did it happen less frequently?" The supervisor can even ask the counselor to rate her own "level of incompetence" on a 1–10 scale. The phrasing may be surprising, but its purpose is to get to where the "stuck" feeling is and then transform it into a more hopeful vision by reminding the counselor of past successes and future alternatives. "Was there ever a time when you felt more competent? Where were you then on the 1–10 scale? How will you know when your supervision is working for you? How will you know when you're more effective? When you are more competent, what will you be doing then? How will you be feeling?" This boundary profiling technique shows how de Shazer's model incorporates insight with a behavioral focus and is expressed in concrete, practical terms.

Setting Goals

To construct a vision of change and find the solution to the problem, realistic goals and objectives must be set. To do this, the supervisor asks "how" questions: "How will you be doing things differently if you practice this skill? How will you be thinking?

feeling? Specifically, what would you like to do differently? When you are acting the way you want to act, what will you do differently? What will be different?"

In setting goals, it is helpful to break down the skills sought into changeable, measurable chunks of behavior, again using a 1–10 scale. "Where do you see yourself now on a scale of 1–10 (10 being best)? If you were a 10 now, how would things be different?" "Where are you today, in this session? Where would you like to be when we're finished? To go from 4 to 8, what do you need to focus on, to talk about in supervision?"

In reality there is no "3" or "4"; these are only labels, ways of scaling how one feels about one's work. Scaling provides a non-qualitative measure of success, thus avoiding either-or or good-bad language, together with a concrete image of the desired end state. "How could you improve on that response? How have you changed so far? How are you able to do that now? How did you teach the client to do that? What are you doing differently now?"

Other questions useful in goal setting are: "What will be different about your work when you are doing better—say, at a 10 level? What will members of your work team notice about you when you're working at a 10 level?" The supervisor can bring other observers metaphorically into the supervision room by asking, "What would your colleagues notice if you were doing it differently?"

Externalizing the Issue

To help the counselor avoid taking on an immobilizing weight of responsibility, the supervisor attempts to externalize the issue, as if the problem existed independently of the counselor. "There are ways you have been able not to have the problem bother you. How are you able to do that? What allows you not to let it bother you? Were there times in the past when the problem got in your way, but you were able to resolve it?"

Talking about "the frustration" or "the problem" distances the issue from the supervisee and his feelings of inadequacy. "How has the problem not been a problem for you before? In what ways is the problem affecting you, keeping you from moving forward? If you had another supervisor, what would she say about the problem? Would she see it as a problem? What if the other supervisor were a man? What would he say about the problem?" When the supervisor uses this kind of language to externalize the issue, it is not to give the counselor a way of denying responsibility. Rather, it helps restore realistic boundaries between what is and is not the counselor's responsibility. For example, "I can't move this family along" might be rephrased as, "This family seems stuck."

Identifying Exceptions to Problem Perceptions

In solution-focused supervision, it is essential for the client and counselor not to be stymied by the problem, as if it always had been and always will be the way it is now. Exceptions, or times when the problem was not there, are a starting point for refocusing from problem to solutions. "Are there certain times when the problem does not occur? When the problem does not occur, how does that come about? Does anyone else notice that it is not a problem? How do you stop the problem from happening?" These questions enable the supervisee to see that the problem need not be over-whelming and can be overcome.

Making Sense of Exceptions

One can practice the solution-focused approach by mimicking behaviors until they fit. Another saying often heard in AA is, "Put the body there and let the mind follow." That is essentially how behavioral therapy works. Similarly, solution-focused supervision works by introducing new concepts to the supervisee, changing specific behaviors, and mimicking the new, desired outcomes. Supervisors ask, "How else could you ask that question, to make it more concise? What in your response helped you to be able to do that? Did you know before you experienced the change that you'd be able to do that? How did you know? What was different about that situation from the way it was when the problem was more in charge of you? What would your colleagues say about how you did that?"

Thus, if the counselor does not perform successfully at this time, the supervisor has given the counselor permission to have a problem: "If the problem isn't getting better, what are you doing to keep it from getting worse? How have mistakes made you a better therapist in the past? If you could imagine the case going well, what would you be doing to be successful?" If, on the other hand, the counselor succeeds, it is a win-win situation: "How did you decide to do that? How did you teach the client to do that? Did this escape from the problem come easily for you? I know this case is difficult, for it has been difficult for most counselors. How is it difficult for others and easy for you?"

Future Orientation

By adopting a future orientation for the solution, the supervisor guides the counselor toward shaping an image or vision of change for the next session. "If you could change anything you chose about this situation, what would it look like then? If a miracle happened today and tomorrow morning you woke up and did not have this problem, what would you notice as different about your life? What would others notice?" The supervisor assumes a positive outcome regardless of the severity of the problem. "You seem to be an optimist, so let's assume you'll be able to beat this obstacle. What will be different? What do you want me to look for this week that you can feel good about in your counseling? Where are you getting better?"

Cheerleading

A supervisor should always find ways of complimenting any positive behaviors. "That's great. Wow! No kidding. There you go." If a supervisor said nothing more after viewing a videotape than "Wow!" (with a positive tone), the supervisee would go out knowing nothing new but feeling wonderful. Most people, not expecting praise, are pleasantly surprised when it comes. Some complimentary expressions a supervisor can use are:

"You should be pleased it went so well."

"That was excellent."

"Tell me how you did that."

"How did you manage to stay calm in the midst of such a troubling session? How did you even stay in the room? I have to tell you *I* felt like walking out in frustration."

"What other responses on your part might also have worked?"

Encouraging the Change to Continue

When schoolchildren have their tests graded, the red markings highlight their relatively small percentage of errors, while their many correct answers are taken for granted. In any kind of education or training, individuals should be reinforced for their successes, not their failures. In supervision, the counselor should be encouraged constantly to continue on the path of positive behavioral change. At this stage the supervisor can say, "Do more of that. Did you like what you did just then? I did! It worked. Do that again." This feedback, instead of giving the supervisee answers to her problems, helps her learn how to learn by interpreting and evaluating outcomes.

The supervisor's ongoing guidance should be directed toward helping the supervisee find her own solutions. Some useful supervisory locutions include:

"What did you like about that session in spite of the fact that you thought it was terrible?"

"That hasn't happened in a session yet, but when it does, what will you do?"

"What is it like to be . . . ? I'm wondering if things will be different for you."

"When did you think about whether you were overcontrolling the session, and how did you manage to keep that behavior from occurring sooner?"

"Because of the last case you had like this, you've learned to do things differently. How might your future choices be affected by this change?"

"As a result of your life experiences, what do you do differently when this happens? What else in your life can you draw upon for a solution?"

"How would you explain that to someone else who does not know how to stay calm in a session?"

"What would you like to take on to become more proficient?"

Solution-focused techniques in supervision give counselors positive reinforcement of specific behaviors, both before and after the fact. These techniques work well with alcoholism and drug abuse counselors who lack formal academic training, as well as with level 1 counselors who are overly self-critical. By focusing on solutions— that is, on what counselors can do to improve their methods of counseling, to bring about positive change in the lives of their clients, and to feel better about their work—the supervisor helps counselors learn specific skills while also gaining insight into their actions.

IN VIVO SUPERVISION

To supplement the standard methods of observation (videotape, cofacilitation, one-way mirror, and so forth) and contexts of supervision (group and peer supervision) discussed in Chapter Twelve, Brodsky and Myers (1986) have proposed an innovative methodology that combines the didactic and experiential components of supervision. In vivo supervision involves a rotation between the teaching of therapeutic techniques and live observation of the supervisor and/or supervisee in action. Each supervision session includes a 45-minute therapy session with the supervisor in the room, a 30-minute group discussion about the therapy session with the client observing (a unique concept), and a 15-minute debriefing between the therapist and the client. Brodsky and Myers have found this to be an intense and productive learning experience for the supervisor, supervisee, and client.

The use of the mirror, which is basic to most live methods of supervision, plays no part in in vivo supervision. Instead, the client and counselor sit at one end of a large counseling room while the supervisor and other observers sit at the other end. Only air space separates the therapist and client from the supervisor and other observers. There is no conversation among the observers during the counseling session.

The contract with the client specifies that all supervision is to occur within the session. There is no supervisee-to-supervisee, supervisor-to-supervisee, or client-to-supervisee discussion at any time outside the counseling room. Thus, all learning occurs for the supervisee, the client, and the supervisor together, in various configurations. All comments are made in the presence of one another. Furthermore, there is no cross-talk between the observers and the other participants. The observers never interact directly with the client. They are simply critical onlookers who sit there for their own edification. The counselor is the focus of the clinical interactions. Brodsky and Myers (1986) assert that the impact of this experience is a profound one for all participants: "Just as the new client often moves from a cautious, valuative mode to an understanding and trusting mode, so both trainees and the supervisor, when they are not serving as the active therapist, move from trying to guide the sessions to trying to understand and trust them. At least the roles of therapist, evaluator, and observer get sorted out" (p. 99).

Those unfamiliar with this method might well ask, "What about the client in all this? Aren't his confidences violated? How does the client feel about this process?" According to Brodsky and Myers, the client's silent presence at the supervision session can be a powerful therapeutic tool. The client gains trust and courage faster, becomes more introspective, and feels less tension in the counseling session as a result of observing the supervision. "The accessibility of not just one, but several therapeutic styles and vocabularies may contribute as well" (p. 100).

Clients must be carefully selected for in vivo supervision, with interviews to screen out those who are inappropriate. Clients must have an intact personality organization and sufficient coping skills to deal with the stress that may result from the observation process. They must have the capacity to process and assimilate the information generated. They should be well-functioning individuals with reasonably good verbal skills. "Also, care must be taken in the initial [screening] interview to clarify the practicum format with the prospective client. Since this is a somewhat unorthodox therapy mode, the client is usually offered referral into a more traditional individual or group therapy at the end of the semester" (Brodsky and Myers 1986, p. 102). Clearly this interesting and ambitious method of supervision is not for all clients, supervisees, or supervisors.

ASSUMING THE SUPERVISORY ROLE

Making the transition from the role of counselor to that of clinical supervisor can be a difficult and painful process. There are a number of steps a new supervisor must take to make the transition successfully. The new supervisor must be a quick learner. He must master the intricacies of affirmative action and equal employment opportunity policies and procedures, budgeting and finance, how to interview and hire staff, how to train and orient new and existing staff to job tasks and functions, how to run productive staff meetings, and how to conduct performance appraisals. The new supervisor must learn expeditiously to define and match tasks and roles. He must develop his own decision-making style. He must learn how to resolve conflicts among staff members as well as between management and line staff. He must learn how to identify and address staff stress and burnout. Most important, the new supervisor needs to learn how to celebrate with staff, how to enjoy the job, and how to be open and vulnerable to new supervisees.

The transition to being a supervisor entails the following tasks:

1. Request an orientation period to review policies and procedures, to talk with middle and upper management, and to observe daily activities of all departments. This is especially important if the supervisor is new to the agency.
2. Identify an internal or external mentor to assist with the initial learning process. The supervisor's mentor should be someone who knows the politics of the agency, the needs of the counseling staff, and the client population served. The mentor, who should be a skilled supervisor, should aid the supervisor in setting initial tasks, priorities, and ground rules for supervision. The mentor is also a coach and cheerleader to help the new supervisor through difficult times.
3. Assemble a core staff and build a cohesive working team. The supervisor needs to develop rapport with her new boss and supervisees through regular and frequent meetings and direct supervision of the supervision. The supervisor should seek management and supervisory training as needed.
4. Solicit feedback and take it seriously. The supervisor must constantly ask "How am I doing?" and be open to the answers, positive or negative.

An essential task for supervisors is always to be sensitive to their own stress and burnout levels. Burnout has been defined as "a progressive loss of idealism, energy, and purpose experienced by people in the helping professions as a result of the conditions of their work" (Edelwich and Brodsky 1980, p. 14) and as "a syndrome of emotional exhaustion, depersonalization and reduced personal accomplishment that can occur among individuals who do people work" (Maslach 1986, p. 98). Although burnout is typically thought of as an end-stage phenomenon, a function of years of overwork and frustration, it is very much the concern of the newly promoted supervisor. As Edelwich and Brodsky show, the seeds of burnout are planted in the initial stage of enthusiasm, when the novice has unrealistic expectations of success, recognition, and fulfillment.

Supervisors often report emotional strain and reduced morale due to multiple and conflicting responsibilities, an overload of paperwork, and the necessity of enforcing rules that do not improve performance. They do not believe that they are truly a part of management (Kadushin 1976; Olmstead and Christensen 1973). Overall, role conflict and role ambiguity are prominent among the occupational stressors that put supervisors at risk for burnout.

Role conflict is defined as "the simultaneous occurrence of two or more sets of pressures, such that compliance with one would make more difficult the compliance with the other" (Kahn and others 1964, p. 19). Middle managers, including clinical supervisors, are highly susceptible to role conflict because of their unique position as mediators and coordinators between management and staff and because they are at the critical point at which the organization's administrative structure impinges on the individual line worker.

Role ambiguity is defined as "the discrepancy between information available to the person and that which is required for adequate performance of his role" (Kahn and others 1964, p. 73). This is an occupational hazard in publicly funded alcoholism and drug abuse agencies where information does not flow downward to line staff. The supervisor must cope simultaneously with the incompleteness of the information available to her and the even greater gaps in the information available to counselors. Clearly, the widespread adoption of the networked, team-based organizational structure described in Chapter Three would help reduce the role ambiguity imposed by hierarchical organizations.

As an antidote to burnout, supervisors should:

1. Maintain sufficient self- and other awareness so as to know when they are burning out.
2. Have a mentor and supervision of their supervision. It is strongly recommended that groups of clinical supervisors meet monthly as peers to share concerns that may lead to burnout as well as clinical techniques they have learned.
3. Maintain some client load to stay in touch with the very purpose for which they went into counseling in the first place: to help people. Supervisors who detach themselves from client care by giving up the caseload altogether may lose that crucial sense of vocation and leave themselves vulnerable to burnout by becoming the "manager" they never wanted to be (Edelwich and Brodsky 1980).
4. Seek external counseling when personal issues interfere with their effectiveness. Burnout can result from both professional and personal stressors. When one's family life is under stress, the effects are likely to be felt on the job.
5. Constantly grow, professionally and personally. By maintaining balance in life, by having vital connections outside work, by never ceasing to grow, supervisors have the best chance to remain relatively sane in an otherwise stressful job.

Chapter Fifteen

Ethical and Legal Concerns

The focus on the ethical and legal responsibilities of clinicians and supervisors in all human services fields has become clear. A tightening of ethical standards, as expressed in the ethics codes of the various professions, has accompanied an escalation of malpractice claims and awards based on various kinds of negligence and conflict of interest. Although all professionals must attend to the requirements of the law and must exercise reasonable prudence to avoid potential liability, especially in a litigious climate, the underlying issues are not legalistic. Rather, they are a matter of discharging ethical responsibilities toward the client, the agency, and the counselor. Supervisors and counselors alike need to uphold standards of practice that reflect professional integrity and pride. Indeed, forensic experts in the mental health field have concluded that high-quality clinical care, grounded in genuine empathy and alliance building, is the best form of malpractice prevention (Gutheil and Appelbaum 2000; Gutheil and others 1991).

Whether they are aware of it or not, supervisors are constantly making ethical choices, many of which have legal ramifications as well. Like the counselors they supervise, they are vulnerable to compromising situations and to potential litigation, for both their own conduct and that of their supervisees. Instances of grossly unethical practice eventually are resolved in state licensing boards, professional credentialing bodies, and courts of law. For example, for a clinician to have sexual relations with a client is universally recognized to be unethical and grounds for malpractice, and in several states it has been made a crime. Of more constant and immediate concern to supervisors are the day-to-day behaviors of clinicians that stray into ethical boundary zones—for example, the voyeuristic probing into sexual or other personal material that the clinician has neither the ability nor the time to deal with in counseling, the inappropriate use of touch in counseling, and the inability to maintain an appropriate professional distance with respect to a client (which may occur, for example, when the counselor and client attend the same AA meetings). All of these are issues to manage in supervision.

In upholding the ethical standards of the profession, supervisors are responsible for the professional development of those whom they train, a mandate that includes guiding trainees' ethical sensibilities (ACES 1989). Supervisors are responsible for exercising reasonable oversight with respect to the ethical conduct of those whom they supervise. These responsibilities involve the supervisor in issues such as informed consent, confidentiality and its limits, the duty to warn, boundary maintenance, dual relationships, social and sexual intimacies with clients, misrepresentation, and professional credibility. Not surprisingly, many of these issues have an isomorphic quality. If the counselor is to learn to respect clients' confidentiality, the supervisor should show the counselor the same respect. As the counselor learns to obtain informed consent from clients, the supervisor should model that process by being open with the counselor about supervisory procedures. The counselor can best learn to avoid dual relationships (social, sexual, business) with clients in an atmosphere in which the supervisor observes proper boundaries with regard to the counselor. The same principles of respect, fairness, nonexploitation, and clarity of expectations govern the supervisory relationship as the counseling relationship.

Ethical and legal concerns are central to supervision, and their exploration within supervision is crucial, for several reasons:

1. Supervision is a training experience in which one learns the practice of counseling and therapy. It is on this training ground that one is taught the rules of therapy, including ethical and legal principles and the behavioral mandates that follow from them. Thus, the attention given to ethical and legal concerns follows from the very definition of supervision.

2. The clinical supervisory relationship, like the therapeutic relationship, involves inherent inequalities of status, power, and expertise. It is therefore vulnerable to abuse.

3. The supervisory relationship also resembles therapy insofar as self-evaluation occurs in conjunction with assessment by an authoritative figure. Personal growth is a goal of supervision. The supervisor's powerful role in this process creates the potential for impropriety (Newman 1981).

4. A supervisor, as well as the employing agency, may be held liable for inadequate supervision of a counselor whose negligence causes harm to others.

This chapter provides an overview of some of the larger ethical and legal themes of the supervisory relationship. This dimension of supervision encompasses the supervisor's and supervisee's ethical obligations to each other, as well as the supervisor's responsibility to monitor the ethical conduct of the supervisee. For more detailed guidance, the reader is referred to the many texts on ethical and legal considerations in clinical practice (Cormier and Bernard 1982; Newman 1981; Stadler 1986; Upchurch 1985; Van Hoose and Kottler 1985). The most comprehensive current guides to mental health law and its implications for day-to-day clinical decision making can be found in Gutheil and Appelbaum (2000) and Gutheil and others (1991).

DUAL RELATIONSHIPS

A dual relationship occurs when one person interacts with another in more than one capacity at the same time, so as to suggest the possibility of an ethical compromise or conflict of interest. Public outrage at revelations of sexual abuse of clients by therapists has caused the mental health professions to subject the slightest extratherapeutic contact between clinician and client to intense scrutiny. Even the most innocent-seeming boundary crossings are questioned, lest they begin a slippery slope ending in sexual, emotional, or financial exploitation (Borys and Pope 1989; Kitchener 1988). Whether out of concern for the vulnerability induced by transference or for the clinician's fiduciary responsibility toward the client, the ethics codes of the various professions have proscribed virtually every form of dual relationship. In this respect, they are running just a step ahead of (or behind) the courts. For example, a therapist who profits financially from information revealed by a client in therapy may be subject not only to civil liability for malpractice but also to prosecution for insider trading (Edelwich and Brodsky 1991).

When it comes to the supervisor-supervisee relationship, the picture is more complicated. Separate ethics codes for supervisors are only beginning to be formulated. To date, only the North Atlantic Regional Association for Counselor Education and Supervision (NARACES) has developed standards for educators and supervisors. ACES, the parent organization, has established a committee to develop guidelines for supervision. Other disciplines have incorporated their standards for supervision into their general codes of ethics.

Thus, the American Psychological Association's Ethical Principles of Psychologists (1981) addresses the functions of a supervisor. Principle 7d states that "psychologists do not exploit their professional relationships with supervisees, students, employees, or research participants sexually or otherwise." Principle 6 states that "psychologists should make every effort to avoid dual relationships that could impair their professional judgment or increase the risk of exploitation. Examples of such dual relationships include, but are not limited to, research with and treatment of employees, students, supervisees, close friends, or relatives."

A decade later, the American Association for Marriage and Family Therapy's (AAMFT) code of ethics (1991) has taken a similar position but with greater specificity and elaboration. Code 3.5 addresses sexual harassment or exploitation of supervisees. Code 4.1 speaks to the supervisor's influential position and the importance not only of avoiding dual relationships but also of taking appropriate precautions to prevent exploitation. This code also states, "Provision of therapy to students, employees, or supervisees is prohibited. Sexual intimacy with students or supervisees is prohibited." The 1991 revision warns that dual relationships contain the potential for impaired judgment and exploitation. According to the code, when a dual relationship cannot be avoided, it is imperative to take appropriate professional precautions (such as supervision of supervision) to ensure that judgment is not impaired.

As the language of these codes suggests, a supervisor is not the same as a therapist. A supervisor is more like a teacher, though often with the authority of an employer and sometimes (depending on the model of therapy) with overtones of a therapist. In supervision, therefore, the standards, while still tilted strongly against the exploitation of an unequal power relationship, are not so uniformly black-and-white as in the therapist-client relationship. There is a consensus that a therapist should not have lunch or play golf with a client, but it is harder to set such boundaries with regard to a supervisee. As a mentor/coach/work director, the supervisor does form a collegial relationship with the supervisee that may involve some kinds of extracurricular activities. Where the line is drawn depends on the individuals and the circumstances. Each relationship is different. What is appropriate with one supervisee may not be appropriate with another.

Boundaries and Guidelines

Among the different types of dual relationships that may occur between counselor and supervisor, some are clearly proscribed, while others involve gradations of judgment. The following examples establish some key boundaries.

Sexual involvement is an unequivocal and unethical exploitation of the supervisory role (Conroe and Schank 1989). In a national survey of clinical psychologists, Pope, Levenson, and Schover (1979) and Pope, Schover, and Levenson (1980) found that 17 percent of the women and 3 percent of the men had been sexually involved with a supervisor while in training. Cormier and Bernard (1982) reported that 10 percent of students in psychology training programs had had sexual contact with an instructor. When this unethical behavior occurs, it is essential that the counselor be assigned a new supervisor and that disciplinary action be taken against the supervisor by the agency and/or the profession in which the supervisor is credentialed.

One does not supervise one's spouse. Intimate partners, married or unmarried, cannot supervise each other.

A supervisor, especially one who has administrative authority over a supervisee, is not to act as the supervisee's personal therapist or counselor. Agencies should have an employee assistance program (EAP) for counselors when personal issues interfere with their job performance. This boundary may be blurred somewhat in models of supervision that emphasize insight and personal growth, where supervision may have an inherently therapeutic component. However, when psychodynamic models are used in work settings (as opposed to training institutions), the dual relationship should be closely monitored, with precautions taken to maintain essential boundaries.

A supervisor should not sponsor a supervisee in AA. The dual relationship of a counselor who is in a twelve-step recovery program for alcoholism or drug abuse and runs into clients at meetings after work hours, unique to the alcoholism and drug abuse field, is fraught with unavoidable gray areas and judgment calls. One relatively clear guideline, however, is to avoid forming the close personal bond of sponsorship with a supervisee, just as one would with a client in therapy.

Supervisors and supervisees who are friends should maintain boundaries carefully. Bernard (1987) comments on another type of dual relationship: "Often persons working together who have a good deal in common become close friends. When the relationship makes objective assessment extremely difficult or impossible, a dual relationship has evolved. It is not always imperative to remove a supervisor in this case, but at the very least outside consultation should be sought by the supervisor to affirm that his or her evaluation of the supervisee is accurate" (p. 53).

Counselors can become personally close to their supervisor during the supervisory relationship, or they may have been good friends already, especially if they came to the same agency as peers. Friendships between supervisors and supervisees are common, inevitable, and generally positive. Nonetheless, the welfare of the client and the supervisee remains the highest priority. Clients have a right to expect that their counselor is receiving competent supervision, with the supervisor maintaining the distance necessary to be objective. Therefore, the precarious boundary between friendship and dual relationships must be carefully monitored.

On the supervisor's part, it may be necessary to say, "Now that I've been promoted to be your supervisor, I can't do some of the things I used to do with you. Our relationship is different now." In addition, it is recommended that the supervisory role be monitored by an objective third party to ensure appropriate boundaries. That is, supervision should be supervised by a member of the facility's clinical staff. Cosupervision with a colleague is another mechanism for monitoring dual relationships. If a dual relationship occurs, it is not preordained that the supervisor be removed from that position. The severity of the problem must be assessed. Outside consultation may be necessary to protect the supervisee and future supervisory relationships.

Finally, supervisees are not to be coerced into friendships and social relationships with supervisors any more than they are to be coerced into sexual relationships. In case of doubt about any of these questions, a good rule of thumb is to err on the side of distance and keep the boundaries clean.

Dilemmas at the Boundaries

Although it is easy to counsel avoiding dual relationships, it may not be so easy to do so in practice. Here are some typical dilemmas that a supervisor might face.

The "Only Game in Town" Syndrome

- You are the best family therapist in town to deal with children with a particular problem. Should you avoid dual relationships with a supervisee who has referred his child to you for care?
- You are counseling an individual referred to you by a supervisee, only to find out that the individual is a distant relative of the supervisee.
- The supervisee who has referred a client to you is pressing charges against the client for theft. You might be called to testify against your own supervisee on behalf of the client.
- You live in a small town and are in private practice with an associate who is the best therapist in that town for the treatment of depression. Among the people she is treating for this condition is the spouse of your supervisee.
- You are part of a small, closely knit gay community whose members know and socialize with one another. You are assigned to supervise another member of this community, whom no one else in the agency is as well qualified to train.
- A client reveals she is having an extramarital affair and identifies her lover as a married clinician whom you are supervising.

What do you do with this information? Do you continue to treat the client? Do you continue to supervise the counselor? If you decide to end the supervisory relationship, how do you explain this while maintaining client confidentiality?

The "We Grew Up Together" Syndrome

- You were promoted from being a counselor on the staff to being the supervisor. You are younger than the other counselors, but because you alone have a master's degree, you were offered the job in compliance with Joint Commission on Accreditation of Healthcare Organizations (JCAHO) and third-party reimbursement regulations. Can you continue to socialize with the whole staff as you did before? Can you accept theater tickets from a supervisee? Can you let one of them fix you up with a date?
- How differently do you act in your new role at social occasions, such as the agency's annual picnic? Are you more reserved? Do you share personal information about your family with supervisees?
- How do you establish credibility with former peers? What if one of the supervisees assigned to you is a close personal friend? spouse? How do you separate your personal from professional responsibilities? Is there anyone you must transfer to someone else's supervision?
- What do you do with private information previously divulged to you as a friend or peer of the individuals you now supervise? How do you ensure that this information does not contaminate the performance review process?

"Two-Hatter" Issues for the Substance Abuse Counselor and Supervisor

- What if you are recovering and the rest of the staff is not? How do you use the recovery history to your advantage while not holding it over the staff?
- Do you go to the same AA meetings with supervisees? What if you live in a small town, and there are no other meetings available to you? This is the only women's meeting for miles. What if you do not have a car to go to meetings? Should you accept

a ride to a meeting with a supervisee? If meetings are held at your facility, should you attend? participate? speak? What if it is a closed meeting?

- You have been attending your home group meeting in AA for a decade. Having just been promoted to supervisor, you find out that a new supervisee attends that meeting too. Do you need to act differently now toward that supervisee? What if that person has a far longer sobriety history than you?
- Are there any circumstances under which you might sponsor a supervisee in AA? What do you do when you believe a supervisee is about to relapse? How do you intervene while maintaining dual-relationship boundaries?

What Should I Tell You About Myself?

- How much self-disclosure is appropriate between supervisor and supervisees? What complications might result from too much exposure? Do I want you to know about my pending divorce? my children's problems in school? My fears, hopes, dreams? How much of this do I want to know from my supervisees?
- How do gender issues affect the extent of my self-disclosure to coworkers? Does male bonding lead me to reveal more to the other male staff members than the female staff? Or do I disclose more to the more nurturing women in the agency while I keep up a competitive edge with the men? When does this differential treatment border on sexism or even sexual harassment?

These questions have no definitive answers. In sorting out the dilemmas they pose, there is no substitute for peer consultation, supervision of one's supervision, and supervisee feedback. When it comes to dual relationships, professional ethics codes cover little more than the extremes. In between the extremes, it is up to the individual to make responsible decisions by taking into account all the variables. This is a skill that supervisors learn as they mature. As a rule, level 3 supervisors develop an integrated ethical perspective that enables them to sort out the shades of gray in what level 1 supervisors perceive as a black-and-white world.

If, after careful consideration and consultation, any question remains about the propriety of a given course of conduct, the supervisor is advised to put the question through the three acid tests proposed by Blanchard and Peale (1988):

1. Is it legal? Will I be violating either civil law or company policy?
2. Is it balanced? Is it fair to all concerned in the short term and long term? Does it promote win-win relationships?
3. How will I feel about it myself? Does it make me feel proud? What if it were published in a newspaper? Would I feel good if my family knew about it?

The third set of questions is the real acid test, because they measure the proposed conduct against the standard of personal values. If any feeling of uneasiness remains, it is best to err on the side of caution.

PROFESSIONAL CREDIBILITY

Principle 2 of the Ethical Principles of Psychologists states that psychologists "only provide services and use techniques for which they are qualified by training and experiences" (APA 1981). Similarly, code 4.2 of the American Association for Marriage and Family Therapy's Code of Ethics (AAMFT 1991) provides that "marriage and family therapists do not permit students, employees, or supervisees to perform or to hold themselves out as competent to perform professional services beyond their training, level of experience, and competence." These sound principles, however, do not provide all the necessary guidelines for their own implementation. The dilemma for supervisors is to decide when a supervisee is competent to use techniques and skills she has never tried before. Clients must be informed that they are being counseled by trainees (ACES 1989; Bray, Shepherd, and Hays 1985; Kaslow 1986a; Margolin 1982; Wilcoxon 1986; Wilcoxon and Fennell 1983).

Similarly, the supervisor who is new to a particular task or role should make an honest disclosure to the supervisee: "Look, I'm new at this game. I'm learning. I need to learn from you. We're growing together." This disclosure can be part of the supervisor's overall briefing, which includes the supervisor's theoretical model, the goals of supervision, and the level of competencies expected. The supervisor's openness about these questions fosters an atmosphere of mutual trust in which the supervisor can readily raise questions of misdiagnosis, unethical conduct, and incomplete learning of techniques if these arise. In this way, supervision becomes a forum for resolving, rather than evading or concealing, questions that bear on professional qualifications, adequacy of training, and competence.

The 1991 revision of the AAMFT's Code of Ethics includes several provisions that could serve as a model for other fields, insofar as they represent the maturing of the discipline of supervision into a profession with sophisticated ethical standards. For example, codes 3.3 and 4 emphasize the importance of scholarship and the need to remain abreast of developments in the field. Supervisee confidentiality, within certain guidelines, is ensured in code 4.3. Codes 7, 7.3, and 7.4 recommend clear and fair fees for supervision. Code 8.9 states that supervisors may advertise themselves under that designation but may not represent it as an advanced clinical status.

EVALUATION

Evaluation is part of the ongoing work of supervision. Furthermore, it is the responsibility of the supervisor to provide counselors with feedback when there are serious concerns about their clinical skills and practice and to screen out those who should not be working in this field. Due process must be observed throughout the evaluation process. Supervisees must know what is expected of them, the means of evaluation, and the consequences of the evaluation. Feedback must be given periodically and in a constructive manner. This feedback should include a written statement, reviewed by both parties, of the supervisee's strengths and weaknesses (Canon and Brown 1985; Hart 1982).

RESPECT

According to the ACES (1988) code, "Counselor educators and supervisors should have the same respect for their trainees as counselors have for their counselees" (p. 245). Supervisors must accord supervisees the same respect and dignity they do clients with regard to confidentiality, fair treatment, clarity of expectations, and boundary setting. Supervisors should respect the racial, ethnic, social, religious, and political diversity of their supervisees at all times. The code goes on to state that "expectations should be made clear. Allowances should be made for freedom of choice. Under no circumstances should counselor educators and supervisors attempt to sway trainees to adopt a particular theoretical belief or point of view." In other words, supervisors do not remake supervisees into their own image or clone themselves in counselors. Instead, they help counselors shape themselves after their own fashion.

INFORMED CONSENT

The supervisor has a responsibility to the client to be certain that the client is informed of the supervisory process and the means of observation and gives voluntary, uncoerced consent. A signed release from the client must be obtained if a session is to be taped. The client must be informed of the uses to be made of any material (video- or audiotapes) and of any limits placed on confidentiality, either by the clinical and training procedures of the agency or by laws mandating reporting of child abuse or threats of violence toward third parties. Failure to obtain informed consent constitutes grounds for legal action irrespective of clinical negligence or malpractice.

CONFIDENTIALITY

Principle 5a of the Ethical Principles of Psychologists (APA 1981) states that "information obtained in clinical or consulting relationships, or valuative data concerning children, students, employees, and others is discussed only for professional purposes and only with the persons clearly concerned with the case." This principle applies to supervision as well as to counseling. What the supervisor learns in supervision is not for cafeteria conversation, as in, "You wouldn't believe what that new counselor did yesterday. He really messed up that case!" Supervisee confidentiality is analogous to client confidentiality in the respect for boundaries it entails.

Client confidentiality itself has become a complex ethical and legal issue in the light of the case law and statute law that have developed around the notion of a clinician's duty to warn. This doctrine originated with the case of *Tarasoff* v. *Regents of the University of California* (1976), in which a university counselor and supervisor were found liable (confidentiality notwithstanding) for failing to take adequate steps to warn an identified victim of a patient's threat of violence. Subsequent court decisions and state laws have interpreted and modified this doctrine in various ways. Supervisors must be aware of the laws and regulations governing confidentiality in their state, including the duty to warn as well as mandatory reporting statutes (for example, concerning child abuse or sexual misconduct by therapists), and instruct their supervisees accordingly.

SUPERVISEE ETHICS

Supervisees have ethical responsibilities that in many ways are the same as, or the reciprocal of, those that apply to supervisors. Chief among these are the following:

1. *To uphold professional standards of practice.* This principle encompasses a wide range of areas, including clinical competence, informed consent, client confidentiality, respect for boundaries, and refraining from unprofessional conduct.
2. *To recognize and deal with personal problems when they interfere with clinical effectiveness.* This requirement has been incorporated into the ethics codes of the APA (1981, principle 2f) and the AAMFT (1991, code 3.2). When disruptive personal problems arise, counselors must seek competent help through their EAP. In addition, they should inform their supervisor that they have taken this step and indicate how they believe their personal problems might be affecting their clinical practice.
3. *To treat the supervisor with respect and dignity.* This principle entails living up to the terms of the mutually agreed-upon contract. It is the responsibility of both parties to resolve any conflicts that arise between supervisor and supervisee.
4. *To treat the information shared in supervision with the highest degree of confidentiality.* Gossiping by a supervisee about the supervisor is as unacceptable as the other way around. Given the limited

training available to supervisors and the paucity of material available to supervisees regarding what to expect in supervision, it is not surprising that boundary violations and breaches of confidentiality occur. However, every effort must be made to train counselors to enter into the supervisory relationship with the same professionalism as the counseling relationship.

Counselors mature in their understanding and ability to implement professional codes of ethics over the course of their training. Typically, level 1 counselors have learned codes of ethics by rote and need help in applying textbook statements to actual situations. Level 2 counselors are better able to differentiate ethical dilemmas, but this nascent appreciation of complexity only adds to their frustration and confusion. The anxiety that results may block effective clinical judgment and action. As they mature, counselors no longer automatically respond with anxiety to situations in which contradictory ethical principles may apply. Level 3 counselors have well-formed and integrated ethical systems, so that they can distinguish between healthy and unhealthy dilemmas (Stoltenberg and Delworth 1987).

LEGAL LIABILITY FOR SUPERVISORS

The demands of the law are felt increasingly on all aspects of clinical practice. With changing civil liabilities reinforced by accountability to credentialing bodies, third-party payers, malpractice insurers, and managed care overseers, clinicians and supervisors must consider a host of legal and regulatory ramifications as they conduct their daily practice (Cormier and Bernard 1982; Gutheil and Applebaum 2000; Gutheil and others 1991; Slovenko 1980). State statutes clearly specify the requirements of practice, but these mainly focus on mandatory disclosures and failure to warn. A much greater proportion of the legal constraints and potential liabilities affecting clinicians comes out of case law, which is constantly evolving.

An aspect of mental health case law that is crucial for supervisors to understand is summarized by Slovenko (1980, p. 462): "The psychotherapy supervisor assumes, in general, clinical responsibility much as if the patient were under his (or her) own personal care." This is known as the principle of vicarious liability. "According to this doctrine, someone in a position of authority or responsibility, such as a supervisor, is responsible for acts of his or her trainees or assistant. Stated another way, supervisors are ultimately legally responsible for the welfare of clients counseled by their supervisees" (Cormier and Bernard 1982, p. 488). The supervisor assumes a heavy responsibility for the quality of care that is rendered, especially (but not exclusively) when a counselor has provided services he was not competent to perform or when a client was not informed that she was being treated by a trainee. Anyone remotely involved in a client's case, including a supervisor not employed by the same agency as the counselor, may be caught up in the net of litigation. Moreover, the counselor's and supervisor's liability extend up the line to the agency itself.

Vicarious liability made itself felt in the *Tarasoff* case, which set the initial legal precedent concerning the duty to warn. In that landmark case, the plaintiff's attorney implied that if the supervisor had personally examined the patient and made a considered decision that the client was not dangerous, the plaintiff might not have had a case. In fact, the clinical supervisor was implicated in the finding of a negligent failure to warn the prospective victim (Slovenko 1980).

This trend has continued in cases involving other grounds for liability. In a 1989 New York State trial, a supervisor and agency were found liable for malpractice for failure to oversee adequately the functioning of a counselor—that is, to make a reasonable effort at supervision. The court ruled that it is the responsibility of the supervisor to ensure quality care and to document that a reasonable effort was made to supervise the staff. The same holds true in the explosive area of sexual exploitation of patients by clinicians. In *Birkner* v. *Salt Lake County* (1989), the Supreme Court of Utah ruled that a county mental health clinic could be held liable for negligent supervision of a sexually exploitive therapist if such negligence could be proved. Any dual relationships entail evident legal risks. Sexual harassment, in particular, constitutes obvious grounds for supervisory liability for failure to maintain an appropriately professional atmosphere in an agency.

The message is clear: supervisors cannot escape responsibility for the care and well-being of their supervisees' clients on the basis of ignorance of the law. Supervisors are legally and ethically responsible to be informed and aware of the actions of their counselors; further, they must make a reasonable effort to supervise counselors and to monitor their activities. These legal requirements are not impossibly stringent. As Borders and Leddick (1987) correctly point out, "Ironically, if the supervisor is aware of the case, but makes an incorrect judgment regarding the case, he/she probably will not be found to be liable. The law does not ask the supervisor to be infallible, but rather, to be involved" (p. 55).

With regard to violence or the threat of violence, for example, supervisors must observe the following guidelines:

1. Follow any applicable state or federal laws.
2. When a counselor has direct knowledge of potential harm to an individual, group, or property, the counselor *under supervisory guidance* must determine: (a) the client's propensity (desire plus ability) to perpetrate violence; (b) the client's intention to perpetrate violence; and (c) whether a specific victim has been identified.
3. When a credible threat of violence exists according to the above criteria, the counselor *under supervisory guidance* must, as appropriate: (a) seek a commitment from the client not to act violently; (b) take action to eliminate the threat; (c) inform the police and the identified victim.
4. It is the supervisor's responsibility to ensure that the counselor understands the concept of the duty to warn and that specified actions are taken. Federally mandated reporting is exempt from the requirement of confidentiality. Such limits on confidentiality should be made clear to the client as part of obtaining informed consent to treatment. Furthermore, it is sometimes possible to involve the client in the process of warning the prospective victim or the police, thereby strengthening both the therapeutic alliance and the client's sense of responsibility (Wulsin, Bursztajn, and Gutheil 1983).

Two of the best ways to demonstrate supervisory involvement are through consultation and documentation, considered the two pillars of malpractice prevention (Gutheil and Applebaum 2000). A clinician who cared enough to seek a colleague's advice and who cared enough to write it down probably exercised considered clinical (or supervisory) judgment. It is strongly recommended that a supervisor maintain a personal record of dates and times when supervision was provided, the names of those supervised, and the general areas and clinical issues discussed. This notation should also include the names of clients discussed during the supervisory sessions (Van Hoose and Kottler 1985). The report need not be more than a few sentences long; as the prominent forensic psychiatrist Thomas Gutheil says, "Don't write more; write smarter." When a supervisor is sued for something a counselor did a year or two earlier, the supervisor will not remember when the individual was supervised, let alone what was discussed. The supervisor's notebook provides documentation that a reasonable effort at supervision was made. What constitutes a reasonable effort at supervision for a given time, place, and profession should be discussed with the agency's legal counsel or forensic mental health specialists.

As a general rule, supervision should be scheduled on a regular basis, offering careful assessment and oversight of counselors. It is also advisable for the supervisor to make an independent assessment of severely disturbed or dangerous patients. Finally, it is normal prudence to know and adhere to the laws of practice for one's state, including those pertaining to mandated reporting of infractions (Cormier and Bernard 1982).

To take one specific (and highly salient) example, clinical supervision plays a vital role in preventing or responding appropriately to sexual misconduct on the part of clinicians (Bursztajn 1990; Schoener 1989; Schoener and Conroe 1989; Strasburger, Jorgenson, and Sutherland 1992). Edelwich and Brodsky (1991, p. 145) summarize the essence of this supervisory responsibility:

> Supervision comes into play not only when a suspicion of wrongdoing arises, but, more important, in the normal, ongoing vigilance that keeps both individuals and the organization out of trouble. Clearly, supervisory intervention becomes more focused when (on the basis of a complaint, rumor, staff member's observation, or tip from another agency) there is reason to believe that a clinician has a personal stake in his or her relationship with a client. Nonetheless, the same skills of observation and inference are to be deployed in routine weekly supervision.

Supervisors should also inform themselves about the trend toward criminalization of sexual misconduct by therapists (six states had enacted such laws as of 1991) and about the evolving professional and legal debate over the impropriety of therapists' sexual involvement with former clients. The latter trend has led to a web of conflicting state laws and professional ethics codes, some of which set time periods during which a clinician may face disciplinary action, civil liability, or criminal prosecution for having sex with a former client (Edelwich and Brodsky 1991). Mandatory reporting of complaints of sexual misconduct by therapists is now provided for by some state laws, so as to track offenders and prevent further abuses in other agencies or locations (Strasburger, Jorgenson, and Randles 1990). Finally, the nature and limits of organizational liability for such offenses have been established by laws such as a Minnesota statute that provides for background checks of prospective employees, responses to background inquiries from other employers, and appropriate action in response to client complaints (Sanderson 1989). These are examples of what supervisors need to know about the law. Most of all, supervisors need to achieve the highest possible level of competency. This is the best insurance policy against ethical compromise and legal vulnerability.

NEW ETHICAL AND LEGAL CONCERNS

The legal and ethical landscape for managers and supervisors has changed dramatically since the first edition of this book was published. The information that follows represents the most significant changes drawn from the current case rulings reported in Janet Elizabeth Falvey's book *Managing Clinical Supervision: Ethical Practice and Legal Risk Management* (2002). The reader is referred to Falvey's book for detailed analysis of recent case law affecting managers and supervisors.

Supervisory Competence

In recent years the number of professional organizations credentialing clinical supervisors has grown. The professional organizations that regulate the ethical and legal practices of supervisors are the National Board for Certified Counselors (NBCC), the National Association of Social Workers (NASW), the American Association for Marriage and Family Therapy (AAMFT), and in the alcohol and drug abuse field, the International Certification & Reciprocity Consortium (IC&RC).

These organizations and the courts have posed critical questions for assessing supervisory competence and defining the range and scope of clinical supervision. Courts in particular, in ruling on malpractice cases, have defined a standard of care and practice in supervision, one that reflects the testimony of experts in the field.

- Does the supervisor have the skills to perform the requisite supervisory functions?
- Does the supervisor make an adequate effort to supervise? *Adequate* is defined by the profession in which the person practices. Most professions define adequate as one hour of supervision for every twenty hours of client contact or approximately one hour of supervision per week for a full-time therapist.
- Do the supervisor and the agency have a formal process for providing feedback and evaluations to counselors?
- Does the supervisor teach the tenets and legal and ethical standards of the profession?
- Does the supervisor maintain adequate documentation of the supervision process?

Court rulings (for example, *Gilmore* v. *Board of Psychological Examiners*, 1986, cited in Falvey 2002) have pointed to several common legal and ethical errors that occur in supervision. Some of these errors are discussed in the Introduction to the 1993 Edition and earlier in this chapter.

- Confusing supervision with case management.
- Focusing on the client's needs rather than the supervisee's development.
- Relying on the supervisor's clinical skills in supervision, thereby turning supervision into therapy with a supervisee.
- Adopting a laissez-faire attitude, with supervision occurring on a sporadic basis.

- Conducting quasi-casual case conferences and crisis-management supervision.
- Using supervisory power inappropriately.

Court rulings have affirmed the importance of clarifying the roles and expectations of clinical supervision, correcting these common legal and ethical errors. The two most important issues considered in these rulings have been: (1) Did the supervisor make a reasonable effort to supervise? (2) Was the supervisor competent (as demonstrated by credentialing, training, and experience) to perform the tasks of a supervisor?

Supervisory Accountability

The legal criterion for malpractice is a breach of duty, that is, of one's fiduciary responsibility to protect the welfare of another. The breach may take the form of an action or inaction that is deemed by the profession not to have met the applicable standard of care and that has a harmful outcome judged to have been foreseeable. The extent to which injury (physical, emotional, or financial) has resulted directly from the dereliction of duty determines the degree of liability of a counselor or supervisor. Although only 2 percent of psychotherapeutic malpractice claims in 1998 were due to a failure to supervise a counselor, there is a growing concern that supervisors are to be held accountable for the actions of their supervisees.

Vicarious liability occurs when damage to a client results from a supervisor's dereliction in carrying out supervisory responsibility for the supervisee's work, from his giving inappropriate advice to the supervisee to the detriment of the client, from his failing to listen carefully to the supervisee's report about a client, or from his assigning tasks to a counselor who is inadequately trained to perform those tasks. Falvey (2002) points to a number of landmark cases that made these distinctions. For example, *Jaffee* v. *Redmond* (1996; cited in Falvey 2002) established that psychotherapeutic communication between a client and a licensed practitioner is privileged, not differentiating between disciplines. However, unlicensed supervisees may not be covered under the regulations for privileging of a licensed supervisor. This is determined by state regulations, and ultimately judges are the interpreters of the scope of privileged communication. This is significant for the alcohol and drug abuse field because many states certify but do not license substance abuse counselors. Thus, they may not be covered under the regulations for privileged psychotherapeutic communication.

Other landmark cases from Falvey (2002) affecting supervisory accountability include *Gilmore* v. *Board of Psychological Examiners* (1986), *Steckler* v. *Ohio State Board of Psychology* (1992), *Peck* v. *Counseling Service of Addison County, Inc.* (1985), and *Almonte* v. *New York Medical College* (1994).

Confidentiality and Its Limits

The most significant legal and ethical issues affecting supervisors concern client confidentiality, with breaches of confidentiality being one of the top five charges in successful suits against psychotherapists. Pope and Bajt (1988) provide startling data from a 1985 survey of 60 senior psychologists, all of whom were members of state or national ethics committees and authors of texts on legal and ethical issues in counseling: 57 percent of senior psychologists acknowledged violating legal and/or ethical mandates concerning confidentiality at least once in the interest of a client's welfare, 21 percent had divulged confidential information, and 27 percent had refused to carry out a duty to report child abuse or to warn a victim of a dangerous situation. Most strikingly, 75 percent stated that at times caregivers should violate formal legal and ethical standards.

Falvey (2002) cites *Roe* v. *State Board of Psychology* (1995), which rejected the claim of lack of adequate training on confidentiality as a defense in the case of a supervisee's violation. The court determined that it was the supervisor's responsibility to train the supervisee in the limits of confidentiality. On the other hand, courts have also affirmed a client's right to privacy by insisting that a counselor inform the client of the limits of confidentiality at the start of counseling. This is termed "the psychological Miranda warning."

Tarasoff v. *Regents of the University of California* (1976), discussed earlier in this chapter, has been used by several states as the standard for duty to warn. Most states place at least symbolic value on this landmark case in defining the duty to warn and thereby to protect identified victims of threatened violence. Two cases in Falvey (2002) address duty-to-warn situations. *Jablonski* v. *the United States* (1983) addressed the predictability of violent acts based on the patient's psychological profile. *Pesce* v. *J. Sterling Morton High School, District 201* (1987) lays out guidelines for mandatory child abuse reporting, while taking into account the child's safety, cultural differences in child rearing, the age of the child, and the type of abuse.

In 2003, the federal government, through regulations implementing the Health Insurance Portability and Accountability Act (HIPAA), established new guidelines that limit confidentiality. The guidelines specify that each provider must issue a "Notice of Privacy Practices" that makes explicit with whom medical information may be shared and how it may be used. The U.S. Department of Health and Human Services (HHS), under the Patriot Act, has been given unrestricted access to medical records to monitor compliance. The new regulations have been challenged in the courts by privacy advocates. It is imperative that supervisors become familiar with these HIPAA guidelines and other HHS regulations and with the court decisions in the area of patient rights that will follow, for these developments will dramatically affect therapeutic and supervisory relationships.

Juxtaposed to the HIPAA regulations, as stated in the Introduction to the 2004 edition, are HHS regulations put into effect in 2003, in response to the terrorist threat against the United States, that allow the federal government and law enforcement to examine an individual's medical records without that person's knowledge or consent. This policy likewise portends great changes in the doctor-patient relationship as traditionally understood and practiced. Clinicians and patients' rights advocates have voiced grave concerns that patients will now withhold information physicians and therapists need for proper diagnosis and treatment. Even when patients do volunteer sensitive information, clinicians may not enter it into the records, which thus are left incomplete. According to a study by the Association of American Physicians and Surgeons, 78 percent of physicians surveyed withheld information from a patient's records because of concerns about privacy. Moreover, 87 percent reported that patients had requested the withholding of information from their medical records (Falvey 2002).

Regardless of how the courts rule on these changes in confidentiality regulations, it is imperative that the supervisor and manager remain current with the ever-changing rules on confidentiality.

Clinical Oversight: Dangerous Liaisons

Court rulings have emphasized that supervisees must know the qualifications of their supervisor, patient information critical to the performance of their clinical duties, treatment logistics, insurance reimbursement procedures, record-keeping requirements, and the risks and benefits of alternatives to treatment.

Falvey (2002) cites four cases concerning clinical oversight. *Simmons* v. *United States* (1986), *Pesce* v. *J. Sterling Morton High School, District 201* (1987), *Jablonski* v. *United States* (1983), and *Andrews* v. *United States* (1984) made clear the supervisor's responsibility to oversee the counseling relationship between a supervisee and a client. Ignorance of the nature of that relationship is no longer an acceptable excuse for a supervisor. The courts further expect the supervisor to confront the supervisee about any allegations of impropriety, document the recommendations made and actions taken, and place a critical incident report in the supervisee's file pending resolution. Courts have also upheld that the supervisor must question the client wherever feasible and clinically viable, consult with colleagues about the alleged impropriety, and monitor the supervisee's cases. Finally, the supervisor is expected to report the allegation to investigative services, state boards, and relevant ethics committees.

A growing concern in supervision is nondisclosure of information by a supervisee to the clinical supervisor. Falvey (2002) points to a study by Welfel (1998) that found 97 percent of supervisees withheld information from their supervisors, 60 percent withheld personal information relevant to their counseling practice, 90 percent withheld negative feelings about the supervisor, 44 percent withheld information about their clinical mistakes, 36 percent withheld countertransferential information, and 9 percent withheld the fact of their attraction to at least one client. Given this evidence of the prevalence of nondisclosure, it is imperative that supervisors establish an open and trusting atmosphere so that supervisees will be more likely to share information.

Finally, supervisors can take these actions to help avoid dangerous liaisons between supervisees and clients. Supervisors should meet the supervisees' clients whenever possible. They should have supervisees review and sign the code of ethics of the counseling profession. They should regularly audiotape or videotape counseling sessions conducted by supervisees and document all recommended actions. Direct observation of counselors in action is no longer a luxury. It is now imperative that supervisors regularly observe the clinical work of staff. As stated in Chapter Twelve, the definition of "reasonable effort" in supervision now encompasses direct observation of counselors' clinical work.

Supervisory Contracting

Falvey (2002) discusses two cases that addressed supervisory contracting. *Ray* v. *Delaware* (1997) and *Steckler* v. *Ohio State Board of Psychology* (1992) defined the standards of supervision and the limits of supervision with an unlicensed counselor. From these rulings, it is clear that some form of written supervisory contract signed by supervisor and supervisee is imperative. This contract should include:

- An individualized training plan for the supervisee.
- The schedule, format, duration, roles, responsibilities, goals, and objectives of supervision.
- Information on the supervisor's training and model of supervision.
- Emergency and crisis-management procedures, including the availability of 24/7 coverage in the event of a clinical emergency.
- Clarification of the roles of an academic supervisor (if any).
- The ratio of the number of clients to the number of supervision hours (such as the 20-to-1 ratio recommended earlier).
- Formative and summative evaluation procedures.
- Disciplinary procedures, due process, rights of the supervisee, and sanctions.

Peck v. *Counseling Service of Addison County, Inc.* (1985) defined the need for a formal crisis management policy (Falvey 2002). Agencies should have a crisis plan that states how crises and duty-to-warn situations will be handled. What mechanisms are in place for responding to crises, especially after normal working hours? Who is on call after hours, and how quickly is information concerning a potentially lethal clinical situation to be reported to the supervisor and management of the organization? What policies and procedures are in place to handle crisis situations? How will duty-to-warn procedures be enacted after normal work hours?

Supervisee Selection, Assignments, and Documentation

Few supervisors identify client screening as an aspect of supervision, despite court rulings that supervisors can be held liable if they do not determine the supervisee's competence before assigning responsibilities. It is imperative that supervisors protect the welfare of the client by:

- Knowing the clinical competencies and limitations of each of their supervisees.
- Assessing the complexity of client issues prior to assigning a case to a supervisee.
- Determining whether the supervisee is adequately trained to assume the case.
- Ensuring that the supervisee does not have too many cases to be able to provide proper services to clients.
- Protecting the supervisee from having too many difficult-to-treat cases in her caseload.
- Identifying and resolving learning and personal problems that may compromise the supervisee's effectiveness.
- Ensuring that there is sufficient supervision time for the cases assigned.

According to a number of court rulings (*Almonte* v. *New York Medical College*, 1994; *Hill* v. *Kokosky, M.D.*, 1990; *Emory University* v. *Porubiansky*, 1981), the supervisor should review the résumés of all employees, assess their areas of strength and areas in which additional training is needed, and require formal training and close supervision for the deficit areas (Falvey 2002).

Falvey (2002) provides a workbook of appropriate forms for documenting clinical supervision. The use of these forms is highly recommended. Documentation should review emergency procedures and the supervisee's employment profile. Records of all clinical supervision sessions should be maintained. Documentation of all cases discussed in supervision is required. Case termination procedures should be documented in the supervisory log. The written and mutually signed supervision contract should be maintained.

Conclusion

As stated in the 1993 edition of this book, it is imperative that supervisors uphold the highest legal and ethical standards of the profession. Now recent court rulings no longer see the fiduciary responsibility of a supervisor as a "nice thing to do." The way to protect an organization and individuals from vulnerability to claims of malpractice is to practice quality clinical supervision. The best way to ensure against the practice of the bad is the practice of the better.

Chapter Sixteen

Special Issues in Supervision

As the field of supervision has become more sophisticated, so has the awareness of special issues affecting the supervisory process. Whereas the early literature largely limited itself to generic issues in supervision, the late 1980s and 1990s have witnessed an expansion of information about a wide array of highly specialized issues. These roughly correspond to the contextual factors—characteristics of the client, counselor, supervisor, and setting that affect the environment of supervision—added to the pyramid diagram (Figure 5-1).

There is a growing body of literature on how gender, ethnicity, and cultural variations influence the supervisory process, as well as on the influence of feminism on counselor training. Of special interest to the alcoholism and drug abuse field is the problem of the resistant or impaired counselor. The addiction field's mission to promote recovery creates a heightened concern for the relapsed counselor or staff member who is abusively using alcohol or drugs. The individual counselor is not, however, the only source of resistance. There is also the resistant milieu—an organizational environment that must provide a range of services to a diverse population, often with limited resources and under frustrating bureaucratic constraints. Of all the contexts that affect the environment of supervision, none is more crucial than the front-line treatment setting in a public or private agency.

The integration of these contextual issues into the philosophy of supervision is a project yet to be undertaken, and the body of research and literature remains to be filled out and synthesized.

Training programs offer courses on specialized subjects such as women in treatment but have yet to integrate them into a coherent therapy or training model. Eventually these special concerns must be incorporated into more comprehensive training objectives— for example, addressing supervision from a feminist perspective. Additional time will be required in training and supervision to deal adequately with these dimensions of clinical care. This chapter gives an overview of current knowledge in these areas, pending their integration into the blended model of supervision, as well as other models.

CONTEXTUAL FACTORS

Anyone who takes on the task of supervision assumes a complex, multidimensional responsibility, as the diversities and conflicts of contemporary society are mirrored in the counseling and supervisory relationships. The supervisor must address questions of race, ethnicity, culture, gender, religion, age, and socioeconomic status continuously throughout the treatment and training process, lest the counselor and supervisor develop contextual blindness, for context shapes the content and outcomes of supervision, as supervisors and supervisees represent multiple levels of experience, background, and clinical resourcefulness.

A supervisor's or supervisee's worldview can have both limiting and liberating effects on the pair's collective ability to break through problems creatively. To maximize the positive effects, the supervisor should aim to create a collaborative, nonjudgmental, and nonpejorative atmosphere that facilitates learning and growth. A willingness to listen, to understand as well as be understood, and an appreciation of every individual's unique qualities strengthen the outcomes of supervision and training. "When supervisor-supervisee relationships are based on mutual respect, understanding, and a willingness to listen and to test out one's opinions, values, beliefs, biases and prejudices, clients as well as others in these systems become beneficiaries" (Roberts 1992, p. 2).

As a first step in contextualizing the supervisory relationship, one should be aware of oneself and of one's own historical and cultural context. For example, I grew up in New York City in a theological ghetto of conservative Protestant fundamentalism, which clearly shaped my early impressions of people, sexuality, relationships, and culture. Later, it made me receptive to the spirituality of the recovery movement. At this writing I have been married for twenty-one years and have two adolescent children. I live now in rural Connecticut next to a pasture. All of these factors contribute to defining who I am when I sit down in a counseling or supervisory session. An understanding of how such a personal background influences a session is critical in order to be aware of transferential issues, to separate personal factors that can get in the way of learning, and thereby to increase effectiveness. Also critical is an awareness of how stereotypical assumptions about race, culture, gender, income levels, and so forth can be reinforced in supervision.

Supervisors and supervisees must be willing to acknowledge and respond to attitudes, ideas, and behaviors that reflect typical roles, prejudices, and stereotypes as they arise in the supervisory relationship. Stereotypes inhibit learning by not allowing people to see the uniqueness of each individual. For example, a Hispanic male supervisee who is unaccustomed to seeing women in positions of authority may be working with a Caucasian female supervisor who has little experience with the Hispanic community. She may be on guard against anticipated "macho" behavior, while he may bring to supervision his feelings of alienation from the women's movement. These differences must be discussed openly. Similarly, a middle-class supervisor working with a new supervisee in an agency serving the poor and underinsured must confront these socioeconomic issues and whatever bearing they may have on the therapeutic and supervisory relationships. One who is supervising an African American counselor in the inner city must engage with the counselor's frustration at white suburban clients who see him for crisis counseling, only to go back to their own communities for therapy when the crisis is over. A supervisor who was in graduate school while the counselor (or client) was serving in the Vietnam War must consider the effects of that major historical trauma on the experiences and presuppositions of the generation that went through it.

Merely being aware of and sensitive to contextual issues is not sufficient. An effective supervisor engages actively with these interpersonal currents, bringing them out into the open, exploring how they are affecting treatment and supervision, and developing specific strategies for working through them. Supervisors must help trainees identify clearly all relevant contextual variables by articulating who the client, supervisee, and supervisor are (in terms of race, class, gender, culture, and so forth) and considering the implications of the setting in which the supervision and counseling take place. The supervisor and supervisee can then examine what contextual issues may arise among these different constituents and how they are to be dealt with.

There are five ways of maximizing the beneficial use of contextual factors in supervision.

1. Context can be used to create and deepen the attachment between client and counselor, supervisee and supervisor. Supervision models a boundaried yet caring context. By bringing out the multiple contexts in supervision with analogies drawn from daily life, the supervisor can evoke certain universal or collective experiences to build commonality, familiarity, and a respectful working partnership.

2. Contextual factors can be used to promote and enhance competency through support and challenge. By intervening in the supervisee's way of thinking and by challenging and expanding the supervisee's belief system, the supervisor can strengthen techniques and facilitate skill building.

3. Context can be used to enhance manageability. Too often, supervision is overloaded with competency-diminishing information, too much of the wrong data about all that is going wrong in counseling. Agencies collect piles of unnecessary information to meet credentialing requirements. By instead using contextual information about the client and supervisee, the supervisor is able to experience these individuals in a totally different way. Such perceptual breakthroughs can lead to new and more productive avenues of intervention.

4. Contextual supervision can differentiate among the universal, transcultural, culture-specific, and idiosyncratic behaviors of all parties. This differentiation makes it possible to emphasize universal and transcultural similarities while recognizing that all individuals and groups have culture-specific and idiosyncratic behaviors.

5. Contextual analysis provides a relativistic framework for assessment and intervention. This framework makes it possible

to recognize culture-bound concepts and behaviors that lead to ethnocentric biases. By bringing contextual factors to the surface, the supervisor can discriminate between cases where these factors may be clinically relevant and those where they are tangential.

Supervisees can learn about contextual issues through didactic lectures, readings, and experiential exercises. For background reading about the influence of gender, ethnicity, culture, and economics on supervision, the following sources are recommended: Caust, Libow, and Raskin (1981); Falicov (1988); Piercy and others (1982); Peterson (1991); Reid and others (1987); Wheeler and others (1985). Finally, the Supervision Department of the American Association for Marriage and Family Therapy publishes a full listing of references on contextual issues in marriage and family therapy supervision (AAMFT Supervision Department, 112 South Alfred Street, Alexandria, VA 22314-3061).

GENDER AS A FACTOR IN SUPERVISION

Gender comes into play in supervision from a number of angles. First, there is the question of gender matching of supervisors and supervisees. Research to date suggests that supervisees prefer supervisors of the same sex (Hoffman 1990; Petty and Odewahn 1983; Stoltenberg and Delworth 1987) and approximately their own age or slightly older (Hoffman 1990). Although some authors advocate cross-gender matching in supervision as an essential professional experience (Alonso and Rutan 1978; Brodsky 1980), there seems no harm in allowing supervisees to choose supervisors of the gender they prefer (usually the same as their own) unless cross-matching has a particular training value in a given situation. In any case, self-selection usually is possible only in academic and training institutions; in the working world, one does not get to choose one's boss.

Gender matching is only one aspect of the larger issue of how gender affects the supervisory relationship. Research has begun to identify numerous effects of gender that a supervisor must take into account. Further research and experience are needed to answer questions such as the following: Are these real differences?

How can gender differences be used to provide better supervisee-supervisor matching in particular cases? Does labeling a style or approach as gender related simply reinforce sexist stereotyping, or does it free the supervisor and supervisee to deal with real differences? To what extent can men and women transcend the differences in counseling or supervisory style that appear to separate them? Are there times when gender differences can be utilized to enhance learning, so as to cope more effectively with a competitive work environment?

The gender-based attributes identified by a growing body of research (Alderfer 1991; Belenky and others 1986; Gilligan 1992; Kaslow 1986a; Rosener 1990; Tannen 1990; Weber 1991) have been masked until recently by the fact that women have largely been responsible for clinical care in treatment agencies whereas men have been largely responsible for theory and policymaking. It has been far more common for women to be supervised by men in authoritative positions than for men to be supervised by women. Munson (1987) comments, "Women supervising women was a common occurrence in the past, while women supervising men was an unusual, brief encounter in the man's rise to higher levels of administration" (p. 237). This picture is changing as more women rise to decision-making roles in agencies.

There is evidence that some women in supervisory relationships value nurturance and relational skills to the point of avoiding task-oriented work. Their idea of support may resemble caretaking (Alderfer 1991; Reid and others 1987). "The beneficence of a woman supervisor may curtail the encouragement of her female supervisee to develop autonomy. Each may lose sight of her own needs in deference to the other" (Alderfer 1991, p. 53). Although male attributes in supervision have received even less attention in the literature than female attributes, traditional male roles may unbalance the supervisory process as much as female roles, to the extent that men focus on cognitions and tasks to the exclusion of affective or interpersonal issues. Men may deny the interconnectedness of feelings and relationships. They may form judgments based largely on moralistic thinking about the client and themselves. Women think of morality in terms of responsibility and in a context of relationships, whereas men see morality as fairness tied to rules and rites (Gilligan 1992).

Women tend to be characterized in the research literature as valuing relationships, connectedness, and beneficence, while men are characterized as valuing autonomy, separation, task, principles, and structure (Chodorow 1978; Gilligan 1992; Hare-Mustin and Maracek 1986). In same-gender supervision, these characteristics, if applicable, may allow for little room to grow (inasmuch as the supervisor simply reinforces the status quo in the counselor), while in cross-gender supervision, the clash between styles may lead to an adversarial relationship that also hinders growth. As Okun (1983) states, "A major gender issue is the possibility of the supervisor-trainee relationship falling into destructive traditional patterns, as indicated in several ways: submissive or seductive behavior in women; a patronizing or seductive attitude in men; male trainees not taking female supervisors seriously; male therapists' ideas, behaviors, and progress valued above those of women" (p. 45).

There is general agreement that these stereotypical gender roles reflect different developmental and socialization patterns in men and women (Belenky and others 1986; Chodorow 1978; Gilligan 1992; Keller 1985). In addition to the polarity between autonomy and relatedness (Gilligan 1992; Gould 1983; Miller 1986), men and women have been found to differ in their use of power. Men are assumed to have more power and to value power more than women. This inequality has a heavy impact on the supervisory relationship, with its inherent power dynamics. Same-gender male supervision may take the form of a struggle for power. Stereotyping behaviors may result, and gender roles may be rigidly reinforced, thereby impeding both parties' freedom and development in supervision.

Termination of supervision presents another gender difference, one that follows from women's affective overinvolvement and men's underinvolvement. Men have a tendency toward premature closure of supervisory relationships, whereas women have difficulty bringing the relationship to a close (Gilligan 1992). In other words, women have trouble saying goodbye in supervision, while men (who say goodbye all too easily) have trouble saying hello (Stoltenberg and Delworth 1987).

Thus, the supervisory relationship can be compromised by both the traditional female roles of nurturance, self-disclosure, lack of firmness, high verbal capability, personalizing behaviors, dependence, contextual and relational thinking, submissiveness, noncompetitiveness, and subjectivity (Avis 1985; Gilligan 1992; Maccoby and Jacklin 1974; Reid and others 1987) and by traditional male roles such as achievement, autonomy, abstract thinking, principledness, dominance, physical action, denial of feelings, competitiveness, and adventurousness (Doyle 1983; Goldberg 1976; Ipsaro 1986; Kaplan 1985). In contrast, supervision needs to decrease the effects of role stereotyping and to construct a reality based on actual behaviors rather than perceptions or self-fulfilling expectations of behaviors. It is critical for supervisors to understand, and guide supervisees in understanding, the gender stereotypes and role expectations that both of them bring to supervision. Where appropriate, the supervisory environment can be adjusted to counteract counselors' gender bias—for example, by emphasizing cognitive interventions with female counselors and affective interventions with male counselors.

Weber (1991) has contributed more specific findings about how gender differences manifest themselves in supervision. Given the expectations and roles into which they are socialized, women tend to prefer small supervisory groups with independent reading, collaborative discussion, and shared power in group supervision. On the basis of these findings, Weber recommends that supervisors should aid female supervisees in expressing their "inner voices" and intuitions while seeking to be behaviorally concrete. The supervisory relationship should be demystified to reduce power concerns, especially if the supervisor is male. Female supervisees should be reaffirmed for their personal investment in learning and empowered to express their anger and conflicts over anger. They should be taught that negative feedback need not be internalized as, "What did I do wrong?"

Furthermore, according to Weber, self-disclosure by women in supervision should be fenced to protect against overdisclosure. The traditional caretaker role should be avoided, and care should be taken not to elicit feelings of fear, mistrust, loyalty, and abandonment. Weber views some of women's traditional ways of thinking as advantageous for supervision, including the emphasis on relatedness and the use of multidimensional, holistic, nonlinear, circular thinking as opposed to the compartmentalized, linear, hierarchical thought processes characteristic of men (Weber 1991).

Finding the delicate balance between taking contextual and gender issues into account and reifying stereotypes of male and female supervisees is part of the art of supervision. To deny gender differences is shortsighted, yet to categorize all men or women in some limited way is prejudicial and sexist. All supervisors must come to terms with their own gender biases and use those biases, along with the supervisee's, as a springboard for exploration.

ETHNICITY AS A FACTOR IN SUPERVISION

There has been increasing attention to ethnicity, both as a treatment variable and as a factor in counselor development. In the coming years, any model of counseling and supervision will be judged in part by how it deals with ethnic issues. "If we are to promote maximum growth in minority supervisees, we must attend to and stimulate their efforts to incorporate ethnic identity with professional identity" (Vasquez and McKinney 1982, p. 60).

The first step is to be aware of and sensitive to ethnic differences. For example, commitment to family is one of the salient characteristics of Latin American culture. Common themes that run through many cultures in that region are familism, which emphasizes family relations over individual ones, and patriarchy, which emphasizes a family structure in which authority is vested in the male head of the family. A corollary is that complex of values known as machismo, which has a strong double standard of sexual morality, with masculinity demonstrated through display of physical and sexual prowess.

Another example is the significance attached to different degrees of eye contact in Asian cultures. Eye contact and gaze behavior show wide cultural variations. For African Americans, not looking another person in the eye is a recognition of that person's authority, whereas whites interpret this as shiftiness and unreliability. When blacks roll their eyes, it is a sign of hostility, impudence, and disapproval, often unrecognized as such by whites. In Japan, smiling may represent embarrassment, sorrow, or anger. Extending the arm with palm up and waving the fingers would be interpreted as "come here" by people in some cultures, "goodbye" in others. Extending the arm with palm down to indicate height might be understood in many places, but in Colombia it would be insulting if used to refer to a person.

Other intercultural and racial differences that a supervisor and counselor might address are facial expressions of emotions, kinesthetics, posture, haptics (touch), proxemics (use of space), paralinguistics (vocal qualities, vocalizations, and the use of silence), and olfactory behavior (smell). In sum, according to Sue and Sue (1990), there are numerous sources of conflict and misinterpretation in counseling, including culture-bound values (individual centered; verbal, emotional, and behavioral expressiveness; communication patterns; issues pertaining to openness and intimacy; and clear distinctions between mental and physical well-being), class-bound values (adherence to time schedules, ambiguous or unstructured approaches to problems, and goal setting), and language variables (emphasis on verbal communication and the use of standard English). Knowledge of the existence of such differences will help minimize inaccurate and prejudicial inferences from observed behavior and make it easier to learn new meanings for familiar behavioral patterns. This openness to new meanings, plus the use of those universal behavioral patterns that do exist, can serve to promote better intercultural understanding for counselors and supervisors.

Second, these cultural variations must be explored as they relate to supervision. There is a dearth of research and literature on the subject of ethnicity and supervision. What has been written falls under the general heading of contextual issues, where gender tends to be emphasized at the expense of ethnicity. Yet research on minority mental health and substance abuse issues has documented the numerous ways in which ethnicity influences the psychological well-being of minority adults and families. Ethnicity shapes belief systems about what constitutes mental illness, as well as the manifestation of symptoms, defensive styles, and patterns of coping with anxiety, depression, fear, guilt, and anger. Some ethnic groups reinforce *acting-in* neurotic symptoms, others reward *acting-out* characterological symptoms, and still others reward somatic symptoms. People learn patterns of illness and dysfunctional behavior that are culturally reinforced and tolerated.

Third, ethnicity largely determines help-seeking patterns and conditions the way people utilize and respond to treatment. Initial level of trust and openness, attitude toward self-disclosure, willingness to discuss sensitive subjects, motivation to participate in insight-oriented treatment or supervision—all of these aspects of clinical care are filtered through the screen of ethnicity.

There are several individual psychosocial issues to be assessed in the counseling and supervision process: physical appearance, affect, self-concept and self-esteem, interpersonal competence, attitudes toward autonomy, attitudes toward achievement, management of aggression and impulse control, coping and defense mechanisms, family relationships, peer relationships, relationships with peers in the community, and adaptation to the community. These variables become more intelligible, meaningful, and useful in the context of ethnicity, culture, and other contextual frames.

Vasquez and McKinney (1982) studied counselor development at a bicultural level using the Loganbill, Hardy, and Delworth (1982) model of development. They examined minority counselors at each stage of their development, particularly with respect to issues such as competition and articulation. For example, level 2 counselors may experience both external and internal pressures to work "in the trenches" in their ethnic communities rather than in mainstream agencies. Sue and Sue (1990) identified four stages of minority counselor development, moving from unawareness of cultural issues to the establishment of a bicultural identity.

According to Ivey (1986, p. 320), "Empathy demands awareness of both the individual and the culture." Both Caucasian and minority counselors must be aware of how cultural, racial, and ethnic factors influence the processes of counseling and supervision. Supervisees should challenge supervisors to develop greater cultural sensitivity. All concerned should work to have supervisors of diverse ethnic backgrounds trained and placed in prominent positions.

WORKING WITHIN THE SYSTEM

A comment often heard at my workshops on clinical supervision is, "My supervisor ought to be here receiving this training." Another variation is, "This is excellent information, but it will never work in the bureaucracy where I work." The work setting is where one must apply the principles and practices of supervision in agencies that are driven by other demands, such as financial solvency or profit making, maintaining bed census, acquiring JCAHO accreditation, or managing power struggles within a linear, hierarchical organization. How does one deal with a resistant boss, reluctant agency, or recalcitrant milieu—one that regards quality clinical training and supervision as mandated frills, to be provided for only after all the other bills are paid? How does one work within that sort of system?

First, all clinicians must be realistic about what can be achieved within a particular working environment. The principles and practices presented in textbooks are prototypes that must be adapted to the unique needs and problems of each agency. Bureaucratic structures, power struggles, personalities, financial constraints, and work cultures are part of the contextualizing of any model of supervision.

Second, the implementation of any model of supervision should be broken down into specific steps that can be implemented sequentially or in a nonlinear manner, depending on practical factors. For example, although live observation of counseling is recommended in the blended model, initially there may be great resistance from counselors to this approach. Gradual desensitization is therefore in order. The first step might be to allow supervisees to observe the supervisor in action, as a form of modeling and permission giving. Next, the supervisor might introduce herself into the counseling process when problem cases arise and the supervisee requests help. Progressive implementation also is called for in response to a resistant boss who does not see the value of clinical supervision. In this case, the supervisor might begin to educate the boss by giving her articles and books about the economic, marketing, and risk-management advantages of good supervision. (Purchasing copies of this book for all staff is an excellent idea.)

Third, the supervisor who faces resistance should begin by implementing a supervision program in a microcosm of the agency, within a small group of supervisees. He can create a groundswell of interest and excitement about supervision and model positive accomplishment, so that the word gets around that something special is happening when that supervision group meets on Friday mornings. A supervisor can begin with just one needy counselor who desires help and training. Building on the interest and enthusiasm of that one individual, the supervisor can introduce the opportunity for learning as the word spreads. If other units in the agency continue to scoff at the idea of supervision, this person can still champion the practice of supervision within his workgroup, creating a model of effective supervision. Even if the rest of the units never buy into the concept, at least his immediate group members have become converts, which means half a dozen new messengers for supervision in their next employment situation.

Fourth, resistant staff and employers should be encouraged to participate in education and training programs that address the value of supervision. Trade association meetings such as the National Association of Alcoholism and Drug Abuse Counselors' (NAADAC) Annual Conference or the International Certification & Reciprocity Consortium's (IC&RC) Committee on Supervision provide information and education on the value of supervision. Training programs sponsored by the Commission on Accreditation of Rehabilitation Facilities (CARF) and JCAHO also emphasize the legal and ethical requirements that mandate supervision. Management training programs sponsored by alcoholism and drug abuse programs as well as non-health-care-related courses, such as those provided by the American Management Association, emphasize the value of quality supervision. Training programs on Total Quality Management (TQM) teach the value of supervisory awareness of the activities of supervisees, even in a hierarchical system.

Fifth, sometimes a supervisor has to take some risks to maintain her integrity and effectiveness. For example, in an alienated organization where the climate does not promote trust, a supervisor may hesitate to ask counselors for feedback for fear it may be reported to management and held against the supervisor. What about the counselors, then, who run that risk routinely? How can a supervisor do evaluations of counselors if she is unwilling to leave herself vulnerable to the impact of an evaluation? There are fundamental principles of mutuality and reciprocity for which she may have to put her job on the line.

Finally, keep in mind that systems are inherently frustrating. That is why burnout is not a special pathology but an ever-present occupational hazard that varies only in degree of intensity (Edelwich and Brodsky 1980). All of the operative forces seem to be arrayed against the principles of TQM, quality care and supervision, and institutional reform. According to the second law of thermodynamics, heat will, of its own accord, flow only from a hot object to a cold object; thus, no engine can be completely efficient. Even in a perfect system, only part of the heat supply is converted into work. The rest (to apply the analogy to a human work environment) goes into gossip, backbiting, individual and organizational self-protection, power struggles, and sabotage.

No model of supervision can be perfectly efficient in reforming all aspects of an agency. Yet rather than give up because "nothing can be done in this place," a supervisor should remember that it is better to allow heat to flow from one "hot" partnership (an enthusiastic supervisor and supervisee) to a few somewhat interested individuals than to generate no heat at all. Institutional change takes time, and in some systems time moves very slowly. Some agencies may not change during one's term of employment there or may never change at all. Still, microcosms of the larger system may adopt a program of supervision that will eventually take root at that facility or spread its seeds to other places.

RESISTANT COUNSELORS: AGE AND RECOVERY ISSUES

It is not surprising that counselors who resist supervision are to be found in the kind of milieu just described. People go to graduate schools and other training institutions because they want to learn professional skills. In a service agency, on the other hand, there may be staff members who just want to cover the day's caseload with as little oversight as possible. Sometimes these individuals are picking up the negative attitudes of agency administrators who are determined to keep their census high even if it means cutting corners and processing clients in a perfunctory way. Some counselors who were hired too soon after their active substance abusing careers and with too little professional training in the interim may still be acting out and testing limits. Academic elitism is conveyed by some master's-level counselors who, having completed their education, do not believe they need further training and supervision, especially not from a supervisor who has less formal academic education. Resistant counselors may present an additional frustration to supervisors in that civil service protections may make it nearly impossible to discipline or fire them.

A special kind of resistance can occur when recovery issues are combined with the age factor. The substance abuse field is unusual, perhaps unique, in having many level 1 counselors who are middle-aged and older. Some of them came late to counseling (in a midlife career change associated with their recovery), while others have been content to work from their recovery background for years without acquiring additional professional training. Many of these individuals are fine counselors. To regard them as unskilled or incompetent merely on the basis of their age and status raises the question of another kind of prejudice—ageism—that must be worked through in supervision.

Nonetheless, some senior counselors are indeed rigidly set in their ways, unresponsive to supervision, and resistant to change. They may act as if they have nothing to learn from younger supervisors, especially (in the case of older male counselors) from young female supervisors. It is important to show respect for these counselors and for the experience they bring to their work. Depending on the individual, they may require varying degrees of flexibility ("Just because I'm your supervisor doesn't mean that I always know more than you, or that I'm right and you're wrong; let's try out some different things together") and firmness ("I understand, but I'm your supervisor, and I'm going to tell you some things I feel you need to change"). In the most stubborn cases, a supervisor may not be able to do any more than find a safe place in the agency where the counselor can practice his limited skills and pursue his limited goals.

No definitive guidelines can be offered for dealing with resistant counselors because the appropriate interventions are so largely a function of the individual and the situation. In agencies where resistance is endemic or where morale problems affect a significant part of the staff, the group counseling techniques developed by Edelwich and Brodsky (1992) for resistant clients can be adapted to on-the-job problem solving and decision making. A problem-solving exercise I use in my clinical supervision workshops, featuring questions like "Who is your worst staff member?" and "What is your worst organizational problem?" (or, for counselors, "Who is your worst client?"), can, with appropriate safe-guards for confidentiality, be used in such process groups or in more informal groups for counselors or supervisors.

Finally, the words of one supervisor are worth noting and fil-ing away for the tough moments: "To understand my staff I have to think back and recall how difficult *I* was to supervise. One of my supervisors told me I was unsupervisable. I didn't understand what he meant; since I got top performance ratings, I thought he didn't have anything to offer me. But I understand it now."

THE IMPAIRED COUNSELOR

Although the emotional functioning of a counselor should be a concern for all disciplines, the impaired counselor is a particu-lar concern in the alcoholism and drug abuse field, with its empha-sis on personal recovery from addictions. Obviously, personal use and abuse of substances such as alcohol, drugs, tobacco, and food can interfere with a counselor's job performance. The policy of the National Association of Alcoholism and Drug Abuse Counselors (NAADAC) is that "it is our duty to help our impaired colleagues to accept that their health and their professional roles are adversely affected by their impairment. Additionally, we believe that appro-priate treatment should be available for impaired counselors and family members to enable them to reenter the profession as ac-countable and reliable professionals" (Lisnow 1990, p. 37).

The supervisor plays a critical role in the identification and referral of the impaired professional. Yet all too often the helping professions deny it when their own peers do what they counsel clients not to do. Treatment delivery systems often fail to identify the professional in need of help, and few effective case-finding techniques have been developed to motivate the impaired profes-sional into treatment in a positive way. Supervision remains the most effective tool to do so.

As in any other job performance appraisal system, the clinical su-pervisor should look for the following signs of impairment, whether that impairment is a result of substance abuse, personal conflicts at home, or emotional factors. These indicators are presented by Bell, Gorski, and Troiani (1985) as a progression through seven phases:

Phase 1. The impaired worker tends to be a compulsive overworker, working harder and longer than previously. He may express great feelings of loyalty and a strong need to have his work recognized or rewarded. He will be very productive in this early stage of impairment, making crucial contributions to the work unit. The assertion, explicit or implicit, is that everything is okay. The worker is talking about being indispensable while beginning to criticize management's decisions.

Phase 2. There is a change in work behavior and attitude. The impaired worker makes compulsive attempts to prove how good a counselor he is. However, his relations with co-workers and supervisor are beginning to be strained. He avoids his superiors and associates while rigidly following job instructions so as to maintain a safe haven. He dwells defensively on the positive aspects of his performance as a counselor and becomes restless when things do not work out just right. He may begin to denigrate AA and the counseling program.

Phase 3. This phase is marked by crises. There is a progressive deterioration of job performance in all areas. Work requires greater effort, and there may be problems with concentration or memory. The impaired worker has difficulty recalling errors made on the job and further isolates himself from fellow counselors. Procrastination and errors of judgment make their appearance. Morale problems with co-workers surface. There will be occasional tardiness and self-generated stress.

Phase 4. This phase is characterized by a general immobilization and "if only . . ." thinking. Daydreaming and frequent tardiness result.

Phase 5. This is a state of confusion and overreaction to the supervisor's recommendations as well as to any real or imagined criticism. Complaints from co-workers become more frequent, and violations of rules result.

Phase 6. The impaired worker shows signs of depression, apathy, cynicism, laziness, and lack of cooperation. Physical appearance may decline. The counselor will leave work early and miss deadlines.

This downward spiral can be averted if the supervisor intervenes in the early phases, identifying job performance impairment as it evolves.

Phase 7. The seventh and final phase is discipline and termination, which all too often come about as a result of poor supervision.

What should the agency and supervisor do if a counselor is abusing substances? First, the agency needs to have a policy in place concerning abusive use of substances. This policy, developed in consultation with legal counsel, should specify what substances it covers. The policy must not discriminate against the recovering alcoholic or addict by imposing a stricter standard on those who have disclosed their recovery history. Rather, the policy must apply to all employees: "The agency will not tolerate abusive use of any substances. Such behavior is to be considered grounds for disciplinary action."

If abuse is found, as soon as the problem is identified, the counselor should be taken out of counseling functions. If the person is suspected but not proved to be abusing substances, the counselor should be informed that the supervisor is aware of the rumors and that the counselor will be closely observed to protect clients. The supervisor might say, "This is what I've been hearing. I'm not accusing you, but in case it's true, I'm reminding you of what our policy is." The observation should continue until such time as the supervisor can be assured that the counselor is not abusing substances.

The agency policy will be respected only if it is enforced consistently. If the field specifies that a person must have two years without abusive use of substances to function as a counselor, that rule should apply to everyone. Thus, a counselor who abuses should be taken off line for two years. In reality, since most agencies do not have other jobs that a person can fill for two years, the policy in effect means termination as a counselor from that agency. The counselor's professional credentialing organization should be informed of this violation of the profession's code of ethics. This policy may seem strict, especially if a recovering person has had many years of sobriety previously. Nonetheless, although the field is still unable to define clearly how much sobriety a person must have to be effective, the best that can be done is to adhere to the only rule that is in place, which specifies no abusive use of substances for two years.

The abusive use of food raises more complex issues. How far overweight does a counselor have to be before this condition becomes a matter of concern for the supervisor, especially if the treatment program emphasizes healthy life-styles, including eating patterns? What if the program treats compulsive overeaters? And to make the issue even more complex, what about compulsive overworking? There are no easy answers to these questions. However, all supervisors and agencies must attempt to advocate and model healthy life-style patterns for staff and clients while realizing that some unhealthy life-style patterns are inevitable. Ultimately—and always with a view toward the effect on patient care—the supervisor must decide how much is too much and when to intervene.

Finally, how sick can a counselor be in less tangible ways before he is taken off line? How codependent need he be before the supervisor intervenes? Fitness-for-duty issues are very unclear in the helping professions, especially in the alcoholism and drug abuse field, which deals directly with codependency and personal recovery. Questions of fitness can range from the counselor who has excellent clinical skills but is arrogant and condescending toward co-workers (professional demeanor) to the counselor who has been seeing a client for fifteen years, only to have the client relapse every time the counselor tries to terminate (codependency). Again, the touchstone is job performance, the quality of the clinical services delivered. The best answer to the fitness-for-duty question is found in frequent and close clinical supervision should a problem be suspected.

AN EVER-EXPANDING CONTEXT

To bring the discussion of contextual factors full circle, here are some questions about the variety of complex contextual dilemmas a supervisor may face:

Discrimination and Harassment

- What is my responsibility to model nondiscriminatory hiring, firing, and interviewing practices among staff? How about sexual harassment practices? Is there a way I can be part of the banter in the kitchen so as to avoid giving sanction to sexual harassment and yet not be seen as a prude who no longer laughs at jokes the way I used to before I was a supervisor?

- What is my responsibility to model positive vocabulary for my staff with respect to the use of four-letter words, sexual innuendo, double-entendre, and so forth? What about my eating and work habits? How am I to be a role model concerning the use of any substances (alcohol, tobacco, food, sugar, prescription drugs) or other potentially addictive experiences (work, sex, codependency)?

The Americans with Disabilities Act

- What is my responsibility for my attitudes and prejudices regarding disabilities? What attitudes toward disabilities should I model in the workplace?
- What legal and ethical responsibilities does the Americans with Disabilities Act impose on a supervisor? Do these conflict with other clinical and ethical responsibilities I seek to fulfill? Will my upholding these unfamiliar legal standards create problems in my supervisory relationships? How does all this affect my AA dealings, since alcoholism is considered a disability?

Sexual Preference

- Should I behave differently toward a supervisee because both of us are homosexual? Is that situation any different, ethically or politically, from that of two opposite-sex heterosexuals? Will it have any impact on supervisory relationships? What if other staff members suspect preferential treatment of the gay supervisee?

The Americans with Disabilities Act (ADA) of 1990 prohibits employment discrimination against qualified individuals with disabilities and requires employers to make reasonable accommodations for qualified employees and applicants with disabilities unless to do so would impose "undue hardship" on the employer's business. The ADA undoubtedly will create new role conflicts for supervisors, who must sort out an increasingly complex web of legal and administrative responsibilities. Likewise, sexual harassment and sexual preference promise to be major contextual factors in the 1990s. There is no limit to the evolving network of contexts that may demand a supervisor's attention in an era when more and more human relationships are being scrutinized, sanctioned, proscribed, or protected.

Chapter Seventeen

New Directions for the Future

A supervisor needs to have super-vision, to be able to see ahead and to forecast the trends in the field so as to best prepare staff for the future. The 1993 edition of this book outlined key issues facing the field to the year 2000, such as changes in the patient population, treatment systems and services, credentialing, funding, and drug policies. Most of these issues remain critical concerns for the behavioral health field. The 1993 edition also stated that "third-party reimbursement will remain the driving force behind treatment decisions." That is even more the case in the alcohol and drug abuse field ten years later.

As for other trends projected a decade ago, the United States continues to recriminalize and restigmatize addiction even as articulate reformers challenge both punitive, prohibitionist drug policies and treatment models that call addiction a disease. The addiction field still needs to do a better job of defining itself. The role of the alcoholism and drug abuse professional continues to evolve, with increasing competencies demanded of the counselor and with greater licensing, certification, and accreditation requirements placed on professionals and agencies. Cultural diversity training remains essential as the concern for counselor cultural competency grows. Close scrutiny by funding sources of clinical decisions, attention to patient matching, and placement criteria continues. Some things change, some things remain the same.

The trends addressed in the 1993 edition continue to unfold. At the same time, several emerging trends will have a dramatic impact on the behavioral health field in the next decade.

PREDICTIONS

The following are predictions for what the alcohol and drug abuse field might look like in 2013. These predictions address trends in therapy, finances, and integration of care.

Therapeutic Trends

In 1982 and every ten years since then, a panel of sixty-two clinicians and researchers has predicted key trends for the next decade in the behavioral health field. The latest report, compiled by John Norcross and Melissa Hedges of the University of Scranton and James Prochaska of the University of Rhode Island, was published in the June 2002 issue of *Professional Psychotherapy: Research and Practice*. These predictions are consistent with my experience and expectations as well.

- The field will focus on brief therapy models, with counseling conducted by master's-level clinicians.
- There will be an increased emphasis on changes the client can make in therapy and independently through tasks such as completion of therapeutically oriented homework assignments.
- The use of classic models of psychotherapy (gestalt, psychoanalytic, Adlerian, transactional, Jungian, and humanistic) will continue to decline as the field moves to therapy approaches that employ treatment manuals and printed materials that clients can use independently of a therapist.
- Most states will move toward mandatory licensing of master's-level counselors and specialists.
- For many addiction counselors with only undergraduate degrees now in practice, the push for master's-level academic training and credentialing will continue to be a major issue for alcohol and drug abuse clinical supervisors.
- The job market for doctoral-level clinicians will shrink.
- There will be a significant trend toward *distance* therapies, those conducted over the telephone and especially the Internet. The scope and range of on-line counseling and *virtual reality* techniques will rapidly expand, raising new legal and

ethical issues and training needs for clinical supervisors. Solid research concerning the efficacy of on-line treatment will be a necessity, as use of empirically supported approaches will expand. Telephone and Internet therapy fits the trend toward economic efficiencies, with escalating pressure from managed care organizations to use designated *treatments of choice.*

- On-line supervision will become a major means of clinical oversight, especially for counselors working in remote locations where regular supervision may not be readily available.

- Supervisors will need training in the competencies required to conduct Internet or telephone counseling so that they can assess counselor skills in these areas. The low overhead, flexible hours, and possibility of doing therapy in one's pajamas may make many therapists engaged in such counseling forget that they are practicing a kind of therapy for which they may not have been trained. Close supervision of on-line therapy is needed.

- Managers and supervisors will need to ensure that their professional liability insurance policies (individual and organizational) cover the new forms of clinical practice. Paperwork will need to be revised to reflect the use of new technologies, as well as to incorporate third-party billing and claim forms. Discussions of confidentiality will need to warn clients and supervisees that electronic conversations may be intercepted.

- Cognitive-behavioral therapy and systems approaches, especially in marriage and family therapy, will remain the poster child of counseling.

- *Integrated care* will be the watchword as the arbitrary distinction between mental and physical health is eliminated and health care delivery systems address the whole person: medical, psychological, relational, and spiritual. The health field is awakening to the reality that all physical illness has behavioral and psychological dimensions. Supervisors and counselors need to become proficient in health psychology, the application of behavioral and psychological techniques to medical conditions.

- Integrated care in a seamless web of "carved-in" services will profoundly affect how and where psychotherapy is practiced, as health care administrators feel the continuing pressure to reduce spiraling costs, especially for the patient who repeatedly seeks treatment.

- Many clinicians and supervisors will lead time-limited, evidence-based, psychoeducationally oriented group sessions that have been shown empirically to reduce medical costs and improve patients' functioning more than traditional medical treatment does.

- Patient problems will be grouped according to the nature of the illness. For example, one set of illnesses might be called the *disease management* group, which would include common medical conditions that are chronic and have no biomedical cure, such as rheumatoid arthritis, asthma, and diabetes. Substance abuse, depression, and many psychological problems that are not primarily medical but that might impinge on the medical delivery system might fall into a *population-based* group.

- The vocabulary concerning addiction and chemical dependence will be corrected to speak more about alcohol and drug abuse and dependence, as *DSM-IV* does and *DSM-V* likely will. The alcohol and drug abuse field might even broaden its definitions of substance and behavioral abuse and dependence to take in all compulsive behaviors, some with physical and medical complications.

These trends will have a great impact on the nature and content of clinical supervision. Ongoing training in the ever-evolving structures, models, and methods of care will be necessary for counselors and supervisors if they are to remain current in the field.

Financial Trends

After the advent of managed care in the early 1990s, the cost of the delivery of services remained steady through the end of that decade. However, just when the medical and psychiatric field thought it had seen the worst of managed care, the Band-Aid broke. In the early twenty-first century, health care costs skyrocketed again and are predicted to continue to rise through the year 2010. Employers are again seeing 10 to 20 percent increases in health insurance costs, reminiscent of the early 1990s. Medical inflation is back! The reasons for these increases are myriad and complex.

- Spending for health care continues to rise as a result of new and more expensive pharmaceuticals, new technologies for diagnosis and treatment, increased consumer demand, better-educated patients, and the growing ability of providers to avoid managed care cuts.
- Most important, America is getting older. The median age continues to rise. As the baby boomers age and try to take their youth into old age, demands on the health care system will continue to increase. Issues related to chronic illness will dominate the health care system. Since 65 percent of the pharmaceuticals used in the United States are consumed by people over the age of sixty-five, as boomers age, the costs of medications will also rise.
- Despite other changes in the U.S. health care system during the 1990s, there was a lack of structural change. The United States continues to have a fragmented health care system, with "stovepipe," or categorical, funding streams. Until funding for health care can be integrated and consolidated into single-payer, single-source funding, categorical funding will result in a continued waste of scarce health care dollars and resources.
- The tendency of Americans to resort to litigation to address problems places a great burden on practitioners, with increasing costs of malpractice insurance. Until tort reform is implemented, health care costs will likely continue to escalate.

In addition to managing the therapeutic changes addressed above, the behavioral health field will have to cope with continued pressure for cost containment and salary suppression. As a result, for instance, a master's-level clinician will be reimbursed at the same rate previously paid to a bachelor's-level counselor.

Continued administrative and technological solutions will be sought through electronic procedures, capitation, and case-rate protocols. The impact of this pressure on supervisors will be significant, as they will be asked to do more with fewer resources. Supervisors will feel caught "between a rock and a hard place," as the legal and ethical pressures outlined in this book necessitate close supervision and training and at the same time funding sources seek to reduce overhead and indirect costs, such as training and supervision services.

It is imperative that providers uphold the highest standards of the profession, advocating for patients and for quality care, and not give in to the increasing pressure to reduce quality in the interest of cost containment. Purchasers and payers must be reminded of the importance of patients' rights and challenged to uphold the highest legal and ethical standards of care. If the leaders in the behavioral health field do not do so, no one else likely will.

Trends in the Integration of Care

Many states are merging alcohol and drug abuse and mental health services into a seamless system of care. The focus on co-occurring disorders will continue to increase. As stated in the Introduction to the 2004 edition, when systems merge, often substance abuse counselors are at a disadvantage in retaining their jobs. It is imperative that the alcohol and drug abuse clinical supervisor urge staff members to pursue advanced degrees and credentialing wherever possible. Counselors need to understand the comorbidity of addictions and mental disorders, seeking common ground between disciplines in terms of the methods of treatment employed. Together with their counterparts in mental health, alcohol and drug abuse counselors and supervisors need to determine mutual core competencies for the behavioral health field. Most important, substance abuse and mental health counselors need to stand together as patient advocates.

Further, supervisors should encourage their organizations to move toward a seamless continuum of services, with integrated funding streams and coordinated patient placement and referral processes. Managers and supervisors who bridge the mental health and addiction systems should establish uniform management systems and multidisciplinary teams.

CONCLUSION

These financial and program changes will require that clinical supervisors move to a new dimension, to a place they may not have been before. Supervisors will now be responsible not only for their own and their supervisees' professional development but also for helping to bring about organizational changes that support that development, and with it the well-being of clients. Yet, while addressing program and financial management issues, they must not slight clinical supervisory functions. Thus, it is imperative that the clinical supervisor adapt to the ever-changing clinical environment and be disciplined and methodical in seeking program changes while retaining a focus on clinical quality and counselor skill development.

Appendix A:
Competencies of Supervisors

I. Conceptual Skills and Knowledge   Rating

    A. Generic Skills

       The supervisor is able to demonstrate knowledge and conceptual understanding of the following:

       1. The methodology of supervision, including:

          a. Facilitative processes (consultation, counseling, education, or training and evaluation)   _____

          b. Basic approaches (e.g., psychotherapeutic, behavioral, integrative, systems, developmental) _____

       2. A definition or explanation of supervision   _____

       3. The variety of settings in which counselor supervisors work   _____

       4. The counselor's roles and functions in particular work settings   _____

       5. The developmental nature of supervision   _____

       6. Appropriate supervisory interventions, including:

          a. Role playing   _____

          b. Role reversal   _____

          c. Live observation and live supervision   _____

          d. Reviewing audiotapes and videotapes   _____

This list was adopted by the ACES Supervision Interest Network at the American Association for Counselor Development (AACD) Convention, New York, April 2, 1985. Reprinted from Borders and Leddick (1987, pp. 65–70) with the permission of the American Counseling Association.

   e. Giving direct suggestions and advice   _____

   f. Leading groups of two or more supervisees _____

   g. Providing didactic experiences   _____

   h. Microtraining   _____

   i. Interpersonal Process Recall (IPR) _____

   j. Other   _____

  7. Credentialing standards for counselors _____

  8. Counselor ethical practices _____

  9. Various counseling theories _____

  10. His or her own personal theory of counseling _____

  11. His or her assumptions about human behavior _____

  12. Models of supervision _____

  13. The meaning of accountability and the supervisor's responsibility in promoting this condition _____

  14. Human growth and development _____

  15. Motivation and needs theory _____

  16. Learning theory _____

  17. Resources and information to assist in addressing program goals and client needs _____

B. Supervision of Practicing Counselors
The supervisor is able to demonstrate knowledge and conceptual understanding of the following:

  18. Legal considerations affecting counselor practice _____

  19. Various intervention activities and strategies that would complement the counseling program goals _____

C. Supervision of Counselors-in-Training (covered under Generic Skills, above)

D. Program Management/Supervision
The supervisor is able to demonstrate knowledge and conceptual understanding of the following:

  20. His or her basic management theory _____

  21. Various program development models _____

  22. Decision-making theory _____

  23. Organization development theory _____

  24. Conflict resolution techniques _____

  25. Leadership styles _____

26. Computerized information systems   _____

27. Time-management techniques   _____

II. Direct Intervention Skills

    A. Generic Skills

      The supervisor is able to demonstrate intervention techniques in the following ways:

      1. Provide structure for supervision sessions, including:

        a. Stating the purposes of supervision   _____

        b. Clarifying the goals and direction of supervision _____

        c. Clarifying his or her own role in supervision   _____

        d. Explaining the procedures to be followed in supervision   _____

      2. Identify the learning needs of the supervisee   _____

      3. Determine the extent to which the supervisee has developed and applied his or her own personal theory of counseling   _____

      4. Provide specific feedback about supervisee's:

        a. Conceptualization of client concerns   _____

        b. Process of counseling   _____

        c. Personalization of counseling   _____

        d. Performance of other related duties   _____

      5. Implement a variety of supervisory interventions (see Conceptual Skills and Knowledge)   _____

      6. Negotiate mutual decisions regarding the needed direction of learning experiences for the supervisee   _____

      7. Use media aids for assisting with supervision   _____

      8. Develop evaluation procedures and instruments to determine program and supervisee goal attainment   _____

      9. Monitor the use of tests and test interpretations   _____

     10. Assist with the referral process, when appropriate   _____

     11. Facilitate and monitor research to determine the effectiveness of programs, services, and techniques   _____

    B. Program Management/Supervision

      The supervisor is able to demonstrate intervention techniques in the following ways:

     12. Develop role descriptions for all staff positions   _____

13. Conduct a needs assessment _____

14. Write goals and objectives _____

15. Monitor the progress of program activities _____

16. Monitor the progress of staff's responsibilities _____

17. Utilize decision-making techniques _____

18. Apply problem-solving techniques _____

19. Conduct and coordinate staff development training _____

20. Implement management information systems _____

21. Employ group management strategies _____

22. Schedule tasks and develop time lines according to the needs of supervisees and the program _____

23. Maintain appropriate forms and records to assist with supervisory duties _____

24. Monitor supervisee report-writing and record-keeping skills _____

25. Diagnose organizational problems _____

26. Employ systematic observation techniques _____

27. Plan and administer a budget _____

28. Conduct follow-up studies and applied research _____

29. Establish consistent and quality hiring and affirmative action practices _____

30. Delegate responsibility _____

III. Human Skills

    A. Generic Skills

    The supervisor is able to apply the following interaction skills in a supervisory capacity:

      1. Deal with the supervisee from the perspective of:

        a. Teacher _____

        b. Counselor _____

        c. Consultant _____

        d. Evaluator _____

      2. Describe his or her own pattern of dealing with interpersonal relationships _____

      3. Integrate knowledge of supervision with own style of interpersonal relations _____

4. Create facilitative conditions (empathy, concreteness, respect, congruence, genuineness, and immediacy) _____

5. Establish a mutually trusting relationship with the supervisee _____

6. Establish a therapeutic relationship when appropriate _____

7. Identify supervisee's professional and personal strengths, as well as weaknesses _____

8. Clarify supervisee's personal needs (behavior mannerisms, personal crises, appearance, etc.), as well as professional needs that affect counseling _____

9. Elicit supervisee feelings during counseling or consultation sessions _____

10. Elicit supervisee perceptions of counseling dynamics _____

11. Use confrontation skills when identifying supervisee's inconsistencies _____

12. Elicit new alternatives from supervisee for identifying solutions, techniques, responses, etc. _____

13. Demonstrate skill in the application of counseling techniques (both individual and group) that are appropriate for the work setting _____

14. Assist the supervisee in structuring his or her own self-supervision _____

15. Conduct self-evaluations as a means of modeling appropriate professional growth _____

16. Identify own strengths and weaknesses as a supervisor _____

17. Model appropriate behaviors expected of supervisees _____

18. Demonstrate and enforce ethical/professional standards _____

B. Traits and Qualities
The supervisor possesses the following traits or qualities:

1. Demonstrates a commitment to the role of supervisor _____

2. Is comfortable with the authority inherent in the role of supervisor _____

3. Has a sense of humor _____

4. Is encouraging, optimistic, and motivational _____

5. Expects supervisees to own the consequences of their actions _____

6. Is sensitive to individual differences   _____

7. Is sensitive to supervisee's needs   _____

8. Is committed to updating his or her own counseling and supervisory skills   _____

9. Recognizes that the ultimate goal of supervision is helping the client of the supervisee   _____

10. Maintains open communication between supervisees and the supervisor   _____

11. Monitors the "energy level" of supervisees to identify possible signs of counselor burnout in advance of possible crises   _____

12. Recognizes own limits through eliciting self-evaluation and feedback from others   _____

13. Enjoys and appreciates the role of supervisor   _____

Appendix B:
Role Delineation Study
for Clinical Supervisors

Performance Domain: Management and Administration

Task 1

Assist in developing quality improvement guidelines, implementing those procedures and standards with staff involvement in a continuing quality improvement plan, in order to monitor and upgrade clinical performance.

Knowledges

1. Knowledge of regulatory agencies' quality improvement requirements which apply to alcohol and drug counseling.
2. Knowledge of the consequences of non-compliance with quality improvement requirements.
3. Knowledge of assessment procedures, to include patient care, staff performance, caseload management, program evaluation and record keeping.
4. Knowledge of monitoring techniques.

Skills

1. Skill in developing quality improvement guidelines.
2. Skill in implementing policies and procedures.
3. Skill in monitoring techniques of quality improvement guidelines.
4. Skill in evaluating clinical performance.
5. Skill in evaluating patient care.
6. Skill in evaluating program outcomes.
7. Skill in evaluating caseload management.
8. Skill in record keeping.

Reprinted by permission from *Role Delineation Study for Clinical Supervisors,* pp. 39–49, published in 1972 by the National (currently International) Certification Reciprocity Consortium/Alcohol and Other Drug Abuse, Inc., under the direction of Columbia Assessment Services, 3725 National Drive, Suite 213, Raleigh, N.C.

Task 2

Monitor compliance with federal and state regulations, implementing existing Quality Improvement mechanisms, in order to protect supervisee's and clients' rights.

Knowledges

1. Knowledge of federal and state regulations.
2. Knowledge of clients' rights.
3. Knowledge of agency policy and procedures.
4. Knowledge of confidentiality laws.
5. Knowledge of grievance process.
6. Knowledge of consequences of violations of client rights and confidentiality.
7. Knowledge of monitoring techniques.

Skills

1. Skill in interpreting federal, state, and agency regulations regarding client confidentiality, client rights, and following procedures to protect those rights.
2. Skill in explaining confidentiality and clients' rights to others.

Task 3

Evaluate and monitor agency policies and procedures using accreditation standards to ensure compliance.

Knowledges

1. Knowledge of agency policies and procedures.
2. Knowledge of accreditation bodies' standards regarding policy and procedure.
3. Knowledge of consequences of non-compliance with policies and procedures.
4. Knowledge of evaluation techniques.
5. Knowledge of monitoring techniques.

Skills

1. Skill in interpreting agency policy and procedures.
2. Skill in monitoring compliance with agency policy and procedures.
3. Skill in interpreting accreditation standards.

Task 4

Plan and coordinate the activities of supervisees to promote effective management in order to maintain clinically effective programming, through the review of daily schedules, consultation, knowledge of onsite and community resources, etc.

Knowledges

   1. Knowledge of management practices.
   2. Knowledge of systems theory.
   3. Knowledge of clinical programming.
   4. Knowledge of staff resources.
   5. Knowledge of budgetary parameters of agency.
   6. Knowledge of scheduling strategies.
   7. Knowledge of concepts of patient care.
   8. Knowledge of treatment practices and goals.
   9. Knowledge of consultation strategies.
  10. Knowledge of linkage and networking strategies.
  11. Knowledge of community resources.
  12. Knowledge of the agency grievance procedure.

Skills

   1. Skill in planning and coordinating resources.
   2. Skill in scheduling staff and clinical activities.
   3. Skill in matching clients to appropriate staff and level of care.
   4. Skill in utilizing community resources.
   5. Skill in problem solving and conflict resolution.
   6. Skill in responding to grievances.

Task 5

Meet with new staff to orient them to all program components and professional expectations in order to enable new staff to adhere to program's performance standards.

Knowledges

   1. Knowledge of program components.
   2. Knowledge of motivating the supervisee to perform specific tasks.
   3. Knowledge of motivational skills.
   4. Knowledge of performance standards.
   5. Knowledge of specific roles within the therapeutic team.

6. Knowledge of policy and procedures.
7. Knowledge of orientation procedures and practice.

Skills

1. Skill in basic communication.
2. Skill in imparting orientation information.
3. Skill in following and enforcing policy and procedures.
4. Skill in interpreting policy and procedures.
5. Skill in supervisee motivation.
6. Skill in documenting understanding of policy and procedures.
7. Skill in the evaluation and maintenance of performance standards.

Task 6

Identify and assess program needs utilizing available mechanisms in order to formulate a plan for enhancing clinical services and program development.

Knowledges

1. Knowledge of program assessment methods.
2. Knowledge of program development methods.
3. Knowledge of program components.
4. Knowledge of performance standards.
5. Knowledge of roles within therapeutic team.
6. Knowledge of staff development.

Skills

1. Skill in identifying program needs.
2. Skill in formulating program plan.
3. Skill in assessment methods.
4. Skill in implementing program changes.
5. Skill in analyzing treatment trends.
6. Skill in analyzing population trends.
7. Skill in identifying staff training needs.
8. Skill in providing staff training.
9. Skill in evaluating staff performance.

Task 7

Coordinate consultation services with supervisee utilizing additional resources for the purpose of providing continuity of quality care for clients.

Knowledges

1. Knowledge of difference between consultation and supervision.
2. Knowledge of rationale for consultation.
3. Knowledge of consultation theories (approaches).
4. Knowledge of continuum of care issues in management.
5. Knowledge of strengths, limitations of peers, self and agency.
6. Knowledge of terminology of profession.

Skills

1. Skill in clarity of written/oral communication.
2. Skill in developing trust and rapport.
3. Skill in case management activities.
4. Skill in assessing needs and interpreting them.
5. Skill in identifying resources for provision of consultation.

Task 8

Recommend, in accordance with agency policy and procedures, the employment and termination of clinical staff by participation in review, selection, and evaluation processes in order to retain quality clinic staff.

Knowledges

1. Knowledge of agency's hiring policies.
2. Knowledge of termination policies.
3. Knowledge of interviewing process.
4. Knowledge of grievance process.
5. Knowledge of performance appraisals.
6. Knowledge of agency staffing pattern.

Skills

1. Skill in interviewing.
2. Skill in conducting performance appraisals.
3. Skill in communication.
4. Skill in consultation.
5. Skill in assessment.

List of Performance Domains and Tasks

I. Assessment and Evaluation

Task 1: Assess the supervisee's experience with and/or knowledge of the field of alcohol and other drug abuse, social and behavioral science, and 12 step philosophy and tradition, by interview, questioning, exploration, and/or discussion in order to determine the supervisee's strengths and weaknesses.

Task 2: Assess supervisee temperament, leadership style, interpersonal strength or weakness, and reactions to stress within the work setting by use of interviews, observations, and assessment instruments in order to promote supervisee growth.

Task 3: Analyze supervisee performance of tasks related to the 12 core functions in order to identify levels of performance by interview, direct observation, review of case records, and use of evaluation tools.

Task 4: In order to become familiar with the supervisee's levels of clinical functioning, explore his/her ability to utilize various therapeutic approaches by direct, ongoing observation.

Task 5: Evaluate the supervisee's strengths and weaknesses by interviews, observations, and feedback solicited from other appropriate sources in order to make appropriate work assignments and to formulate a plan for the supervisee's ongoing development.

II. Counselor Development

Task 1: Build with the supervisee a developmental framework for a supervisory relationship through the use of assessment activities, case presentation, demonstration, and dialogue, for the purpose of facilitating supervisee development.

Task 2: Promote a career development process with the supervisee through the use of mutual planning, assessment activities, and motivational techniques, in order to stimulate a desire for continuing personal and professional growth.

Task 3: Work with the clinical staff to facilitate clinical teamwork behaviors by using observational tools, staff discussion, demonstration, and reading/writing tasks, for the purpose of improving and maintaining clinical staff resource utilization and effectiveness.

Task 4: With supervisee participation, develop and implement a clinical training and education program based on an assessment of the supervisee's learning needs in order to operationalize clinical training and educational practices for the purpose of strengthening the supervisee's clinical competence.

Task 5: Provide direct clinical supervision to supervisees, using a variety of supervisory methods, in order to build supervisees' clinical skills.

III. *Professional Responsibility*

Task 1: Participate actively in professional organizations to model and encourage professional involvement by the supervisee.

Task 2: Promote, maintain and safeguard the best interests of the supervisee by adhering to established codes of ethics in order to encourage high standards of conduct.

Task 3: Pursue personal and professional development by participating in related professional and educational activities in order to improve supervisory competence.

Task 4: Strive to maintain or improve personal, physical, and mental health by participating in activities which promote professional effectiveness.

Task 5: Recognize the uniqueness of the individual supervisee by gaining knowledge about personality, culture, lifestyle, personal feelings, and other factors in order to influence the supervisee in the process of his/her development.

Appendix C:
Assessing One's Preparation as a Clinical Supervisor

Following are questions to ask when assessing the ability to do clinical supervision. There are no baselines or cut-off scores to determine the supervisor's level of competency; these questions are merely suggestive for self-exploration by the clinical supervisor.

	Number of Hours
1. What clinical supervision have you received?	
Individual supervision	_____
Group supervision	_____
Total	_____
2. What clinical supervision have you given to others?	
Individual supervision	_____
Group supervision	_____
Total	_____
3. What supervision of your supervision have you had?	
Individual supervision	_____
Group supervision	_____
Total	_____

	Check All That Apply
4. What supervision methods have been used by your supervisor?	
Process notes/verbatims	_____
Cofacilitation of counseling sessions	_____
Entering room during a counseling session	_____

Adapted from the writings of Stoltenberg and Delworth (1987), Mead (1990), and others.

Bug-in-the-ear   _____
Feedback during a session   _____
Phone-ins   _____
Audiotaping   _____
Videotaping   _____
One-way mirror observation   _____
Other   _____

In assessing your own supervisory skills, determine your level of competency, from 1 (needing improvement) to 5 (excellent). This is a self-assessment tool.

Level of
Competency
(1–5)

1. Interviewing skills
   Supporting and accepting the counselor   _____
   Nonblaming behavior   _____
   Using warmth, empathy, humor in supervision   _____
   Confrontation and self-disclosure in supervision   _____

2. Assessment skills   _____

3. Determining counselor's technical skills
   Eliciting counselor's preferred theoretical model   _____
   Determining counselor's awareness of self and others   _____
   Determining counselor's motivation   _____
   Determining counselor's degree of autonomy/dependence   _____
   Determining counselor's developmental level   _____

4. Determining supervision goals
   Determining counselor's and supervisor's goals for
   supervision   _____
   Sharing goals   _____
   Establishing mutual goals with supervisee   _____
   Case assignments based on these goals   _____

5. Using observation methods
   Establishing observation and assessment methods   _____
   Establishing intervention methods   _____
   Presenting supervision plans   _____

6. Using intervention methods   _____

7. Your own observation skills   _____

8. Structuring supervision sessions
    Reviewing homework assignments   _____
    Setting agendas   _____
    Using lectures, discussion, role plays, simulations   _____
    Meeting resistance   _____
    Ending session, summarizing, establishing homework
    assignments, ending with rapport   _____

9. Using technical skills
    Case conceptualization and hypothesizing   _____
    Delivery of interventions   _____
    Handling ethical and professional issues   _____

10. Evaluation skills
    Evaluating case files and assessments   _____
    Using confrontation with the counselor   _____
    Determining counselor progress, strengths, deficits,
    need for further training   _____
    Writing counselor development and training plans   _____

Appendix D: Determining Readiness to Be a Supervisor

The following twenty statements may be used to assess general preparedness to be a supervisor, using a scale of "agree" (A), "disagree" (D), or "no opinion" (N).

1. I like to set my own goals and do things my own way. _____
2. I have a keen sensitivity to the interests of other people. _____
3. I see my work as only a means to an end, rather than as a main focus of my life. _____
4. When I know a job needs to be done well, I will do it myself. _____
5. I don't want to take the responsibility for someone else's work, good or bad. _____
6. I consider myself an attentive listener. I don't interrupt. _____
7. Given a fair chance, most people want to do a good job. _____
8. I live according to the rule of "better late than never." _____
9. When working with a group of other people on a project, I often find myself prodding them to get the job done. _____
10. I have a lot to learn about management and supervision. _____
11. Good employees work safely, obey the rules, and are willing to give a fair day's work. _____
12. My friends know that I won't criticize them when they come to me with their hard-luck stories. _____
13. People who break the rules should be prepared to pay the penalty. _____
14. I like to show other people how to do things. _____
15. The thought of working overtime without extra pay seems extremely unfair. _____

16. Most of my bosses have been a hindrance rather than a help to me and my co-workers. _____

17. I consider myself to be a good explainer: I can make things clear to other people. _____

18. In handling my personal affairs, I rarely fall behind in what I set out to do. _____

19. When assessing a situation, I find that there is likely to be some good in it as well as the bad and the ugly. _____

20. When things go wrong, that's a sign that a problem needs to be solved rather than a person blamed. _____

Scoring: Score 1 point for each "agree" answer to statements 2, 6, 7, 9, 10, 11, 12, 13, 14, 17, 18, 19, and 20 and 1 point for each "disagree" answer to statements 1, 3, 4, 5, 8, 15, and 16. There are no points for answering "no opinion."

A person who scores between 15 and 20 points is ready to be a supervisor. A person who scores between 9 and 14 points needs to gain a better understanding of the role of a supervisor. One who scores less than 9 points should look at other career options. Supervision may not be the right choice.

Appendix E:
Counselor Evaluation
of the Supervisor

Assessment of the supervisor by the supervisee is an essential part of the evaluation process. A supervisor's willingness to be evaluated by supervisees indicates that the supervisor is not making the mistake of asking staff members to do something he is not willing to do. The following evaluation form, which a counselor can use in assessing a supervisor, gives the supervisor valuable feedback while it gives the counselor a sense of responsibility and involvement in the design and development of supervision.

Use the following rating scale:

1 = strongly disagree

4 = neither agree nor disagree

7 = strongly agree

Rating

1. Provides useful feedback regarding counselor behavior   _____
2. Promotes an easy, relaxed feeling in supervision   _____
3. Makes supervision a constructive learning process   _____
4. Provides specific help in areas needing work   _____
5. Addresses issues relevant to current clinical conditions   _____
6. Focuses on alternative counseling strategies to
   be used with clients   _____
7. Focuses on counseling behavior   _____
8. Encourages using alternative counseling skills   _____
9. Structures supervision appropriately   _____

Adapted from Borders and Leddick (1987).

10. Emphasizes the development of strengths
and capabilities   _____

11. Brainstorms solutions, responses, and techniques that
would be helpful in future counseling situations   _____

12. Involves the counselor in the supervision process   _____

13. Helps the supervisee feel accepted and respected as a person   _____

14. Appropriately deals with affect and content   _____

15. Motivates the counselor to assess counseling behavior   _____

16. Conveys a sense of competence   _____

17. Is helpful in critiquing report writing   _____

18. Helps to use tests constructively in counseling   _____

19. Appropriately addresses interpersonal dynamics
between self and counselor   _____

20. Can accept feedback from counselor   _____

21. Helps reduce defensiveness in supervision   _____

22. Encourages expression of opinions, questions,
and concerns about counseling   _____

23. Prepares the counselor adequately for the next counseling
session   _____

24. Helps clarify counseling objectives   _____

25. Provides an opportunity to discuss adequately
the major difficulties the counselor is facing with
clients   _____

26. Encourages client conceptualization in new ways   _____

27. Motivates and encourages the counselor   _____

28. Challenges the counselor to perceive accurately
the thoughts, feelings, and goals of the client   _____

29. Gives the counselor the chance to discuss
personal issues as they relate to counseling   _____

30. Is flexible enough to encourage spontaneity
and creativity   _____

31. Focuses on the implications and consequences
of specific counseling behaviors   _____

32. Provides suggestions for developing counseling skills   _____

33. Encourages the use of new and different techniques   _____

34. Helps to define and achieve specific, concrete goals   _____

35. Gives useful feedback   _____

36. Helps organize relevant case data in planning
    goals and strategies with clients   _____

37. Helps develop increased skill in critiquing
    and gaining insight from counseling tapes   _____

38. Allows and encourages self-evaluation   _____

39. Explains the criteria for evaluation
    clearly and in behavioral terms   _____

40. Applies criteria fairly in evaluating
    counseling performance   _____

Appendix F:
Evaluation of
the Counselor

Supervisee _____ Date of Evaluation _____

Supervisor _____

Section I: Theoretical and Technical Knowledge

Goal: insight into human development and life issues; knowledge of theory; familiarity with various counseling techniques; ability to describe a client's difficulties within an intellectual framework; understanding and use of an integrated model of counseling

COMMENTARY

Level of Knowledge
or Performance
(1–5)

1. Life context
   - Understands family life issues, development, what can be expected at various life stages _____
   - Focuses on fundamental life questions in the light of this knowledge _____

2. Theory
   - Knows various counseling models under which the counselor is supervised _____
   - Is aware of key issues in the field _____
   - Has knowledge of alcoholism and drug abuse counseling issues _____
   - Has knowledge of family therapy models _____
   - Has knowledge of therapy with children and adolescents _____

Adapted from Stoltenberg and Delworth (1987).

- Has developed a comprehensive and integrated
  model of change in counseling _____
3. Professional activity _____
   - Reads journals/books _____
   - Attends conferences/seminars/training _____
   - Writes papers/presents at conferences _____
4. Case conceptualization
   - Is able to formulate case hypotheses _____
   - Is able to express conceptual hypotheses _____
   - Is able to formulate counseling strategies
     and interventions _____

Section II: Procedural Knowledge

Goal: knowledge of fundamental procedures of profession; ability to demonstrate skills; flexibility in working with clients

COMMENTARY

1. Is able to apply affective and facilitative skills
   (warmth, empathy, genuineness); is able to form
   a strong therapeutic alliance with clients _____
2. Is able to apply advanced counseling skills (makes
   relevant links, derives clinical material, facilitates
   client's self-exploration) _____
3. Is able to apply challenging skills (self-disclosure,
   confrontation, probing, immediacy) _____
4. Is able to apply crisis intervention skills (suicide,
   homicide, abuse) _____
5. Is able to draw client's decisions about issues _____
6. Knows when to seek consultation, supervision, refer _____
7. Is able to conduct intake sessions _____
8. Collaborates effectively with other staff _____
9. Seeks formal and informal clinical supervision
   as needed _____
10. Supports other staff as needed _____
11. Relates appropriately to agency management _____
12. Community skills: understands environmental
    factors affecting clients _____

13. Cultural skills: works well with different cultural, racial, ethnic, and sexual orientations   _____

14. Legislation: knows relevant laws, policies, and procedures related to patients, including those of the courts and the welfare and foster care systems   _____

15. Case conceptualization skills: is able to articulate case-related issues in an appropriate and thorough manner   _____

Section III: Judgment

Goal: high quality of judgment, understanding, and communication about issues, based on data; sense of where progress is possible for clients; self-knowledge of own limitations; sense of ethics and exemplary ethical practice based on sound judgment

COMMENTARY

1. Is able to take the long view, to be aware of the limits of available strategies for problem solving; can make judgments in the midst of uncertainty   _____

2. Is aware of own limitations   _____

3. Accepts limitations   _____

4. Has an understanding of ethical principles of confidentiality, competency, boundaries, and professional dealings with clients   _____

5. Has an appropriate respect and admiration for the profession, with appropriate critique   _____

6. Is committed to the profession, to further training   _____

Section IV: Insight

Goal: insight into persons and systems; systemic understanding; ability to see own role in system; ability to understand and interpret work environment; sufficient resolution of major conflict in counselor's life that he or she can help others; spontaneity

COMMENTARY

1. Displays intuition: able to see clearly, aware of limits   _____

2. Has an appropriate systemic focus: understands roles in the counseling relationship; knows how counseling interacts, assesses personal impact on patient, and uses that impact therapeutically; and uses own experience and experience of client to determine themes   _____

3. Has necessary personal qualities: appears to have resolved conflicts in personal life sufficiently for them not to unduly interfere in counseling, has the humility to choose the best possible solution, and exhibits appropriate involvement with clients   _____

4. Displays spontaneity and creativity in counseling: varies counseling methods and ways of being in sessions, is flexible when things do not go according to plan, and is willing to experiment   _____

Section V: Roles and Activity in Supervision Sessions

Goal: maintenance of professional behavior throughout clinical and administrative supervision; understanding of roles and activities of counseling and clinical supervision

COMMENTARY

1. Prepares for supervision sessions, is punctual, has materials prepared as directed, and prepares case notes, keeping a log book of supervisor's comments; is willing to prepare "life material" for supervision   _____

2. Receives feedback in a healthy, constructive manner, is willing to examine own role with clients   _____

3. Is willing to relate relevant personal material to case discussion; is willing to explore countertransferential issues affecting counseling and supervision   _____

4. Is able to critique self in a realistic fashion   _____

5. Can be spontaneous in supervision sessions, initiates in sessions   _____

6. Displays appropriate autonomy from supervisor and has a sense of professional self; is self-aware; maintains stable motivation for counseling   _____

Appendix G:
Individual Development Plan

Forms developed by ETP Inc., based on the twelve core functions as presented in National Certification Reciprocity Consortium, *NCRC Case Presentation Method Trainer's Manual* (Atkinson, N.H.: NCRC, 1990).

Individual Development Plan

Student/Intern/Counselor: _____

Supervisor: _____

CORE FUNCTIONS

	Strengths:	Weaknesses:
1. SCREENING The process by which a client is determined appropriate and eligible for admission to a particular program.		
2. INTAKE The administration and initial assessment procedures for admission to a program.		
3. ORIENTATION Describing the general nature and goals of the program to the client.		
4. ASSESSMENT Those procedures whereby the client's strengths, weaknesses, and needs are identified for the development of a treatment plan.		

Individual Development Plan

Student/Intern/Counselor: _____

Supervisor: _____

NOTE: An asterisk (*) next to any item indicates a strength or weakness and has been further addressed on the Supplemental Sheet.

CORE FUNCTIONS

	Strengths:	Weaknesses:
5. TREATMENT PLANNING The process whereby the client and counselor identify and rank problems, establish agreed upon goals, and decide on treatment methods and resources to be used.		
6. COUNSELING The utilization of special skills to assist individuals, families, or groups in achieving objectives.		
7. CASE MANAGEMENT Bringing resources and people together within a planned framework of action to achieve established goals.		
8. CRISIS INTERVENTION The response to the client's need during acute distress.		

Individual Development Plan

Student/Intern/Counselor: _____

Supervisor: _____

CORE FUNCTIONS

	Strengths:	Weaknesses:
9. CLIENT EDUCATION The providing of information regarding alcohol and other drug abuse to the client.		
10. REFERRAL Identifying the needs of the client that cannot be met by the counselor or agency and assisting the client to utilize the support systems and community resources available.	Strengths:	Weaknesses:
11. REPORT AND RECORD KEEPING Charting the results of the assessment and treatment plan; writing reports, progress notes, discharge summaries, and other client-related data.	Strengths:	Weaknesses:
12. CONSULTATION Relating with professionals in regard to client treatment/services, to assure comprehensive, quality care.	Strengths:	Weaknesses:

Individual Development Plan

Student/Intern/Counselor: _____

Supervisor: _____

NOTE: An asterisk (*) next to any item indicates a strength or weakness and has been further addressed on the Supplemental Sheet.

CORE FUNCTIONS

	Strengths:	Weaknesses:
13. ALCOHOL/DRUG ABUSE AND EATING DISORDERS		
14. GROUP COUNSELING	Strengths:	Weaknesses:
15. PROFESSIONAL GROWTH	Strengths:	Weaknesses:

Individual Development Plan

Student/Intern/Counselor: _____

Supervisor: _____

NOTE: An asterisk (*) next to any item indicates a strength or weakness and has been further addressed on the Supplemental Sheet.

CORE FUNCTIONS

	Strengths:	Weaknesses:
16. FAMILY AND SIGNIFICANT OTHERS		
17. PREVENTION AND OUTREACH	Strengths:	Weaknesses:

INDIVIDUAL DEVELOPMENT PLAN
(Supplemental Sheet)

Core Function # _____

Goal(s)	Objectives (includes methods and frequency)	Objective Dates			Implementer
		Open	Target	Close	

Student/Intern/Counselor Name: _____ (print)

Supervisor Name: _____ (print)

Program Manager's Name: _____ (print)

Student/Intern/Counselor Signature: _____

Supervisor Signature: _____

Program Manager's Signature: _____

GROUP SUPERVISOR

_____ _____
(Signature)   (Date)

CLINICAL EDUCATION SUPERVISOR:

_____ _____
(Signature)   (Date)

EDUCATION SPECIALIST:

	1	2	3	4
Test Scores:				
Retakes:				

_____ _____
(Signature)   (Date)

PRACTICUM COORDINATOR:

_____ _____
(Signature)   (Date)

OTHER: CERTIFICATION EXAM: *PASSED/FAILED _____
                                              (Date)

(* Students who pass the certification exam must still complete the minimum one year structured internship and be recommended for certification by their clinical supervisor, program manager, and Commanding Officer.)

_____ _____
(Signature/Title)   (Date)

STUDENT'S COMMENTS:

Internship Start Date: _____

Program Manager: _____
                      typed/printed

Clinical Supervisor: _____
                          typed/printed

Projected Certification Date: _____

Projected Re-certification Date: _____

Appendix H:
Use of the Sociogram

Although little has been written about the use of the sociogram in clinical supervision, other than the information published in the 1993 edition of this book, some have used this technique extensively in their supervision practice. Scott Graham, who practices in Vermont, has made it his standard practice to do a sociogram for each group counseling session he observes and then to use that sociogram as a valuable tool in supervision. The following information is based on modifications to the technique that I have made since the 1993 edition and on the valuable contribution to the field made by Scott Graham.

Graham initially used the sociogram to provide a starting point for debriefing groups that he observed. Over time, however, his use of the sociogram grew from an elementary formulation of the tool to an evaluative process for delineating the roles of counselors as group facilitators and identifying group processes. He has collected the equivalent of EKGs for heart patients or seismographs for geologists; he has written records of group process over a particular period of time for the counselors he supervises. The sociogram is a significant part of his supervisory process, including the counselor evaluation functions. By adapting and adding to the original tool, Graham has created a procedure that nonjudgmentally records the process.

It is helpful to use the sociogram repeatedly with any given group so as to see the changes in the group over time. Also, as one would expect to see a different process in a psychoeducational or task-oriented group than in a process-oriented group, it is helpful to differentiate on the sociogram the type of group observed.

The sociogram takes a composite picture of the group process without analysis or interpretation of that process. Thus, it can be used when working with individuals who have different theoretical models and orientations. The sociogram is not tied to any particular view or theory of counseling. It does not report that saying "X" is more effective than saying "Y." It allows for *equifinality*, multiple avenues toward the same result. The sociogram is simply a recording of what happened in the group, a two-dimensional map of the group process. A verbatim or process recording offers some of the same information but with more drawbacks, as stated in Chapter Twelve.

Although the sociogram is independent of models of counseling, it is important that the supervisor have a philosophy of what a "good" group looks like, according to her model of counseling. The sociogram provides an objective, unbiased picture of how the counselor led the group session, which can then be compared with the supervisor's model of group process as derived from her philosophy of counseling.

The following observations are based on experience with the sociogram as it evolved in supervision over the years. Each section includes a description of an enhancement to the sociogram, an explanation of the value of that particular enhancement, and, where appropriate, an example of the enhancement in action.

Create a Vision

First, the supervisor should educate and train staff about what a sociogram is and how it reflects group dynamics and processes. Then, the supervisor should develop, draw, and distribute a "perfect" sociogram for a specific group format, one that reflects either her philosophy and model of group counseling or that of the organization. For example, a supervisor might state, "This drawing identifies what we would see in a standard ('perfect') therapy group at this agency." This "perfect" sociogram becomes the template for group process for that agency. Additional templates should then be developed that reflect the stages of group development and variations in group dynamics resulting from the composition of the group (for example, gender differences or role variation among group members—the dominating member, the quiet member, the "group leader"). These templates serve as an excellent tool for training staff on how the group process is conducted for different stages of group development and different group members in that agency.

Identifying the "perfect" sociogram from the beginning establishes grounds for comparison and an avenue for solution-focused supervision. A picture is worth a thousand words. With representations of what is observed and of what is desired, rather than just an example of one group session, the supervisor can hold the "perfect" and the actual group side by side for comparison. The sociogram becomes more than just a tool that generates discussion about what is happening in a particular group.

It becomes a measuring stick and a nonjudgmental, objective feedback instrument that identifies the process in a group at a particular time. It creates an opening for facilitating counselor awareness and skill development.

In debriefing with the counselor after group, a supervisor might say, "Let's compare what you did in group to what you want to do in group." Or, "Let's compare what you did in group to what we expect you to do in group." Then supervision can move into problem solving and identifying specific strategies for moving the group toward the shared vision. The supervisor can ask the supervisee, "As you compare the sociogram of your group with the sociogram of our agency's 'perfect' group, what are some facilitation strategies that you can use in your group to move it toward an optimal group process?" The supervisor can then ask, "As you apply strategies to facilitate the group, what can I expect to see when I observe your group next week? What will the sociogram look like then?" The supervisor can also work with the supervisee to draw a sociogram that reflects what the supervisee is working toward in his facilitative efforts.

Observe the Same Group Regularly

Direct observation of sessions should be a priority, as discussed in Part Three. It must be scheduled in advance. Since writing the 1993 edition, the authors have seen the importance of scheduling supervision ahead for three to six months. Also, it is important that the supervisor make an effort to observe the same group whenever possible. Identifying a specific group to observe and scheduling the observations ensures that the supervisor is committed to observing on a consistent basis. Further, the supervisor can then develop sociograms that act as "snapshots of growth" and can assess over time the impact of identified interventions and changes recommended by the supervisor to the supervisee. By observing the same group on a specific schedule, the supervisor is in a better position to evaluate the counselor's skills. A meteorologist can determine a more complete picture of temperature trends over a season by recording the temperature at the same time and location every day. So too can a supervisor use the sociogram to identify patterns and processes of the group and the counselor's interventions.

Take Out Your Crayons

Experience has demonstrated that it is useful to use colors to distinguish counselor communication processes and gender dynamics. The counselor might consistently be drawn with a red pen and the clients with a black one, or male clients might be drawn with a blue pen and female clients with a brown one. Any colors will work as long as they are used consistently. It is helpful to use no more than three colors, however. When the supervisor uses the sociogram to provide feedback to the clinician, having many colors (for example, one for each client) distracts the focus from the clinician's communication patterns. It can also diffuse the impact and the discussion that ensues because it interferes with consistent observation and recording of the group process and the clinician's contribution to that process.

Making tick marks to represent multiple communication events between the same persons (recommended in the first edition of this book) was a helpful technique and simplified the diagram. But the use of multiple lines that parallel each other allows the sociogram to better represent the impact of the communication processes and the dominance of the group by any member or members. Using another example from meteorology, consider the difference between a graph that shows simply a monthly record of daily temperatures and a graph of these same numbers that also shows the frequency of days within certain temperature ranges. The second graph contains the same information as the monthly record but also conveys information about interrelationships and trends that may not be apparent from the raw data.

Further, it is helpful to use the same color key code for all one's sociograms, including the sample "perfect" sociogram. A consistent color key allows for more accurate assessment, comparison, and evaluation of each counselor's performance. Used in this manner, the sociogram becomes primarily a tool for counselor skill improvement and secondarily a tool for increased knowledge and understanding of group dynamics and processes.

Record Volume Using Multiple Lines

The drawback of using tick marks to indicate multiple interactions between the same persons was that the supervisor was unable to determine who spoke to whom when an arrow was drawn on both sides of the line. A better alternative is to record the volume of comments using multiple lines between those communicating. (*Volume* refers here to the airtime occupied by the interaction, not the loudness of the conversation.) Each time a person communicates to another or to the group, the observer creating the sociogram draws a new line instead of making a tick mark. The wider the line, the longer the comments made by the speaker. The result is that the final sociogram is made up of multiple lines that more clearly illustrate communication patterns in the group. As the group process unfolds and the sociogram is mapped, the individual lines build on one another. The breadth of conversations during group can be seen in the final sociogram by the width created by the accretion of lines between participants.

Someday, perhaps, technology will give us a way to plot frequency of comments, their length and duration, and their intensity and decibel volume.

Compile Sociograms in a Three-Ring Binder and Share with Staff

By compiling the sociogram data in a binder, the supervisor creates a scrapbook of counselor progress over time and a set of reference points that mark skill improvement along the way.

The supervisor increases the power of the sociograms by putting them all together, allowing for intragroup comparisons. By collecting ongoing group data in a binder, the supervisor can map group process for the entire program, for multiple groups, and for different group facilitators. The binder can also be used to educate, train, and orient new personnel; to clarify the group process; and to encourage peer support and consultation. This increases staff buy-in to the expected group facilitation strategies and model of the agency. Over time, the supervisor will collect an accurate picture of the types of groups and the group process at that agency.

Using the Sociogram with New Supervisees

When working with a new counselor, or supervisee, the supervisor can state, "As part of your orientation, I want you to observe Elaine's group. While I observe the group, you will sit behind the one-way mirror [or in the group if there is no mirror available] and complete a sociogram. A sociogram is . . . [explain the sociogram and orient the new counselor to its use and benefits]." When supervising an entry-level counselor, the supervisor might want to have the new supervisee observe a high-performing group facilitated by a skilled clinician who will ensure that the communication pattern provides the desired example of the "perfect" sociogram.

Alternately, a video can be recorded of a mock group, and new counselors can complete a sociogram on this group. When several new counselors complete a sociogram on the same group, the supervisor can compare the sociograms for accuracy.

With either approach, the new counselor will see that the sociogram represents the way the group functions. The new counselor now has two maps of what is expected from the group process: the "perfect" sociogram and the actual group he observed. The new counselor also has an understanding of the evaluative tool that will be used in his agency.

Freeze-Frame

A limitation of the sociogram is that it might not fully describe what is truly occurring in the group. The end product of the sociogram is a compilation of the discrete communication events that transpired during the observed group, drawn parallel to one another and forming a final picture, or map, of that group. However, this map may not be an accurate representation of the process.

For example, a counselor may facilitate a group in a clockwise manner (that is, she starts by engaging the person to her left and then moves to the person to the first person's left). This is often seen in groups that "check in" about how members are doing from session to session. The group process is disjointed as each individual checks in, and the interactions between participants are mostly unrelated one to another. Although the final sociogram may convey a picture of a highly interactive, dynamic group with multiple conversations and actions, it does not accurately reflect the group process as it developed.

The solution to this dilemma is to *freeze-frame* the group process, using unlined white paper and a few sheets of tracing paper in addition to the usual colored pens. This strategy requires some preparation before the group starts. First, the supervisor draws the circle of group participants on the unlined white paper, as she would for a typical sociogram, and then she overlays a sheet of tracing paper and traces the circles for participants. She repeats this process with a second sheet of tracing paper. Each sheet is labeled and includes space at the top to record the time and date of the observed session. The tracing paper is set aside, and the supervisor begins recording the group process on the unlined white paper. At some point in the session, perhaps after one-third of the time has passed, the supervisor stops recording on the original sheet, overlays the tracing paper, and continues the process. At a later point, perhaps after two-thirds of the time has passed, the supervisor begins recording on the second sheet of tracing paper.

The result is a sociogram that reflects the group but also offers the overlays of various scenes, or frames, of the same group that can be analyzed independently of the entire sociogram of the group process. Comparing these scenes or frames shows how the group process developed at different stages.

The reader is encouraged to try these techniques in using the sociogram and to explore other options with this valuable tool.

Appendix I: Suggested Outline for Case Presentations

Client name:

Town or residence:

Age:

Marital status (number of marriages, number and ages of children):

Occupation or trade:

Employment status:

Referral source:

Presenting complaints (verbatim and counselor's impression):

Diagnosis:

History of Present Problem

- Years drinking
- Longest period of sobriety
- Recent drinking patterns
- Medical complications, history

- Hospitalizations, number, length of time, dates
- Arrests, charges, amount of time spent in jail
- Suicidal or homicidal ideation, gestures
- Job or situational changes
- Previous treatment

Interview Results

Behavior and Appearance

- Preliminary attitudes
- Entry into room
- Brief physical description, cleanliness, clothing (typical/atypical, bizarre, unusual)
- Unusual physical characteristics
- Attire, build
- Quality of rapport
- Orality, withdrawing, manipulative, seductive
- Posture (tension, rigidity, appropriateness)
- Facial expressions
- Cooperativeness, domineering, provocative, suspicious, overly compliant, hyperactive, depressiveness
- Lethargy, distractibility, shyness, dependency
- Anxiety, hostility, friendliness, fears, apprehensions
- Mannerisms, suggestive verbalizations
- Handedness
- Recurring themes
- General body movements (accelerated, decreased, inappropriateness, fidgety, restlessness)
- Amplitude and quality of speech (slurring, stammering, loud, soft)

Affect

- Appropriateness, flat, absence of affect
- Depressed, anxious, happy, anger, bizarreness

- Mood differences or changes (euphoria, elation, apprehension)
- Blandness, lability of affect

Intellectual Functioning

- Efficiency, mental deficiency, abstraction ability and calculation ability
- Reality testing, disorientation to person, place, and time
- Thought disordering (obsessions, compulsions, phobias, depersonalizations, derealization, suicidal or homicidal ideations)
- Clarity, goal directedness, insight ability, blaming
- Appropriateness, coherence
- Attention, concentration, breaks, impaired level of consciousness
- Discrepancy, perseverations, delusions, ideas of influence/reference
- Process tendencies (associational disturbances)
- Perceptions (illusions, auditory/visual hallucinations)
- Memory (immediate recall, recent and remote memory)
- Judgment about daily living and making reasonable life decisions

Interpersonal Relationships (Social and Emotional Functioning)

- Functioning: marriage, job
- Interpersonal defenses
- Historical: significant figures, conflicts
- Quality of relationship to male/female figures
- Unconscious material, relevant parental information

Self-Concept

- Statements about self (conscious and unconscious)
- Ego strength and self-image

Character Structure and Diagnosis

- Organicity, brain damage
- Major defenses (intrapersonal, interpersonal), root conflicts, problems, areas of strength and weakness

Prognosis

- Reality factors, environmental
- Recommendations for treatment
- Prognosis

Appendix J:
Counselor Assessment Forms

This appendix contains the following counselor assessment forms for use in supervisory evaluation:

- Supervisory Record Form
- Supervision Observation Form
- Live Supervision Form
- Supervision Evaluation Form
- Supervisory Consultation
- Supervision Form

An agency should adapt these forms to its philosophy of treatment, model of therapy, core competencies, and individualized administrative requirements.

These forms appear in the *AAMFT Forms Book* (Washington, D.C.: American Association for Marriage and Family Therapy, 1989). Those under copyright are reprinted by permission of their respective authors as indicated.

Supervisory Record Form

Date:_____

Supervisee: _____

Session #:_____

IDENTIFYING INFORMATION

Case:_____ Supervisee Concern:_____

_____

_____

_____

_____

_____

_____

Supervisory Goals: _____

_____

Supervisory Activity	**Supervisory Recommendations**
1. Supporting Documents	1. Treatment: _____
a. Case Record: _____	
b. Audiovisual Record: _____	
c. Other: _____	
2. Theoretical Issues: _____	2. Training: _____
3. Process Observations:_____	
4. Therapist Self-Awareness: _____	3. Other Comments:_____
5. Treatment Evaluation:_____	

AAMFT Forms Book

Originally developed by Loy O. Bascue, Ph.D. (as referenced in *AAMFT Forms Book*).

Supervision Observation Form

Therapist: _____ Date: _____

This is Session #_____ with this family.   Supervisor: _____

Family Situation:	Therapeutic Plan for this Session:

Joining Skills	0	1	2	3	4	5	_____
Tracking Skills	0	1	2	3	4	5	_____
Thorough Assessment (Problem/Goal/Attempted Solutions/ Alcohol/World View/Developmental Stages)	0	1	2	3	4	5	_____
Probing, Flexible Questions (Circularity/Neutrality/ Hypothesizing/Strategizing)	0	1	2	3	4	5	_____
Clarification, Confrontation	0	1	2	3	4	5	_____
Directing Transactions	0	1	2	3	4	5	_____
Examining Transitional Patterns	0	1	2	3	4	5	_____
Direct Interventions	0	1	2	3	4	5	_____
Indirect Interventions	0	1	2	3	4	5	_____

Comments: _____

_____

_____

Code:					
0 - Skill not required	1 - Skill required but not used	2 - Introductory skill level	3 - Competent skill level	4 - Very good skill level	5 - Creative, flexible use of skills

AAMFT Forms Book

Originally developed by James E. Morton, M.S.W. (as referenced in *AAMFT Forms Book*).

The Live Supervision Form

Date	Time	Room	Session/Contract

Therapist: _____   Clients: _____

Session Objectives:
1. Follow-up on assignment

2.

3.

4.

Prearranged Live Intervention Format:
☐ Phone-in   ☐ Knock   ☐ Walk-in
Midsession Conference at: +30___ +40___ Other___
Specific Intervention Style: _____
Other Request of Observers:

Therapist's Theoretical Orientation:	Skill Development Goals:	Session Themes and Hypotheses:

Observations and Comments: _____
_____
_____
_____
_____
_____

Messages and/or Assignment: _____
_____
_____

Summary of Observations and Comments:
1.

2.

3.

Recommendations for Future Sessions:
1.

2.

3.

Next Appointment:

Day	Date	Time

AAMFT Approved Supervision Credit

Hours & Minutes

Supervisor's Initials

AAMFT Forms Book

Reprinted by permission from Heath, A. 1983. The Live Supervision Form: Structure and Theory for Assessment in Live Supervision. In B. Keeney, ed., *Diagnosis and Assessment in Family Therapy,* Rockville, Md.: Aspen Systems Corp., pp. 143–154.

Supervision Evaluation Form

	Superior	Excellent	Acceptable	Low	ND
1. Professional Decorum					
2. Demonstrates appropriate relationship skills.					
3. Demonstrates joining skills with dyad/family.					
4. Lays down procedural rules for therapeutic process.					
5. Help family define their problem and goals.					
6. Collects detailed information about etiology of identified problem.					
7. Shifts approach when one way of gathering information is not working (flexibility).					
8. Uses specific and clear communication.					
9. Demonstrates ability to elicit specific information from family members.					
10. Demonstrates sense of caring and concern for family members.					
11. Explicitly structures or directs interaction among family members.					
12. Avoids becoming triangulated by the family.					
13. Maintains an objective stance.					
14. Concentrates on the interactions of the system rather than just intrapsychic dynamics.					
15. Directs interaction between family members.					
16. Helps the family establish appropriate boundaries.					

AAMFT Forms Book

Reprinted by permission of David M. Lawson, Ph.D.

Supervisory Consultation

Family Name:_____   Date:_____

Therapist's Name: _____

<table>
<tr><td colspan="3">Type of Consultation:</td></tr>
<tr><td>☐ Live</td><td>☐ Video</td><td>☐ Other</td></tr>
</table>

Guidelines for Therapist:

1. Summary of work to date.
2. Bring a complete genogram for distribution to supervisor and peers.
3. Write a brief problem formulation regarding the family process.

4. State briefly information in your personal family relevant in the treatment of this family.
5. This form must be signed by consulting supervisor and placed in case record.

Summary: _____
_____
_____
_____
_____
_____
_____

Focus your supervision by defining your goal for the supervision session, identifying where you are having difficulty with the family and postulating reasons for these difficulties. **Be Specific.**

_____
_____
_____
_____
_____
_____

Problem Formulation: major triangles

_____
_____
_____
_____
_____

_____
_____

Treatment Plan
(to be listed after supervisory consultation)

Personal Issues (Therapist's) Relevant In Treatment of This Family:

_____
_____
_____
_____
_____
_____

a. _____
_____

b. _____
_____

c. _____
_____

d. _____
_____

Supervisor _____

AAMFT Forms Book

Originally developed by Family Institute of Westchester (as referenced in *AAMFT Forms Book*).

Supervision Form

Therapist's Name: _____ Month and Year: _____

Supervision Received

Indicate the faculty supervisor's initials, the date, the number of hours (quarter-hours), "I" if it was an Individual supervision or "G" if it was Group supervision, and "L" if it was Live supervision or "C" if it was Case consultation. If audio or video tapes were reviewed, record the amount of supervision time spent on each (e.g. .5 hour V, 1.25 hours A, etc.)

Initials of Faculty Supervisor	Date (mo./day/yr.)	Hours	Ind/ Group	Live/ Case	Audio/Video Time

AAMFT Forms Book

Reprinted by permission of Fred P. Piercy.

References

Abels, P., and M. Murphy. 1981. *Administration in Human Services: A Normative Systems Approach.* Englewood Cliffs, N.J.: Prentice Hall.

Abroms, G. M. 1977. Supervision as Metatherapy. In F. W. Kaslow and Associates, *Supervision, Consultation, and Staff Training in the Helping Professions,* 81–99. San Francisco: Jossey-Bass.

Aiken, J., S. Smits, and D. J. Lollar. 1972. Leadership Behavior and Job Satisfaction in State Rehabilitation Agencies. *Personnel Psychology* 25, 65–73.

Alderfer, C. 1991. The Effects of Gender on the Supervisory Process. Ph.D. dissertation, University of Massachusetts.

Aldrich, L., and A. K. Hess. 1983. The Parallel Process in Psychotherapy Supervision. Paper presented at the annual Southeastern Psychological Association Convention, Atlanta.

Alexander, C. N., and E. J. Langer, eds. 1990. *Higher Stages of Human Development: Perspectives on Adult Growth.* New York: Oxford University Press.

Allen, G. J., S. J. Szollos, and B. E. Williams. 1986. Doctoral Students' Comparative Evaluations of Best and Worst Psychotherapy Supervision. *Professional Psychology: Research and Practice* 17, 91–99.

Alonso, A. 1983. A Developmental Theory of Psychodynamic Supervision. *Clinical Supervisor* 1 (3), 23–36.

Alonso, A. 1985. *The Quiet Profession.* New York: Macmillan.

Alonso, A., and J. Rutan. 1978. Cross-Sex Supervision of Cross-Sex Therapy. *American Journal of Psychiatry* 135, 928–931.

American Association for Marriage and Family Therapy. 1984, 1989, 1991. *The AAMFT Code of Ethical Principles for Marriage and Family Therapists.* Washington, D.C.: Author.

American Psychological Association. 1981. Ethical Principles of Psychologists. *American Psychologist* 36, 633–638.

Amidon, E. J. 1965. A Technique for Analyzing Counselor-Counselee Interaction. In J. E. Adams, ed., *Counseling and Guidance: A Summary View.* New York: Macmillan.

Ansbacher, H., and Ansbacher, R. 1956. *The Individual Psychology of Alfred Adler.* New York: Basic Books.

Association for Counselor Education and Supervision. 1988, 1989. Standards for Counseling Supervision. Draft.

Autry, J. 1991. *Love and Profit.* New York: Avon Books.

Avis, J. 1985. The Politics of Functional Family Therapy: A Feminist Critique. *Journal of Marital and Family Therapy* 11, 127–138.

Baker, S. B., E. Johnson, M. Kopala, and N. Strout. 1985. Test Interpretation Competence: A Comparison of Microskills and Mental Practice Training. *Counselor Education and Supervision* 25, 31–44.

Baker, S., M. Scofield, W. Munson, and L. Clayton. 1983. Comparative Effects of Training Basic Counseling Competencies Through Brief Microskills Practice Versus Mental Practice. *Counselor Education and Supervision* 23, 71–83.

Baltes, P. B., H. W. Reese, and J. R. Nesselroade. 1977. *Life-Span Developmental Psychology: Introduction to Research Methods.* Belmont, Calif.: Wadsworth.

Barrett-Lennard, G. T. 1964. *Relationship Inventory.* Armidale, Australia: University of New England.

Bartlett, W. E. 1983. A Multidimensional Framework for the Analysis of Supervision of Counseling. *Counseling Psychologist* 11 (1), 9–17.

Bascue, L. O., and J. A. Yalof. 1991. Descriptive Dimensions of Psychotherapy Supervision. *Clinical Supervisor* 9 (2), 19–30.

Beck, A. 1976. *Cognitive Therapy and the Emotional Disorders.* New York: International Universities Press.

Belenky, M. F., B. M. Clinchy, N. R. Goldberger, and J. M. Tarule. 1986. *Women's Ways of Knowing: The Development of Self, Voice, and Mind.* New York: Basic Books.

Bell, T. L., T. T. Gorski, and J. E. Troiani. 1985. *On the Job Warning Signs: Field Diagnostic Handbook for Relapse Prevention.* Campbell, Calif.: O'Connor Hospital.

Berger, M. M., ed. 1978. *Videotape Techniques in Psychiatric Training and Treatment.* Rev. ed. New York: Brunner/Mazel.

Berger, M. M., and C. Dammann. 1982. Live Supervision as Context, Treatment, and Training. *Family Process* 21, 337–344.

Bernard, J. M. 1981. Inservice Training for Clinical Supervisors. *Professional Psychology* 12, 740–748.

Bernard, J. M. 1987. Ethical and Legal Considerations for Supervisors. In L. D. Borders and G. R. Leddick, *Handbook of Counseling Supervision,* 52–57. Alexandria, Va.: Association for Counselor Education and Supervision.

Bernard, J. M., and R. K. Goodyear. 1992. *Fundamentals of Clinical Supervision.* Boston: Allyn & Bacon.

Bernstein, B. L., and C. LeComte. 1979. Supervisory-Type Feedback Effects: Feedback Discrepancy Level, Trainee Psychological Differentiation, and Immediate Responses. *Journal of Counseling Psychology* 26, 295–303.

Best, D. L., and M. L. Rose. 1997. *Quality Supervision: Theory and Practice for Clinical Supervisors.* London: W. B. Saunders.

Biddle, L. R., and J. W. Newstrom. 1990. *What Every Supervisor Should Know.* New York: McGraw-Hill.

Birch and Davis Corporation. 1986. *Development of Model Professional Standards for Counselor Credentialing.* Dubuque, Iowa: Kendall/Hunt.

Birkner v. Salt Lake County, 771 P.2d 1053 (1989).

Blanchard, K., and S. Johnson. 1982. *The One Minute Manager.* New York: Morrow.

Blanchard, K., and N. V. Peale. 1988. *The Power of Ethical Management.* New York: Fawcett Crest.

Blocher, D. H. 1983. Toward a Cognitive Developmental Approach to Counseling Supervision. *Counseling Psychologist* 11 (1), 27–34.

Blocher, D. H., E. R. Dustin, and W. E. Dugan. 1971. *Guidance Systems.* New York: Ronald Press.

Blount, C. M., and D. Glenwick. 1982. A Developmental Model of Supervision. Part of a Symposium: Psychotherapy Supervision: Expanding Conceptual Models and Clinical Practices, Annual Meeting of the American Psychological Association, Washington, D.C., August.

Blumberg, A. 1970. A System for Analyzing Supervisor-Teacher Interaction. In A. Simon and G. Boyer, eds., *Mirrors for Behavior.* Vol. 3. Philadelphia: Research for Better Schools.

Borders, L. D., and G. R. Leddick. 1987. *Handbook of Counseling Supervision.* Alexandria, Va.: Association for Counselor Education and Supervision.

Bordin, E. S. 1983. A Working Alliance Based Model of Supervision. *Counseling Psychologist* 11 (1), 35–42.

Borys, D. S., and K. S. Pope. 1989. Dual Relationships Between Therapist and Client: A National Study of Psychologists, Psychiatrists, and Social Workers. *Professional Psychology: Research and Practice* 20, 283–293.

Boyd, J. D., ed. 1978. *Counselor Supervision: Approaches, Preparation, Practices.* Muncie, Ind.: Accelerated Development.

Boyd, J. D., and N. K. LaFleur. 1974. Self Management: A Basic Counseling Goal. *Focus on Guidance* 7, 1–10.

Boyd, J. D., J. Nutter, and S. Overcash. 1974. A Psychobehavioral Approach to Counseling Supervision. Program and paper presented at the American Personnel and Guidance Association Convention, New Orleans.

Bradley, L. J. 1989. *Counselor Supervision: Principles, Process, and Practice.* 2d ed. Muncie, Ind.: Accelerated Development.

Bramley, W. 1996. *The Supervisory Couple in Broad-Spectrum Psychotherapy.* New York: Free Association Books.

Brammer, L. M., and A. C. Wassner. 1977. Supervision in Counseling and Psychotherapy. In D. J. Kurpius, R. D. Baker, and I. D. Thomas, eds., *Supervision of Applied Training: A Comparative Review,* 43–82. Westport, Conn.: Greenwood Press.

Bray, J. H., J. N. Shepherd, and J. R. Hays. 1985. Legal and Ethical Issues in Informed Consent to Psychotherapy. *American Journal of Family Therapy* 13 (2), 50–60.

Breunlin, D. C., B. M. Karrer, D. E. McGuire, and R. A. Cimmarusti. 1988. Cybernetics of Videotape Supervision. In H. A. Liddle, D. C. Breunlin, and R. C. Schwartz, eds., *Handbook of Family Therapy Training and Supervision,* 194–206. New York: Guilford Press.

Breunlin, D. C., H. A. Liddle, and R. C. Schwartz. 1988. Concurrent Training of Supervisors and Therapists. In H. A. Liddle, D. C. Breunlin, and R. C. Schwartz, eds., *Handbook of Family Therapy Training and Supervision,* 207–232. New York: Guilford Press.

Bridges, N. A., and J. W. Wohlberg. 1999. Sexual Excitement in Therapeutic Relationships: Clinical and Supervisory Management. *The Clinical Supervisor* 18 (2), 23–34.

Brodsky, A. M. 1980. Sex Role Issues in the Supervision of Therapy. In A. K. Hess, ed., *Psychotherapy Supervision: Theory, Research, and Practice,* 509–522. New York: Wiley.

Brodsky, S., and H. H. Myers. 1986. In Vivo Rotation: An Alternative Model for Psychotherapy Supervision. In F. W. Kaslow, ed., *Supervision and Training: Models, Dilemmas, and Challenges,* 95–104. New York: Haworth Press.

Bruner, J. S. 1963. *The Process of Education.* New York: Random House.

Burgoyne, R. W., S. Santini, F. Kline, and F. R. Staples. 1976. Who Gets Supervised? An Extension of Patient Selection Inequity. *American Journal of Psychiatry* 133, 1313–1315.

Bursztajn, H. J. 1990. Supervisory Responsibility for Prevention of Supervisee Sexual Misconduct. Paper presented at the International Congress of Psychiatry and the Law, Toronto.

Butcher, E., M. E. Scofield, and S. B. Baker. 1985. Clinical Judgment in Planning Mental Health Treatment: An Empirical Investigation. *AMHCA Journal* 7, 116–126.

Cade, B. W., B. Speed, and P. Seligman. 1986. Working in Teams: The Pros and Cons. In F. W. Kaslow, ed., *Supervision and Training: Models, Dilemmas, and Challenges*, 105–118. New York: Haworth Press.

Caligor, L., P. M. Bromberg, and J. D. Meltzer, eds. 1984. *Clinical Perspectives on the Supervision of Psychoanalysis and Psychotherapy*. New York: Plenum.

Canada, R. M., and M. L. Lynch. 1975. Systems Techniques Applied to Teaching Listening Skills. *Counselor Education and Supervision* 15, 40–47.

Canon, H. J., and R. D. Brown, eds. 1985. Applied Ethics in Student Services. In *New Directions for Student Services*. San Francisco: Jossey-Bass.

Caplan, G. 1970. *The Theory and Practice of Mental Health Consultation*. New York: Basic Books.

Carkhuff, R. R. 1969. *Helping and Human Relations*. Vol. 2. New York: Holt, Rinehart and Winston.

Carkhuff, R. R., and C. B. Truax. 1965. Training in Counseling and Psychotherapy: An Evaluation of an Integrated Didactic and Experiential Approach. *Journal of Consulting Psychology* 29, 333–336.

Carlson, J. R. 1980. Audiotape and Videotape Procedures: A Study of Subjects' Reactions. *Journal of Counseling Psychology* 27, 605–610.

Caruth, E. G. 1990. Interpersonal and Intrapsychic Complexities and Vulnerabilities: The Psychoanalytic Supervisory Process. In R. C. Lane, ed., *Psychoanalytic Approaches to Supervision*, 181–193. New York: Brunner/Mazel.

Caust, B. L., J. A. Libow, and P. A. Raskin. 1981. Challenges and Promises of Training Women as Family Systems Therapists. *Family Process* 20, 439–447.

Center for Substance Abuse Treatment. 2003. Manpower Study, 2003. Bethesda, Md.: Center for Substance Abuse Treatment.

Charny, I. W. 1986. What Do Therapists Worry About? A Tool for Experimental Supervision. In F. W. Kaslow, ed., *Supervision and Training: Models, Dilemmas, and Challenges*, 17–28. New York: Haworth Press.

Chazan, S. E. 1990. On Being Supervised and Supervision. In R. C. Lane, ed., *Psychoanalytic Approaches to Supervision*, 25–28. New York: Brunner/Mazel.

Cherniss, C., and E. Egnatios. 1977. Styles of Clinical Supervision in Community Mental Health Programs. *Journal of Consulting and Clinical Psychology* 45, 1195–1196.

Chodorow, N. 1978. *The Reproduction of Mothering: Psychoanalysis and the Sociology of Gender*. Berkeley: University of California Press.

Colby, A., and L. Kohlberg. 1987. *The Measurement of Moral Judgment*. Vol. 1. New York: Cambridge.

Commons, M. L., C. Armon, L. Kohlberg, F. A. Richards, T. A. Grotzer, and J. D. Sinnott, eds. 1990. *Adult Development,* Vol. 2: *Models and Methods in the Study of Adolescent and Adult Thought.* New York: Praeger.

Commons, M. L., J. Demick, and C. Goldberg. 1995. *Clinical Approaches to Adult Development.* Norwood, N.J.: Ablex.

Commons, M. L., F. A. Richards, and C. Armon, eds. 1984. *Beyond Formal Operations,* Vol. 1: *Late Adolescent and Adult Cognitive Development.* New York: Praeger.

Commons, M. L., J. D. Sinnott, F. A. Richards, and C. Armon, eds. 1989. *Adult Development,* Vol. 1: *Comparisons and Applications of Adolescent and Adult Development Models.* New York: Praeger.

Conroe, R. M., and J. A. Schank. 1989. Sexual Intimacy in Clinical Supervision: Unmasking the Silence. In G. R. Schoener, J. H. Milgrom, J. C. Gonsiorek, E. T. Luepker, and R. M. Conroe, eds., *Psychotherapists' Sexual Involvement with Clients: Intervention and Prevention,* 245–262. Minneapolis: Walk-In Counseling Center.

Corey, G., M. S. Corey, and P. Callahan. 1987. *Issues and Ethics in the Helping Professions.* 3d ed. Monterey, Calif.: Brooks/Cole.

Cormier, S., and J. M. Bernard. 1982. Ethical and Legal Responsibilities of Clinical Supervisors. *Personnel and Guidance Journal* 60, 486–491.

Covey, S. 1992. *Principle-Centered Leadership.* New York: Simon & Schuster.

Curran, D. 1983. *Traits of a Healthy Family.* Minneapolis: Winston Press.

Cutcliffe, J. R., T. Butterworth, and B. Proctor, eds. 2001. *Fundamental Themes in Clinical Supervision.* London: Routledge.

D'Andrea, M. 1989. Person-Process Model of Supervision: A Developmental Approach. In L. J. Bradley, ed., *Counselor Supervision: Principles, Process, and Practice,* 257–298. 2d ed. Muncie, Ind.: Accelerated Development.

Delaney, D. J. 1969. Simulation Techniques in Counselor Education: Proposal of a Unique Approach. *Counselor Education and Supervision* 17, 293–299.

Delaney, D. J. 1972. A Behavioral Model for the Supervision of Counselor Candidates. *Counselor Education and Supervision* 12, 46–50.

Denton, K., and D. Krebs. 1990. From the Scene to the Crime: The Effect of Alcohol and Social Context on Moral Judgment. *Journal of Personality and Social Psychology* 59, 242–248.

De Pree, M. 1989. *Leadership Is an Art.* New York: Dell.

de Shazer, S. 1988. *Clues: Investigating Solutions in Brief Therapy.* New York: W. W. Norton.

Dewey, J. 1963. *Experience and Education.* New York: Collier. (Originally published 1938.)

Disney, M. J., and A. M. Stephens. 1994. *Legal Issues in Clinical Supervision*. Vol. 10. Alexandria, Va.: American Counseling Association.

Dodge, J. 1982. Reducing Supervisee Anxiety: A Cognitive-Behavioral Approach. *Counselor Education and Supervision* 22, 55–60.

Doyle, J. 1983. *The Male Experience*. Dubuque, Iowa: Wm. C. Brown.

Duval, S., and R. A. Wicklund. 1972. *A Theory of Objective Self-Awareness*. Orlando, Fla.: Academic Press.

Edelwich, J., and A. Brodsky. 1980. *Burnout: Stages of Disillusionment in the Helping Professions*. New York: Human Sciences Press.

Edelwich, J., and A. Brodsky. 1991. *Sexual Dilemmas for the Helping Professional*. Rev. ed. New York: Brunner/Mazel.

Edelwich, J., and A. Brodsky. 1992. *Group Counseling for the Resistant Client: A Practical Guide to Group Process*. New York: Lexington Books.

Eitington, M. 1937. An Address to the International Training Commission. *International Journal of Psychoanalysis* 18, 346–348.

Ekstein, R. 1960. Report of the Panel on the Teaching of Psychoanalytic Technique. *Journal of the American Psychoanalytic Association* 8, 167–174.

Ekstein, R., and R. Wallerstein. 1972. *The Teaching and Learning of Psychotherapy*. 2d ed. New York: International Universities Press.

Ellis, A. 1973. *Humanistic Psychotherapy: The Rational-Emotive Approach*. New York: McGraw-Hill.

Emch, M. 1955. The Social Context of Supervision. *International Journal of Psychiatry* 36, 298–306.

Erikson, E. 1959. *Identity and the Life Cycle*. New York: International Universities Press.

ETP Inc. 1991. *The Alcoholism and Drug Abuse Field: Planning for the Year 2000*. Windsor, Conn.: ETP.

Falicov, C. 1988. Learning to Think Culturally. In H. Liddle, D. Breunlin, and R. Schwartz, eds., *Handbook of Family Therapy Training and Supervision*, 335–357. New York: Guilford Press.

Falvey, J. E. 1987. *Handbook of Administrative Supervision*. Washington, D.C.: Association for Counselor Education and Supervision.

Falvey, J. E. 2002. *Managing Clinical Supervision: Ethical Practice and Legal Risk Management*. Pacific Grove, Calif.: Brooks/Cole.

Feltham, C., and W. Dryden. 1994. *Developing Counselor Supervision*. London: Sage.

Fingarette, H. 1988. *Heavy Drinking: The Myth of Alcoholism as a Disease*. Berkeley: University of California Press.

Fiscalini, J. 1985. On Supervisory Parataxis and Dialogue. *Contemporary Psychoanalysis* 21, 591–608.

Fish, D., and S. Twinn. 1997. *Quality Clinical Supervision in the Health Care Professions: Principled Approaches to Practice.* London: Butterworth and Heinemann.

Flanders, N. A. 1970. Interaction Analysis in the Classroom: A Manual for Observers. In A. Simon and G. Boyer, eds., *Mirrors of Behavior.* Vol. 2. Philadelphia: Research for Better Schools.

Fleming, J. 1967. Teaching the Basic Skills of Psychotherapy. *Archives of General Psychiatry* 16, 416–426.

Fleming, J., and T. Benedek. 1966. *Psychoanalytic Supervision: A Method of Clinical Teaching.* New York: Grune and Stratton.

Foundation for Addictions Research and Education. 1998. Wisconsin Clinical Supervision Training Project. [www.fare-wi.org/FARERtoPWIClinSupTrngModelSummary].

Frankel, B. R., and F. P. Piercy. 1990. The Relationship Among Selected Supervisor, Therapist, and Client Behaviors. *Journal of Marital and Family Therapy* 16, 407–421.

Friedlander, M. L., and L. G. Ward. 1984. Development and Validation of the Supervisory Styles Inventory. *Journal of Counseling Psychology* 31, 541–557.

Gaoni, B., and M. Newmann. 1974. Supervision from the Point of View of the Supervisee. *American Journal of Psychotherapy* 23, 108–114.

Garfield, S. L. 1986. Research on Client Variables in Psychotherapy. In S. L. Garfield and A. E. Bergin, eds., *Handbook of Psychotherapy and Behavior Change,* 213–256. 3d ed. New York: Wiley.

Gediman, H. K., and F. Wolkenfeld. 1980. The Parallelism Phenomenon in Psychoanalysis and Supervision: Its Reconsideration as a Triadic System. *Psychoanalytic Quarterly* 49, 234–255.

Gibbs, J. C. 1977. Kohlberg's Stages of Moral Judgment: A Constructive Critique. *Harvard Educational Review* 47, 43–61.

Gilbert, M. C., and K. Evans. 2000. *Psychotherapy Supervision: An Integrative Relational Approach to Psychotherapy Supervision.* Buckingham, U.K.: Open University Press.

Gilligan, C. 1992. *In a Different Voice: Psychological Theory and Women's Development.* 2d ed. Cambridge, Mass.: Harvard University Press.

Gleick, J. 1987. *Chaos: Making a New Science.* New York: Penguin Books.

Glickman, C. D., ed. 1992. *Supervision in Transition: 1992 Yearbook of the Association for Supervision and Curriculum Development.* Washington, D.C.: Association for Supervision and Curriculum Development.

Goldberg, H. 1976. *The Hazards of Being Male: Surviving the Myth of Masculine Privileges.* Plainview, N.Y.: Nash.

Goodyear, R. K., and F. O. Bradley. 1983. Theories of Counselor Supervision: Points of Convergence and Divergence. *Counseling Psychologist* 11 (1), 59–67.

Gould, C., ed. 1983. *Beyond Domination: New Perspectives on Women and Philosophy*. Totowa, N.J.: Rowman & Allenheld.

Grater, H. A. 1985. Stages in Psychotherapy Supervision: From Therapy Skills to Skilled Therapist. *Professional Psychology: Research and Practice* 16, 605–610.

Greben S. E., and R. Ruskin. 1994. *Clinical Perspectives on Psychotherapy Supervision*. Washington, D.C.: American Psychiatric Press.

Greenberg, L. 1980. Supervision from the Perspective of the Supervisee. In A. K. Hess, ed., *Psychotherapy Supervision: Theory, Research, and Practice,* 85–91. New York: Wiley.

Greenleaf, R. 1977. *Servant Leadership*. Chicago: Paulist Press.

Gutheil, T. G., and P. S. Appelbaum. 2000. *Clinical Handbook of Psychiatry and the Law*. 3d ed. Baltimore: Lippincott Williams & Wilkins.

Gutheil, T. G., H. J. Bursztajn, A. Brodsky, and V. G. Alexander, eds. 1991. *Decision Making in Psychiatry and the Law*. Baltimore: Williams & Wilkins.

Haber, R. 1996. *Dimensions of Psychotherapy and Supervision: Maps and Means*. New York: W. W. Norton.

Hackney, H., and L. S. Nye. 1973. *Counseling Strategies and Objectives*. Englewood Cliffs, N.J.: Prentice Hall.

Haley, J. 1976. *Problem-Solving Therapy*. San Francisco: Jossey-Bass.

Haley, J. 1988. Reflections on Supervision. In H. A. Liddle, D. C. Breunlin, and R. C. Schwartz, eds., *Handbook of Family Therapy Training and Supervision,* 358–367. New York: Guilford Press.

Handley, P. 1982. Relationship Between Supervisors' and Trainees' Cognitive Styles and the Supervision Process. *Journal of Counseling Psychology* 29, 508–515.

Hansen, J. C., R. Pound, and C. Petro. 1976. Review of Research on Practicum Supervision. *Counselor Education and Supervision* 16, 107–116.

Hare-Mustin, R., and J. Maracek. 1986. Autonomy and Gender: Some Questions for Therapists. *Psychotherapy* 23, 205–212.

Hart, D. H., and D. J. Prince. 1970. Role Conflict for School Counselors: Training Versus Job Demands. *Personnel and Guidance Journal* 48, 374–380.

Hart, G. M. 1982. *The Process of Clinical Supervision*. Baltimore: University Park Press.

Hawthorne, L. 1975. Games Supervisors Play. *Social Work* 20, 179–183.

Hayes, R. 1980. The Democratic Classroom: A Program in Moral Education for Adolescents. Ph.D. dissertation, Boston University.

Henderson, C. E., C. S. Cawyer, and C. E. Watkins. 1999. A Comparison of Student and Supervisor Perceptions of Effective Practicum Supervision. *The Clinical Supervisor* 18 (1), 47–74.

Henry, W. E., J. H. Sims, and L. S. Spray. 1971. *The Fifth Profession.* San Francisco: Jossey-Bass.

Heppner, P. P., and P. G. Handley. 1981. A Study of the Interpersonal Influence Process in Supervision. *Journal of Counseling Psychology* 28, 437–444.

Heppner, P. P., and H. J. Roehlke. 1984. Differences Among Supervisees at Different Levels of Training: Implications for a Developmental Model of Supervision. *Journal of Counseling Psychology* 31, 76–90.

Hess, A. K., ed. 1980. *Psychotherapy Supervision: Theory, Research, and Practice.* New York: Wiley.

Hess, A. K. 1986. Growth in Supervision: Stages of Supervisee and Supervisor Development. In F. W. Kaslow, ed., *Supervision and Training: Models, Dilemmas, and Challenges,* 51–67. New York: Haworth Press.

Hill, C. E., D. Charles, and K. G. Reed. 1981. A Longitudinal Analysis of Changes in Counseling Skills During Doctoral Training in Counseling Psychology. *Journal of Counseling Psychology* 28, 428–436.

Hill, C. E., and K. E. O'Grady. 1985. List of Therapist Intentions Illustrated in a Case Study and with Therapists with Varying Theoretical Orientations. *Journal of Counseling Psychology* 32, 3–22.

Hill, W. F. 1965. *Hill Interaction Matrix.* Los Angeles: Youth Study Center, University of Southern California.

Hoffman, L. W. 1990. *Old Scapes, New Maps: A Training Program for Psychotherapy Supervisors.* Cambridge, Mass.: Milusik Press.

Hoffman, M. L. 1984. Empathy: Its Limitations, and Its Role in a Comprehensive Theory. In W. M. Kurtines and J. L. Gewirtz, eds., *Morality, Moral Behavior, and Moral Development.* New York: Wiley.

Hogan, R. A. 1964. Issues and Approaches in Supervision. *Psychotherapy: Theory, Research and Practice* 1, 139–141.

Holloway, E. L. 1982. The Interactional Structure of the Supervision Interview. *Journal of Counseling Psychology* 29, 309–317.

Holloway, E. L. 1987. Developmental Models of Supervision: Is It Developmental? *Professional Psychology: Research and Practice* 18, 209–216.

Holloway, E. L. 1995. *Clinical Supervision: A Systems Approach.* London: Sage.

Holloway, E. L., and R. Johnson. 1985. Group Supervision: Widely Practiced but Poorly Understood. *Counselor Education and Supervision* 24, 332–340.

Holloway, E. L., and B. E. Wampold. 1983. Patterns of Verbal Behavior and Judgments of Satisfaction in the Supervision Interview. *Journal of Counseling Psychology* 30, 227–234.

Holloway, E. L., and P. A. Wolleat. 1980. Relationship of Counselor Conceptual Level to Clinical Hypothesis Formulation. *Journal of Counseling Psychology* 27, 539–545.

Horan, J. J. 1972. Behavioral Goals in Systematic Counselor Education. *Counselor Education and Supervision* 11, 162–170.

Hubble, M. A., B. L. Duncan, and S. D. Miller. 1999. *The Heart and Soul of Change: What Works in Therapy.* Washington, D.C.: American Psychological Association.

Imber, S. D., E. H. Nash, and A. R. Stone. 1955. Social Class and Duration of Psychotherapy. *Journal of Clinical Psychology* 11, 281–284.

International Certification & Reciprocity Consortium. 1992. *Role Delineation Study for the Clinical Supervisor.* Raleigh, N.C.: Columbia Assessment Services.

Ipsaro, A. 1986. Male Client–Male Therapist: Issues in Therapeutic Alliance. *Psychotherapy* 23, 257–266.

Issacharoff, A. 1982. Countertransference in Supervision: Therapeutic Consequences for the Supervisee. *Contemporary Psychoanalysis* 18, 455–472.

Ivey, A. E. 1971. *Microcounseling: Innovations in Interviewing Training.* Springfield, Ill.: Charles C. Thomas.

Ivey, A. E. 1986. *Developmental Therapy: Theory into Practice.* San Francisco: Jossey-Bass.

Ivey, A. E., C. Normington, C. Miller, W. Morrill, and R. Haase. 1968. Microcounseling and Attending Behavior: An Approach to Pre-Practicum Counselor Training. *Journal of Counseling Psychology* (Monograph Supplement) 15 (Part 2), 1–12.

Jakubowski-Spector, P., R. Dustin, and R. George. 1971. Toward Developing a Behavioral Counselor Education Model. *Counselor Education and Supervision* 10, 242–250.

Kadushin, A. 1976. *Supervision in Social Work.* New York: Columbia University Press.

Kadushin, A. 1992. What's Wrong, What's Right with Social Work Supervision. *Clinical Supervisor* 10 (1), 3–19.

Kagan, H. 1975. Influencing Human Interaction—Eleven Years with IPR. *Canadian Counselor* 9, 74–97.

Kahn, R., D. Wolfe, R. Quinn, D. Snock, and R. A. Rosenthal. 1964. *Organizational Stress: Studies in Role Conflict and Ambiguity.* New York: Wiley.

Kahn, W. J. 1976. Self-Management: Learning to Be Our Own Counselor. *Personnel and Guidance Journal* 55 (4), 176–180.

Kaplan, A. 1985. Female or Male Therapists for Women Patients: New Formulations. *Psychiatry* 48, 111–121.

Kaslow, F. W. 1986a. Commentary: Individual Therapy Focused on Marital Problems. *American Journal of Family Therapy* 14, 264.

Kaslow, F. W. 1986b. *Supervision and Training: Models, Dilemmas, and Challenges.* New York: Haworth Press.

Katz, S. J., and A. E. Liu. 1991. *The Codependency Conspiracy: How to Break the Recovery Habit and Take Charge of Your Life.* New York: Warner.

Keen, S. 1991. *Fire in the Belly.* New York: Bantam Books.

Keller, E. 1985. *Reflections on Gender and Science.* New Haven, Conn.: Yale University Press.

Keller, J. F., and J. Protinsky. 1986. A Self-Management Model for Supervision. *Journal of Marital and Family Therapy* 10, 281–288.

Kermish, I., and F. Kushin. 1969. Why High Turnover? Social Work Staff Losses in a County Welfare Agency. *Public Welfare* 27, 134–137.

Kitchener, K. S. 1988. Dual Role Relationships. What Makes Them So Problematic? *Journal of Counseling and Development* 67, 217–221.

Koenig, H. 1999. *The Healing Power of Faith.* New York: Simon & Schuster.

Kohlberg, L. 1981. *The Philosophy of Moral Development: Moral Stages and the Idea of Justice.* San Francisco: Harper & Row.

Kohlberg, L. 1984. *Essays on Moral Development,* Vol. 2: *The Psychology of Moral Development: Moral Stages, Their Nature and Validity.* San Francisco: Harper & Row.

Kohlberg, L., ed. 1987. *Child Psychology and Childhood Education: A Cognitive-Developmental View.* New York: Longman.

Koplowitz, H. 1984. A Projection Beyond Piaget's Formal-Operational Stage: A General System Stage and a Unitary Stage. In M. L. Commons, F. A. Richards, and C. Armon, eds., *Beyond Formal Operations,* Vol. 1: *Late Adolescent and Adult Cognitive Development,* 272–296. New York: Praeger.

Kramer, J. R., and M. Reitz. 1980. Using Video Playback to Train Family Therapists. *Family Process* 19, 145–150.

Kris, E. 1956. Some Vicissitudes of Insight in Psychoanalysis. *International Journal of Psychoanalysis* 37, 445–455.

Krumboltz, J. D. 1966. Behavioral Goals for Counseling. *Journal of Counseling Psychology* 13, 153–159.

Kugler, P., ed. 1995. *Jungian Perspectives on Clinical Supervision.* Zurich, Switzerland: Daimon.

Kuhn, D. 1978. Introduction to *Stage Theories of Cognitive and Moral Development.* Reprint no. 13. Cambridge, Mass.: Harvard Educational Review.

Lane, R. 1985. The Recalcitrant Supervisee: The Negative Supervisory Reaction. *Current Issues in Psychoanalytic Practice* 2, 65–81.

Lane, R. C., ed. 1990. *Psychoanalytic Approaches to Supervision.* New York: Brunner/Mazel.

Lawson, G. W., D. C. Ellis, and P. C. Rivers. 1984. *Essentials of Chemical Dependency Counseling.* Rockville, Md.: Aspen.

Lebovici, S. 1970. Technical Remarks on the Supervision of Psychoanalytic Treatment. *International Journal of Psychoanalysis* 51, 385–392.

Leddick, G., and H. A. Dye. 1987. Effective Supervision as Portrayed by Trainee Expectations and Preferences. *Counselor Education and Supervision* 27, 139–155.

Lesser, R. M. 1983. Supervision: Illusions, Anxiety, and Questions. *Contemporary Psychoanalysis* 19, 120–129.

Levenson, E. A. 1984. Follow the Fox. In L. Caligor, P. M. Bromberg, and J. D. Meltzer, eds., *Clinical Perspectives on the Supervision of Psychoanalysis and Psychotherapy,* 153–167. New York: Plenum.

Levering, R. 1988. *A Great Place to Work.* New York: Random House.

Liddle, H. A. 1988. Systematic Supervision: Conceptual Overlays and Pragmatic Guidelines. In H. A. Liddle, D. C. Breunlin, and R. C. Shwartz, eds., *Handbook of Family Therapy Training and Supervision,* 153–171. New York: Guilford Press.

Liddle, H. A., D. C. Breunlin, and R. C. Schwartz, eds. 1988. *Handbook of Family Therapy Training and Supervision.* New York: Guilford Press.

Lisnow, F. 1990. Is Impairment a Current Issue Facing Alcoholism and Drug Abuse Counselors? In *The Counselor.* Arlington, Va.: National Association of Alcoholism and Drug Abuse Counselors.

Littrell, J. M., N. Lee-Bordin, and J. R. Lorenz. 1979. A Developmental Framework for Counseling Supervision. *Counselor Education and Supervision* 19, 129–136.

Loevinger, J. 1976. *Ego Development: Conceptions and Theories.* San Francisco: Jossey-Bass.

Loevinger, J. 1977. Ego Maturity and Human Development. *Pupil Personnel Services Journal* 6, 19–24.

Loganbill, C., E. Hardy, and U. Delworth. 1982. Supervision: A Conceptual Model. *Counseling Psychologist* 10 (1), 3–42.

Loganbill, C., and C. D. Stoltenberg. 1983. A Case Conceptualization Format: A Training Device for Practicum. *Counselor Education and Supervision* 22, 235–241.

Lorr, M., M. M. Katz, and E. A. Rubenstein. 1958. The Prediction of Length of Stay in Psychotherapy. *Journal of Consulting Psychology* 22, 156–160.

Maccoby, E., and C. Jacklin. 1974. *Psychology of Sex Differences*. Stanford, Calif.: Stanford University Press.

Mager, R. F. 1972. *Goal Analysis*. Belmont, Calif.: Fearon.

Mahler, M., F. Pine, and A. Bergman. 1975. *The Psychological Birth of the Human Infant*. New York: Basic Books.

Mahoney, M. J., and C. E. Thoresen. 1974. *Self-Control: Power to the Person*. Monterey, Calif.: Brooks/Cole.

Margolin, G. 1982. Ethical and Legal Considerations in Marital and Family Counseling. *American Psychologist* 37, 788–801.

Maslach, C. 1986. Burnout in the Social Services: A Critique. *Journal of Social Service Research* 10 (1), 95–105.

McNeill, B. W., C. D. Stoltenberg, and R. A. Pierce. 1985. Supervisees' Perceptions of Their Development: A Test of the Counselor Complexity Model. *Journal of Counseling Psychology* 32, 630–633.

Mead, D. E. 1990. *Effective Supervision: A Task-Oriented Model for the Mental Health Professions*. New York: Brunner/Mazel.

Mead, D. E., and D. Crane. 1978. An Empirical Approach to Supervision and Training of Relationship Therapists. *Journal of Marriage and Family Counseling* 4, 67–75.

Merriam-Webster's Collegiate Dictionary. 10th ed. 1988. Springfield, Mass.: Merriam-Webster.

Miars, R. D., T. J. Tracey, P. B. Ray, J. L. Cornfield, and C. J. Gelso. 1983. Variation in Supervision Process Across Trainee Experience Levels. *Journal of Counseling Psychology* 30, 403–412.

Michaels, L. F. 1982. The Development of an Anchored Rating Scale for Evaluating Psychotherapy Skills. Ph.D. dissertation, Colorado State University.

Miller, G. D. 1977. Developmental Theory: High Promise for Guidance Practice. *Pupil Personnel Services Journal* 6, 1–17.

Miller, J. B. 1986. *Toward a New Psychology of Women*. Boston: Beacon Press.

Miller, S. D., B. L. Duncan, and M. A. Hubble. 1997. *Escape from Babel: Toward a Unifying Language for Psychotherapy Practice*. New York: W. W. Norton.

Minuchin, S., and H. D. Fishman. 1981. *Family Therapy Techniques*. Cambridge, Mass.: Harvard University Press.

Mueller, W. J., and B. L. Kell. 1972. *Coping with Conflicts: Supervising Counselors and Psychotherapists*. New York: Appleton-Century-Crofts.

Munson, C. E. 1979. *Social Work Supervision: Classic Statements and Critical Issues*. New York: Free Press.

Munson, C. E. 1983. *An Introduction to Clinical Social Work Supervision*. New York: Haworth Press.

Munson, C. E., ed. 1984. *Family of Origin Applications in Clinical Supervision.* New York: Haworth Press.

Munson, C. E. 1987. Sex Roles and Power Relationships in Supervision. *Professional Psychology: Research and Practice* 18, 236–243.

Munson, C. E. 1999. *Clinical Social Work Supervision.* New York: Haworth Press.

Naisbett, J., and P. Aburdene. 1990. *Megatrends 2000.* New York: Morrow.

National Certification Reciprocity Consortium. 1992. *Role Delineation Study for the Clinical Supervisor.* Raleigh, N.C.: Columbia Assessment Services.

National Institute on Alcohol Abuse and Alcoholism. 1978. *Counseling Alcoholic Clients.* Rockville, Md.: Author.

Newirth, J. W. 1990. The Mastery of Countertransferential Anxiety: An Object Relations View of the Supervisory Process. In R. C. Lane, ed., *Psychoanalytic Approaches to Supervision,* 157–164. New York: Brunner/Mazel.

Newman, A. S. 1981. Ethical Issues in the Supervision of Psychotherapy. *Professional Psychology* 12, 690–695.

Nichols, W. C., D. P. Nichols, and K. V. Hardy. 1990. Supervision in Family Therapy: A Decade Restudy. *Journal of Marital and Family Therapy* 16, 275–285.

Norcross, J. C., M. Hedges, and J. O. Prochaska. 2002. The Face of 2010: A Delphi Poll on the Future of Psychotherapy. *Professional Psychology: Research and Practice* 33, 316–322.

Oberman, N. C. 1990. Supervision and the Achievement of an Analytic Identity. In R. C. Lane, ed., *Psychoanalytic Approaches to Supervision,* 194–206. New York: Brunner/Mazel.

Okun, B. 1983. Gender Issues of Family Systems Therapists. In B. Okun and S. Gladdings, eds., *Issues in Training Marriage and Family Therapists.* Ann Arbor, Mich.: ERIC/CAPS.

Olmstead, J., and H. E. Christensen. 1973. *Effects of Agency Work Contexts: An Intensive Field Study.* Research Report 2. Washington, D.C.: Department of Health, Education and Welfare.

Page, S., and V. Wosket. 2001. *Supervising the Counselor: A Cyclical Model.* East Sussex, U.K.: Brunner-Routledge.

Patterson, C. H. 1983. A Client-Centered Approach to Supervision. *Counseling Psychologist* 11 (1), 21–25.

Peabody, S. A., and C. J. Gelso. 1982. Countertransference and Empathy: The Complex Relationship Between Two Divergent Concepts in Counseling. *Journal of Counseling Psychology* 29, 240–245.

Peele, S. 1995. *Diseasing of America: How We Allowed Recovery Zealots and the Treatment Industry to Convince Us We Are Out of Control.* San Francisco: Jossey-Bass.

Peele, S., A. Brodsky, and M. Arnold. 1991. *The Truth About Addiction and Recovery: The Life Process Program for Outgrowing Destructive Habits.* New York: Simon & Schuster.

Perry, W. G., Jr. 1968. *Forms of Intellectual and Ethical Development in the College Years.* New York: Holt, Rinehart and Winston.

Peterson, F. K. 1991. Issues of Race and Ethnicity in Supervision: Emphasizing Who You Are, Not What You Know. *Clinical Supervisor* 9 (1), 15–31.

Petty, M. M., and C. A. Odewahn. 1983. Supervisory Behavior and Sex Role Stereotypes in Human Service Organizations. *Clinical Supervisor* 1 (2), 13–20.

Piaget, J. 1971. *Biology and Knowledge: An Essay on the Relations Between Organic Regulations and Cognitive Processes.* Chicago: University of Chicago Press.

Piercy, F., A. Hovestadt, D. Fennell, G. Franklin, and D. McKeron. 1982. A Comprehensive Training Model for Family Therapists Serving Rural Populations. *Family Therapy* 9, 239–249.

Pope, K. S., and Bajt, T. R. 1988. When Laws and Values Conflict: A Dilemma for Psychologists. *American Psychologist* 43, 828–829.

Pope, K. S., H. Levenson, and L. R. Schover. 1979. Sexual Intimacy in Psychology Training: Results and Implications of a National Survey. *American Psychologist* 34, 682–689.

Pope, K. S., L. R. Schover, and H. Levenson. 1980. Sexual Behavior Between Clinical Supervisors and Trainees: Implications for Professional Standards. *Professional Psychology* 11, 157–162.

Powell, D. J. 1976. *Manpower Needs in the Alcohol Field.* Bloomfield, Conn.: Eastern Area Alcohol Education and Training Program, Inc.

Powell, D. J. 1980a. *Clinical Supervision: Skills for Substance Abuse Counselors: Manual.* New York: Human Sciences Press.

Powell, D. J. 1980b. *Clinical Supervision: Skills for Substance Abuse Counselors: Workbook.* New York: Human Sciences Press.

Powell, D. J. 2003. *Playing Life's Second Half: A Man's Guide for Turning Success into Significance.* San Francisco: New Harbinger.

Prochaska, J. O., J. C. Norcross, and C. C. DiClemente. 1994. *Changing for Good.* New York: Avon Books.

Rabinowitz, F. E., P. P. Heppner, and H. J. Roehlke. 1985. Descriptive Study of Process and Outcome Variables of Supervision over Time. *Journal of Counseling Psychology* 33, 292–300.

Ralph, N. B. 1980. Learning Psychotherapy: A Developmental Perspective. *Psychiatry* 43, 243–250.

Raphael, R. D. 1982. Supervisee Experience: The Effect on Supervisor Verbal Responses. Paper presented at the Annual Meeting of the American Psychological Association, Washington, D.C., August.

Reid, E., S. McDaniel, C. Donaldson, and M. Tollers. 1987. Taking It Personally: Issues of Personal Authority and Competence for the Female in Family Therapy Training. *Journal of Marital and Family Therapy* 13, 157–165.

Reiser, S. J., H. J. Bursztajn, P. S. Appelbaum, and T. G. Gutheil. 1987. *Divided Staffs, Divided Selves: A Case Approach to Mental Health Ethics.* Cambridge, U.K.: Cambridge University Press.

Reising, G. N., and M. H. Daniels. 1983. A Study of Hogan's Model of Counselor Development and Supervision. *Journal of Counseling Psychology* 30, 235–244.

Rest, J. 1973. Comprehension Preference and Spontaneous Usage in Moral Judgment. In L. Kohlberg and E. Turiel, eds., *Recent Research in Moral Development.* New York: Holt, Rinehart and Winston.

Rice, D. G. 1986. Supervision of Cotherapy. In F. W. Kaslow, ed., *Supervision and Training: Models, Dilemmas, and Challenges,* 119–142. New York: Haworth Press.

Richardson, B. K., and L. J. Bradley. 1984. Microsupervision: A Skill Development Model for Training Clinical Supervisors. *Clinical Supervisor* 2 (3), 43–54.

Robertiello, R. C., and G. Schoenewolf. 1987. *101 Common Therapeutic Blunders: Countertransference and Counterresistance in Psychotherapy.* London: Aronson.

Roberts, H. 1992. Contextual Supervision Involves Continuous Dialogue with Supervisees. AAMFT. *Supervision Bulletin* 5 (3), 2.

Rogers, C. R. 1951. *Client-Centered Therapy: Its Current Practice, Implications and Theory.* Boston: Houghton Mifflin.

Rosenblatt, A., and J. E. Mayer. 1975. Objectionable Supervisory Styles: Students' Views. *Social Work* 20, 184–189.

Rosener, J. 1990. How Women Lead. *Harvard Business Review* 68 (6), 119–125.

Rozsnafszky, J. 1979. Beyond Schools of Psychotherapy: Integrity and Maturity in Therapy and Supervision. *Psychotherapy: Theory, Research and Practice* 16, 190–198.

Russell, R. K., and F. Wise. 1976. Treatment of Speech Anxiety by Cue-Controlled Relaxation and Desensitization with Professional and Paraprofessional Counselors. *Journal of Counseling Psychology* 23, 583–586.

Ryan, T. A. 1969. Systems Techniques for Programs of Counseling and Counselor Education. *Educational Technology* 9, 7–17.

Ryan, T. A., and F. R. Zeran. 1972. *Organization and Administration of Guidance Services.* Danville, Ill.: Interstate.

Saba, G. W., and H. A. Liddle. 1986. Perceptions of Professional Needs, Practice Patterns and Critical Issues Facing Family Therapy Trainers and Supervisors. *American Journal of Family Therapy* 14, 109–122.

Sanchez-Craig, M. 1976. Cognitive and Behavioral Coping Strategies in the Reappraisal of Stressful Social Situations. *Journal of Counseling Psychology* 23, 7–12.

Sanderson, B. E. 1989. Employer Liability for Sexual Exploitation of Clients. In B. E. Sanderson, ed., *It's Never OK: A Handbook for Professionals on Sexual Exploitation by Counselors and Therapists,* 147–152. St. Paul: Minnesota Department of Corrections.

Sansbury, D. L. 1982. Developmental Supervision from a Skills Perspective. *Counseling Psychologist* 10 (1), 53–57.

Savickas, M., C. Marquart, and C. Supinski. 1986. Effective Supervision in Groups. *Counselor Education and Supervision* 26, 17–25.

Saylor, R. H. 1976. Managing Competency-Based Preparation of School Counselors. *Counselor Education and Supervision* 16, 195–199.

Schoener, G. R. 1989. The Role of Supervision and Case Consultation: Some Notes on Sexual Feelings in Therapy. In G. R. Schoener, J. H. Milgrom, J. C. Gonsiorek, E. T. Luepker, and R. M. Conroe, eds., *Psychotherapists' Sexual Involvement with Clients: Intervention and Prevention,* 495–502. Minneapolis: Walk-In Counseling Center.

Schoener, G. R., and R. M. Conroe. 1989. The Role of Supervision and Case Consultation in Primary Prevention. In G. R. Schoener, J. H. Milgrom, J. C. Gonsiorek, E. T. Luepker, and R. M. Conroe, eds., *Psychotherapists' Sexual Involvement with Clients: Intervention and Prevention,* 477–493. Minneapolis: Walk-In Counseling Center.

Schofield, W. 1964. *Psychotherapy: The Purchase of Friendship.* Englewood Cliffs, N.J.: Prentice-Hall.

Schwartz, E. 1990. Supervision in Psychotherapy and Psychoanalysis. In R. C. Lane, ed., *Psychoanalytic Approaches to Supervision,* 84–95. New York: Brunner/Mazel.

Searles, H. F. 1965. Problems of Psycho-Analytic Supervision. In *Collected Papers on Schizophrenia and Related Subjects,* 584–604. New York: International Universities Press.

Shaw, B. F., and K. S. Dobson. 1988. Competency Judgments in the Training and Evaluation of Psychotherapists. *Journal of Consulting and Clinical Psychology* 56, 666–672.

Shemberg, K. M., and D. B. Leventhal. 1978. A Survey of Activities of Academic Clinicians. *Professional Psychology* 9, 580–586.

Shipton, G., ed. 1997. *Supervision of Psychotherapy and Counseling: Making a Place to Think.* Philadelphia: Open University Press.

Shulman, L. 1993. *Interactional Supervision.* Washington, D.C.: NASW Press.

Silverstein, L. M. 1977. *Consider the Alternative.* Minneapolis: Compcare.

Simon, S., ed. 1985. *Managing Finances, Personnel, and Information in Human Services.* New York: Haworth Press.

Singer, J. L. 1990. The Supervision of Graduate Students Who Are Conducting Psychodynamic Psychotherapy. In R. C. Lane, ed., *Psychoanalytic Approaches to Supervision*, 165–178. New York: Brunner/Mazel.

Slavin, S., ed. 1985. *Social Administration: The Management of the Social Services.* Vol. 1. New York: Haworth Press.

Slovenko, R. 1980. Legal Issues in Psychotherapy Supervision. In A. K. Hess, ed., *Psychotherapy Supervision: Theory, Research, and Practice.* New York: Wiley.

Spivack, J. D. 1972. Laboratory to Classroom: The Practical Application of IPR in a Master's Level Pre-Practicum Counselor Education Program. *Counselor Education and Supervision* 12, 3–16.

Stadler, H., ed. 1986. Professional Ethics (Special Issue). *Journal of Counseling and Development* 64 (5).

Steinhelber, J., V. Patterson, K. Cliffe, and M. Legoullon. 1984. An Investigation of Some Relationships Between Psychotherapy Supervision and Patient Change. *Journal of Clinical Psychology* 40, 1346–1353.

Stenack, R. J., and H. A. Dye. 1982. Behavioral Descriptions of Counseling Supervision Roles. *Counselor Education and Supervision* 21, 295–304.

Stoltenberg, C. D. 1981. Approaching Supervision from a Developmental Perspective: The Counselor Complexity Model. *Journal of Counseling Psychology* 28, 59–65.

Stoltenberg, C. D., and U. Delworth. 1987. *Supervising Counselors and Therapists: A Developmental Approach.* San Francisco: Jossey-Bass.

Stoltenberg, C. D., U. Delworth, and B. McNeill. 1998. *IDM Supervision: An Integrated Developmental Model for Supervising Counselors and Therapists.* San Francisco: Jossey-Bass.

Stoltenberg, C. D., R. A. Pierce, and B. W. McNeill. 1987. Effects of Experience on Counselor Trainees' Needs. *Clinical Supervisor* 5 (1), 23–32.

Stoltenberg, C. D., G. S. Solomon, and L. Ogden. 1986. Comparing Supervisee and Supervisor Initial Perceptions of Supervision: Do They Agree? *Clinical Supervisor* 4 (3), 53–61.

Strasburger, L. H., L. M. Jorgenson, and R. Randles. 1990. Mandatory Reporting of Sexually Exploitative Psychotherapists. *Bulletin of the American Academy of Psychiatry and the Law* 18, 379–384.

Strasburger, L. H., L. M. Jorgenson, and P. Sutherland. 1992. The Prevention of Psychotherapist Sexual Misconduct: Avoiding the Slippery Slope. *American Journal of Psychotherapy* 46, 544–555.

Sue, D. W., and D. Sue. 1990. *Counseling the Culturally Different.* 2d ed. New York: Wiley.

Taibbi, R. 1995. *Clinical Supervision: A Four-Stage Process of Growth and Discovery.* Milwaukee: Families International.

Tannen, D. 1990. *You Just Don't Understand: Women and Men in Conversation.* New York: Ballantine Books.

Tarasoff v. Regents of the University of California, 131 Cal Reptr 14 (Cal 1976).

Tennyson, W. W., and S. M. Strom. 1986. Beyond Professional Standards: Developing Responsibleness. *Journal of Counseling and Development* 64, 298–302.

Thomas, F. 1992. Solution Focussed Supervision. Paper presented at the American Association for Marriage and Family Therapy Fiftieth Anniversary Conference, Atlanta.

Thoresen, C. E. 1969. The Systems Approach and Counselor Education: Basic Features and Implications. *Counselor Education and Supervision* 9, 3–17.

Tomm, K. M., and L. M. Wright. 1982. Multilevel Training and Supervision in an Outpatient Service Program. In R. Whiffen and J. Byng-Hall, eds., *Family Therapy Supervision: Recent Developments in Practice,* 211–227. London: Academic Press.

Trimpey, J. 1992. *The Small Book: A Revolutionary Alternative for Overcoming Alcohol and Drug Dependence.* New York: Delacorte.

Truax, C. B., and R. R. Carkhuff. 1967. *Towards Effective Counseling and Psychotherapy: Training and Practice.* Chicago: Aldine.

Upchurch, D. W. 1985. Ethical Standards and the Supervisory Process. *Counselor Education and Supervision* 75, 90–98.

Van Hoose, W. H., and J. A. Kottler. 1985. *Ethical and Legal Issues in Counseling and Psychotherapy.* 2d ed. San Francisco: Jossey-Bass.

Vanier, J. 1998. *Becoming Human.* New York: Paulist Press.

van Ooijen, E. 2000. *Clinical Supervision: A Practical Guide.* London: Churchill Livingstone.

Vasquez, M. J., and D. McKinney. 1982. A Conceptual Model—Reactions and an Extension. *Counseling Psychologist* 10 (1), 59–63.

Wagner, F. F. 1957. Supervision of Psychotherapy. *American Journal of Psychotherapy* 11, 759–768.

Wallace, J. 1985. *Alcoholism: New Light on the Disease.* Newport, R.I.: Edgehill.

Ward, L. G., M. L. Friedlander, L. G. Shoen, and L. G. Klein. 1985. Strategic Self-Preservation in Supervision. *Journal of Counseling Psychology* 32, 111–118.

Weber, G. 1991. Feminist Models of Supervision. Paper presented at the American Association for Marriage and Family Therapy Annual Conference.

Welfel, E. R. 1998. *Ethics in Counseling and Psychotherapy: Standards, Research, and Emerging Issues.* Pacific Grove, Calif.: Brooks/Cole.

Wetchler, J. L., F. P. Piercy, and D. H. Sprenkle. 1989. Supervisors' and Supervisees' Perceptions of the Effectiveness of Family Therapy Supervisory Techniques. *American Journal of Family Therapy* 17, 35–47.

Wheeler, D., J. M. Avis, L. A. Miller, and S. Chaney. 1985. Rethinking Family Therapy Education and Supervision: A Feminist Model. *Journal of Psychotherapy and the Family* 1 (4), 53–72.

Whiffen, R., and J. Byng-Hall, eds. 1982. *Family Therapy Supervision: Recent Developments in Practice.* London: Academic Press.

Wilcoxon, S. A. 1986. One-Spouse Marital Therapy: Is Informed Consent Necessary? *American Journal of Family Therapy* 14, 265–270.

Wilcoxon, S. A., and D. L. Fennell. 1983. Engaging the Non-Attending Spouse in Marital Therapy Through the Use of Therapist-Initiated Written Communication. *Journal of Marital and Family Therapy* 9, 199–203.

Wiley, M. O'L. 1982. Developmental Counseling Supervision: Person-Environment Congruency, Satisfaction, and Learning. Paper presented at the Annual Meeting of the American Psychological Association, Washington, D.C., August.

Wiley, M., and P. Ray. 1986. Counseling Supervision by Developmental Level. *Journal of Counseling Psychology* 33, 439–445.

Williams, A. 1995. *Visual and Active Supervision: Roles, Focus, Technique.* New York: W. W. Norton.

Wilner, W. 1990. The Use of Primary Experience in the Supervisory Process. In R. C. Lane, ed., *Psychoanalytic Approaches to Supervision,* 58–70. New York: Brunner/Mazel.

Winnicott, D. W. 1971. *Playing and Reality.* London: Tavistock.

Wolf, S. 1974/1975. Counseling—for Better or Worse. *Alcohol Health and Research World,* 27–29.

Wolkenfeld, F. 1990. The Parallel Process Phenomenon Revisited: Some Additional Thoughts About the Supervisory Process. In R. C. Lane, ed., *Psychoanalytic Approaches to Supervision,* 95–112. New York: Brunner/Mazel.

Worthington, E. L., Jr. 1984. An Empirical Investigation of Supervision of Counselors as They Gain Experience. *Journal of Counseling Psychology* 31, 63–75.

Worthington, E. L., Jr. 1987. Changes in Supervision as Counselors and Supervisors Gain Experience: A Review. *Professional Psychology: Research and Practice* 18, 189–208.

Worthington, E. L., Jr., and H. J. Roehlke. 1979. Effective Supervision as Perceived by Beginning Counselors-in-Training. *Journal of Counseling Psychology* 26, 64–73.

Wrenn, C. G. 1962. *The Counselor in a Changing World.* Washington, D.C.: American Personnel and Guidance Association.

Wulsin, L. R., H. Bursztajn, and T. G. Gutheil. 1983. Unexpected Clinical Features of the *Tarasoff* Decision: The Therapeutic Alliance and the "Duty to Warn." *American Journal of Psychiatry* 140, 601–603.

Yalom, I. D. 1995. *The Theory and Practice of Group Psychotherapy.* 4th ed. New York: Basic Books.

Yalom, I. D. 2002. *The Gift of Therapy.* New York: HarperCollins.

Yogev, S. 1982. An Eclectic Model of Supervision: A Developmental Sequence for Beginning Psychotherapy Students. *Professional Psychology* 13, 236–243.

Zucker, P. J., and E. L. Worthington, Jr. 1986. Supervision of Interns and Post-Doctoral Applicants for Licensure in University Counseling Centers. *Journal of Counseling Psychology* 33, 87–89.

About the Authors

DAVID J. POWELL, PH.D., LADC, CCS, is president of the International Center for Health Concerns, Inc., a health consulting company. He assists worldwide in the education and training of behavioral health professionals. Formerly he was president of ETP Inc. for twenty-five years, and in that capacity oversaw clinical supervision training programs for the U.S. Navy and Marine Corps worldwide. He has trained managers, counselors, and clinical supervisors in every state and many countries. He is a licensed alcoholism and drug abuse counselor, certified clinical supervisor, certified sex therapist, and licensed marriage and family counselor. In addition to two previous books on clinical supervision, he is the author of *Playing Life's Second Half: A Man's Guide for Turning Success into Significance* (2003) and *Alcoholism and Sexual Dysfunction* (1984). For information on supervision training, write to David J. Powell, P.O. Box 831, East Granby, CT 06026, or e-mail him at djpowell1@aol.com.

ARCHIE BRODSKY is senior research associate at the Program in Psychiatry and the Law, Massachusetts Mental Health Center, Harvard Medical School. He has also been a research associate at the Heller Graduate School, Brandeis University. He is the coauthor of numerous books, including *The Truth About Addiction and Recovery* (1991) and the forthcoming *Preventing Boundary Violations in Clinical Practice*.

Index

CPSIA information can be obtained
at www.ICGtesting.com
Printed in the USA
BVOW06s1755120917

494676BV00006B/11/P